CONSCIENCE:
ITS FREEDOM AND LIMITATIONS

THE PASTORAL PSYCHOLOGY SERIES,
NUMBER 6

CONSCIENCE:
ITS FREEDOM AND LIMITATIONS

Edited by
WILLIAM C. BIER, S.J.

FORDHAM UNIVERSITY PRESS · NEW YORK

© Copyright 1971 by FORDHAM UNIVERSITY PRESS
Library of Congress Catalog Card Number: 79–125029
ISBN 0–8232–0905–9

Printed in the United States of America

Table of Contents

Preface

The series of Pastoral Psychology Institutes sponsored by the Psychology Department of Fordham University began in 1955. With the single exception of 1967 when an Institute was not offered, they have been presented on an alternate-year basis since their inception. The current volume contains the papers presented in the 1969 Institute.

These Institutes, intended originally for the clergy and initially open only to clergymen, dealt with a series of topics selected because they represented areas in which the behavioral sciences were in a position to contribute understanding and viewpoints helpful in dealing with the kind of problems encountered in pastoral work. The first two Institutes, those of 1955 and 1957, dealt rather briefly with a series of topics and were combined for publication into a single volume, the first in the series: *Personality and sexual problems in pastoral psychology*. Subsequent Institutes were devoted to single topics which received more detailed treatment. The 1959 Institute concerned itself with addiction, before the drug problem assumed the proportions found today, and appeared as volume two in the series: *Problems in addiction: Alcohol and drug addiction*. The 1961 Institute focused on the teenager and provided the material for volume three in the Pastoral Psychology Series: *The adolescent: His search for understanding*. Marriage was the topic of the 1963 Institute and volume four in the series: *Marriage: A psychological and moral approach*. The 1965 Institute turned its attention to the topic of woman in the Church and the world today and appeared as volume five under the title *Woman in modern life*.

All the Institutes have conformed to the same overall pattern of arrangement. They have been conducted from a Monday through a Friday of a week in the latter half of June. The Institute reported in the present volume ran from the 16th to the 20th of June, 1969. This general time has been selected so as to fit between the end of the academic year and the start of summer school or other summer commitments. In a five-day span it is obviously impossible to impart counseling techniques or skills, and the Institutes have never had any such goals. Rather they have focused upon the imparting of information on a selected topic and the developing of attitudes with reference to this topic, goals which are attainable within the time-span available.

A significant feature of the Institutes has been their interdisciplinary approach. The contributions of the behavioral sciences have been central so that there always were in each of the Institutes representatives of such disciplines as psychology, psychiatry, and sociology, with frequent assists from such other disciplines as philosophy, theology, and social work. Because "conscience" was the topic of the 1969 Institute, representatives of the legal profession and of political science were included as well.

The Institutes have provided a concentrated week-long experience focused on a pre-selected topic, and the interchange in both formal discussion and informal conversation between the contributors, who gave the papers, and the participants, who attended, has been a notably valuable feature of the Institutes. Not all of the contributors were able to remain for the entire Institute, although some did; but most of them remained for at least a full day. Luncheons, for instance, on the three middle days of the Institute, and dinner on one evening, were made part of the Institute attendance in order to maximize the opportunity for interchange and discussion. Consistently the discussion period after the formal papers has been viewed as an important part of the Institute. Valuable, however, as discussions of this kind are for those who are present, experience indicates that this discussion's significance is limited almost entirely to the face-to-face confrontation and the spontaneous interchange of opinions and viewpoints it provides. It is impossible to recapture this atmosphere afterwards, and this volume, like its predecessors, makes no attempt to do so. This experience, which is a living one, is the bonus which is reserved for those who are able to spend the week required to attend the Institute—as opposed to those who must be content with the reading of the published volume. We believe, however, that the published proceedings have a contribution to make to a far larger group than those who are able to attend the Institute sessions, especially since the topics of the more recent Institutes have been broadened beyond problems encountered in pastoral work and attendance at the Institutes has been opened to other professional persons in addition to clergymen. The reception accorded the previous volumes in the Pastoral Psychology Series would seem to attest the validity of this conviction.

The planning Committee for the 1969 Institute selected *Conscience* as the topic to be considered because it seemed that this concept had moved recently into a central position both in the Church and in the world. With the Declaration on Religious Freedom of Vatican II, with the appeal to conscience in dissent from the teaching of *Humanae Vitae* on birth control, and with the raising of the entire question of the exercise of authority in the

Church, it was quite evident that a consideration of conscience had become unquestionably central in the life of the Church. With the continuation of the war in Vietnam and with the rise in selective conscientious objection to the draft, together with the extensive increase in civil disobedience as a means of protest against the war and against "establishment" policies in general, it is hardly less evident that conscience now occupies a central position in civic affairs as well. What the Committee conceived itself as attempting to do with this topic in the Institute was to put the concept of conscience in proper perspective. This we sought to do by the subtitle: *Its freedom and limitations.* We wanted indeed to vindicate, as adequately and fully as we could, freedom of conscience for the individual, but we felt it equally necessary to consider what are the necessary limits to freedom of individual conscience, which the tempo of the times seems sometimes to repudiate.

A glance at the table of contents reveals that there are eight sections to the material presented in this volume. The first three sections provide the background, at least as the planning Committee saw it, for the consideration of conscience in contemporary society, which was the focus of the Institute. Section I tries to place conscience in the historical and theological perspective of the Judaeo-Christian tradition, while Section II furnishes a more contemporary background by considering the contributions of the behavioral sciences—notably psychology, psychiatry, and sociology—in the development of conscience. Section III provides a more theoretical background with its focus on *freedom* of conscience in the perspective of four disciplines: philosophy, theology, psychiatry, and law.

The role of conscience in contemporary society is treated in sections IV and V. Section IV considers various aspects of conscience and civil authority, while section V is devoted entirely to civil disobedience, because the latter seems to have become a focal point with reference to the individual conscience and civil order in our country today. Sections VI and VII turn to consideration of conscience and the Church. Section VI treats of certain select aspects of conscience and the contemporary Church, with particular reference to the question of conscience and Church authority. Section VII is given over to the encyclical *Humanae Vitae,* treated obviously from the viewpoint of conscience with respect to certain representative groups within the Church—namely, the various national hierarchies, the professional theologian (Biblical and dogmatic), the confessor, and the lay penitent.

The final section, VIII, turns to a consideration of the mature conscience as this is seen in the perspective of our different disciplines: philosophy, theology, psychiatry, and political science. Today there is considerable awareness of the commitment which each one must have for personal growth, an important and even central aspect of which must be maturity of conscience.

As editor of the Proceedings and as chairman of the Institute Committee, I am pleased to pay grateful tribute to the contributions of my fellow Committee members: Rev. Francis P. Canavan, S.J., Rev. David W. Carroll, S.J., Dr. Ewert H. Cousins, Rev. Joseph G. Keegan, S.J., Rev. Matthew J. O'Connell, S.J., Rev. Edwin A. Quain, S.J., and Dr. Werner Stark. Planning for the Institute took place during the academic year 1968–69, at which time all on the Committee were faculty members of Fordham University, although several of them are now engaged in other work. A particular debt of gratitude is gratefully acknowledged as owing to Rev. David W. Carroll, S.J., Vice-chairman of the Institute Committee, who with his secretary, Mrs. Antoinette Florio, handled the publicity for the Institute and all of the arrangements with the participants.

WILLIAM C. BIER, S.J.

May, 1970

CONSCIENCE:
ITS FREEDOM AND LIMITATIONS

I
CONSCIENCE IN
THEOLOGICAL PERSPECTIVE

Conscience in the Bible

JAMES C. TURRO

Father James C. Turro received an A.B. degree from Seton Hall University and an M.A. from New York University. Special degrees include an S.T.L. from Catholic University (Washington) and an S.S.L. from the Biblical Institute (Rome). A member of the Catholic Biblical Association, the Society for Biblical Literature, the Catholic Theological Society, and the Modern Language Association, Father Turro is a contributor to a number of theological and Biblical periodicals including Theological Studies *and the* Catholic Biblical Quarterly. *He has taught courses in Scripture at La Salle College, Philadelphia, Marist College, Poughkeepsie, and Mary Rogers College, Maryknoll. Father Turro is currently professor of New Testament at Darlington Seminary, Ramsey, New Jersey.*

Any current attempt to study the Bible's teaching on conscience must acknowledge at least two embarrassments. The first is that our society has not as yet succeeded, it would seem, in formulating a hard and fast definition of conscience that is agreeable to all. Consequently the exegete is not altogether sure what he must look for as he pursues his examination of the Biblical text. This may be putting it too strongly, however. We may not be as disabled as all that, for there are certain elements that find their way into most contemporary definitions of conscience which are easy enough to isolate in Scripture. It is some of these which this paper attempts to present and scrutinize.

A second difficulty that must be candidly confronted is this: Scripture, as the word of God, was spoken primarily into a special set of circumstances, into life situations that quite differed from our own. The result is that Scripture's interests and preoccupations with conscience do not always parallel our own. Every age generates its own questions regarding conscience and fundamental reality in general. The concerns of society in one age do not always coincide with those of society in a later age. This is to say that the Biblical world assumed its own angle of vision on conscience and was taken up with aspects of it that do not particularly engage us. At the same time, certain implications of conscience which seem paramount to us are considered either not at all or barely so in the Bible. The danger, obviously, to be guarded against is that of extrapolation from the Biblical setting to our own. Krister Stendhal (1964) in his article on the Introspective Conscience in Paul has convincingly warned against this, specifically in any study of conscience in Scripture.

CONSCIENCE IN THE OLD TESTAMENT

With these reservations duly noted, we can take up our task. To begin at the beginning, with the Old Testament, it might be observed that this segment of Scripture is notoriously unpsychological in its descriptions of human behavior. Köhler in his study of Old Testament theology is compelled to write that ". . . the idea of conscience was never valued in the Old Testament" (Köhler, 1957, p. 202). If any mention is made of a person's motivation or sense of remorse, it is very generally a surface reference; the deeper aspects are left blithely unexamined. The potential role of conscience is diminished still more by the notion—frequently encountered in the Old Testament—of material sin and guilt. After all, if a man can perpetrate a crime or commit a sin without any awareness that he is doing wrong, there cannot be much point to conscience. It might be added that in Maurer's view the absence in the Old Testament of a developed concept of conscience may result from Old Testament anthropology which considers God's word as opening up self-understanding to man (Maurer, 1964).

A modest number of texts can be adduced that allude to one facet or other of conscience. Wisdom of Solomon 17:11 may serve as an example: "For wickedness is a cowardly thing, condemned by a witness of its own. And being distressed by conscience has always exaggerated hardships." Attention might be called to the phase of conscience pointed to here—namely, remorse, or the pain that arises from an awareness of having done wrong. As this study develops, this fact will be shown to be of some significance.

Before relinquishing the discussion of conscience in the Old Testament, some note must be taken of the view indulged in by some who feel that the Old Testament offers subtle evidence of an evolving concept of conscience. According to this view, a beginning is made in various theophanies through which God functions as the conscience of the whole nation of Israel. Later, it is averred, the prophets speaking in God's name fulfill a similar role in Israel. As time progresses, the prophets begin to stress individual responsibility (Jer. 31:29–30; Ez. 14:1–8). Finally, they predict a time when God will plant His law in the heart of man. Finally, one attains to a situation roughly akin to conscience in man. Thus, by a very orderly progression, conscience which begins as the voice of God is transformed in time into a natural fixture built into the life of man. Besides being too pat an arrangement of the data of Scripture, this view assumes rather venturesomely, it would seem, that conscience can sometimes be defined as a reality extrinsic to man—as, for example, the voice of God, an angel, or a prophet. W. D. Davies, for example, feels that he must define conscience as "a witness *within* man which condemns his sin" (emphasis added; Davies, 1962, p. 671). Furthermore, it is rather loose reasoning to equate conscience with "the law written in the hearts of men." Conscience does not make the law, nor is it itself a law, but rather it recognizes law and by it assesses conduct. So much for the Old Testament witness to conscience.

CONSCIENCE IN THE NEW TESTAMENT

In the New Testament—and, one might add, in Scripture in general—reference to conscience is found in sharpest focus in Paul's use of the word συνείδησις and also in the employ of that term made in the Letter to the Hebrews. It has been satisfactorily established by Pierce (1955) that both word and meaning were plucked by the New Testament writers from current Greek popular usage. In the main, the connotation of the word remained unaltered in the hands of the New Testament authors.

An analysis of the currency of συνείδησις in the Greek world of that day reveals the following:

1. the word was conceived as a facet of human nature. God (the gods) devised it as one of the checks and balances in a carefully regulated universe.
2. it was thought to bear internal witness to specific acts. It testifies to character only to the extent that character is determined and articulated in definite acts.
3. it was believed to concern itself with the nature of a person's own acts; not at all with the quality of other men's deeds or attitudes.
4. its proper object was held to be only past acts, that is to say, conscience can

be triggered into operation only by a definite act as antecedent cause. It makes no difference whether the act done in the past was immediately complete in itself or whether it represented the beginning of an extended process.
5. finally, the reference of συνείδησις is to acts, conditions, or characters that are bad. Consequently the function of conscience is described as
   a) pain,
   b) inflicting pain, or
   c) feeling pain.

Bultmann (1951, Vol. I, pp. 211–220) clarifies some of these aspects of conscience by distinguishing συνείδησις from νοῦς.

A characteristic description of the activity of conscience as understood in those times is found in Philo. It runs as follows:

> For every soul has for its birth-fellow and house-mate a monitor whose way is to admit nothing that calls for censure, whose nature is ever to hate evil and love virtue, who is its accuser and its judge in one. If he be once roused as accuser he censures, accuses and puts the soul to shame, and again as judge, he instructs, admonishes and exhorts it to change its ways. And if he has the strength to persuade it, he rejoices and makes peace. But if he cannot, he makes war to the bitter end, never leaving it alone by day or night, but plying it with stabs and deadly wounds until he breaks the thread of its miserable and ill-starred life [Philo, The Decalogue, 87*].

Plutarch proceeds in a similar vein. He contends that conscience is like a sore:

> My conscience since I know I've done a dreadful deed like an ulcer in the flesh, leaves behind it in the soul regret which ever continues to wound and prick it. For the other pangs reason does away with, but regret is caused by reason itself, since the soul, together with its feeling of shame, is stung and chastised by itself. For as those who shiver with ague or burn with fevers are more distressed and pained than those who suffer the same discomforts through heat or cold from a source outside the body, so the pangs which Fortune brings, coming as it were, from a source without are lighter to bear; but that lament: none is to blame for this but me myself, which is chanted over one's errors, coming as it does from within, makes the pain even heavier by reason of the disgrace one feels [Plutarch, On tranquility of mind, 476F–477A†].

The connotation which συνείδησις bore in popular Greek parlance may therefore be summarized as follows: man is so constituted by God that, should he ever go beyond the moral limits of his nature, he will sense pain —the pain of συνείδησις: conscience.

As remarked above, there appears to be good warrant for saying that the

---

* Loeb Classical Library, Philo (trans. by F. H. Colson) Vol. 7, p. 51.
† Loeb Classical Library, Plutarch's Moralia (trans. by W. C. Helmbold) Vol. 6, pp. 235–237.

New Testament writers accepted this term and its meaning as current in the Greek world and they used it as such without significant variation.

As already intimated, Paul's use of συνείδησις can be taken as normative for the New Testament and for the whole of Scripture. Therefore one may profitably introduce at this point some sample instances drawn from Paul's epistles to show that the New Testament conception of conscience is very much in accord with the Greek notion as analyzed above.

In Rom. 13:3–5, in a text referring to submission to governing authorities, Paul speaks as follows:

> For rulers are not a terror to good conduct but to bad. Would you have no fear of him who is in authority? Then do what is good and you will receive his approval for he is God's servant for your good. But if you do wrong, be afraid, for he does not bear the sword in vain; he is the servant of God to execute his wrath on the wrongdoer. Therefore one must be subject not only to avoid God's wrath but also for the sake of conscience.

In this text Paul has put conscience on a par with the punitive power of lawful authority—both afflict a man *after* he has transgressed. Also instructive in this passage is Paul's bracketing of conscience with God's wrath. Elsewhere in this same Letter to the Romans, Paul indicates that he believes conscience plays a role coordinate to God's wrath in human life—that is, he believes conscience and God's wrath function as dual controls, one from within, the other from without, acting to keep a man on course.

In Rom. 9:1 Paul alludes to the function of conscience in a more oblique fashion.

> I am speaking the truth in Christ, I am not lying: my conscience bears me witness in the Holy Spirit that I have great sorrow and unceasing anguish in my heart.

In declaring that he feels "great sorrow and unceasing anguish" in his heart, Paul knows himself to be completely honest, for he perceives no "twinge of conscience" as one might say. His conscience does not internally accuse him of falsehood. And as Spicq (1947, pp. 29–38) has noted, commenting on this passage, neither does the Holy Spirit indict him. Absence of the pain of conscience corroborates his sincerity. Paul has equivalently said: "I have no painful consciousness of lying"—that is, "my conscience does not testify against me in this assertion of the grief I feel for Israel."

These two texts will at least suggest the way in which conscience is usually thought of and spoken of in the New Testament. This statement is qualified by the word "usually" because, on occasion, conscience is pictured otherwise—but these instances must be viewed as exceptional. In brief, then, conscience is considered to be the painful awareness in a man of his own past misbehavior. It is the reaction of his nature to his past attempts to transgress the bounds of his nature. It is not God, nor the voice of God in man's soul, nor the law of God in man's heart, but rather a response, a reaction to God's word. It is a device engineered by God to keep man within the confines of his nature. This, as may be readily seen, is conscience viewed in a much narrower sense than is usual today. Deman (1968) points out how wide the gulf separating Biblical from modern thinking on conscience is. Consequently, it ought to be remarked that many of the problems which animate contemporary discussions of conscience are not even suggested in Scripture.

REFERENCES

Bultmann, R. K. *Theology of the New Testament* (trans. by K. Grobel) (2 vols.) New York: Scribners, 1951.

Davies, W. D. Conscience. In G. E. Buttrick *et al.* (Eds.) *Interpreter's dictionary of the Bible* (4 vols.) New York: Abingdon, 1962. Vol. 1, pp. 671–676.

Deman, T. The school of conscience. *New Blackfriars*, 1968, *50*, 129–135.

Köhler, L. *Old testament theology*. Philadelphia: Westminster, 1957.

Maurer, C. σύνοιδα. In G. Kittel (Ed.) *Theologisches Wörterbuch zum Neuen Testament* (8 vols.). Stuttgart: Kohlhammer, 1964. Vol. 7, pp. 897–918.

Pierce, C. A. *Conscience in the New Testament*. London: SCM Press, 1955.

Spicq, C. *Les épîtres pastorales*. Paris: Gabalda, 1947.

Stendhal, K. The apostle Paul and the introspective conscience. In S. H. Miller & G. E. Wright (Eds.) *Ecumenical dialogue at Harvard*. Cambridge: Harvard University Press, 1964. Pp. 236–256.

Conscience in the Catholic Theological Tradition

JOSEPH V. DOLAN, s.j.

Father Joseph V. Dolan, S.J. is assistant professor of philosophy at Fordham University, where he received his A.B. and M.A. degrees. His licentiates in philosophy and in theology are from Woodstock College, Maryland. After finishing doctoral studies at Laval University in Quebec City, he taught at Canisius College in Buffalo before coming to Fordham University in 1964. Father Dolan has published several articles on natural law and jurisprudence in Laval Théologique et Philosophique *and in* Pacific Philosophy Forum.

My topic is a rather wide one to attempt to handle in any comprehensive way within the limits of a brief essay. It would take considerable time to distinguish the multiple senses of the term "conscience" alone (Stelzenberger, 1962). I will treat a single aspect of the subject which I judge to be of some importance for an institute in pastoral psychology.

LEGISLATIVE CONSCIENCE

The psychologist usually operates with a broader notion of conscience in mind than the theologian or moral philosopher. He is more likely to focus on the affective states associated with its activity such as guilt, anxiety, and remorse. Or he may understand it as a person's system of values. The theologian knows these senses too (St. Thomas, *Summa theologica,* I q. 79, a. 13; *De veritate* q. 17, aa. 1–4), but his principal concern is with conscience in its primary and specific function of passing judgment on the moral quality of a proposed particular action. Conscience does not, in other words, tell me that murder is wrong or that Macbeth's waylaying of Banquo was wrong. It forbids my prospective act of murder. This is what is called antecedent (or legislative) conscience: conscience commanding or forbidding. It is distinguished from consequent (or judicial) conscience which approves or blames in retrospect. The theologian and the moralist are chiefly interested in the first of these functions. All the properly moral problems are here.

While legislative conscience is a universally recognized phenomenon, St. Paul seems to have been the first to use the term συνείδησις in this sense and it is from this that our English "conscience" derives from the Latin equivalent of the Greek. Paul is dealing with what we call today a "case of conscience." (I believe that it is the first instance in the New Testament of the use of casuistry: distinguishing the different circumstances under which the Christian may or may not eat meat sacrificed to idols [I Cor. 8; 10:23–30; Rom. 14].) He solves it on the basic principle that conscience is the norm of morality: one may act with a certain conscience and one may not act against conscience or with a wavering one (I Cor. 8:7; Rom. 14:23). But what is in itself lawful may yet be inexpedient and the Christian's exercise of his rights in this matter will be guided by the superior principle of charity and regard for the "weakness" of his brothers for whom it might prove a stumbling-block (I Cor. 8:9ff.; Rom. 14:15).

As Eric D'Arcy notes (1961, p. 15), the essential elements of a theology of conscience are here. The development, however, was sidetracked and complicated owing to the scholastics' fascination with a famous gloss of St. Jerome on a text of Ezechiel in which he introduces another classic but curious term, συντήρησις (itself possibly understood through a corruption of συνείδησις), which he calls "the spark of conscience" (*scintilla conscientiae*). Scholastic commentators spent a good deal of time posing questions about it. Is it a separate faculty? Is it cognitive or affective? Is it inextinguishable (since it was not smothered even in Cain)? Is it just another term for natural law (D'Arcy, 1961, pp. 1–19)? These are not at all idle questions even for moral theology. St. Thomas considers them in the *Summa theologica* (I q. 79, aa. 12–13) but he also resumes the specifically moral problem of conscience as we understand it today.

THE OBJECTIVE ROLE OF CONSCIENCE

Here we must make some general but crucial remarks on the setting of a Catholic theology of conscience. The Catholic moralist sees man as included within a created and therefore radically intelligible universal order. Individual men have a common human essence (or nature) and share a common destiny. For all the uniqueness of the person—its "incommunicability" and power of self-determination—the human nature in which that personality is rooted has its objective exigencies and conditions of development. In so far as these depend for realization on the use man makes of his characteristic power of freedom, they found an objective moral order mediated to him through what is called, for better or worse, the natural moral law. This is not an extrinsically obtruded norm but one communicated to him as reason's own discernment of right and wrong. Thus one comes to the classical definition of natural law as "the rational creature's participation in the eternal law" (*participatio legis aeternae in rationali creatura*)—a participation possessed by man as "image of God" sharing in a finite analogous way God's own judgment of good and evil. St. Thomas puts it as follows:

> And so after saying: *Offer up the sacrifice of justice,* the Psalmist (as though some were asking what the works of justice are) continues: *There are many who say "Who will show us what is good?"* In answer to this he says: *The light of your countenance, O Lord, is sealed upon us* as much as to say that the light of natural reason whereby we distinguish good and evil, which is the function of natural law, is nothing else but the impress upon us of the divine light itself [*Summa theologica,* I–II q. 91, a. 2].

Conscience is simply the extension or application of this natural law to a particular act.

Evidently there is no sympathy here for a "morality of intention" that bypasses the objective order and requires only that we be sincere in action and mean well; or for a type of situation ethics which so highlights the uniqueness of the person in his immediate and loving confrontation with God as Father, as to reject a universal moral law which would suppose a common human nature (the scholastic *natura absoluta*) as its basis. Least of all is there room for a secularist or existentialist notion of freedom where the individual conscience is considered the source of its own values and decrees and thus finally answerable only to itself. The Catholic view of conscience stresses its function of registering the demands of an objective moral order and the prevailing importance of a right conscience over a peaceful one. This does not do away with all problems by any means. But where a case of conscience arises the Catholic moralist finds different factors to compose and different tensions to resolve (Fuchs, 1952, pp. 107–128).

In the first place, from the fact that conscience applies a moral law, its judgment binds (*obligat*). While the expression can mislead and confuse the judgment of conscience with its accompanying emotional resonances, we can still aptly describe it as "the voice of God," which is the basic con-

ception of conscience presented by Vatican II in its treatment of the subject
in its Pastoral Constitution on the Church in the Modern World (Vatican
Council II, 1966, n. 16, pp. 213–214). There is thus a religious dimension
involved. To act against conscience is not just to go against one's own
better judgment or one's own system of values. It is to go against God's
authority and therefore to sin. Hence the Catholic wariness of potentially
mischievous expressions like "rights of conscience," "right to dissent," "right
to make up one's mind." The conscience is not, properly speaking, a subject
of rights, nor does it choose its positions. It is a surrogate—*quasi ratio Dei.*

CONSCIENCE AS ULTIMATE SUBJECTIVE NORM

On the other hand, as with natural law itself, conscience is man's own
judgment inasmuch as it is formed by his own mind operating on its own
final estimate of the facts. Even when he seeks counsel of others or follows
a religious authority as objective norm, the individual must assume responsibility for following it (St. Thomas, *De veritate,* q. 17, a. 5 ad 4). Neither
counselor nor prelate, nor even the objective moral law itself, can supplant
the individual conscience as the *immediate* norm of action, for there is no
other way a man can judge his obligation than as he himself finally sees it
when all the data are in. If it be his human act then his conscience must
have the last word as ultimate subjective norm of morality (Fuchs, 1952,
pp. 111–112; Pius XII, 1952). Yet this inviolable norm of action can be in
error and, what is more aggravating, can be in doubt.

Problems at once suggest themselves. Can there be a genuine obligation
to violate the objective moral law? May one act or abstain from acting
while unsure that a decision to act or not act is right? What has been called
the objective bias of Catholic moral theology did in fact lead some medieval
theologians to judge severely an action placed according to an erroneous
conscience (though they seem for the most part to have been reprehending
rather a presumed culpable ignorance as the occasion for it). Even St.
Thomas, who opposed them and argued the necessity of following an erroneous conscience, was not prepared to call the corresponding action itself
good (*Summa theologica,* I-II, q. 19, a. 6). Be that as it may, there has
long been agreement that a certain conscience, whether correct or not, is
normative for the individual (for whom *ex hypothesi* there will be no personal problem anyhow). Otherwise no conscience could bind, the reason
again being that the immediate norm of action is not the "object" as it is
in itself but as apprehended by reason (*Summa theologica,* I-II, q. 19, aa.
3, 5; Fuchs, 1952, p. 116).

PROBABILISM: SOLUTION FOR A DOUBTFUL CONSCIENCE

Stormy and historic quarrels came with the discussions centering on the doubtful conscience. These have issued in the famous "moral systems": tutiorism, probabiliorism, aequiprobabilism, and probabilism—so named for the different spirit in which they employ the so-called reflex principles for converting a speculatively doubtful conscience to one which is certain in practice (as all insist it must be before one may act on it). Here we need only note that, after many reverses and some fierce opposition (notably Pascal's), probabilism, the most lenient of these systems, appears to have won out and is today generally followed in practice. It holds that when there exists a "solidly probable" reason "favoring liberty," one may act on it despite the agent's own awareness of the simultaneous presence of other and even "more probable" reasons in its disfavor. The appeal is to the principle of jurisprudence that a doubtful law does not bind (*lex dubia non obligat*). Described in this summary fashion it may appear to smack of legalism, even dishonesty, and in some instances its practice degenerated into the abuse of laxism with which some would identify it. It should be remarked, however, that, as opposing probabilities increase, the solidity of the favoring grounds begins to dissolve, and that an obligation, too, can be practically certain despite a merely theoretical doubt about it. Furthermore, all systems presuppose a conscience sincere in its inquiry. Finally, the virtue of prudence, a requisite for a healthy conscience, itself demands that one follow the course of action which is thoroughly safe. The individual can do this and still be systematically a probabilist.

THE INFLUENCE OF VOLUNTARISM

The treatise on conscience, as we now know it, originated in the sixteenth century by way of elaboration on St. Thomas' treatment in the *Summa theologica* of the erroneous conscience. As it developed into its present form in the standard manuals of moral theology, it represents even in its prominence an approach to morality quite alien to that of the scholastic period. It has been noted (Pinckaers, 1966, p. 216) that Thomas has no question in the *Summa* dealing *ex professo* with obligation. He has relatively little to say of conscience in its role of commanding and forbidding, and he is ninety questions deep into the *Pars secunda* before taking up the treatise on law (which, it is seldom noted, culminates in the articles on the *lex nova*, the "law of liberty" and grace).

Several factors account for this shift in orientation and what appears as a somewhat less generous view of the moral life. After the Council of Trent, treatises on moral theology were designed largely with the needs of confessors and the requirements for valid administration of the sacrament of penance in mind. Hence the emphasis on the treatise *de peccatis*, identifying sins over-nicely according to species, and determining, for example, whether it constituted a numerically distinct sin to resume one's lubricious thoughts after a five-minute distraction. The virtues, which constitute the substance of morality and are thoroughly treated in the *Summa*, are now summarily handled and, instead of in their natural order, by contrived arrangement under some convenient overlapping precept of the Decalogue or of the Church (e.g. chastity, which is part of the virtue of temperance, under the sixth commandment). A consequence of all this was what has been called (Pinckaers, 1966, p. 224) the atomization of human activity—a preoccupation with individual acts to the neglect of habits as the more significant element of morality.

But this was only symptomatic of a prior and more deep-seated deterioration of traditional moral theology that set in during the fourteenth century with the diffusion of nominalism and voluntarism. The chief agent here was William of Ockham who proposed a radically new concept of the will and its freedom. This was the notion of "liberty of indifference," later effectively sponsored by Suarez, which severed the will's essential connection with intellect. No longer defined as intellectual appetite (St. Thomas, *Summa theologica*, I q. 19, a. 1) predicated upon intellect and oriented by very nature toward the good apprehended by reason, the will is here conceived as an autonomous power completely indeterminate and free even with respect to the Beatific Vision itself. Regulation of it comes, as a consequence, not from practical reason directing it as formal cause from within, but from law—an extrinsic principle obligating and constraining it. The moral good is no longer realized in man's rational pursuit of the good but in the subjection of the will to law—that is to say, in obedience which now displaces prudence as chief cardinal virtue since an action now becomes evil for no other reason than that it is forbidden (*malum quia prohibitum*). So too the idea of law itself has been radically deformed. In the Thomistic scheme it is defined as an "ordinance of reason" (St. Thomas, *Summa theologica*, I-II, q. 90, a. 4)—that is to say, reason's own illuminating and interiorized direction of the will. It is thus presented as a principle of liberty because, provided it be a good law, it is ultimately in harmony with the will's basic aspiration toward the good. Now, however, law emerges as a gratuitous and arbitrary check upon it. By a kind of Kantianism before the fact, obligation supplants the idea of the good as keystone in the structuring of moral theology. Law and liberty no longer complement but confront each other. And conscience is on hand, not to work in harness with prudence in preparing its decision, but to mediate the rival claims of law and liberty and determine which of the two is "in possession" (another legal formula).* As Pinckaers remarks:

> The moral science whose object is law and obligation will as a consequence be characterized by a basic "extrinsecism." Its commands and prohibitions, its moral precepts, cannot have their roots in liberty nor awaken any deep resonances within it; no aspiration or desire can answer their appeal where liberty's first principle is the affirmation of its own indetermination, its independence of all affectivity and its radical indifference [Pinckaers, 1966, p. 228].†

One can easily surmise the opportunities such a perspective offers for the flourishing of a legalistic ethics with its consequent deformation of conscience (White, 1953, pp. 157ff.).

In the opening article of the treatise on human acts in the *Summa,* St. Thomas understands the morally good life as a *plenitudo essendi* (St. Thomas, *Summa theologica,* I-II, q. 18, a. 1)—the actualization of innate human capacities, with the moral virtues, the acquired and infused habits of good action under the direction of prudence as their "eye," conferring a connaturality with the good and, as "second natures," guiding in a quasi-instinctive way to the right decision (St. Thomas, *Summa theologica,* II-II, q. 45, a. 2). Now, on the contrary, actions are regulated by an externally imposed law, and moral theology itself becomes patterned on jurisprudence. Laws of conduct, particularly ecclesiastical laws, are interpreted and applied, not in virtue of one's own prudence, but by recourse to "approved authors" and to the use of extrinsic probability. The virtues, in fact, are no longer conceived according to the classical scheme as "excellences" or powers informing and educating the passions—temperance, for example, working within the concupiscible appetite itself, not to repress but to transform it (White, 1953, p. 157). With the downplay of the sphere of sensibility the principal function of the virtues becomes the negative and repressive one of keeping the passions out of the will's way in its act of obedience to law.

The consequences of all this were costly. One was the effective suppression of the treatise on prudence itself (Pieper, 1959). We need only remark the connotation of "prudence" for the ordinary person today to appreciate what ignominious fate has overtaken this brave "charioteer of the virtues." Another and related consequence was the practical absolutizing of positive law. Rigid objective norms—two-and-a-half ounces; twelve minutes—were prescribed to secure against abuses with the result that the claims of a particular situation were often muted because the responsibility of the individual for

---

* As Gilby (1966, p. 184) notes, it is the purpose of conscience to serve prudence, and not the other way around (cf. St. Thomas, *Summa theologica,* II-II, q. 47, aa. 1, 3, 8).
† I have made liberal use of this essay of Pinckaers'. The translation here is my own.

assessing them had been usurped. The sometimes elaborate casuistry designed to temper the rigors of a literalist interpretation often enough issued
only in new absolutes. Even a moralist of Gerald Kelly's stature and originality could at times be intimidated by the prevailing *"impérialisme juri-
dique"* (Delhaye, 1964), as when, apparently against his own better judgment on the merits, he balked at departing from the position that the omis-
sion of a single small hour of the breviary constituted grave matter, for no
other reason than that the common opinion so held (Kelly, 1963).

RENEWAL AND RETURN

Of course, in rehearsing this development within so short a space, there is
danger of injustice and oversimplification of issues. Nothing we have said
is meant in despite of the great moralists of the past four centuries who had
to grapple with fresh and intricate problems, especially in the treatise *de jure
et justitia,* and who made immense contributions to their discipline. The
Christian will always need their guidance and have recourse to their systems.
Principles do not of themselves reach to particulars, and the contingencies
with which human actions are concerned are not the object of demonstration.
Paradoxically, it is the mature and sensitive conscience which is most likely
to be hesitant and perplexed, and if it is not to remain anxious and paralyzed
it will need the help of reflex principles along with the counsel and support
of genuine authority. In practical matters the judgment of the expert—that
is, the experienced—is itself a principle (St. Thomas, *Summa theologica,*
I-II q. 95, a. 2, ad 4, citing Aristotle).

We have been describing an abuse and deviation in order to indicate the
background of the current malaise that has prompted today's "renewal of
moral theology." This marks in many respects a return to a healthier pre-
Reformation tradition. It draws more heavily for inspiration on scriptural
sources, is more closely allied with ascetical theology from which it had
been practically divorced, and is moving away from the minimalist perspectives of allowable and forbidden, which the method of the standard manual
seems to have encouraged or at least occasioned. More account is now taken
of the dynamics of Christian life understood as a development of internal
finalities of nature and grace (Gilby, 1966), rather than in terms of an
ethics of avoidance or conformity to an extrinsic (in the sense of personally
unassimilated) moral code (Brunner, 1966). In the development of a Christian life, law, as external principle, is a pedagogue (Gal. 3:24) looking to
its own elimination as command and dictate, though not as regards its substance since it is presumably a prescription of "right reason." It has become
part of the mature Christian's own inner imperatives, making him "a law
to himself" (St. Thomas, *Summa theologica,* I-II, q. 93, a. 6, ad 1), a true
liber et legalis homo. For such "there is no law" (I Tim. 1:9; Gal. 2:18)

but only "spirit and life" (Rom. 8). Without that spirit informing our actions, as Augustine warns (*De spiritu et littera,* ch. 21), even the letter of the Gospel itself can kill. The Christian's activity is meant to be the fruit and manifestation of the presence within him of that Holy Spirit who is his Law (Rom. 8; St. Thomas, *Summa theologica,* I-II, q. 106, a. 1).

It is in the logic of this approach to stress the formation of conscience as a principle of growth and resonator of values natural and Christian. This is of primary importance for the contemporary Catholic who must live with today's religious and cultural pluralism when he can no longer find the automatic support for his values in the environment; when there is no idea without its astute propagandists, and where the complexities of personal, civic, and professional life make many more demands than heretofore on his own power of moral judgment (Rahner, 1964).

EDUCATING THE CATHOLIC CONSCIENCE TODAY

The educational task here indicated is a formidable and delicate one. It will not improve things if, for example, in impatient reaction and overeagerness to dissociate ourselves from past excesses, we were now to bid the faithful who seek direction, simply and *sine addito* to "follow your own conscience" in a context equivalently suggesting that they may ignore an unwelcome teaching of the magisterium. Docility—teachability—is an integral part of prudence (St. Thomas, *Summa theologica,* II-II q. 48, a. 1), and, factor for factor, an authentic teaching of the Church should be for the Catholic the single weightiest, even when not all-controlling, of the objective elements to consider. Besides, it would not really leave them any more adult or self-directed than before. It would merely substitute the prestige of one "authority" for another—that of their local theologian for the pope's—and by exploiting their present state of confusion and exposure to whatever winds of doctrine happen to be gusting at the moment, might only serve to make a rationalizing process already under way more comfortable to live with. It should not be forgotten that under the term "conscience" are often subsumed superstitious fears, taboos, and a superego wholly unrelated to concern for moral rectitude (De Broglie, 1964), and, further, that the erroneous conscience even when at peace can be an objectively guilty one owing to "bad faith." This is why Aristotle considered the intemperate man worse off than the incontinent or "morally weak" who do wrong "knowingly" (Stewart, 1892, Vol. II, p. 201). He has come to terms with a corrupt style of life and is so thoroughly installed in his habit that he experiences no qualms or remorse, as does the incontinent, and can now act unchastely with ease and "in good conscience." So too the "sincerity" with which some people claim to act is a purely emotional one. They will argue that they grasp moral truth "contextually" or existentially "in a lived experience" and not by childish recourse to an abstract principle or extrinsically imposed law, whereas the unflattering fact is that practical intellect is under the sway of appetite and swamped by desire. It is like the adrenally conditioned sincerity with which an angry man "honestly judges" he should punch another's nose.

This is the importance of the habitual moral dispositions for conscience: not only for supporting its verdict loyally in those circumstances of particular action where the passions—love, hatred, anger, fear—are engaged, but even more so perhaps for the integrity of the verdict of conscience itself. *Qualis unusquisque est talis finis videtur ei*—As a man *is* so the good appears to him. Conscience does not involve a detached "objective" kind of knowledge such as the scientist's or mathematician's; it is an "interested" judgment of what is good and evil for me. As such it is a function of the moral state of the agent—of character: which explains why it will warn and gnaw (*remorsus*) only when the action contemplated or perpetrated goes against one's habitual way of acting and there is a "better self" with which it is in conflict (Allers, 1931, p. 230).

When this better self no longer exists we have the blinding of moral vision (*obcaecatio*) and the hardening of moral sensibility (*obduratio*) which characterize what we call the dead conscience and which are not a mere result but the penalty of wrongdoing (Rom. 1). Here, we may finally note, lies the great peril in trifling with the conscience either by open disregard of it or by undercutting it through the more subtle maneuver of rationalization. If we fail to act as we really judge, we come in time to judge as we act. A basic condition for spiritual growth is then lacking for we no longer truly discern. "Qui facit veritatem. . . . He who *does* the truth comes to the light" (Jn. 3:21).

REFERENCES

Allers, R. *The psychology of character.* New York: Macmillan, 1931.

Brunner, A. (s.j.) Gesetz und Gnade. *Stimmen der Zeit,* 1966, *178,* 185–197.

D'Arcy, E. *Conscience and its right to freedom.* New York: Sheed & Ward, 1961.

De Broglie, G. (s.j.) *Le droit naturel à la liberté religieuse.* Paris: Beauchesne, 1964.

Delhaye, P. *La conscience morale du Chrétien.* Tournai: Desclée, 1964.

Fuchs, J. (s.j.) *Situation und Entscheidung.* Frankfurt: Knecht, 1952.

Gilby, T. (o.p.) (Ed. & trans.) *Summa theologiae,* Vol. 18: *Principles of morality.* New York: McGraw-Hill, 1966.

Kelly, G. (s.j.) Notes on moral theology. *Theological Studies,* 1963, *24,* 626–651.

Pieper, J. *Prudence* (trans. by R. & C. Winston). New York: Pantheon, 1959.

Pinckaers, S. (o.p.) (Ed. & trans.) *Somme théologique—les actes humains* Paris: Desclée, 1966.

Pius XII. De conscientia Christiana in juvenibus recte efformanda. Radio address on occasion of Family Day, promoted by Italian Catholic Action, March 23,

1952. *Acta Apostolicae Sedis,* 1952, *44,* 270–278. English translation: Forming the Christian conscience of youth. *Catholic Action,* 1952, *34* (5), 17–19.

Rahner, K. (s.j.) *Nature and grace: dilemmas in the modern church* (trans. by D. Wharton). New York: Sheed & Ward, 1964.

Stelzenberger, J. Gewissen. In H. Fries (Ed.) *Handbuch theologischer Grundbegriffe* (2 vols.) Munich: Kösel, 1962. Vol. I, pp. 519–528.

Stewart, J. A. *Notes on the Nicomachean ethics of Aristotle* (2 vols.) Oxford: Clarendon Press, 1892.

Vatican Council II. W. M. Abbott (s.j.) (Ed.) *The documents of Vatican II.* New York: Herder & Herder, 1966.

White, V. (o.p.) *God and the unconscious.* Chicago: Regnery, 1953.

A View of Conscience Within the Protestant Theological Tradition

David Little received his A.B. degree from Wooster College (Ohio) in 1955, his B.D. degree from Union Theological Seminary in 1958, and his Th.D. degree from the Harvard Divinity School in 1963. He is the author of two books: American foreign policy and moral rhetoric *(1965) and* Religion, order and law: A study in pre-revolutionary England *(1969). Previously, Dr. Little was instructor in ethics at the Harvard Divinity School; currently he is professor of Christian ethics at the Divinity School, Yale University.*

Roman Catholics need no reminder that it is important to think about the conscience. They have been pondering it with a good deal of sophistication for a long time. And if studies like Eric D'Arcy's (1961) *Conscience and its right to freedom* are any indication, the tradition is by no means deteriorating.

Protestants, on the other hand, have not of late engaged in much systematic reflection on the subject of the conscience. This is odd, too, because Protestants are usually eager to claim "freedom of conscience" as one of the great contributions of Protestantism to the rise of modern society. Still, one looks in vain for any sort of extended discussion of conscience in the writings of influential Protestant theologians like Emil Brunner, Karl Barth, Dietrich Bonhoeffer, and Reinhold Niebuhr.

One contemporary Protestant theologian who has attempted to overcome this deficiency is Paul Lehmann of Union Seminary. In his book *Ethics in a Christian context*, he has properly identified the conscience as a central problem in the Protestant tradition, and he has set about to recapture "the distinctive contribution of the Reformation" toward reformulating and resolving the problem. Though I have some very serious difficulties of my own regarding Lehmann's way of "doing the conscience over," as he puts it, I believe he has performed an immense service by challenging us all to think about the conscience anew.

Lehmann's main point is summarized as follows:

> Ethical thinking in the tradition of the Reformation has not yet fully and faithfully explored the insights into the bearing of Christian faith upon behavior by means of which the original Reformers, especially Luther and Calvin, broke fresh ethical ground. . . . [There has been a] failure to perceive the methodological revolution in ethical thinking effected by the Reformers' rediscovery of the Bible and their soteriological stress upon grace and faith alone. . . . [As against all moral philosophy and moral theology,] what the Reformation meant for the methodology of ethical theory was the liberation from the attempt to give shape to behavior in terms of *principial foundations* and *perceptual directives* [Lehmann, 1963, p. 345].

Both moral philosophy and moral theology have, according to Lehmann, distorted a proper understanding of the conscience by abstracting principles and precepts out of the actual situation or context in which people make their moral decisions. For example, on this score, he finds little to choose between an Aristotelian-Thomistic and a Kantian view of conscience. When an agent relies on a set of allegedly self-evident moral principles as one of the foundations of conscientious decisions, such as Thomas proposes with his notion of συντήρησις, then, says Lehmann, the agent looks in the wrong direction for moral guidance. Rather than turning his attention to abstract principles and therefore away from his concrete situation, he ought to focus upon the situation—to examine what is already going on around him. Only then can he avoid the woodenness and the externalism that Lehmann believes are the logical consequence of Thomas' understanding of conscience.

Likewise, Kant's theory of conscience as "practical reason holding man's duty before him" (Kant, 1964, p. 60) introduces simply another form of "external authority." Lehmann contends that with his unrelenting emphasis upon objective duty Kant has produced an "authoritarian conscience," and has thereby contributed to the decline and fall of the conscience. For, Lehmann says, "it is this authoritarian conscience which has so conspicuously lost its ethical persuasiveness and force today" (Lehmann, 1963, p. 336). Lehmann believes that Freud has once and for all undermined the basis for any sort of abstract or external view of conscience. Freudian analysis purportedly shows that Thomistic and Kantian theories of conscience "dehumanize" because they are hostile to real human fulfillment and maturity. They enslave men to external authorities rather than set them free.

Now, Lehmann's argument is that the Reformation "stress upon grace and faith alone" does succeed in liberating the conscience. For Luther and Calvin the emphasis is not upon abstract moral principles and precepts which it is the duty of conscience to try to implement in various situations. On the contrary, the emphasis is upon what has already been done and is continuing to be done by God for man. This is the building of a *koinonia,* or a community of mature individuals, whose consciences are formed by "what it takes to make and to keep human life human" in concrete, here-and-now situations. Thus, to be conscientious, according to Lehmann, is to acknowledge what is already taking place "by the grace of God," and to act upon that insight.

My difficulties with Lehmann's approach to the conscience are basically two, though they are closely related to each other: 1.) I believe that he sells short moral philosophy and moral theology, at least in their Thomistic and Kantian versions; and 2.) in part because of this, he gives an inadequate account of conscience in the Reformers.*

CONSCIENCE IN THOMAS AND KANT

It seems to me that Lehmann has misunderstood the place and function of practical reason in both the Thomist and the Kantian theory of conscience. While there are, as I shall argue, important differences between them, both figures suggest that, whatever else he is, *moral man is a reason-giving animal.* To be man is to give reasons for action, and particularly so when an act affects or interferes with the action of another person. To alter the way of life of another without being able to justify or to give good reasons for doing so is what is meant by arbitrariness or irrational action. For both Thomas and Kant, arbitrariness or unjustifiable action is the opposite of freedom. It is action that seeks to control another "whether he likes it or not"; it is action that disregards the other's feelings and responses. In short, it is action that seeks to enslave another. By contrast, when one gives reasons for action affecting another, he is in that very process respecting the right of the other to hear and consent to those reasons; and he is thereby honoring the other's freedom.

Correspondingly, for both men the conscience is the activity of giving

* I shall not deal with Luther, but only with Calvin.

oneself reasons (or justifications) for and against an action. In neither Thomas nor Kant is the conscience purely a rational matter, for it necessarily involves subjective feelings of approval or disapproval. But these feelings, we might say, cause the court of conscience to convene. They raise the question whether, say, the feelings of remorse which I have about forgetting my wife's birthday are in fact justified or not. This whole process of standing in judgment on myself, of hearing reasons for and against my behavior, of applying to myself the same standards I apply to others enables me to get free of myself and to examine myself from an intersubjective point of view —in this case, from the point of view of my wife.

On this account, the rational component of conscience is certainly not external to man, or "authoritarian" in any sense. It is one of the necessary conditions of overcoming arbitrariness, of making man a *moral* agent, by enabling him to look at himself, not only from his own point of view, but also from the point of view of others. To be rational in this sense is one of the conditions of being free. Incidentally, this connection between rationality and freedom is found not only in Thomas and Kant, but also—so those tell me who know more than I do—in Freud himself.

Thus far the positions of both Thomas and Kant seem in agreement, and they appear to me to supply an indispensable starting-point for further thinking about the conscience. I am not at all convinced, as I reflect on my own behavior and that of others, that the process of giving myself reasons for action, or looking at my own behavior from an intersubjective or rational point of view, is either dehumanizing or in danger of losing significance in human life.

But there are differences between Thomas and Kant regarding the conscience, and by noting them we shall better understand some of the divergent emphases between the Catholic and the Reformed traditions on the problem of conscience. Lehmann himself observes a difference of the greatest interest to us.

> Whereas Aquinas had analyzed the conscience as a faculty of judgment, Kant makes an important addition. Conscience for Kant is *juridicial as well as judgmental*. It functions not simply as the intellect or reason in the act of distinguishing good from evil but as a *tribunal* [Lehmann, 1963, p. 335].

Whatever the reasons for the difference, it seems clear that Kant does place greater stress upon conscience as accuser and judge than as guide and director, which is Thomas' emphasis. For Thomas, conscience, properly associated with the principles of συντήρησις, directs man, above all, to his good, or his ultimate happiness. Because of this conception, conscience and the principle of prudence get on happily together in Thomist thought. Indeed, if Josef Pieper is right " 'conscience' is well-nigh interchangeable with the word 'prudence' " for Thomas (Pieper, 1959, p. 27).

But Kant will not agree that conscience is first of all grounded in the rational pursuit of happiness, or in prudence.

> We must . . . differentiate between the judgment of prudence and the judgment of conscience. . . . He who goes in fear of being prosecuted for a wicked deed, does not reproach himself on the score of the wickedness of his misdemeanour, but on the score of the painful consequences which await him; such a one has no conscience, but only a semblance of it. *But he who has a sense of the wickedness of the deed itself, be the consequences what they may,* has a conscience [emphasis added; Kant, 1963, p. 130].

In order fully to appreciate this argument, we need to put Kant's famous definition of conscience alongside it:

> Every man has a conscience and finds himself watched, threatened, and, in general, kept in an attitude of respect (of esteem coupled with fear) by an inner judge; and this power watching over the law in him is not something that he himself (arbitrarily) makes, but something incorporated in his being. It follows him like his shadow when he plans to escape. . . . He can at most, in the extremity of corruption, induce himself to pay no more attention to it, but he still cannot help hearing it. Now . . . although the business [of the conscience] is an affair of man with himself, man yet sees himself necessitated by his reason to carry it on *as if at the bidding of another person.* . . . Hence, *for every duty man's conscience will have to conceive someone other than himself* . . . [emphasis added; Kant, 1964, pp. 103–104].

What is crucial in these passages and crucial for understanding Kant in general is that morality and conscience *start by presupposing someone else alongside the self*—"for every duty man's conscience will have to conceive some one other than himself." Conscience has not initially to do with prudential calculations—of assessing the probable rewards or punishments for the self of a given act. It has to do initially and basically with what is owed or not owed to another. Consequently, to have a conscience is, for Kant, to give consideration or "respect" or "reverence," to use his terms, to someone else alongside oneself. The very act of conceiving of another is, for Kant, to conceive of one to whom respect is owed. Conscience normally acts as a judge and accuser after the fact because man readily inclines to forget his moral nature and to determine his life, including his relations with others, on the basis of what brings *him* maximum gratification, whether heavenly or earthly in nature. Such action is the heart of arbitrariness or irrationality because it forgets to accord to others the same measure of respect it accords to itself. It readily inclines to treat others as means to one's own gratification rather than as ends in themselves.

CALVIN'S VIEW OF CONSCIENCE

As I said, my second difficulty with Lehmann's analysis is that because he sells moral philosophy short—and particularly Kant's position—he does not adequately grasp Calvin's view of the conscience.

It is striking that, although Lehmann is concerned with the problem of conscience, and with the contribution of the Reformation to resolving that problem, he does not deal in any depth with Calvin's own treatment of the subject. Were he to have done so, he could not have missed the similarities between the views of Kant and Calvin, at least in formal terms. Calvin says:

> When men have an awareness of divine judgment adjoined to them as a witness which does not let them hide their sins but arraigns them as guilty before the judgment seat—this awareness is called "conscience." It is a certain mean between God and man, for it *does not allow man to suppress within himself what he knows,* but pursues him to the point of making him acknowledge his guilt [emphasis added; Calvin, Bk. IV, ch. 10, par. 3; McNeill, 1960, p. 1181].

> For our conscience does not allow us to sleep a perpetual insensible sleep without being an inner witness and monitor *of what we owe God,* without holding before us the difference between good and evil and *thus accusing us when we fail in our duty* [emphasis added; Calvin, Bk. II, ch. 8, par. 1; McNeill, 1960, p. 368].

The first thing the conscience tells Calvin, as it tells Kant, is that there is an Other to whom duty is owed. It is this which, for Calvin, man knows deep within himself and which conscience will not "allow him to suppress." At the same time, this "inner witness" constantly accuses man of ignoring his debts, and of seeking as vigorously as he can to escape the Other—to disregard Him.

Now, Calvin is quite prepared to give "good reasons" why man owes duties to God. These reasons consist in what I would call the "logic of gratitude." Indeed, much of Calvin's theology can be charted according to the various aspects of the concept of gratitude. Moreover, by examining Calvin's emphasis on gratitude, one can readily grasp the "Kantian" element in his thought.

> Although our mind cannot apprehend God without rendering some honor to him, it will not suffice simply to hold that there is One whom all ought to honor and adore, unless we are also persuaded that he is the fountain of every good. . . . Thus we may learn to await and seek all these things from him, and *thankfully to ascribe them, once received, to him.* . . . I call "piety" that reverence joined with love of God which the knowledge of his benefits induces. For until men recognize *they owe everything to God,* that they are

nourished by his fatherly care, that he is the Author of their every good, that they should seek nothing beyond him—they will never yield him willing service [emphasis added; Calvin, Bk. I, ch. 2, par. 1; McNeill, 1960, pp. 40–41].

What man ought to know, and does know, deep within his conscience, is that the Other—God—has already gone out of His way to act on man's behalf. Were it not for this Other and His action, man would be nothing— he would not even have "a self" at all. But, it is this debt of gratitude that man so "naturally" neglects, and to which his conscience ever and again calls him. Man is inclined to see himself as his own creator, and thus to conceive his duties and obligations as owed primarily to himself, and to his own gratification. This, for Calvin, is man's chief sin (which is the same as "arbitrariness" for Kant). In both Calvin and Kant, "sin" is to adopt one's own gratification as the starting-point of moral reflection. "And we are not allowed to pretend ignorance without our conscience itself always convict-ing us both of baseness and ingratitude" (Calvin, Bk. I, ch. 6, par. 15; McNeill, 1960, pp. 68–69).

But for Calvin what man owes God, according to the logic of gratitude, is nothing short of *a willing spirit of appreciativeness* (or love). That is, for a debt of gratitude to be properly understood, one ought to want to respond thankfully to a benefactor. He ought not to have to be shamed or coerced into giving thanks. For example, parents often reprimand a child for ingratitude, and yet they will normally add, "I ought not to have to tell you to say 'thank you'; you ought to want to say it." According to our ordinary understanding, gross ingratitude is certainly blameworthy, but what is most blameworthy of all is that the "ingrate," as we call him, does not feel any obligation himself to his benefactor. He does not want— freely and of his own accord—to repay his debts or to "do his duty."

It is this lack of willing response or lack of a freely self-initiated sense of obligation to God that man's conscience constantly reminds him of. Man "under the law" in Calvin's view misunderstands this. He responds to God grudgingly, or on the basis of a calculation of personal rewards and punishments. Consequently, his conscience is "terrorized" or "in bondage." It is so because it misconstrues "the reason" for which the conscience accuses man. It accuses him in the first instance not because he inadequately serves himself by failing to consider the consequences of his action in terms of rewards and punishments—that is, because he is imprudent. It accuses him *in the first instance* because he does not recognize and ac-knowledge his obligation or duty freely to serve the one who has freely served him. It accuses him because he is an "ingrate" in the fullest sense of that term.

It is against this background that Jesus Christ as "the liberator of the conscience" must be seen. For Calvin, Christ shows the way of voluntary gratitude to the Father. He does not obey because of the "curse of the

Law," which is the terror of God's punishment. Rather, He absorbs the curse of the law and overcomes it by freely electing to obey God. "In Christ" men understand the true character of their obligation of gratitude to God.

> The second part [of Christian freedom] . . . is that consciences observe the law, not as if constrained by the necessity of the law, but that freed from the law's yoke they willingly obey God's will. For since they dwell in perpetual dread so long as they remain under the sway of the law, they will never be disposed with eager readiness to obey God unless they have already been given this sort of freedom [Calvin, Bk. III, ch. 19, par. 4; McNeill, 1960, p. 836].

> The gist of true piety does not consist in a fear which would gladly flee the judgment of God, but . . . rather in a pure and true zeal which loves God altogether as Father, and reveres him truly as Lord, embraces his justice and dreads to offend him more than to die [cited by McNeill, 1960, p. 40, fn. 1].

Freedom of this sort is possible precisely because of the preceding or prior existence and "grace" of Another.

SUMMARY

We may now, in conclusion, summarize the similarities between the approaches of Kant and Calvin to the problem of conscience. In formal terms, both seek to root the notion of conscience in the irreducible apprehension of obligation to another. "Freedom of conscience" for both consists in the self-initiated and self-conscious awareness of a debt to another, including "respect," "reverence," "honor," and "gratitude." In both men, the conscience is precisely not free, so long as it adopts as a starting-point prudential calculations. Calvin would wholeheartedly agree with Kant's formulation: "We must differentiate between the judgment of prudence and the judgment of conscience. . . . He who has a sense of the wickedness of the deed itself, be the consequences what they may, has a conscience." In neither Kant nor Calvin is the consideration of "happiness" ruled out, even in moral reasoning. But it is not the starting-point of moral reflection. As Kant put it, "for every duty man's conscience will have to conceive someone other than himself." *For both Kant and Calvin, conscience is first of all moral consciousness of another.* That awareness must be the foundation of moral reasoning.

It has not been my objective to oversimplify the connections between Kant and Calvin. There are many differences between them, and many subtleties of emphasis, even on the question at hand, that we have not even begun to explicate. But in the way I have outlined, I do believe Kant and Calvin share basic similarities of outlook in their approach to the conscience. If I am right, perhaps moral philosophers and Reformation theologians need not be quite so suspicious of each other as they so often are.

REFERENCES

D'Arcy, E. *Conscience and its right to freedom.* New York: Sheed & Ward, 1961.

Kant, I. *Lectures on ethics* (trans. by L. Infield). New York: Harper & Row, 1963.

Kant, I. *The doctrine of virtue* (trans. by M. J. Gregor). New York: Harper & Row, 1964.

Lehmann, P. L. *Ethics in a Christian context.* New York: Harper & Row, 1963.

McNeill, J. T. (Ed.) *Calvin: Institutes of the Christian religion* (trans. by F. L. Battles). (2 vols.; Vols. 20–21 in Library of Christian Classics.) Philadelphia: Westminster Press, 1960.

Pieper, J. *Prudence* (trans. by R. & C. Winston). New York: Pantheon, 1959.

Conscience in the Documents of Vatican II

RICHARD J. REGAN, s.j.

Father Richard J. Regan, S.J. earned his A.B. degree at St. Peter's College, Jersey City, his S.T.L. degree at Woodstock College, Maryland, and his Ph.D. degree at the University of Chicago. He is a member of the American Political Science Association, and the author of two books: American pluralism and the Catholic conscience *(1963) and* Conflict and consensus: Religious freedom and the 2nd Vatican Council *(1967). Father Regan is an assistant professor of political science at Fordham University.*

In one sense, the whole work of the Second Vatican Council can be said to deal with problems of "conscience," at least the conscience of Catholics. But in the narrower sense of the rights and responsibilities of individual conscience in relation to authority, or even in conflict with it, one document of Vatican II, in particular the Declaration on Religious Freedom (Vatican Council II, 1966, pp. 675–696), spoke explicitly.

DECLARATION ON RELIGIOUS FREEDOM

The Declaration on Religious Freedom proclaimed unequivocally the right of the human person to religious freedom, i.e., to immunity from coercion on the part of any human power

... in such wise that in matters religious no one is to be forced to act in a manner contrary to his own beliefs . . . nor is anyone to be restrained from acting in accordance with his own beliefs, whether privately or publicly, whether alone or in association with others, within due limits [Vatican Council II, 1966, n. 2, p. 679].

The word "conscientia" in the Latin text was used in the generic sense of "beliefs" or "convictions." Hence the Declaration affirmed the equal rights of believers and non-believers to freedom in religious matters. Second, the right to religious freedom was defined in negative terms, i.e., a "freedom from" coercion. The Declaration thus avoided any question of the truth or falsity of religious beliefs and any implication that there is a right to believe what is false or to do what is wrong—an implication which would be moral nonsense. Third, the right to religious freedom was not even made dependent on the sincerity of conscience; the right to immunity from coercion in religious matters was declared to be a right simply inherent in the dignity of the human person.

An argument for the principle of religious freedom from the right and duty of individuals to follow their conscience had been central to the first two drafts of the Declaration, but conservatives and many liberals objected to the argument on several grounds (Regan, 1967, pp. 53–70). First, opponents contended that this argument constituted an illicit transition from the subjective world of individual conscience to the objective world of social consequences. In their view, an argument for religious freedom should establish not only the right of the individual to be free from compulsion to act against his conscience, but also his right not to be impeded from acting according to conscience. The argument for religious freedom from the right and duty to follow conscience was said to raise the question whether an individual's action is in fact good or bad for society, and, without recourse to man's personal dignity as a free agent and the corresponding constitutional limitation of the role of government in matters of religion, was said to be vulnerable to the thesis that religious error harms the common good. Moreover, the argument was said to give no ground for an insincere conscience to claim a right to religious freedom, to invite governments to judge which consciences are sincere, and thus to risk making religious freedom a concession from governments rather than a matter of right.

The argument for religious freedom from the right and duty of individuals to follow their conscience was represented in the final draft of the Declaration in a subsidiary rather than central role:

In all his activity a man is bound to follow his conscience faithfully. . . . It follows that he is not to be forced to act in a manner contrary to his conscience. Nor, on the other hand, is he to be restrained from acting according to his conscience, especially in matters religious [Vatican Council II, 1966, n. 3, p. 681].

But, as John Courtney Murray observed in a footnote which he contributed for the Declaration on Religious Freedom:

> . . . the Declaration does not base the right to the free exercise of religion on "freedom of conscience." Nowhere does this phrase occur. And the Declaration nowhere lends its authority to the theory for which the phrase frequently stands, namely, that I have a right to do what my conscience tells me to do simply because my conscience tells me to do it. This is a perilous theory. Its particular peril is subjectivism—the notion that, in the end, it is my conscience and not the objective truth which determines what is right or wrong, true or false [Murray, 1966, p. 679].

LIMITS ON THE RIGHT TO RELIGIOUS FREEDOM

The Council was conscious that the right to religious freedom, like all rights exercised in society, is subject to regulatory norms. The Declaration stated in the first place a moral norm, namely, the principles of personal and social responsibility which are imposed by individual moral consciousness: "Men are to deal with their fellows in justice and civility" (Vatican Council II, 1966, n. 7, p. 686). More difficult was the formulation of juridical norms according to which governments should limit the exercise of religious freedom, and the Declaration appealed to "public order" as the normative concept for restrictions of religious freedom by governments (Vatican Council II, 1966, n. 7, pp. 686–687). This "public order," a part of the universal moral order, was given a threefold content. First, the order of society was said to involve an order of justice in which the rights of all citizens need to be effectively safeguarded and conflicts of rights peacefully resolved. Second, the order of society was said to involve a political order in which peace should be preserved within a context of justice and adequate processes for the resolution of grievances. Third, the order of society was said to involve a moral order in which certain minimal standards of public conduct need to be enforced.

These juridical norms on the limits to the exercise of religious freedom, of course, were couched in general terms, and their application to particular situations will not always be easy. What are the rights of others which governments should protect against various exercises of religious freedom? When is the public peace seriously disrupted by such exercises? What are the responsibilities of government in the matter of public morals? But at least the Declaration defined the issues on which rational argument should take place. It eliminated religious reasons as an acceptable norm for restrictions on religious freedom and established secular considerations as the exclusive basis for such restrictions. For the rest, the issues were left to be resolved by a calculus of casuistry.

The Declaration did not state any limits to the right of persons not to be coerced to act contrary to their conscience in religious matters, but this should not be taken to imply that it recognized no limits to this principle. In fact, the third draft of the Declaration had labeled this principle "absolute," but subsequent drafts omitted such a sweeping description of the principle (Regan, 1967, pp. 122–124). The reason for the change was the recognition that there are cases in which governments apparently force citizens to do things that their consciences forbid—and with good reason. Thus, although it is against the religious convictions of some sects, governments often insist on the medical care of children, transfusions for pregnant mothers in danger of death from loss of blood, and vaccination.

Actually, the third text's attempt to absolutize the right not to be coerced to act against conscience was based on two important differences between a dictate of conscience which forbids an action and a dictate of conscience which commands an action. In the typical case, the former is unconditional for the circumstances for which it is enunciated, while the latter requires favorable conditions and frequently allows a choice of the means of implementation. This is due, of course, to the structure of negative precepts. Moreover, inaction by citizens for reasons of conscience is less likely to conflict with the rights of others or the public interest than action according to conscience. The right to immunity from coercion to act against conscience, therefore, ought to be broader than the right to act according to conscience, both because of the inner character of conscience itself and because of the relation of its dictates to the social context. Since these points were unnecessary to a conciliar affirmation of religious freedom, however, succeeding drafts of the Declaration simply dropped altogether the word "absolute" to describe the right not to be coerced to act against conscience.

SYNTHESIS OF SACRAL AND SECULAR ORDERS

If the basic work of distinguishing the sacral and the secular orders was accomplished by the Declaration, a new, more formidable task of synthesis confronts Christians, who are members of both orders. The secular must be distinguished from the sacred, but both orders must also be integrated into the thought and action of citizens whose destiny transcends the earthly city. In the sacral society this process of integration was so total that it confused the identity of the two orders; in the secular society a new synthesis is necessary which will respect the proper independence and autonomy of each. The integrity of the believer as a rational human being requires the effort. To decline it would invite intellectual and practical schizophrenia.

Indeed, the Dogmatic Constitution on the Church strongly commended the search for harmony:

> Because the very plan of salvation requires it, the faithful should learn how to distinguish carefully between those rights and duties which are theirs as members of the Church and those which are theirs as members of human society. Let them strive to harmonize the two, remembering that in every temporal affair they must be guided by a Christian conscience [Vatican Council II, 1966, n. 36, p. 63].

As a result of current movements of social protest in the United States and the prominent participation of clerics and religious, the American political community is confronting a new dimension of the age-old problem of asserted rights to disobey laws in the name of conscience. Citizens in Western society have long reserved the right to disobey laws deemed unjust and, ultimately, to revolt against a government deemed tyrannical when the degree of injustice to self or fellow-citizens outweighs the consequences of resistance to other individuals or to society. What is new on the contemporary American scene is the asserted right to disobey an admittedly just law in order to protest another law or system of laws deemed unjust. The exercise of practical reason necessary in these cases of civil disobedience is similar to that of the more traditional cases of disobeying allegedly unjust laws and revolting against tyranny: the degree of alleged injustice in a law or system of laws must be weighed against the cost of particular acts of disobedience to individual citizens and to the community, including the disvalue of encouraging disobedience to all law.

The Declaration did explicitly mark and encourage the religious responsibility of citizens for the society in which they live: "Religious freedom . . . ought to have this further purpose and aim, namely, that men may come to act with greater responsibility in fulfilling their duties in community life" (Vatican Council II, 1966, n. 8, pp. 687–688). Of course, the Declaration did not consider specifically the phenomenon of civil disobedience; it would have been inappropriate for the Council of the universal Church in its statement on the general subject of religious freedom to comment on the peculiar problem of the United States. But this problem is clearly pertinent to the Declaration's affirmation of the right to act according to conscience in religious matters and its invitation to the religious consciences of men to exercise social concern.

The Declaration's qualification that conscience act responsibly can be applied to cases of civil disobedience: prudence is necessary on the part of individuals participating in acts of civil disobedience and on the part of society judging these acts. Individuals cannot appeal to the rights of conscience as a formula of absolution from their obligation as citizens to justify rationally disobedience of society's laws. On the other hand, society cannot simply appeal to citizens' general obligations to obey legal prescriptions without weighing the actuality and degree of the injustice alleged by the civil disobedients. In any case, clerics and religious can claim no special charism exempting them from the obligation of justifying rationally their disobedience. Still less can they plead "benefit of clergy" if society disallows particular acts of civil disobedience.

Not only is the Declaration on Religious Freedom significant for the secular order; it also has meaning for the internal life of the Church. Although the Declaration did not deal explicitly with freedom in the Church and the role of individual conscience, and one introductory report specifically disclaimed any intention to treat the subject, it stands as symbol of change, a recognition of the historical evolution of human institutions and human consciousness. In this context, the Church's affirmation of the value of freedom in the polity is bound to influence the evolution of freedom in the Church herself. The relation of freedom to authority clearly depends on the nature of the community involved. Since the Church and the polity are communities with different, if complementary, goals, the relation of freedom to authority in the one cannot be applied without distinction to the other. But since freedom is a value inherent in the dignity of the human person, it ought to exist in every community as far as possible.

CONSCIENCE IN THE PASTORAL CONSTITUTION ON THE CHURCH IN
THE MODERN WORLD

Another conciliar document, the Pastoral Constitution on the Church in the Modern World (Vatican Council II, 1966, pp. 199–308), also dealt with the role and rights of conscience on contemporary moral issues. In the first chapter of that Constitution, the Council expressed itself as follows:

> In the depths of his conscience, man detects a law which he does not impose upon himself, but which holds him to obedience. . . . Hence the more that a correct conscience holds sway, the more persons and groups turn aside from blind choice and strive to be guided by objective norms of morality [Vatican Council II, 1966, n. 16, pp. 213–214].

Indeed, in the next sentence after the above-quoted material, the Council declared: "Conscience frequently errs from invincible ignorance without losing its dignity" (Vatican Council II, 1966, n. 16, p. 214).

When the Pastoral Constitution turned to the moral problem of war confronting contemporary man, it took up the specific responsibility of individual conscience. Noting the persistence of war since World War II and its potential for savagery far surpassing that of the past, the Council recalled ". . . the permanent binding force of universal natural law and its all-embracing principles" (Vatican Council II, 1966, n. 79, p. 292). Since "man's conscience itself gives ever more emphatic voice to these principles . . . actions which deliberately conflict with these same principles, as well as orders commanding such actions, are criminal" (Vatican Council II, 1966, n. 79, p. 292). Not only cannot "blind obedience . . . excuse those who yield to them," but "the courage of those who openly and fearlessly resist men who issue such commands merits supreme commendation" (Vatican Council II, 1966, n. 79, p. 292).

Moreover, the Council urged that ". . . laws make humane provisions for the case of those who for reasons of conscience refuse to bear arms, provided, however, that they accept some other form of service to the human community" (Vatican Council II, 1966, n. 79, p. 292). The Council was quite careful in its statement about the status of conscientious objectors. It made no statement about the truth or falsity of the moral claims of conscientious objectors; it simply appealed to lawmakers to accommodate selective or universal conscientious objectors to war, as far as possible. The judgment of conscience with respect to a particular war or to all war may be morally binding for the individual, but this does not settle the question. Society too must make moral judgments on war, and a conflict between the moral judgment of the individual and that of society can be resolved in practice only by a decision of society on the degree of tolerance to be accorded the dissenter.

It is in this context that the Council's statement should be understood: the dissenter may or may not be correct in his moral evaluation of the objective situations that lead governments to military action, but the Council exhorts governments to tolerance for the moral dilemma of the individual whose judgment of conscience dissents from that of society. It should also be noted that the Council did not retreat from the traditional Thomistic principle that no responsible individual can act against a negative judgment of conscience without moral fault. Rather, the Council assumed that principle without explicit articulation or argument, and, precisely because of it, the Council appealed to governments for tolerance of individuals caught in conflict between the demands of their conscience on moral integrity and the coercive commands of government.

SUMMARY

By way of conclusion, let me suggest the following set of propositions as an integrative summary of the Council's conception of conscience:

1. There is an objective norm of morality to which individual conscience should conform its judgment.

2. A responsible judgment of conscience is the supreme norm of morality for the individual, even if erroneous.
3. Government has no competence in religious matters.
4. For religious reasons, therefore, government should not command any person to act against his conscience or forbid him to act according to his conscience.
5. Government may restrict the freedom of religious exercise for reasons based on requirements of public order.
6. In secular matters, individual conscience ought both to judge the morality of the commands of government and to impel citizens to promote the ideals of justice and charity in responsible ways.
7. In the specific case of conscientious objection to war, governments ought to respect the moral dilemma of dissenters as far as a policy of exemption is consistent with their responsibilities for the common welfare.

REFERENCES

Murray, J. C. (s.j.) Footnote to section 2 of the Declaration on Religious Freedom. In W. M. Abbott (s.j.) (Ed.) *The documents of Vatican II.* New York: Herder & Herder, 1966. Pp. 678–679.

Regan, R. J. (s.j.) *Conflict and consensus: Religious freedom and the second Vatican Council.* New York: Macmillan, 1967.

Vatican Council II. W. M. Abbott (s.j.) (Ed.) *The documents of Vatican II.* New York: Herder & Herder, 1966.

II
CONSCIENCE IN THE PERSPECTIVE
OF THE BEHAVIORAL SCIENCES

Development of the Normal Conscience

DOROTHEA McCARTHY

Dorothea McCarthy received her A.B. and her Ph.D. degrees from the University of Minnesota. She is a fellow of the American Psychological Association, a member of the Society for Research in Child Development, and a diplomate in clinical psychology. She is a former president both of the New York State Psychological Association and of the Division of Developmental Psychology of the American Psychological Association. Dr. McCarthy is also the author of over fifty articles in representative psychological journals. In recognition of her life-time contributions to the fields of child and developmental psychology, she was awarded the honorary degree of Doctor of Science by the College of New Rochelle in 1967. Dr. McCarthy is professor of psychology at Fordham University.

It may be appropriate for me to mention that my approach is that of a developmental psychologist. I shall try to describe what psychologists have contributed to our knowledge of the developing conscience of the child and how they approach the subject. Then I shall point out some of the limitations of methodology and the need for further research in this vitally important area.

In terms of normative outlining of how the child's conscience develops, this area, and the whole broader sphere of moral development, has lagged behind other aspects of child development such as motor behavior and language development. It has frequently been subsumed, even among authors who recognize the area, under the general rubric of socialization of the child, and hence has been given very limited treatment within that context. Until about ten or fifteen years ago the textbooks in child psychology rarely, if ever, mentioned moral development or conscience. This was probably a result of the fact that, as psychology was trying to establish itself as a science, especially by using objective methods, the earlier work was done on the more readily objectifiable aspects of child behavior rather than on this elusive, sensitive area of conscience. In the period when behaviorists were dominating the field of psychology, consciousness and other subjective phenomena were not considered readily subject to scientific investigation. In more recent years, however, learning theorists, psychoanalysts, and developmental psychologists have developed techniques for the study of conscience and various aspects of moral development in children. And in 1968 the topic was considered of sufficient import to be the focus of a conference at the National Institute of Child Health and Human Development. It brought together developmental psychologists as well as psychiatrists, theologians, and clergymen of many denominations (National Institute of Child Health and Human Development, 1969).

PSYCHOLOGISTS' DEFINITIONS OF CONSCIENCE

Much depends on the theoretical orientation of the investigator as to how he defines conscience, what dimensions of it he will choose to investigate, and how he will interpret his data.

In some of the attempts of psychologists to define conscience, one notes a certain self-consciousness and uncertainty in their efforts, for most of them have no religious affiliation and the term has been heard too frequently in religious contexts in which most behavioral scientists are not usually at ease. Sears in his essay on the growth of conscience states:

> The meaning of *conscience* is not very precise in western culture, but the word has an approximate aura which nearly everyone understands. It refers to the standards of right and wrong, and the motivation to abide by these standards, that every normal person carries within himself. It is the incontrovertible dogma of obligation and responsibility, the not-to-be-argued-with moral sense, the deep-lying self-control of pleasure-seeking principles [Sears 1960, p. 92].

Jersild admits that ". . . from a psychological point of view, the conscience is a rather nebulous thing. . . . The conscience usually does not represent a unitary, internally consistent set of principles or sanctions. It has many facets" (Jersild, 1968, p. 512). Sears (1960) identified three such facets as resistance to temptation, feelings of guilt, and the positive side of the moral ledger which he also calls conscience in a narrow sense. Jersild points out that the conscience may be rigorous in some things and too lenient in other matters; it may be strong and prevail over temptation, or weak and succumb to temptation. He even indicates that it may be only the voice of expediency or a sort of gadfly which merely prevents a person from enjoying what he knows he should not do, but often does not keep him from doing it.

Kohlberg offers the following comment on the meaning of conscience:

> Current investigators consider morality or conscience to be the set of cultural rules of social action which have been internalized by the individual. . . . In spite of loose agreement on the notion of internalized rule, there have been important differences of emphasis in researchers' conception of morality [Kohlberg, 1964a, p. 277].

One difficulty of definition frequently encountered in the literature stems from the etymological definition of morality which derives from *mores* or social customs of the group. In tests of moral knowledge, authors often lump together matters of serious violations of moral standards which most societies would agree are wrong—such as stealing or assault—with trivial matters of politeness with only minimal ethical implications—such as spitting on the sidewalk. Much confusion in the literature can result from such superficial labeling and grouping under the same term of behaviors of such diverse implications.

PROBLEMS OF METHODOLOGY

Before reviewing recent research in the various schools of thought, I should draw attention to certain limitations of methodology. In order for a psychologist to gather data on any aspect of behavior he must develop a method with which to measure or observe and quantify the trait or characteristic. He must also cope with the problem of the validity and reliability of his method. Two of the most careful pieces of research I know of in the area of moral development are doctoral dissertations which have been done at Fordham University: one by Father Pius Riffel (1967) on scrupulosity, and another by Father William Novicky (1959) on fraternal charity. In both of these investigations great care was taken to define the dimensions being studied and to validate the scales used for measuring them.

Many laboratory studies have been conducted in efforts to isolate various dimensions of moral development. Some have concentrated on the self-critical ability of the child, others on evidences of guilt shown by the child who has transgressed; from such evidence the presence of a conscience is inferred. Other studies have concentrated on resistance to temptation especially in cheating and lying, and still others on ability to delay gratification. Some of these studies use methods which seem so devious and contrived that many thoughtful readers consider them superficial and doubt the validity of the results as well as the meaning attributed to them. The "ray gun" or shooting-gallery technique developed by Grinder (1961), and subsequently used in a number of other investigations, in which the child has an opportunity to falsify his score and earn a badge of dubious motivational value, is typical of such studies.

Another methodological difficulty concerns the samples used in the various investigations. Since there are no norms nationally or culturally for really large groups, only very limited generalizations can be made from the particular samples involved. Strangely enough, the vast majority of studies on moral behavior have used only males as subjects. Some which have used female subjects, however, have emerged with different results for the two sexes. Yet these researchers, considering the role of the parents in moral training of children, usually find that for preschool- and elementary-school-age children the mother is the chief disciplinarian in our American culture.

Typical of studies concerned with children's moral values is the study by Gump and Kounin (1961) in which over 200 children were asked: "What is the worst thing a child can do at home?"; "Why is that so bad?" and "What is the worst thing a child can do at school?"; "Why is that so bad?" The responses fell into the categories of violation of rules, assaults on other children, breaking and damaging property, non-conformity with the adult leader, and miscellaneous items. Breaking and destructiveness showed the greatest difference between home and school, with the more destructive behavior at home. Boys always reported more assaults on children in school. Talking in school was reported by 1 girl in 4 in first grade, but by third grade this was reduced to only 1 in 8. Play with fire was more frequently reported by boys than by girls, and at third grade 1 in 4 boys reported it at home, and 1 in 16 at school. These authors report that children were increasingly concerned about harm to others and with morally serious incidents with increase in age and less frequently referred to adult punishment as they became older. Especially was there less frequent mention of corporal punishment among the older children than among the younger.

Many of the investigations on the child-rearing attitudes and techniques of parents also leave much to be desired from the standpoint of methodology, for they often depend on retrospective reports of parents, sometimes going back several years, about the methods of control they formerly employed. Another large group of studies depends on a variety of projective techniques such as story completions, and the like, which may not reflect what the child really would do if he were confronted with the actual situation described in the story stem. Ingenious as many of these techniques are in attempting to find the key to this important area, they often do not yield solid scientific data.

Most of the better studies recognize the multifaceted nature of the concept of conscience and attempt to investigate only one content area, such as Eberhart's (1942) study on attitude toward property, Durkin's (1959) study of children's concepts of justice, or Ausubel's (1955) attempt to distinguish between guilt and shame.

RESEARCH AND THEORIES BEARING ON MORAL DEVELOPMENT

As Mussen, Conger, and Kagan (1969) point out in their recent text, although developmental psychology has amassed a vast amount of information about persons of all ages throughout the life span, the field is relatively deficient in explanatory theory. The major influences are those of the cognitive theorists, emphasizing the trait-organization approach; the learning theorists, who stress the influence of the environment and the learning experiences of the individual; and finally the psychoanalytic theorists, who stress the active internalization of rules in the process of moral development. Each of these systems offers partial theories of various aspects of psychological development, and moral development is treated to a limited extent by each of them. As yet no one theory affords sufficiently unifying explanations or hypotheses either of psychological development in general or of moral development in particular.

The Cognitive Theorists

In 1928 there appeared the first volume in the monumental and now classic works of Hartshorne and May (1928–1930) involving studies in deceit and in service and self-control. A variety of situations were set up so that deception, cheating, and lying of various sorts could be detected. Older children were found somewhat more deceptive than younger; there was no difference between boys and girls. In general, brighter children were more honest in the experimental situations than duller ones. Children who were emotionally more unstable on other personality indices were more likely to be deceptive, and children of upper socio-economic levels were less deceptive than those of lower socio-economic levels. These studies, although considered daring and ingenious, were severely criticized. The rather consistent indications were that honesty was not a unitary trait, but was very specific to the situation, since none of the children was always honest and none was always deceitful. Those moral and religious educators who were oriented toward the cultivation of the virtue of "honesty" were rather dismayed by such results indicating the importance of specific environmental factors.

In 1963 Burton applied factor-analytic techniques to the old data of

Hartshorne and May and found evidence for some degree of generality in regard to the concept of honesty. His work suggested a model for the further investigations of Nelson, Grinder, and Mutterer (1969), who gathered new data by presenting six tasks to sixth-grade children. The correlational data essentially confirmed the results of Hartshorne and May, although the data were gathered forty years later, with different subjects performing different tasks. However, in applying Burton's factor-analytic procedures to the new data these investigators also found evidence for conceptualization of a disposition toward honesty *vs.* transgression across a variety of temptation situations. They also applied the more recently developed techniques of analysis of variance and were able to tease apart statistically the influence of persons and of situations. Persons accounted for about 15–26 per cent of the total variance, and tasks for about 14 per cent. The remainder of the variance was accounted for by error and interaction scores (60–71 per cent). These findings have important methodological implications, for the relatively low indices of internal consistency suggest that any *single* behavior measure holds little or no validity as a measure of a general trait of honesty.

The Learning Theorists

Recognizing that conscience is a learned phenomenon, psychologists have been ingenious in developing techniques to try to discover how the child learns to behave in a moral way. As Kohlberg (1964a) puts the question, "How does the amoral infant become capable of morality?" Traditionally there is the explanation of the learning theorists who see the answer in terms of learning good habits by positive reinforcement (or reward) of good or approved behavior and by negative reinforcement (or punishment) of bad or disapproved behavior. Such writers as Eysenck (1960), Sears, Maccoby, & Levin (1957), Mowrer (1950), and Bandura and Walters (1963) regard learning in the moral sphere as similar to learning in other areas, with Eysenck's view being the most simplistic and closest to that of the associationists. Learning in the moral sphere is, however, much more complex than the learning of a motor skill or the learning of the meaning of a word, and more dynamic and motivational forces must be recognized as operative in moral learning. These writers generally agree that morality is conformity to cultural norms; but the learning theorists stress that the child learns to behave in a moral way by the process of reinforcement resulting in modeling behavior, and that the child gradually actively internalizes the standards of society through the societal imposition of restrictions on his behavior. The emphasis is on the environment.

Psychoanalytic Theorists

Writers with a psychoanalytic orientation, such as Freud himself and Erickson (1950), agree with the learning theorists that morality represents conformity to cultural standards, but they tend to stress the affective and motivational aspects involved in developing such conformity. The acquisition mechanism is different in learning theory and in psychoanalytic theory, in the latter the dynamics of family influences being brought in, for the parents are regarded as the transmitters of the culture. By the process of identification the child forms an ego-ideal in terms of consistency with the parent of the same sex. Incidentally, these theories have been much more fully developed for boys than for girls. In today's society more and more children are growing up without the opportunity for parental influence in the traditional sense, and hence become victims of amorality and experience identity crises. The psychoanalytic point of view stresses the child's active efforts to cope with the process of incorporating the rules of society. It is less through an environmental impact of specific rewards and punishments as is the case with the learning theorists, and the internalization of the rules of society is tied in with the formation of the super-ego and the resolution of the Oedipal conflict. The child is seen as the active internalizer of rules rather than as a passive recipient of environmental experience. Freudian theory has led to a number of interesting experimental studies of the child-rearing antecedents of various groups of children. These researches have been very ably summarized by Hoffman (1963).

Another theorist who stressed the affective aspects of moral development, but whose work has not led to much experimental verification, is Erickson (1950)* who has presented the only developmental theory of the formation of the ego. The well-cared-for infant learns very early that when his mother is there, making certain sounds in getting his bottle ready, he will be fed, and that everything will be all right. The child thus learns to wait and trust his mother, and in so doing he also learns to defer immediate gratification of his desires. This has been described by Goldfarb (1955) as the basis of all character formation. Certainly the child who learns to wait and to defer gratification is the one who learns to control impulsivity. Bender (1947) has pointed out that the psychopath has no conscience, and she relates this character deficiency to his never having learned to defer immediate gratification—or to trust others, in Erickson's terms. Some children are also very deficient in their concepts of time and show very slow development of time-words (Brock & Del Giudice, 1963). One cannot help but wonder, therefore, how meaningful legal penalties in terms of "doing

* The integration of Erickson's theory with Catholic philosophy is well developed by McLaughlin (1964).

time" really are for such persons when they become teenagers and young adults.

DEVELOPMENTAL COGNITIVE THEORIES

In addition to the trait-oriented cognitive theorists already mentioned, there are developmental cognitive theories which deserve consideration. As the name would suggest, these theories stress the developmental nature of morality and try to define the stages characteristic of such progress. The best-known of these theories are those proposed by Piaget and Kohlberg.

The Theory of Jean Piaget

Modern workers in the field regard Piaget's volume *Moral judgment of the child* (1932) as a milestone in research on moral development. Concentrating on the cognitive aspects of moral development and using his typical clinical-interview technique, Piaget studied approximately 100 children from six to twelve years of age and identified two distinct stages in the child's moral judgment. The first he called "heteronomous" and the second "autonomous," with the transition between the two occurring at about *seven* years of age in normal children. (It is indeed interesting that developmental psychologists, using their sophisticated techniques, find and describe in their own jargon important qualitative changes in the child's cognitive development around seven years of age which traditionally has been used by wise old Mother Church as "the age of reason.")

Children in these two stages, Piaget reports, have different concepts of right and wrong, and different concepts of justice. In the "heteronomous" stage they judge the seriousness of offenses against property, for example, in terms of the amount of damage done (how many cups broken, regardless of the accidental nature of the event), whereas the "autonomous" children judge the seriousness of the offense in terms of the *intent* of the offender. Similarly, the less mature children were found to believe in immanent justice and the need for expiation. The more mature children tend to believe in naturalistic causation and in the need for restitution rather than for expiation. These trends were found to show increase with age and to hold for many Western cultures.

Piaget not only identified the above-mentioned two major stages in moral development, but on the basis of rather scanty evidence outlined in some detail five types of moral realism and six attributes of the sense of justice. His work in broad outline has been verified by other investigators, but the details of the sequences he postulates have not been substantiated.

Kohlberg (1964a) agrees that eight of Piaget's eleven stages are consistent enough to be considered "genuine developmental dimensions," increasing regularly with age regardless of the culture or situation. He also maintains that the other three dimensions described by Piaget, which are less cognitive, do not appear to be genuine developmental dimensions. Studies of the relations of moral judgment and social pressure and of the child's attitude toward authority yield no support for Piaget's theory. Although the latter's theory leads to the expectation of a positive relationship between peer-group participation and an orientation toward reciprocity, Kohlberg found a trend in the opposite direction, for children who were social isolates made more use of the concept of reciprocity in their moral thinking than those who identified with a peer group. Kohlberg concludes:

> Piaget's theory is . . . validated only in its description of the young child's morality as oriented to obedience and to punishment and as ignoring subjective ends and values, and in its assumption that these features of child morality decline with age and development in various cultural settings [Kohlberg, 1964a, p. 320].

The Theory of Lawrence Kohlberg

After a critical review of Piaget and the psychoanalytically oriented identification theory, Kohlberg (1964a) turns to the developmental approach, which he espouses, in which moral learning is viewed in terms of age-related sequences of changes by which moral attitudes emerge from qualitatively different premoral attitudes and concepts. He sees these differences in *description* of moral learning as being associated with differences in conception of the *process* of moral learning, regardless of content. The developmentalist, Kohlberg explains, does not accept the "superego strength" view of the social environment as "stamping into" the child given cultural rules which persist as internal moral structures throughout life; environment is seen rather as a social world including rules which the child comes to understand through conceptualized role-taking. He concludes:

> The mere process of role-taking the attitudes of others in organized social interaction is believed to transform concepts of rules from external things to internal principles [Kohlberg, 1964a, p. 314].

In Kohlberg's own developmentally oriented research based on lengthy free interviews with 100 boys aged seven to seventeen years concerning ten hypothetical moral-conflict situations, he identified six stages which, he claims, define a genuine sequence in individual development. He concludes that moral internalization relates closely to cognitive development of moral concepts, and that this contrasts markedly with the prevailing ideas of learning theorists interested in overt behavior, psychoanalysts interested in fantasy, and of Piaget who was interested in moral judgment. He points out that these theorists have all assumed that the basic features of adult conscience have developed by early childhood between five and eight years of age and claims that moral judgment data indicate that anything clearly like "conscience" develops relatively late.

Kohlberg (1964b) studied children's ability to judge action in terms of moral standards by asking them to evaluate certain deviant acts which they were told were followed by rewards, and certain conforming acts which they were told were followed by punishment. Each act was judged as good or bad by four-year-olds in terms of the reward or punishment rather than in terms of a rule. Between five and seven years of age, the children generally evaluated the act in terms of its moral label rather than in terms of its reinforcement in the story. It was not until pre-adolescence that the majority of children were able to make "disinterested" moral judgments and to formulate a concept of a good self. Kohlberg's studies support a developmental point of view, and he maintains that moral judgment cannot be explained by a "nondevelopmental" view of moral learning as simply internalization of cultural rules through verbal learning, reinforcement, or identification. Relating his work back to the earlier findings of Hartshorne and May, he points to a "view of overt adolescent moral conduct as a product of the development of broad social-cognitive capacities and values rather than of a 'superego' or of 'introjection of parental standards' " (Kohlberg, 1964a, pp. 324–325). He concludes as follows:

> The development of a morality of identification with authority is dependent upon "natural" social role-taking and the development of concepts of reciprocity, justice, and group welfare in the years from four to twelve [Kohlberg, 1964a, p. 323].

As a final point, Kohlberg, after identifying five types of ego-strength variables from the experimental literature, drew the following conclusion which is very relevant to our concern about the development of conscience:

> The above findings in the aggregate provide some support for the interpretation of moral character as ego, rather than superego strength. This interpretation implies that the major consistencies in moral conduct represent decision-making capacities rather than fixed behavior traits. It is thus consistent with the findings on situational variation which suggested that moral conduct was the product of a situational decision [Kohlberg, 1964b, pp. 391–392].

OTHER DEVELOPMENTAL STUDIES

In an effort to answer the developmental question of whether the early formation of conscience is predictive of good behavior over long periods of the life span, the studies of MacFarlane, Allen, and Honzik (1954), and of Kagan and Moss (1962) may be cited. These studies showed no substantial stability between ages six and thirteen on such traits as parents' ratings of selfishness and psychologists' ratings of aggressiveness over time.

In the Nobles County (Minnesota) longitudinal study reported by Anderson (1960) a "sense of responsibility" as measured by the Harris (1957) scale revealed early improvement in responsibility from nine to eleven years, followed by a plateau until thirteen years of age, and a second growth spurt from thirteen to sixteen years of age. Peck and Havighurst (1960) found considerable stability in moral character as shown by the ratings of community informants over the ages of ten to seventeen. As Kohlberg (1964) points out, however, this may be the result of an increasingly favorable reputation and halo effect in ratings obtained in the small city where the data were gathered, rather than to any real stability in the deeper aspects of moral character. According to Parke (1969), such data "argue against a learning theory interpretation of moral judgments as products of direct cultural instruction." He adds that "a learning theory approach may be more appropriate for explaining moral conduct data, which in contrast to moral judgments, vary greatly with situational and background differences" (Parke, 1969, p. 513). This illustrates the complexity of the field and how difficult it is to isolate different aspects for separate investigation.

In discussing the very sensitive and ingenious study of Aronfreed (1963) on self-criticism (which is essential to the formation of conscience) and reparation, Parke states:

> Self-critical responses are more likely to be made when the socialization agent provides the child with explicit standards of evaluation than when cognitive structure is minimized. Reparation, however, tends to occur when the child, rather than the agent, has active control over the corrective or punitive consequences of transgression [Parke, 1969, p. 512].

Ausubel (1955), in a very insightful presentation on guilt and shame in the socializing process, points out that guilt is one of the most important psychological mechanisms through which an individual becomes socialized and without which child-rearing would be extremely difficult. He conceptualizes guilt as a special kind of negative self-evaluation, when an individual acknowledges that his behavior deviates from a given moral value to which he feels obligated to conform. By conscience Ausubel means an abstraction referring to a feeling of obligation to abide by all internalized values.

Before guilt feelings can be experienced, Ausubel (1955) hypothesizes that certain developmental conditions must have occurred: *a*) the individual must have accepted certain standards as his own, *b*) he must also have accepted the obligation to regulate his behavior to conform to those standards and must feel accountable for any lapses from them, and *c*) he must possess sufficient self-critical ability to recognize when a lapse has occurred. Ausubel (1955) also makes an interesting distinction between moral behavior and conformity to ethical standards. He claims that conformity may be only an indication of submission to authority rather than acceptance of it, and that behavior can first be regarded as manifesting moral properties when a sense of obligation is acquired.

Aronfreed (1964) studied the timing of punishment and found that an undesirable response was more likely to be inhibited if the punishment came at the onset of the action rather than afterwards. The punishment after the deviant behavior had occurred was more effective in producing the acquisition of self-critical responses. Parke concludes that the general implication of Aronfreed's research is that different reactions to transgression "should be treated as distinct moral phenomena and not equivalent reflections of an underlying unitary phenomenon such as conscience" (Parke, 1969, p. 512).

Three other studies of particular relevance deserve special mention, not only because of their scope and careful methodology, but also because of their practical implications for child-rearing. The first of these is *Anger in young children* by Goodenough (1930), in which over 1800 anger outbursts were observed and recorded in detail by the mothers of 42 children. Anger outbursts were found to be related to time of day, state of the child's health, what activity the child was engaged in, and so forth.

Perhaps the most pertinent results of Goodenough's study in the context of moral behavior and conscience concern the parents' methods of handling outbursts. Many of the methods which brought the outbursts to an immediate end were not effective for long-term training in moral development, as they rewarded the child for his misbehavior (bribing, giving in to the child's desire, and the like would come under this category). Many verbal methods such as reasoning, scolding, coaxing, and the like did not terminate the outbursts, but nearly always had to be followed by other methods. This is interpreted as indicating that children often have temper tantrums as a means of getting parental attention, and these verbal methods do just that—give the child plenty of attention! The most effective methods were those usually described by investigators in the field of parent–child relations as withdrawal of love—namely, ignoring or isolation for the severe occurrences. When these techniques are used with a well-adjusted child, the child should always know that he will be back in the family circle as soon as he is ready to behave himself, and what he has to do to reingratiate himself. Small incidents with very young children are often better handled by distraction and a change of activity.

A longitudinal analysis of the individual records kept over a period of several weeks revealed interesting data regarding the consistency of parental discipline. When the cases were divided into those who had more than the average number of outbursts and those who had less, it was found that, with one exception, every case in the former group had parents who used inconsistent discipline so that the children had no opportunity to learn what would happen as a result of their misbehavior. Most after-effects, such as pouting and resentment, were found in the children whose parents were *inconsistent* in their handling. Thus children resent, and consider unfair, punishments based on whims which vary from day to day. After meticulous analysis of her data by statistical techniques, Goodenough concluded with the wise adage which might have been heard from the pulpit generations ago: "Self-control in the parents is after all the best guarantee of self-control in the child" (Goodenough, 1930, p. 247). Although Goodenough's analysis seems to have been suggested by learning theorists, her conclusion is certainly relevant to the modeling and identification aspects of the psychoanalytic tradition.

A rather parallel study on discipline in the home was reported by Clifford (1959) which involved 120 mothers of 60 boys and 60 girls from both upper and lower socio-economic levels. The children were three, six, and nine years of age. The three-year-olds were involved in disciplinary incidents on the average of once a day, the six-year-olds approximately once every other day, and the nine-year-olds only once every fourth day. For all the dimensions examined, age was the most important variable. Disciplinary incidents arose in situations concerning daily routines, establishing sibling and adult relationships, and in displaying behavior adults deem inappropriate. Mothers were primarily responsible for handling the incidents requiring discipline, and the fathers participated only minimally. Evidence was found that parents shift their disciplinary methods with the age of the child. This is attributed to the child's increasing communication skills, for as he becomes older he can communicate his needs and desires more effectively and can better understand the limitations imposed by, and expectations of, the parents. Clifford concludes that the child proceeds from rudimentary concepts to those which are more differentiated, and that the degree to which the child comes to establish his own set of behavioral standards is really the best measure of the success of the discipline. Since the older child was found better able to get along with others, better able to follow routines, and better able to participate in activities without requiring disciplinary measures, Clifford believes that his study showed that the older subjects had learned self-discipline.

A third study by Eberhart (1942) was based on 850 boys in grades 1 to 12 from the West Side of Chicago. Using the method of paired comparisons, he developed a scale of children's attitudes regarding the seriousness of offenses against property. Some of the offenses which were regarded as more serious by older than by younger children were "to swipe flowers from a park," "to swipe your mother's wrist watch and pawn it," "to sneak a rubber ball from a dime store counter." Offenses which older children regraded as less serious than younger children regarded them were: "to keep $1.00 you find on the street without trying to find the owner," "to help yourself to chocolates from a box in your sister's room," "to ride on the street car for half fare when you should pay full fare." About ten per cent of the boys were interviewed in order to determine some of the criteria for the moral judgments they expressed on the written test. Here the findings agreed with Piaget's report of increasing concern with intention and motivation. Offenses were judged more serious in proportion: as they were more likely to bring punishment; as they involved more valuable property; when the property was owned by someone toward whom an obligation was felt; when they injured an actual person; when they must be called stealing rather than "borrowing"; or insofar as they damaged the moral character of the offender. The absence of these features rendered offenses less serious in the judgment of the children. In general, younger boys reported fear of punishment more frequently, and in the upper grades the reason given most frequently was unwillingness to injure others.

PARENT–CHILD RELATIONSHIPS

Hoffman succinctly summarized the studies on the influence of family relationships and child-rearing practices on the child's development of a conscience as follows:

> Affection contributes to identification: psychological discipline which capitalizes on the affectionate relationship (and its resulting identification) fosters the development of internalized moral structures in general; and variations in type of psychological discipline may then account for the particular kind of internalized moral structure that develops [Hoffman, 1963, p. 312].

The same author goes on to conclude that, although in early childhood there may be little behavioral generality and little dynamic consistency, both tend to increase with age. The morality of the young child may be more a matter of rote learning of relatively specific acts and avoidances, but as the child grows older his standards become more integrated around broad principles and are more likely to be generalized from one situation to another.

In summarizing a related group of investigations dealing with children's reactions to transgressions, the same author concludes:

> Despite the diversity of theoretical approaches, measuring instruments, and moral content areas . . . , results have a common core of agreement that is encouraging. . . . We may tentatively conclude that an internalized moral orientation is fostered by an affectionate relationship between the parent and child, in combination with the use of discipline techniques which utilize this relationship by appealing to the child's personal and social motives [Hoffman, 1963, p. 305].

On the other hand, after reviewing a number of investigations on parental punitiveness, Kohlberg (1964a) concludes that there is a consistent positive relationship between conscience and parental punitiveness. Indeed, punitive aggression by the parent leads to aggression by the child, but it does not lead to moral learning. In spite of the experimental and naturalistic evidence of imitation of parental behavior based on power and prestige, it appears, according to Kohlberg, that there is almost no evidence that variations in parental power influence strength of conscience or strength of identification with parents. He also found that there is little evidence for a relationship between the sex of the dominant parent and various measures of conscience.

Probably the most devastating type of parental behavior for children's moral development is that which deliberately and openly flouts the moral principles which parents verbalize and try to instill in their children. The "white lies" parents tell, or ask children to tell for them, and the frequent forgotten or broken promises can do more to undermine a child's trust than preaching and religious education can counteract. Children are very wise and sense inconsistency and insincerity in the behavior of adults at an early age. This is the kind of thing which is present in large amounts in too many homes and which often counteracts the better moments and the good outside influences of school and religious educators. Parents who punish bad language by children, yet constantly present such a language model to their children, or who insist that children attend church, but do not go themselves, are guilty of this type of inconsistency.

One of the most baffling problems for parents, teachers, and religious educators concerned with helping children to develop a right conscience in a variety of areas, is the discrepancy between moral knowledge and conduct. Parents frequently admonish children for wrongdoing with the comment "You should know better!"—and indeed the culprit often does know better. But as so often happens at all ages, we "know better and do worse." This has been one of the greatest pitfalls to the clergy who usually are verbalists par excellence, steeped in abstractions of philosophy and theory during their long years of training, but who find themselves utterly frustrated and incapable of spelling out the abstractions and principles which they have absorbed in sufficiently concrete and specific terms to make them meaningful to small children.

Mothers, too, often become hopelessly entangled in semantic problems as they have become overly attached to the words of prayers or the catechism and find themselves unable to communicate spiritual and moral values to young children in language which they can understand. Children at first think very concretely in terms of their own limited experience. When they first begin to define words, around six years of age, their definitions are most often in terms of use, such as "a hat is to wear," "a stove is to cook on," or "an orange is to eat." Still later, the definitions are in descriptive terms of shape, color, size, or material, and only much later—about ten to twelve years of age—do they think categorically and say that "an orange is a fruit" or "a hat is an article of clothing."

Too often, parents, the clergy, and religious educators give the principles and expect children to be able to apply them in their everyday life situations. For the eight-year-old it is a far cry from learning to love one's neighbor to not hitting Charlie back, on the playground; or from learning to verbalize about respect for the property of others to not taking fruit from a fruitstand or the necessity of paying for candy in the supermarket. Much of the attempted moral training of children has resulted in disappointment because it is too much oriented to the intellectual approach, and when he *knows* better, the child's parents and teachers are baffled by the psychological problem of the motivation for disapproved behavior.

On the other hand, many childish transgressions are committed in utter ignorance that the specific act is dishonest, cruel, or impure according to his as yet imperfectly internalized standards. How often has a young child been called "a little liar" for something he said when he himself has no idea of what "a liar" is. It has been found that about 50 per cent of the lies children tell are told out of fear, usually as quite natural defensive reactions to the threat or expectation of severe punishment. Another high percentage of the lies of four- and five-year-olds are merely fanciful imaginative tales of children who are looking for attention or approval, and who have no intention of deceiving a listener. A great deal of psychological harm is often done to children by well-meaning adults who attempt to read moral meanings into innocent events or extract confessions even in the face of objective facts, or who label as lies the fanciful imaginative stories of creative children who need help in distinguishing between the real and the unreal. Extracting confessions is of little or no value. It often amounts to mental cruelty and never replaces the broken object.

SOCIO-ECONOMIC STATUS AND DELINQUENCY

Burton (1963) cites the work of Kohn (1959) who noted that different value systems have been found to characterize families from different social levels. Working-class families tend to stress the immediate implications of a child's act and want the child to stay out of trouble by not doing the "wrong" thing. In essence their approach seems to be entirely negative and to emphasize the "don'ts." On the other hand, middle-class parents try to help their children to understand the implications of their own behavior, to show them *why* they should not do certain things and to enable them to *choose* to do the "right thing." This fits in with MacRae's (1954) postulation that there are two distinct processes of moral development, the cognitive and the emotional. It would seem that the middle-class families, with their greater language skills enabling better communication and interpretation and generalization about ways to behave, tend to develop the cognitive aspect of moral behavior earlier and to a more effective level; whereas the lower socio-economic families are more concerned with the immediate control of their impulse-ridden children who have not learned to wait, and to trust, and to defer immediate gratification, as required in Erickson's (1950) and Goldfarb's (1955) conceptualizations.

The voluminous literature on delinquency may be mentioned briefly in this connection as it exemplifies the failure of the development of a normal conscience. The evidence is quite impressive that delinquents tend to come from homes where an excessive amount of corporal punishment has occurred. Rejecting parents have relied almost exclusively on physical punishment, often administered in anger with the children not knowing what they were being punished for. "Oh, she was always beatin' on me" is typical of delinquents' descriptions of home discipline. Eventually the children get too big for this kind of blind, unreasoned handling; the necessary affective bond for the normal identification is never formed, and respect for authority is not established in such children. The result is open rebellion in the form of delinquency and serious conduct-problems. In these cases there is no formation of a healthy conscience, and recidivism is common. Hewitt and Jenkins (1946) describe this type of child as the "unsocialized aggressive" youngster who is not helped by the usual psychotherapeutic techniques because

. . . he does not have too much superego: he has too little. One does not need to analyze a superego, rather it is necessary to synthesize one. One does not seek to relieve guilt-anxiety. One seeks to create it. This is done in essentially the same way that taboos are planted at any time of life, whether in the early training period of childhood when the process is normally most intense or in later life adjustments as upon induction into the Army. It requires the use of authority, firmness, planned limitation, and at times punishment. What is necessary for success is, first of all, a warm accepting attitude on the part of the parent or parent substitute [Hewitt & Jenkins, 1946, p. 86].

Since the parents of the above-described children often do not or cannot love them, the job usually falls to a counselor, teacher, or other parent-surrogate. It is necessary first to convince such a child that one has an interest in his welfare. It usually takes a very exceptional personality to be able to tolerate and maintain a warm relationship with these difficult children. The slow process of retraining such children usually has to be done in an institutional setting where *all* transgressions can be corrected. If these children are treated by methods suited to overinhibited, withdrawn children in permissive-play therapy, which leads to further open expression of aggression, behavior only becomes worse.

Not all children who engage in delinquent behavior are of this unsocialized aggressive type. Hewitt and Jenkins (1946) also identified a group of children who were called socialized delinquents who subscribe to the code of the peer group. These children are often the products of parental *neglect* rather than parental *rejection* who have developed gang loyalty which must be redirected. Either the individual children must be isolated from the group, or the whole group treated effectively by strong masculine personalities with capacities for warmth, fairness, and generosity of feeling. More recent work by Kohlberg found a

> . . . morality of reciprocity and equality . . . to be associated with lack of respect for adult authority, but with peer group participation. Judgements in terms of reciprocity, relativism and equality were found to differentiate delinquents from working class controls [Kohlberg, 1964a, p. 320].

RELIGIOUS TRAINING

The developmental psychologist who is trained to deal with the whole child in all the complexities of the total organism has difficulty in accepting the intellectual compartmentalizing of the person engaged in by philosophers and theologians. Piaget, for example, stresses only the cognitive aspects of moral judgment, yet developmental psychologists, clergy, educators, and parents are concerned with the moral conduct and behavior of children. In trying to help children develop a right conscience about their behavior, adults must be concerned also with the emotional and affective aspects of their lives as well, which include the feelings of guilt or shame as elements of conscience, and which to the developmentally oriented psychologist cannot be reduced to isolated intellectualized distinctions used by theologians.

In the home of religious parents, the child's religious motives can also be appealed to, for parents who have a deep, abiding faith in God and who recognize that their authority over their children is God-given inculcate in their children a belief in the Creator. Such parents can appeal to their children's love for their heavenly Father, which is a powerful means of accomplishing conformity to the standards of behavior they are trying to maintain in their home. Emphasis on the positive motivation of conformity because of the love of God and desire to please Him is much sounder psychology than the all-too-frequent and strong emphasis on negative motivation to be good because of fear of God's punishments. It is an aid in achieving perfect contrition rather than imperfect contrition and is much less likely to lead to problems of scrupulosity and overwhelming guilt feelings.

There are a few psychological studies which present some evidence on the influence of religious training. Of special interest in this connection is the study by Boehm (1962) who gave four Piaget-type stories to children from six to nine years of age and found a marked tendency for the children from Catholic parochial schools to make more mature moral judgments in responding to the stories, answering much more often in terms of intentionality than children in public schools. In similar articles on the same populations she had found differences related to intelligence and to socio-economic level. The differences in relation to intelligence and social class were not found in the Catholic school children, as the more mature moral interpretations seemed to have been communicated to the children of the working class in such settings as well as, or sometimes better than, to the children from the middle class.

A somewhat different dimension of what may be conscience as broadly conceived was studied by Novicky (1959) in his research on fraternal charity in Catholic students in parochial and in public schools. The students were matched on background factors so as to minimize the likelihood of finding positive results in favor of the parochial school children. The instrument was carefully validated and was highly reliable. At all grade levels studied—five, seven, nine and twelve—the parochial school children showed strikingly higher scores on fraternal charity. The trait measured by this instrument showed growth over these grades in both school systems, with some slackening at ninth grade and with the girls earning scores superior to those of the boys.

In an interesting study by Kuhlen and Arnold (1944), 547 children and adolescents, aged twelve, fifteen, and eighteen years, responded to a questionnaire consisting of 52 statements representing various religious beliefs and 18 statements dealing with religious issues. Many important age trends appeared in contrasting the beliefs of the twelve- and eighteen-year-olds, indicating an increasing tolerance and a discarding of many specific beliefs as they grew older. Catholics, all of whom were in public schools, wondered about fewer beliefs and checked fewer problems than did non-Catholics. One wonders if the same trend would be found since Vatican II. The study did indicate that many children had religious problems with which they wanted help, but they were dissatisfied with conventional church services and with the help available to them through their churches. In another study, Farber (1959) found that the presence of a mentally retarded child in the home had a less disintegrating effect on Catholic families than on families of Protestant or Jewish background.

An interesting volume by a psychologist (O'Neil) and a priest (Donovan) entitled *Sexuality and moral responsibility* shows the strong impact of Piaget's writings on some of the newer thinking in theology. The basic contention of the book is that "a viable morality must be solidly grounded in the established principles of the behavioral sciences" (O'Neil & Donovan, 1968, p. ix). These authors attempt to build a bridge between psychological findings on cognitive growth and moral development in children and recent theological thinking on the nature of mortal and venial sin. It is on the basis of material of this sort that such controversial changes as deferral of the Sacrament of Penance have gone into effect in some dioceses.* The problem of masturbation has also been reinterpreted especially in reference to the age of the penitent and to a morality of intention rather than of specific acts.

In the past, religious educators have often been disappointed that the catechetical method produced mere mouthings about theological concepts which young children did not really comprehend. The great needs seem to be to translate the abstract material or content into sufficiently concrete language to make it really meaningful to the immature minds of children, and then to find techniques for carrying children through the difficult growing-up and doubting period of adolescence when religious material formerly accepted on the authority of adults becomes accepted as mature beliefs, well integrated with scientific and other areas of knowledge.

It seems that from the psychological point of view religious educators in their current haste to innovate may be discarding something very precious in the early training of the young at their most impressionable age. Because previous methods of teaching have often produced difficult cases of scrupulosity even among the very young, and because of the increasing shortage of priests and the increasing numbers of children to cope with, Piaget's placing of the cognitive stage of "logical operations" as late as eleven to thirteen years has seemed to provide a welcome psychological justification for postponing the reception of the Sacrament of Penance until the adolescent or preadolescent years, when intellectually in Piaget's schema the necessary stage of cognitive growth has been reached for making the moral judgments necessary for an adequate examination of conscience, using the theological definitions of sin both mortal and venial.

Yet, as has been shown, much younger children can do wrong and they give evidence of feelings of guilt about their wrongdoing. It seems as though the early training for confession, when properly given, serves two very useful psychological purposes: a) it gives the child a way of disposing of his guilt at frequent intervals instead of cumulating it to be unloaded on the

---

* The focal point of the controversy is the reception of First Communion without antecedent reception of the Sacrament of Penance. In this connection, it is emphasized that Penance and Eucharist are two distinct and separate sacraments. It is appropriate, therefore, that pastoral concern should be separately directed to the best initial reception of each. Guidelines adopted, for instance, in the Diocese of Brooklyn state: "The theological understanding of sin, the experience of priests and catechists and the studies of developmental psychology lead to the conclusion that young children are not capable of mortal sin. Hence they should not be obliged to confess before First Communion." In keeping with this viewpoint, initial reception of the Sacrament of Penance might be postponed until the age of ten or even early adolescence, because it is judged, largely on the basis of evidence from developmental psychology, that the individual does not have the self-possession or freedom to sin gravely until this time. An indication of how sharply controverted this viewpoint is may be seen from the interchange of articles and letters on this subject appearing in *The Tablet* (Brooklyn) during October, November, and December, 1969, and January, 1970.—Ed.

therapist's couch in adulthood; and *b*) it gives him a feeling of reverence in preparing himself for the reception of the Eucharist. This feeling is also in danger of being lost in the newer methods. Whether these practices have theological validity is another matter, but psychologically it will be very difficult suddenly to expect certain religious practices at eleven to thirteen years of age, when the conscience has not been developed and trained gradually in small matters from the very beginning.

Because religious education has not always used the most effective methods is no reason for deferring the whole process during the child's most important formative years. There will always be a few obsessive-compulsive personalities who will develop problems of scrupulosity regardless of specific content taught. The number and seriousness of these deviations can be lessened by placing the stress on the positive aspects of love of God rather than on the negative aspects of fear of punishment.

Many adults never really achieve Kohlberg's highest level in moral development and frequently rely on techniques and crutches they learned as children, for they never learned to communicate on the level of conscience in an adolescent or adult manner. Individual differences are great, and faulty methods of religious education can be responsible for fixations at immature levels. The techniques and curricula must grow with the child, always a step ahead to challenge him, yet timed not to be so advanced as to be beyond his grasp, but never so repetitious as to bore him. Furthermore, it is only when parents and teachers exemplify in their own lives the principles they are trying to inculcate that they can avoid the current well-deserved accusation of hypocrisy, leveled by the younger generation.

Just as Piaget claims that the psychologist should not tell the educators how or what to teach, but should merely present them with the facts that research has discovered regarding the child's intellectual development, so Kohlberg draws similar conclusions regarding the moral development of children. He wisely points out that "Social scientists can contribute to *clarification* of moral education decisions both of ends and techniques, without imposing their values on others" (Kohlberg, 1964b, p. 424). Such clarification demands the communication of accurate and comprehensive information regarding moral development and functioning to parents and educators in terms they can understand and apply in everyday-life situations in their relationships with children.

REFERENCES

Anderson, J. E. Prediction of adjustment over time. In I. Iscoe & H. Stevenson (Eds.) *Personality development in children.* Austin, Texas: University of Texas Press, 1960. Pp. 28–72.

Aronfreed, J. The nature, variety, and social patterning of moral responses to

transgression. *Journal of Abnormal and Social Psychology,* 1961, *63,* 223–240.
Aronfreed, J. The effects of experiential socialization paradigms upon two moral responses to transgression. *Journal of Abnormal and Social Psychology,* 1963, *66,* 437–448.
Aronfreed, J. The origin of self-criticism. *Psychological Review,* 1964, *71,* 193–218.
Ausubel, D. P. Relationship between shame and guilt in the socializing process. *Psychological Review,* 1955, *62,* 378–390.
Bandura, A., & Walters, R. H. Aggression. *The 62nd yearbook of the National Society for the Study of Education.* Pt. I. *Child psychology.* Chicago: University of Chicago Press, 1963. Pp. 364–415.
Bender, L. Psychopathic behavior disorders in children. In R. M. Lindner & R. V. Seliger (Eds.) *Handbook of correctional psychology.* New York: Philosophical Library, 1947.
Boehm, L. The development of conscience: A comparison of students in Catholic parochial schools and in public schools. *Child Development,* 1962, *33,* 591–605.
Brock, T. C., & Del Giudice, C. Stealing and temporal orientation. *Journal of Abnormal and Social Psychology,* 1963, *66,* 91–94.
Burton, R. V. Generality of honesty reconsidered. *Psychological Review,* 1963, *70,* 481–499.
Clifford, E. Discipline in the home. *Journal of Genetic Psychology,* 1959, *95,* 45–82.
Durkin, D. Children's acceptance of reciprocity as a justice principle. *Child Development,* 1959, *30,* 289–296.
Eberhart, H. C. Attitude toward property. *Journal of Genetic Psychology,* 1942, *60,* 3–35.
Erickson, E. *Childhood and society.* New York: Norton, 1950.
Eysenck, H. J. The development of moral values in children: The contribution of learning theory. *British Journal of Educational Psychology,* 1960, *30,* 11–22.
Farber, B. Effects of severely mentally retarded child on family integration. *Monographs of the Society for Research in Child Development,* 1959, *24* (Whole No. 71).
Goldfarb, W. Emotional and intellectual consequences of psychologic deprivation in infancy: A revaluation. In P. Hoch & J. Zubin (Eds.) *Psychopathology of childhood.* New York: Grune & Stratton, 1955. Pp. 105–119.
Goodenough, F. L. *Anger in young children.* Minneapolis: University of Minnesota Press, 1930.
Grinder, R. New techniques for research in children's temptation behavior. *Child Development,* 1961, *32,* 679–688.
Gump, P. V., & Kounin, J. S. Milieu influences in children's concepts of misconduct. *Child Development,* 1961, *32,* 711–720.
Harris, D. B. A scale for measuring attitudes of responsibility in children. *Journal of Abnormal and Social Psychology,* 1957, *55,* 322–326.
Hartshorne, H., & May, M. A. *Studies in the nature of character.* Vol. I. *Studies in deceit.* Vol. II. *Studies in self control.* Vol. III. *Studies in the organization of character.* New York: Macmillan, 1928–1930.
Hewitt, L. E., & Jenkins, R. L. *Fundamental patterns of maladjustment: The dynamics of their origin.* Springfield, Ill.: State of Illinois, 1946.
Hoffman, M. L. Child rearing practices and moral development: Generalizations from empirical research. *Child Development,* 1963, *34,* 295–318.
Jersild, A. T. *Child psychology.* (6th ed.) Englewood Cliffs, N.J.: Prentice-Hall, 1968.

Kagan, J., & Moss, H. A. *Birth to maturity: A study in psychological development.* New York: Wiley, 1962.

Kohlberg, L. Moral development and identification. *The 63rd yearbook of the National Society for the Study of Education.* Pt I. *Theories of learning and instruction.* Chicago: University of Chicago Press, 1964. Pp. 277–327. (a)

Kohlberg, L. Development of moral character and ideology. In M. L. Hoffman & L. W. Hoffman (Eds.), *Review of child development research.* New York: Russell Sage Foundation, 1964. Pp. 383–432. (b)

Kohn, M. L. Social class and parental values. *American Journal of Sociology,* 1959, *64,* 337–351.

Kuhlen, R. G., & Arnold, M. Age differences in religious beliefs. *Journal of Genetic Psychology,* 1944, *65,* 291–300.

MacFarlane, J., Allen, L., & Honzik, M. P. *A developmental study of the behavior problems of normal children between 21 months and 14 years.* Berkeley: University of California Press, 1954.

MacRae, D., Jr. A test of Piaget's theories of moral development. *Journal of Abnormal and Social Psychology,* 1954, *49,* 14–18.

McLaughlin, B. (s.j.) *Nature, grace, and religious development.* Westminster, Md.: Newman Press, 1964.

Mowrer, O. H. *Learning theory and personality dynamics.* New York: Ronald Press, 1950.

Mussen, P. H., Conger, J., & Kagen, J. *Child development and personality.* (3rd ed.) New York: Holt, Rinehart & Winston, 1969.

National Institute of Child Health and Human Development. *The acquisition and development of values: Perspectives on research.* Report of a Conference, May 15–17, 1968, Washington, D.C. Washington, D.C.: U.S. Government Printing Office, 1969.

Nelson, E. A., Grinder, R. E., & Mutterer, M. L. Variance in behavioral measures of honesty. *Developmental Psychology,* 1969, *1,* 265–279.

Novicky, W. A. A comparison of the attitudes of fraternal charity between Catholic children with two kinds of educational background. Unpublished doctoral dissertation, Fordham University, 1959.

O'Neil, R. P., & Donovan, M. A. *Sexual and moral responsibility.* Washington, D.C.: Corpus Books, 1968.

Parke, R. D. Introduction: Moral development. In R. D. Parke (Ed.) *Readings in social development.* New York: Holt, Rinehart & Winston, 1969. Pp. 507–515.

Peck, R. F., & Havighurst, R. J. *The psychology of character development.* New York: Wiley, 1960.

Piaget, J. *The moral judgement of the child* (trans. by M. Worde). New York: Harcourt, Brace & World, 1932.

Riffel, P. (s.j.) *A psychological study of the personality characteristics of the pastorally scrupulous.* (Doctoral dissertation, Fordham University) Ann Arbor, Mich: University Microfilms, 1967. No. 67–11,496.

Sears, R. R. The growth of conscience. In I. Iscoe & H. Stevenson (Eds.) *Personality development in children.* Austin, Texas: University of Texas Press, 1960. Pp. 92–111.

Sears, R. R., Maccoby, E. E., & Levin, H. *Patterns of child rearing.* Evanston, Ill.: Row Peterson, 1957.

Turiel, E. Developmental processes in the child's moral thinking. In P. H. Mussen, J. Langer, & M. Covington (Eds.) *Trends and issues in developmental psychology.* New York: Holt, Rinehart & Winston, 1969. Ch. 5, pp. 92–131.

Abnormalities in the Development of Conscience

WAYNE M. WEISNER

Wayne M. Weisner received his M.D. degree from the New York Medical College in 1948. He is a psychiatrist with a double diplomate, one from the American Board of Psychiatry and Neurology, and the other from the American Board of Child Psychiatry. Some of his previous positions include: Chief of Psychiatric Service, U.S. Army Hospital, Camp Stewart, Georgia, 1951–1953; Director, St. Charles Child Guidance Clinic, Brooklyn, 1956–1960 and Consultant to Catholic Charities Family Service, Queens, 1960–1962. Currently, Dr. Weisner is assistant pediatric psychiatrist, North Shore Hospital, Manhasset, and is engaged in the private practice of child and adolescent psychiatry.

Both of the two extremes of conscience—the scrupulous person and the psychopath—represent a crisis in conscience, and the Institute is concerned with both crisis and conscience. The psychopath at one time was thought to be suffering from "moral insanity." This term is now outdated: today we have the sociopath. Unhappily, he is still with us. The sociopath is the antithesis of the scrupulous person, although in the severe form of scrupulosity the individual also appears to be suffering from "moral insanity."

Happily, however, with the current ecumenical movement and the recent and rapid changes in the Catholic Church, the scrupulous person, as we have known him, is fast disappearing. We are still left with the pre-morbid personality structure of the scrupulous individual, but, it is hoped, not with the set of symptoms that historically has been recognized and written about by our spiritual fathers over the last four hundred years. If nothing else, I am hopeful that this paper will lend historical perspective on this subject. More recently, Weisner and Riffel (1960) and others have emphasized the emotional and human aspects of scrupulosity to the point where this condition has been pretty well delineated and rendered identifiable as a clinical entity. We may even refer to it as a Scrupulosity Syndrome, if by syndrome we mean a pattern of symptoms that characterizes a particular disorder or disease.

In both the scrupulous and sociopathic personality there is a defect in personality organization, and thus a defect in conscience. In each, an unconscious sadomasochistic element is present; there is a problem in ego-development, and a malformation of the ego-ideal. The sociopath shows an absence of superego development, usually attributable to lack of love and identification in his very early development. He lacks the ability to empathize, to relate in a meaningful way, and fails to develop a conscience although he possesses the ability to exploit and manipulate. In the scrupulous person the superego has been too rigid, literal, and inflexible. Doyle (1964, p. 92) points out that scrupulosity becomes a major problem when concern over committing sin becomes the major concern of the day and disrupts the free flow of emotion. By scruple, as described by Riffel (1958, 1967), we mean an unhealthy and morbid kind of meticulousness which hampers a person's religious adjustment. Scruple means fear and insecurity which tend to make an individual see evil where there is no evil, serious sin where there is no serious sin, and obligation where there is no obligation. In a scrupulous person the infantile, irrational superego is seen as dominating the individual's activities.

DEVELOPMENT OF SCRUPULOSITY

Just as delinquent or sociopathic trends can be spotted by the age of seven or eight, so too is it possible for the clinician to recognize the scrupulously predisposed child by the age of seven or younger. Symptoms of scrupulosity not uncommonly show themselves by the age of seven and around the time of Confession and first Holy Communion. It often reaches full bloom and becomes more obvious to the clinician or confessor, however, at the time of puberty.

What causes this malady? We cannot readily dismiss constitutional factors; temperament does play a part. The scrupulous child has a set of behavioral patterns or personality traits that makes him prone to develop scrupulosity, given a certain environment and religious orientation. In over forty cases of scrupulosity which I have treated privately in the past ten years, mostly consisting of children or adolescents, all have had their grade-school education in Catholic parochial school. Most of the nuns teaching these children were, themselves, a product of parochial-school education. Many were undoubtedly scrupulous, obsessive-compulsive, and perfectionistic. McAllister and Vander Veldt (1965), in a study regarding psychiatric illness in hospitalized Catholic religious, noted that the religious patients outnumbered lay patients 11 to 3 in admission for obsessive-compulsive symptoms. The nun-patients also showed a significantly higher rate of paranoid and schizoid personality disorders.

The incidence of scrupulosity is about the same for both sexes. Not infrequently many of these scrupulous children came from large families and the patient was the only child in the family who developed clinical symptoms of scrupulosity. More often than not, one and occasionally both parents had symptoms of scrupulosity in their past life or admitted to remnants of such. Several parents had been treated for acute anxiety states in their early twenties. This fact suggests that the parents' scrupulosity rubbed off on this particular child who was constitutionally predisposed to develop such a malady.

Unlike the sociopath's, the scrupulous child's family is intact and his parents are productive and contributing members of society who appear to be living in relative harmony. Usually the child fits into that large group referred to as the over-conforming or inhibited child. The child, at birth, is usually described as good, compliant, easy to manage, and later shows a need and wish to please. Consistently the toilet-training of such a child has been without incident. Instead of "acting out" his angry feelings or dealing with his sexual thoughts and integrating them into his personality, the scrupulous child tends to over-intellectualize, is over-controlled, inhibited, and constricted. He has excessive and neurotic guilt with an excessively severe superego.

The scrupulous child has come to feel and believe that any expression of anger or anything associated with sex or sexual awareness is sinful. He suppresses and represses these emotions as well as their associated fantasies. Thus, normal fantasy life and sexual curiosity become too early and too quickly associated with temptation and with what is evil and forbidden. The scrupulous child feels guilty over his own sexual development or over noticing it in the opposite sex. This happens partly because during his early school years the negative aspects of religion and sex have been stressed, such as man's fall in nature, his concupiscence, sin, guilt, and hell. He has been taught about sins of the flesh, before he has learned or understood what the flesh is all about. The young child also tends to see things concretely and to accept things quite literally. He has received information about mortal sin which he cannot understand or conceptualize, especially under emotional stress. The scrupulous child consequently loses his ability to discriminate, and everything becomes a mortal sin. He confesses extra sins to be "safe."

O'Neil and Donovan (1965) contend that prior to the onset of adolescence children are not capable of the cognitive or judgmental acts necessary to commit mortal sin. The research findings they discuss reveal that conceptual thinking and autonomy of judgment are not present consistently in the average child before age twelve or thirteen. In the case of the scrupulous child, unfortunately, willpower, grace, prayer, frequent confession, and reception of the sacraments are inadequate to overcome faulty personality development, immaturity of conscience, anxiety, confusion, and lack of natural childhood spontaneity. In addition, the child has learned that a sin may be committed in thought, word, or deed. The thought becomes the action—an especially disturbing concept to young children with their magical and omnipotent thinking, or in a child with poor reality testing. Thus the child prone to scrupulosity, because of his background, personality, and religious training, wants to please, to do right, to be accepted by God, his parents and teachers (authority). Yet he finds that there are few if any outlets readily available for dealing with his normal developing emotions, feelings, and impulses. Anxiety is generated, he becomes immobilized by fear and indecision, he loses his capacity to discriminate, and finds himself confronted with either/or decisions (black or white).

Extraordinary defensive mechanisms and maneuvers are then called for and we see the resultant ambivalence, intellectualization, denial, reaction formation, panic, hysteria, somatization, and phobic, magical, ritualistic, and obsessive-compulsive (doing and undoing) symptomatology. Depression and crying are not uncommon. This is not a primary depression but is reactive, and is merely the result of the insoluble conflict the child finds himself in. He is literally "damned" if he does act, and "damned" if he does not. These scrupulous children frequently withdraw still further from environmental stimuli. Frank, aged twelve, felt he was "doomed" as he could not make up his mind whether he was doing the right thing or the wrong thing. He became more upset because he could not do anything about it. In this particular case he finally hid in the closet!

Often, passive death-wishes are present to escape the guilt, suffering, and the ordeal being experienced. Not too infrequently, then, the "moral insanity" takes the form of a transitory psychotic episode. This is because the ego is overwhelmed and the defenses break down, or the child becomes so vulnerable that any normal functioning cannot and does not take place. The teacher may note that the child's school marks suddenly begin to drop, his handwriting may become illegible, he may spend hours on his homework, he is slow in performing his normal routines, phobias and rituals develop, and so forth. Treatment usually alleviated these symptoms and prevented further personality malfunction and maldevelopment. It aided them in integrating their personality, improved their judgment- and decision-making capacity, and facilitated their reality-testing.

Mailloux (1964, p. 99) has observed that the scope of scrupulosity is far wider than that suggested by the older formulation that it is an element in the obsessive-compulsive neurotic and that it actually involves a pathological sensitivity of moral conscience which is seen in a large variety of clinical cases. In treating such scrupulous children, I commonly made the diagnosis of personality maladjustment with neurotic traits manifested by acute scrupulosity. They showed anxiety, neurotic guilt, somatic disturbances, depression, obsessive-compulsive and/or hysterical symptoms. Other scrupulous children were neurasthenic, schizoid, or schizophrenic with psychotic episodes of the paranoid, hebephrenic, or catatonic types. I would concur, however, that one of the most frequent or consistent personality traits present is the obsessive-compulsive.

Quite frequently we note that a specific religious event such as first Holy Communion or Confirmation is sufficient stress to precipitate the first acute episode of scrupulosity although the pre-morbid predisposition is present and the die has been cast! Joseph, aged twenty, was the exception to the rule and he had not received his grade-school education in the parochial school. He did, however, receive religious instruction for three years and was converted. Following his baptism he became scrupulous with a concomitant cessation of masturbation. He started numbering his sins, wanted to be more perfect, and felt he was unworthy. He began avoiding girls as they caused him to have impure thoughts. He became unable to make any decisions whatsoever, and was at the priest's door every minute for help. The priest noted rapid deterioration and referred him to me.

AUTHORITY AND TRANSFERENCE

There are similarities between the manner in which the scrupulous child reacts to his parents and to his confessor. The scrupulous child is more often closer to his mother, although quite competitive, and often seemingly emotionally aloof, self-centered, and self-sufficient. With the onset of this horrendous conflict in morality, the scrupulous child, like any sick individual, is forced to become even more dependent. Regression takes place and we find him asking his mother for "permission" to do things. He asks for permission to eat, permission to dress, and, in effect, he asks her to take the decision-making responsibility away from him—"Is it all right?"; "Is it a sin?" —ad infinitum. He seeks her approval, her acceptance, her opinions, in an exaggerated, childish fashion. We find him using such expressions as "I think so," "maybe," "I guess"—so as not to lie and because he doesn't know his own mind. This is a reflection of his caution, self-doubt, indecision, and ambivalence.

The above-mentioned behavior partly explains why in the past the confessor has often taken over the initiative in handling the severely scrupulous penitent. Not infrequently he assumes the decision-making role, assuming responsibility for the penitent, and at times demanding "blind obedience" to his directives. Patricia, aged eight, after using the bathroom, would inquire of her mother if her panties were wet. Mother would reassure her that they were not wet. This relieved Patricia of guilt and the child would then feel that it was "all my mother's fault" should her panties be or later become wet. Under these trying circumstances, the confessor's taking over the decision-making role is perhaps one of the few options he has open to him, especially when the penitent is immobilized by fear and indecision. Unfortunately the confessor soon finds this to be a two-edged sword. Just as the scrupulous child questions his mother and at times even demands that she reply in a certain way each time and often even in a specific tone of voice, so the scrupulous person makes similar demands of his confessor. He is quick to pick up inconsistencies or contradictory advice, or to feel that his confessor did not understand him, or that he had not made himself understood.

Suzan, aged twelve, worried that she might not have given the examining doctor the right answers when he examined her abdomen for appendicitis. She then wondered if the pills he gave her for treatment might be the wrong ones. Frequently, however, the problem is not so much a feeling of being misunderstood as a fact that the scrupulous person is so overwhelmed, overpowered, and controlled by his irrational emotions that he lacks the freedom to follow his confessor's advice. Underneath he is wrestling with his unconscious wish to see or do the forbidden (which frequently might be quite legitimate) or with his unconscious anger and resentment (which frequently might be quite justifiable). Unfortunately the confessor, by demanding "blind obedience" to his orders and suggestions, encourages a dependency relationship rather than alleviates one.

Confession itself is often a stress situation, especially for the scrupulous penitent—arousing much anxiety and mental torment. He is forced to make a decision he cannot make; he has to make himself understood, when he cannot understand even himself; and he has to ask pardon for irrational guilt. This impossible task may be aggravated by the dread of making a sacrilegious (bad) confession. Usually these scrupulous people are unable to make use of the "reasonable doubt" in deciding whether a thing is a sin or not, since they are beyond reason and are acting and reacting irrationally. Bill, aged thirteen, believed that his confessor was "making believe" and had not really given him absolution. To compound his plight, the scrupulous person realizes that it is the teaching of the Catholic Church that, if one believes a sin to be serious and acts upon this belief, he has then in fact committed a serious sin whether it is objectively serious or not. This realization completely paralyzes the scrupulous person as he has come to believe that almost everything is a serious sin no matter how insignificant or trivial.

The scrupulous child is almost always aware that these obsessive thoughts, compulsions, and phobias are foreign to his thinking, "silly," "crazy," and so forth. But he remains at their mercy. Scrupulous individuals refer to their condition as "it," "the thing." If their confessions are very troublesome, I usually advise scrupulous patients to go less often, and to consult their confessor outside the confessional—more as a spiritual adviser. The child himself resumes confession when he feels ready and more comfortable—this taking anywhere from one week to one year.

COMMON FEARS OF THE SCRUPULOUS

I shall enumerate a number of common fears I have encountered in the scrupulous child or adolescent. There is fear of stealing or lying: a boy of twelve years of age would ask his mother for permission to eat an apple; else he felt it would be stealing. There is concern over inadvertently giving a person a bad name or hurting his reputation, as well as physically hurting someone accidentally. Not uncommonly, scrupulous people are disturbed when driving a car for fear that they have accidentally hit someone without knowing it, or that they may run over a stone which will be thrown out and hit someone. Driving also probably unconsciously represents to them freedom, self-expression, self-assertion, masculinity, and perhaps an expression of unconscious sexuality. There is frequently ingrained a deep fear of bodily harm (unconscious castration anxiety).

The scrupulous individual becomes concerned over other people's actions and worries that these people might be hurt, blamed, get in trouble, or sin because of his acts. There is apprehension over sin, dying, being misunderstood, "rash judgments," and "bad thoughts." There may be dread of germs, rabies, tetanus, or of being poisoned, kidnapped, or murdered. I have treated three or four children who were afraid of having sold their souls to the Devil, of being possessed by the Devil, or of asking the Devil for help (this is reminiscent of the Salem witch trials). Michele, aged sixteen, became alarmed and found herself in a double bind when she wondered if she asked the Devil's help in getting rid of impure thoughts. Her need to call on the Devil for help was also related to her anger which she was unaware of. The Devil was symbolic of this anger. When her stubborn dog wanted to go the other way and refused to go into the house, Michele worried that she called on the Devil for help to get him into the house.

Eye symptoms may be present, such as looking back a number of times, beginning with three times because this is related to the Blessed Trinity. Then the scrupulous person finds himself looking back six times, nine times, and so on. Morbid fears of breaking the fast before Holy Communion and of eating meat on Fridays invariably existed under previous Church legislation.

TREATMENT

Treatment of scrupulous persons seems to mobilize their hostility and gives them ego-strength (and permission, if you will) to direct their anger and frustrations outward upon the people they are emotionally closest to, dependent upon, and involved with. These usually are parents, siblings, friends and, of course, the therapist. The mechanism of externalization of their anger during the treatment process permits them to be easier on themselves inwardly (aggression turned outward—with less depression and fewer symptoms). They also begin to express more open curiosity about sex and begin to ask their parents specific questions regarding sex. I have found it unwise therapeutically to get involved over what is or is not a sin, and such patients are referred to their spiritual adviser for this information. Surprisingly enough, this question rarely comes up as an issue during treatment! Scrupulous patients seem content to verbalize their fears, doubts, worries, and conflicts, and seldom ask specifically if the action was or was not a mortal sin. Nor are they disturbed if no direct answer is forthcoming; nor were they specifically advised by the therapist what to do or what not to do. The therapist's interest, empathy, concern, understanding, and acceptance is reassuring to them. Thus, through identification with the therapist and by ego-support the scrupulous person develops a feeling of self-worth, value, and self-acceptance, and is aided in ameliorating his excessively strong conscience or superego. Tranquilizers such as Thorazine, Stelazine, Librium, or Triavil are frequently used on an initial short-term basis.

The underlying personality structure of the child—his past adjustment and present emotional health (or lack of it)—usually determines the prognosis and outcome of treatment rather than the severity of the initial symptoms. Predominantly hysterical personality traits make for a better prognosis than predominantly schizoid traits. In the adolescent, resolution of the problem of scrupulosity seems to go hand-in-hand with acceptance of and adjustment to new-found femininity or masculinity. Toward the conclusion of treatment, these children begin to behave more like typical teenagers. They begin to engage in normal social activities with the opposite sex, and are more role-oriented, with a progressive acceptance of their masculine or feminine identification. This might be another way of saying that they were helped to develop a sense of identity and independence. They became secure and mature enough to reach a decision and act upon it.

Rarely do we find homosexuality among the scrupulous. It is not that they are not sometimes interested in or attracted by their own sex, but more that their scrupulosity represents a stifling of sexual curiosity, awareness, and expression. Certainly their scrupulosity also prohibits any acting-out of any such homosexual urges. I have treated several severely scrupulous adolescents who appeared to have an unconscious homosexual conflict, but these were schizophrenic individuals with paranoid traits. Needless to say, this scrupulosity and developmental process is often worked through by the child without treatment in the course of six months to two years. This is not true, however, in more severe cases. Riffel (1958) has found that one out of every seven Catholic college students is still suffering from scrupulosity.

A CASE OF SCRUPULOSITY

Debbie, aged eleven, and in the sixth grade, developed symptoms of scrupulosity around the time of preparation for Confirmation. Onset was sudden, with agitation, anxiety, despair, tearfulness, sleeplessness, difficulty in completing homework assignments, and a nine-pound weight loss. The acute symptoms began one Saturday while Debbie was at home doing a class punishment assignment. She felt that she was not doing it properly and that she was sinning. She was further bothered by "presumption and despair," and had the feeling "that I'm always doing something wrong." Should she give up trying to avoid committing a venial sin, however, she felt it was despair.

Each day her symptoms became a little worse—"If I touch the table, I'm really offending God." There were tears, she'd get a vacant, faraway look in her eyes, fold her arms and withdraw into deep thought, and she could not be reached. She became terror-struck that she might have offended God by touching a table-top or touching her arms with her hands—and did it mean she was striking God? Although previously very self-reliant, she began showing over-dependency on her mother—following her about the house and kissing her. She felt safe and with less chance of sinning if her mother was in the house with her (her alter superego).

In school when Debbie's nun returned from an errand, she asked the class how many times the girls talked. Debbie confessed to having spoken twelve times! This was for talking and making "breathing noises," none of which her classmates heard. She volunteered and did punishments which she felt were "unfair" as she felt better for having done them. Her nun would say to the class: "Did you talk? Examine your conscience."

At home, Debbie began saying "I don't want to go to school. I don't want to talk about sin." She disliked written punishments, yet she continued to confess to talking "just to have peace of conscience." She began to question if she wanted to sin and she questioned if she might wish to offend God by writing sloppily. Debbie was afraid that if she did not write properly, or if the words were written below the line, it was a mortal sin. This represented a reaction-formation to her preconscious wish to write sloppily and get back at the nun (and God) for "unfair" written punishments she compulsively volunteered to do because of her neurotic guilt and scrupulosity. Debbie felt better for it, as "it relieves my conscience."

Debbie's biggest concern was "Did I take a false oath?"; "Did I lie?" Twice in one night she came downstairs drenched in perspiration, asking "Did I lie?" Occasionally she had thoughts of "selling my soul to the Devil" or fears of being kidnapped or murdered. Debbie's dependency needs and oral conflicts were reflected in her regressive dependency upon and kissing of her mother, her nine-pound weight loss, her fear of breaking the fast before reception of Holy Communion (even with the more liberal one-hour fast regulations), and her belief that breathing was a sin. Repressed oral aggressive tendencies were evident in her fear that she would accidentally say a curse word. During treatment she also became stubborn, argumentative, and exasperating at home. For the first time in her life her mother recalled that she began to show her annoyance with one of her girlfriends.

At our seventh treatment interview Debbie's confession and Holy Communion were over and Confirmation was to take place the next day. At this point her mother was more encouraged and believed that Debbie genuinely wanted to get well. Our eighth and last interview took place two weeks later. Confirmation had gone well and Debbie had been free of all symptoms. Treatment was terminated at Debbie's request and things continued to go well for Debbie. In this case Stelazine, and later Triavil, was used during the treatment process.

ORALITY AND SCRUPULOSITY

One is impressed by the oral element in the scrupulous child, and much of the religious problem experienced is depicted in terms of an oral conflict. This is not surprising as these children are basically conforming, pliant, and passively receptive. I have observed a frequent similarity in the personality of the scrupulous child and of those children who are prone to develop Anorexia Nervosa, which consists in a psychological aversion to food with consequent malnutrition. The clinical picture and dynamics of the severely scrupulous child are often not too dissimilar from the child with Anorexia Nervosa. In one instance, I treated a nine-year-old girl for this condition, and six months later she developed symptoms of scrupulosity! Whereas the aversion to food is more quantitative in Anorexia Nervosa, it is more specific, selective, and religiously oriented in the scrupulous child.

Morbid fears of breaking their fast before receiving Holy Communion and of eating meat on Fridays invariably existed in the scrupulous patients of my experience. One twelve-year-old scrupulous boy would not eat any-thing on Fridays as he came to the conclusion that everything was meat—including fish and all other foods. He concluded that food had micro-organ-isms in it and that they are animals! Oral conflicts in three adolescent girls were illustrated in their eating disturbances—finicky eating, overeating, re-quiring permission to eat, disturbances and anxiety over germs and being poisoned. All three had conflict and fear about accidentally eating meat on Fridays. Their symptoms were commonly worse on Fridays and Ember days. In one of these cases, the proximity of any food to meat would "con-taminate" it, and another child went about all day one Friday with her lips puckered up so as not to swallow. Not uncommonly there is tension between the time of Confession and the reception of Holy Communion. Much of this apprehension is centered on the Host and the fast. In brushing their teeth, they became concerned that a particle of food might have been left in their mouth. There is an unconscious connection between orality and sexuality that often disquiets them. After Holy Communion, many scru-pulous persons fear that the Host is still in their mouth, on their lips, or that they might have gotten a particle of it on their dress, glasses, or other item. White specks on the altar bother them as perhaps indicating that the priest dropped part of the Host.

An international symposium on Anorexia Nervosa reported in *Medical Tribune* helps me illustrate some similarities between these two clinical en-tities or syndromes. In the anorexic, food was severely restricted and was secondary to a frantic attempt to establish control over the body and its functions. This preoccupation occurred in pre-puberty as well as in puberty, and not only in girls.

> Characteristic was an early childhood free of problems, the absence of the normal period of resistance—that is, compliance to an unusual degree. They had been well cared-for children, except there had been no regard for their individual needs. The illness represented a tragic effort to develop a sense of identity and independence. These children also revealed an over-conscien-tious but joyless atmosphere in which a child needed to develop an illness with a "dialogic" function [Bruch, 1965, p. 2].

Wall (1959) in a study of 15 female hospitalized Anorexia Nervosa patients found an active aversion to eating which was accompanied many times by compulsion and obsessive–compulsive features with perfectionistic trends. He reports that their feelings were not deep or warm, and that they moved with difficulty from one level of adjustment to another. These patients were immature and got along poorly with their siblings. All expressed a disgust for excessive weight, and all showed a marked ambivalence toward every-one in their lives. Wall noted a peculiar dependence upon the mother, with a hostile and spiteful attitude toward her. Around adolescence these patients did not wish to grow up, and the theme of renunciation and denial began to appear. They were shy with boys, there was a complete lack of oral impregnation fantasies, and he observed that eating became in some peculiar way equated for them with sex-life. They felt that their aversion to food would keep them from growing up. Finally, Wall observed in the article referred to that more recently younger patients had been referred for treatment and that their reactions had been more neurotic in character with outstanding hysterical, obsessive–compulsive, and depressive features.

From the above descriptions it would appear that the constellation of symptoms, early development and personality traits of the scrupulous child is often not remarkably different from that of the child prone to develop Anorexia Nervosa. In both cases one of the central problems revolves around an oral conflict. In addition, in the scrupulous child, fear, insecurity, doubting, and an unhealthy kind of meticulousness hamper the child's religious adjustment.

A CASE OF ADOLESCENT SCRUPULOSITY

Betty was a rather large, well-developed, mature-looking fourteen-year-old who illustrates quite nicely an acute, transient form of scrupulosity. Onset was sudden, and her parents related the turmoil, confusion, and hysterical spells which had occurred during the past two weeks. Betty became upset as she feared meat had been in the soup her parents ate on Friday. She insisted on seeing a priest immediately, wanted to repeat her confession, and felt that the confessor had not understood her. She kept wanting to see a priest, but his reassurance lasted only a short time. Betty became obsessed with the thought of male genitals. She was rubbing an apple on her stomach to clean it, had pregnancy thoughts, and became upset (oral pregnancy fantasies). She had hysterical spells the past two weeks with pressure in her head and various other pains. Betty accused her mother of stealing when her mother brought home some leftover food from a party given at her aunt's house. She had also been upset for some time by her father's doing odd jobs about the house on Sundays—and she refused to do anything herself on Sundays, such as bringing up the wash from the basement or setting the table.

Betty was the only offspring of older parents. Her mother gave the impression of being rather rigid and proper, whereas her father was more easygoing and not especially religious. Betty's early development was essentially uneventful. She seemed to get along well with people. She was described as being very religious and received Communion daily in grammar school. Her marks were always in the 90s but she worked hard for this. Betty had started high school several months before onset of symptoms, and her menstrual periods had begun at age eleven.

At our first meeting I found Betty to be likeable, friendly, girlish, and giggly. She flushed easily (labile vaso-motor system), yet she was able to speak about what was upsetting her. Betty believed that her difficulty had begun five months previously when she began worrying about meat being in her soup on Fridays. Now "everything" was a mortal sin. Yesterday, for instance, a small mark on her paper bothered her. Last month sexual thoughts became more frequent and strong, and she couldn't get them out of her mind. Betty had met some boys at the beach the previous summer and felt that this possibly might have some connection with her difficulty. Her drawings indicated sexual conflict, and she recently had become upset by seeing a pregnant woman in church. I took the liberty of describing pregnancy, birth, and sexual intercourse to her, as she was confused by this and did not understand it. She found the concepts nauseating and upsetting to her stomach (making a face and holding her stomach). After this first visit I had the feeling that Betty would respond quickly and well to treatment.

Betty was seen for a total of fifteen interviews. The first ten were for one hour and the remaining five for a half-hour.

At our second visit there was a lot of laughing, giggling, and smiling on Betty's part as she felt somewhat self-conscious and uneasy. She had been fine except for several thoughts about what we had spoken of last week, and she again put her hand on her stomach with a nauseous expression. She was disappointed on missing the honor roll with an 88% average. We discussed the tendency for Betty's face and neck to become flushed when she was nervous, excited, or laughed too much. She first noticed this two years ago at the doctor's office when she went for her annual checkup. There had not been any more anxiety spells. Betty was to go to Confession that night for the first time in several weeks. There had been some concern in the past that the priest had not understood her. Betty's father was seen for several minutes and he reported that she had been fine. She was happier, more relaxed, and had not mentioned Confession. Betty had improved, and I felt that the sexual information I had given her in our first interview had been helpful.

Betty would arrive happily. Initially she might mention a disturbing sexual thought or dream she had, and then she spoke of her weekly activities, school, dates, and boys. She had her first argument with her girlfriend whom she had known for years. She remarked that sometimes she was too good, could not get angry at people, and implied that they took advantage of her good nature. Betty also lost her temper with her mother, and had an argument with her "for nagging me." She expressed some difficulty with the girls in her class as they cheated and expected her to cheat and exchange answers. Betty could neither understand nor accept this. Not eating meat on Fridays and working on Sundays came up for discussion. Her impure thoughts were upsetting to her, made her nervous, and she felt "empty inside."

By our twelfth interview Betty appeared more feminine and less girlish and awkward. She began to wear lipstick and her hair was cut shorter and neater. During the treatment Betty was quite active socially and several boys had begun to take an interest in her. She attended school dances and basketball games. Betty also ceased having disturbing sexual thoughts. Her parents reported that Betty was doing more things and enjoying them all. She was happier, slept better, and an occasional sexual thought did not throw her into a panic. She was able to accept reassurance from her parents. The mother saw Betty as "one hundred percent improved." There were no more hysterical spells. She was not disturbed by her father's working around the house on Sundays and even ironed some things for her father on Sunday, which was unheard-of before. Her father was anxious to terminate treatment, and this was done after our fifteenth visit.

Betty never objected to or resisted treatment. Symptoms abated early, and this was because Betty basically was a healthy girl and fairly well-adjusted. There was an hysterical component to her personality and some unconscious exhibitionistic tendencies. Her need to please, to be accepted, and to be good, made it difficult to express any feeling of anger. Acute onset of scrupulosity developed around the adolescent period when she was having difficulty in handling her strong sexual impulses and curiosity. When Betty was able to view this as a normal phase of her development and accept herself more comfortably in her new-found feminine role, the acute symptoms subsided. During this period she kept in touch with her confessor, whom she saw every few weeks. Treatment would have continued longer had there not been pressure from her father to terminate, partly because of financial reasons. Several months after treatment I received a note from Betty's father thanking me for my kindness at a time when they most needed it and "above all for the help you gave Betty, who is now doing very well and is very happy."

A CASE OF A SOCIOPATH

The sociopath is one whose behavior seems to indicate a complete lack of moral scruples. Tommy is a good illustration of this condition. He was under my care between the ages of ten and twelve. During this two-and-a-half-year period I saw him for 118 treatment interviews. His parents were seen in counseling but resisted suggestions that they seek additional help for themselves.

During Tommy's early life no permanent, meaningful relationships were established; no feeling of belonging or trust was allowed to develop, and he lost any love objects by the age of two or three. This resulted in faulty ego- and superego-development (conscience), with subsequent difficulty and lack of concern in distinguishing right from wrong. Tommy lacked a feeling of self-esteem, self-worth, and value. There existed unconscious anger and frustration with self-destructive and self-punitive behavior that culminated in poor grades, trouble with teachers, parents, and, eventually, all authority. His unconscious guilt was acted out by his getting himself punished and restricted. There was no overt evidence of anxiety, and any underlying anxiety and depression were fended off by denial and acting-out behavior, which kept things in a crisis state. This gave him a feeling of well-being and being in contact with reality. It helped him maintain ego-boundaries and staved off more severe ego-disintegration. Any feeling that people were not for him was reinforced by his own provocative and rejecting behavior (injustice collecting). Egocentricity, mild grandiosity, feelings of omnipotence, impulsivity, ingratiating behavior, asocial behavior, narcissism, lack of consideration and empathy for others, living for the present, repetitive behavior patterns, and inability to profit from experience are all descriptive terms of the sociopath. These could be applied nicely to Tommy.

Tommy's mother was a matter-of-fact person who seemed interested in her son, but she was not an especially warm, motherly, or giving person. She had built up her own defenses for survival. His father was impulsive, erratic, and attempted to do violence to Tommy's mother. The family was deserted when Tommy was about one year old, and they had to fend for themselves. The mother returned to work, placing Tommy in a series of homes. There were three or four placements, each lasting about 18 months. At the age of three, Tommy became close to a grandfather who lived in one of these homes but he then died. A longer placement, far from ideal, took place between the ages of six and nine. His mother remarried and Tommy rejoined the home at the age of ten.

At this point Tommy would be a strain on any marriage. His stepfather originally tried to establish a relationship with Tommy and help him. He became disappointed and discouraged, however, in his repeated efforts to reach Tommy. He tended to personalize this and felt hurt by Tommy's lack of response and began to resent Tommy. There continued a series of mishaps and mischievous acts on Tommy's part. The stepfather was rebuffed in all his contacts with teachers, counselors, social workers, the courts, and even his own parents, regarding Tommy—all tended to sympathize with Tommy, take his part, and occasionally saw his parents as villains or culprits. There was some natural rivalry between Tommy and his stepfather for his mother's attention and affection. Her loyalty was torn between her son and husband. The stepfather was also immature in some areas and poorly adjusted socially. Gradually the stepfather began to feel that Tommy was persecuting him. The mother also began to feel this way, and eventually both parents tended to blame any and all of their difficulties on Tommy.

The parents were beside themselves when they brought Tommy to me at the age of ten. He had been a disruptive element in the household since his mother's remarriage, and was a focal point of disagreement between his mother and stepfather. Although a bright boy, he was a chronic under-achiever. Not only was Tommy failing in school, but he aggravated and antagonized his parents and made them angry in many subtle ways. He enjoyed getting a response from them, and was frequently confined to his room for lack of a more effective punishment. He tended to have difficulty with authority but seldom if ever openly rebelled. His rebellion was shown through passive resistance, and through provocative and manipulative behavior. He was generally uncooperative, believed all authority to be unfair, and was quite critical of others and reported adults to one another. He would rebel even when his own health and safety were involved. Tommy's emotions were shallow and superficial and he had little consideration for others. He showed no sincere love for anyone, and had no trust in others; nor could he be trusted. His parents believed him to be a deceitful child, but at times he gave the impression of being friendly, polite, and charming, although he often behaved in a senseless way. He had no friends and tried to get others in trouble, including his teachers. He teased and annoyed in a childish fashion, was unable to take criticism, and tried to change all rules, even in sports. Tommy ran away from home several times but always returned the same day. He showed no remorse or guilt. He smirked when caught in the act. His parents felt that his lack of guilt and conscience, together with his aggressive behavior, made him dangerous to himself or others. His stepfather began to see Tommy as another future "Bird Man of Alcatraz" or as a potential "Lee Harvey Oswald."

On first meeting Tommy I found him to be a bright, talkative youngster who seemed to be preoccupied with planes, war, powers, and the like. He was impulsive and hyperactive. He wished to be boss, craved attention, and looked upon himself as bad and "ugly." Initially he verged on delusions of grandeur and his productions occasionally verged on the bizarre. At first I felt that he was a borderline schizophrenic with behavioral difficulties (schizopath), but during treatment he resembled more the sociopath. It was difficult for Tommy to be good for any length of time; if he was good in school, he was bad at home, or vice versa. He was a constant instigator and provoker, and was most comfortable when everything was in a turmoil. He was adept at playing one person off against the other. When he wished to be good, he could be so for short periods of time.

Tommy had marked feelings of inadequacy and inferiority which he tried to cover up with bravado: he was working on a cure for cancer, or wished to be a famous general or a great baseball player. When pinned down, however, he admitted that he lacked the equipment for any of these. He remained friendly and likable although he continued to relate on a superficial level. Tommy had difficulty, however, in gaining insight—although I continued to point out to him his tendency to collect injustices and that he had a need to prove that people did not like him and rejected him. In turn this justified to himself his subtle, provocative, punishing behavior. He seemed willing to hurt himself in order to punish his parents and others. He presented me with an autobiography that emphasized all the unpleasant happenings in his life. Tommy felt he was not attached to anyone, recalled early possessions he had lost in moving from home to home, and finally felt that he was losing his mother to his stepfather. It was difficult for him to feel that I was genuinely interested in him and he expressed the view that "things would be different if I had a real father."

For the most part Tommy remained reality-oriented, although ego-adequacy was marginal. He was a boy who needed closeness, acceptance, and love very badly, and yet could not trust anyone's expression of positive feelings. Thus he assumed a light, casual, testing air, and thereby maintained a protective distance. He drew himself tightly in as a way of protecting himself and as a way of preserving himself from falling apart. He remained controlled with little capacity for object relations. He was more successful in non-emotional situations, but when emotions entered the picture his defenses would weaken. He would become more tense and anxious, his judgment would become impaired and his ego-controls less effective. Tommy remained an angry, unhappy youngster who felt rejected and different. He assumed a negativistic, mildly defiant, hostile approach to people as his protection against involvement and against further rejection and hurt. He cast his parents in an aggressive, hostile, and threatening role. At times they fulfilled that role because of his provocations. Thus the sadomasochistic, repetitive pattern continued with an unconscious need to be caught and punished —which he always was. Tommy never showed an actual psychotic break and therapy was supportive with the focus on ego-integration. Some attempts were made to change his environment and to change his parents' reactions to his behavior.

As is frequently reported in the literature on the sociopath, Tommy showed an abnormal electroencephalogram and had normal neurological findings. During treatment, various medications were tried without noticeable result, including Dexadrine, Stelazine, Thorazine, and Librium. I felt that, with therapy, he developed a little better opinion of himself. A lot of his aggressive and explosive fantasies subsided. At home, on occasion, he began to shed what appeared to be real tears for the first time in his life. His marks improved, and he passed the fifth grade with a fairly good average.

Tommy attended summer camp for two months, and he was enthusiastic about his camp experience. Like Tommy's nature, the camp report was inconsistent and contradictory. He was described as enthusiastic, eager, interested, and a participant. The counselors found him sociable, well-liked, a leader, intelligent, and ingratiating. He enjoyed all activities and functioned well. On the other hand, he needed individual attention and compliments. He had a low esteem for himself in some areas. Camp counselors also de-

scribed Tommy as domineering, provocative, antagonistic, resistive to authority, exhibitionistic, quick to fight, and impulsive. There was some clowning
and Tommy was inattentive to unpleasant things and easily distracted. He
wanted praise when good but could also be critical and resentful. He would
act out by running away, fighting, being belligerent, antagonistic, and
"easily provoked." His fears came out at night and he latched onto his
counselor's arm on overnight hikes.

Seven months after summer camp the parents got in touch with me and
treatment was resumed. Tommy was doing poorly in the sixth grade, and
remained exasperating to his teachers. As usual, the school report indicated
poor control and little consideration for others. Tommy remained optimis-
tic, however, and felt that in the end everything would work out all right.
As he once put it, even if he knew that he was to die in the electric chair
in two minutes and he had a chance to escape, he would not try to do so,
as he would still hope that something would happen to save him! His drawings became more orderly and less chaotic. Typical pictures drawn were of
two men fencing, a flying saucer from outer space, and a knight in full
armor waving a sword. I lost track of Tommy when he returned to summer
camp for the second time.

At age fifteen Tommy was administered psychological tests prior to his
attending boarding school. Test results showed Tommy to have an IQ of 112,
with a vocabulary-level estimated IQ of 135. His arithmetic level was eleventh
grade, and reading level thirteenth grade. There was much variability in his
test functioning, and his emotional problems interfered with his intellectual
performance. Tommy had much difficulty in maintaining concentration and
attention, and he showed a hostile and negative approach toward learning.
He became annoyed easily with the "loony tests" that "get me confused."
He was so easily annoyed that it was difficult working with him construc-
tively and he had very little frustration tolerance. He was a highly manipulative boy, willing to do anything to get his own way. Test functioning was
very variable: at times he functioned on a relatively high level; at other
times he fell apart. The tester observed that Tommy worked to "get" what
he wanted, and when this was accomplished little else seemed important.
Tommy hid his real thoughts and feelings from adults. He was suspicious of
the world and found it most difficult to trust anyone. There was much sense
of coldness and emptiness about him. He got annoyed when he looked
foolish and was troubled by the projective material that did not have a
correct response for him. In effect, Tommy tried to hide his real feelings
and to manipulate the world to accomplish his whims of the moment. There
was much potentially explosive material in Tommy's testing. The tester concluded that Tommy needed continuing help and that it was probable that
he would require constant supervision to keep him out of trouble.

Tommy was enrolled in a small boarding school geared to dealing with children who had emotional problems. He lasted about a year and a half. Initially he made a rather satisfactory adjustment. He was active and participated in many sport activities. Usually he had a good relationship with the other students and staff, although at times he showed resentment when required to live up to dormitory regulations. His adjustment varied with his moods and there were increasing incidents of a serious nature. When he got discouraged and depressed he resorted to self-punishment in various ways. He ran away on two different occasions, but returned the next day. He admitted to glue-sniffing and to a beer-drinking incident, and seemed quite anxious to get caught. Tommy used pressure to get other things he wanted. He tried to defy the staff, and sometimes seemed to be purposely trying to antagonize certain members of the faculty so that the administration would have to punish or expel him. At least on one occasion he mentioned the possibility of suicide, and began experiencing more frequent moods of depression. He stated that he did not care about the school and was not anxious to continue. It became difficult to keep him in a program. The principal felt it unfortunate that Tommy refused to make use of his potential, as he was liked by the other boys and staff. They believed that he was quite capable of being a good citizen, but it was impossible to motivate him in the proper direction. The guidance department at times found him responsive and capable of relating quite well. On other occasions Tommy was quite negative and resistive to all attempts to motivate him. Much time was spent in an attempt to get him to think in a positive fashion, with little lasting effect. Tommy admitted that he liked the school but just was not interested in education and did not want to be pressured. He claimed to have no real goals and implied that he had no feelings for his parents—thus making it most difficult to work with him.

Tommy became more uncooperative and on numerous occasions was outwardly defiant of school rules. He began to experiment with various types of drugs, and became one of the leaders of the drug group on the campus. He created a problem with his bizarre personal appearance by wearing beads, long hair, and other types of garb that tended to make him conspicuous.

One morning at 7:00 o'clock I received a call from the police. They had a boy under custody who had run away from school but refused to give them his name. He told them he had once been under my care. I prevailed upon Tommy to cooperate with the police. He voluntarily entered a drug-addiction center and after two weeks was accepted in a nearby residential center for drug users. He was thought to be psychologically but not physiologically addicted to drugs. Thus the problem became more one of control and restraint than a resolution of inner conflict. The task became one of re-education and socialization rather than reduction of inner tension.

Dr. Melitta Schmideberg (1960) points out that the offender, the criminal, or the sociopath is the social opposite of the neurotic. The former concerns society at large. He causes others to suffer, he reports for treatment only under pressure, is impulsive, and thinks too little about consequences. He is typically poor and uneducated, is unreliable, dishonest, reluctant to work, and not likely to pay for treatment. In treatment she has noted that the progress of the offender's case is marked by crises and social-legal complications; too much happens. Offenders are antisocial and lack self-control. She feels that the ultimate task is to re-educate and socialize the patient, rather than to relieve him of inner tensions. The immediate task is to help keep him out of jail, not to establish rapport. Nor does she feel that there is time to use any psychotherapeutic methods which do not view the patient's real-life situation as the primary problem of therapy, both ultimately and immediately.

REFERENCES

Bruch, H. Earlier diagnosis improves outlook in anorexia nervosa. *Medical Tribune*, 1965, *6*, No. 111, 2 (September 15, 1965).

Doyle, T. L. Scrupulosity from other points of view: A psychiatrist. In W. C. Bier (s.j.) (Ed.) *Personality and sexual problems in pastoral psychology.* New York: Fordham University Press, 1964. Pp. 90–97.

Mailloux, N. (o.p.) Scrupulosity in pastoral work. In W. C. Bier (s.j.) (Ed.) *Personality and sexual problems in pastoral psychology.* New York: Fordham University Press, 1964. Pp. 68–81.

McAllister, R. J., & Vander Veldt, A. J. Psychiatric illness in hospitalized Catholic religious. *American Journal of Psychiatry*, 1965, *121*, 881–884.

O'Neil, R. P., & Donovan, M. A. Psychological development and the concept of mortal sin. *Insight*, 1965, *4* (2), 1–7.

Riffel, P. A. (s.j.) The detection of scrupulosity and its relation to age and sex. Unpublished master's dissertation, Fordham University, 1958.

Riffel, P. A. (s.j.) *A psychological study of the personality characteristics of the pastorally scrupulous.* (Doctoral dissertation, Fordham University) Ann Arbor, Mich.: University Microfilms, 1967. No. 67–11,496.

Schmideberg, M. Psychiatric program helps to rehabilitate delinquents. *Factor*, 1960. *1* (3), 1 & 14.

Wall, J. H. Diagnosis, treatment and results in anorexia nervosa. *American Journal of Psychiatry*, 1959, *115*, 997–1001.

Weisner, W., & Riffel, P. A. Scrupulosity: Religion and obsessive-compulsive behavior in children. *American Journal of Psychiatry*, 1960, *117*, 314–318.

Superego and Conscience

ROBERT J. CAMPBELL

Robert Jean Campbell, III, M.D. is Director, both of the Division of Community Mental Health, and of the Division of Training and Education, Department of Psychiatry, St. Vincent's Hospital and Medical Center, New York City. He is also associate in psychiatry, Columbia University, College of Physicians and Surgeons, and adjunct professor, Psychology Department, Fordham University Graduate School. Prior to these current positions, Dr. Campbell was Chief, Psychiatry and Neurology Division, Camp Gordon Rehabilitation Training Center, Camp Gordon, Georgia (1951–1953); Senior Clinical Psychiatrist, New York State Psychiatric Institute (1953–1956); and Chief of In-Patient Service, Jacob L. Reiss Mental Health Pavilion, St. Vincent's Hospital, New York (1956–1961). His A.B. degree is from the University of Wisconsin, his M.D. from the College of Physicians and Surgeons, Columbia University, and his diplomate in psychiatry from the American Board of Psychiatry and Neurology. He is the author of over twenty-five professional articles and the editor of both the third and the fourth editions of Hinsie & Campbell's *Psychiatric Dictionary.*

In psychoanalytic psychology, the superego is one of the three major sub-divisions of the psyche; yet important as is the place it has been assigned in the trinity of psychic functioning, its recognition as a separate mental structure came very late in Freud's never-ending refinements of his theories. As early as 1896, to be sure, he had suggested that self-reproaches for forbidden childhood activity were the core of obsessional ideas (Freud, 1896), and in *The Interpretation of dreams* (1899) he referred to a censorship mechanism that kept morally unacceptable ideas from reaching consciousness. But the term superego does not appear until 1923, when he subsumed both conscience and the ego-ideal under his newly named structure. Unfortunately, it is not always clear even in Freud's own writings what part of the superego is being talked about when the word is used—the conscious part called conscience, the unconscious self-critical part, or the partly conscious and partly unconscious part that has to do with self-love and self-esteem. As a result, there has been some degree of misinterpretation of the relationship between psychoanalysis on the one hand and morality, ethics, and value systems on the other. In dealing with patients, for example, most of us are struck with the unrealistically harsh and punitive aspects of the unconscious, self-critical part of the superego, and one of the steps in therapy is to help the patient free himself from his sadistic taskmaster. It is not hard to see that the next step might logically seem to be to free the patient also from the nagging qualms of his conscience. And many did, in fact, proceed along those lines. "Twenty-five years ago, in the heyday of Freudianism, most psychologists, if they were interested in the phenomenon of conscience at all, were concerned only to the extent of discovering how to get rid of it" (Mowrer, 1965, p. 244).

But the earlier theory, that mental health is threatened by too much control or excessive restriction of the drives, has been modified. Nowadays it is recognized that optimal psychic functioning requires that the drives be kept under some degree of control. That control depends not only upon maintenance of an internal equilibrium of mental energies ("ego mastery"), but also upon an external equilibrium that might best be termed social organization. It has long been known that failure of internal mechanisms of control can lead to exaggerated use of inappropriate defenses and thus produce symptoms of neurosis. It is now known that social disorganization too can promote malfunctioning of the mental apparatus. It is largely the superego that exerts such control in post-infancy years; it stands as a watchdog over the internal forces, so as to effect the fullest possible integration within the social units of which the person is a part.

The superego is the representative of society within the psyche. It is a repository of "do's" and "don'ts"—both conscious and unconscious, not only current rules and regulations but also prohibitions and restrictions from the distant past. It sets standards to be followed, establishes values to be adhered to, and sculpts an idealized image of self within the psyche that the ego is relentlessly prodded to attain. Sometimes harshly critical and punitive, sometimes gently approving and laudatory, the superego is a servomechanism that continuously scans and evaluates the activities of the ego, judges its accomplishments in terms of a rigid code of ethics and morality, and measures its achievements against an unrealistic standard, the ego-ideal.

DEVELOPMENT OF THE ARCHAIC SUPEREGO

The superego is the latest part of the psyche to develop. It is a split-off portion of the ego that arises on the basis of identifications with certain aspects of the introjected parents. Yet since introjection and identification are among the first defense mechanisms to appear, it is clear that the beginnings of the superego date back to early infancy. Such precursors consist mainly of the various effects which the demands and prohibitions of parents and parent-surrogates have on the child. The standards and ideals, the tastes, the judgments about what is done or what is not done—all these ways that the significant adults have of assessing reality are transmitted to the infant as those same adults train and control him. Very early in his life, his autarchic fiction of omnipotence is destroyed by them, but he tries to regain that power by making himself into a replica of those masters of his still small world. Even by the age of six months, the child can be seen to be imitating the gestures and actions of his mother as the most effective way of avoiding her rebukes and, later, of gaining her approval. He imitates, of course, what he sees, and later what he hears—but what he sees and hears will be grossly distorted by his imperfect differentiation between self and non-self, by his failure to separate cause from effect, relevant from irrelevant. Further, he tends to perceive external reality in all-or-none terms—either all good or all bad—and in terms of harsh and brutal physical punishment. The period of toilet training—in our culture, the first time of open conflict between mother and child—is particularly likely to intensify the child's fear of physical retaliation for wrongdoing and loss of control. The so-called sphincter morality concerning what can and what cannot be done that develops at this time, while admittedly more a response to immediate demands of the significant others than obedience to an internal authority, nonetheless sets a pattern for the later regulatory system concerned with what *ought* to be done and what *ought not* to be done.

Within the perceptive and anticipatory part of the ego, in other words, is developing a core of rules, regulations, standards, and values—a core that grows by a series of successive identifications with the adults about the child, at least as he perceives them. In the oedipal phase, that core is enormously expanded, and the infantile superego begins to take its final form as an internal authority that stands between ego and id, an internalized environment that compels the person on his own to renounce certain pleasures and metes out punishment in the form of shame and guilt for violations of its orders.

DEVELOPMENT OF THE EGO-IDEAL

So far we have described the development of the harsh, critical, punitive part of the archaic superego. Linked to the same idealization of parental power that led to identifications with the perceived value system of the punishing parents is still another aspect of the superego. The ego-ideal, as it is called, is the love side, rather than the hate side, of early relationships with the parents, and probably begins as a kind of magical union with the omnipotent and loving mother. The imagined participation in her omnipotence sets a standard—unrealistic and unattainable—that the superego uses as a measure of what the ego achieves. The ego-ideal may well be a source of comfort and security to the ego, offering it guidance, protection, and empathetic concern, and keeping its faith in the ego even when all else has failed. But it also has its negative aspects, for persisting failure to draw near to a goal impossible to reach may produce chronic disenchantments and depression, and no achievement seems worthy when compared with the perfection of infantile phantasies (Cameron, 1963).

DEVELOPMENT OF THE OEDIPAL SUPEREGO

The superego as we know it in the adult is mainly an outgrowth of the oedipal phase—as Freud (1923) said, it is the heir of the Oedipus complex. It is a solution to the impulses of this period, which have no prospect of succeeding in reality and which, if allowed to continue, would be dangerous. The phallic phase and the Oedipus complex necessitate new modes of dealing with impulses, aggressive as well as sexual. The love for the mother, and the hatred of the father, must both be withdrawn from the parent objects. As it happens, the defenses used to accomplish this are introjection and identification—and, just as they did earlier with the archaic precursors of the superego, those defenses result in a modification of the ego itself. The part of the ego so modified is termed superego—it contains the sadism that was originally directed against the father, and it also contains the love originally felt for the mother. As before, the internalization of the parents, their standards, their love, and their controls, is an identification with such qualities as they are perceived by the child, and not to the parents as they are in the light of perfect reality testing. Furthermore, the child identifies not only with the conscious and unconscious useful parts of the adults around him, but also with unuseful ways they have of dealing with reality, including ways that they may even dislike in themselves. It must not be assumed that parenthood suddenly confers perfection on people, and their imperfections may well form important parts of their children's superego organizations. Many parents indeed have clinically obvious superego defects, and the child of such parents is likely to develop a superego that will reflect those defects. Since the child may be as alert to unconscious impulses in the parents as to their conscious and deliberate attitudes, his superego may develop on the basis of frustrated parental desires, in recognition of the parent's unconscious wish for the child to act out forbidden impulses. This appears to be particularly true in some cases of antisocial behavior and sexual perversions; in cases of inadequate sex identity and sexual cross-identification, for example, parental psychopathology produces a kind of "superego corruption" and fosters attitudes and interests characteristic of the sex opposite from that of the child (Cameron, 1963). When the personalities of the oedipal parents are the reverse of the usual—that is, when it is the father who is passive and the mother who is domineering and aggressive—one might predict that the boy would fear the mother as the potential castrator. Yet such is not the case; in fact, the more passive and ineffectual the father, the greater the son's anxiety about him is. No matter what the reality, the father is made over into an awesome avenger. This suggests that in part the Oedipus complex is biologically or phylogenetically determined, and that the superego may indeed be a vehicle of racial inheritance as Freud long ago theorized (Rubenstein & Levitt, 1957). It further underlines the extent of the child's own contribution to the structure of his superego. The more intense his drives in relation to the oedipal situation, the more harsh and unyielding will his superego controls be, since they are the major means he has of preventing his own destruction.

To recapitulate what has happened in the oedipal period: the frustrations of that phase have caused the ego to resort to primitive methods of defense —introjection and identification. As a result, the oedipal objects are regressively replaced by identifications, and sexual longing for the maternal object has been replaced by an asexual alteration within the organization of the ego. These newly introjected objects, which replace the sexual and hostile impulses toward the parents, combine with the earlier introjects of the archaic or pre-phallic period, and the superego is formed. While its growth will by no means stop at this stage, it is at the oedipal period that we can see the superego for the first time as an independent internal stabilizer or modifier of behavior with its own rules and codes, rather than merely a storage site or memory depot for the prohibitions and demands arising from the immediate environment.

The superego is now a part of the child's own psyche and not just an intruder given overnight lodgings. It begins to function as an ally and adviser of the ego in testing, evaluating, and adapting to reality, and as a means of controlling instinctual forces which—if expressed—would endanger the ego. It may decide, for example, that an instinctual drive may be gratified, whereupon the ego is free to seek expression for the drive. On the other hand, it may denounce the drive in any form, and force the ego to expel all traces of it through repression. Most commonly, though, it espouses conditional or indirect gratification, and to sustain superego sanction the ego resorts to other defensive maneuvers. Among these are sublimation through desexualization or desagressivization, wherein the original drive is neutralized and expressed as a non-sexual or non-aggressive derivative. Thus an early impulse to watch or listen to the parents' sexual activities may become the counselor's interest in his clients' emotional lives. But if the chief defense is reaction-formation, that early impulse may be reversed into an attack on pornography, or a crusade against smut—the fanatic intensity of which betrays how strong the original impulse was, if such stern measures are necessary to control it.

FEMALE SUPEREGO DEVELOPMENT

We are less certain about superego development in the woman—not, to be sure, that we find her less conscience-ridden or idealistic than the man, but because even for the most brilliant of theorists woman has remained something of a mystery. Her Oedipus complex is different from the boy's, for she has in fact no penis to lose through retaliative castration, and she has less apparent reason to abandon her love objects and convert them into the internalized structure of the superego. Probably her pre-oedipal introjects—and thus her "archaic super-ego"—are the same as the boy's. But how does she ever arrive at the phase of transferring her love from the original maternal object onto the father? There is some reason to believe that while the possibility of castration is the major reason for ending the boy's oedipal phase, it is the major force in beginning that phase in the girl. She finds that she has no penis and may first think that one really is there but has not yet grown. Then she wonders if perhaps she had one once, but lost it. According to some writers, she blames the mother for her loss, and then turns to her father in hopes that he will make up for her inadequacy. Perhaps he can give her his penis, or his love, or perhaps his penis can give her a substitute organ in the form of a baby. She becomes the mother's rival, but fearing further retaliation or mutilation she slowly abandons her hopes and identifies with the mother. Superego formation is thus more prolonged in the girl, and the ego-ideal (in the main, deriving from the mother) is more pronounced, with an emphasis on "inner" values and high standards.

THE POST-OEDIPAL SUPEREGO

Within the post-oedipal superego we can distinguish several subdivisions, at least in theory: the superego proper, the ego-ideal, and conscience. The ego-ideal is predominantly a reflection of the relationship with the mother; it has to do with standards of thought, feeling, and conduct, and serves as a model of what one is, as well as what one would like to be. The superego proper, on the other hand, is predominantly a reflection of the relationship with the father, and imposes an unconscious system of morality on the ego, being particularly concerned with the control of aggressive and destructive impulses. Conscience is the relatively small conscious portion of the superego system; it includes the ideals and aspirations of which the person is aware, and also those recognized internal prohibitions against impulses. One has pangs of conscience, if you will, when he has acted in a way that he consciously knows to be wrong; he has superego pangs when the ego acts, or merely thinks about acting, in a way that is counter to a standard set up so long ago that the ego no longer knows that a rule is being broken. Before the oedipal period, one can see in the child what Piaget (1951) has termed a "morality of constraint"; this morality is heteronomous and externally imposed, rather than autonomous and independently operating, and it directs the child to obey in order to avoid punishment. Only after the massive repression of infantile impulses that begins with the oedipal phase can be seen the beginnings of a "morality of cooperation," which continues to develop through adolescence and adulthood in interactions with peers and in relationship to the values and standards of the whole world with which the person has contact. Introjection, incorporation, and identification—the chief building blocks in superego function—continue to be used throughout life, and over the years one's ideals and codes are changed by relationships established with many different persons. Many of those changes, of course, are conscious, and in relative harmony with reality; but others are unconscious and are absorbed into the web of the superego proper, which is neither totally realistic nor wholly infallible. Rather, it may represent distortions, misinterpretations, or liabilities of the objects who have been introjected, and yet it may demand that the ego act in accord with those distortions. Because of its childish origins, the mode of operation of the superego imposes a kind of archaic logic on ego functioning. It operates by the talon principle, and whenever one of its rules has been broken restitution must be made in kind. Furthermore, it is in touch with unconscious as well as conscious mental life and makes no discrimination between wish and deed; thus unconscious wishes are punished as severely as accomplished deeds. And it is largely with those unconscious portions of superego organization that we concern ourselves clinically; the conscious portions, or conscience, are mainly of concern to us if they are absent. The adolescent, for example, must acomplish at least two tasks that are related to values: establishment of an internal pattern of control over impulses, and the construction of an individual moral philosophy to provide him with a sense of personal identity and a set of values (Knight, 1968). If he does not accomplish these inter-related tasks, we can anticipate that his future functioning will be impaired.

THE SUPEREGO IN ADULT LIFE

Let me now turn briefly to a consideration of some of the superego's functioning in adult life:

1. *Regulation of self-esteem.* In large part, self-esteem is a reflection of how close one has come to his ego-ideal. Lowered self-esteem results from a failure to measure up to that ego-ideal and threatens the person with loss of the superego's love, empathy, and protection. An awareness of not measuring up, particularly with respect to one's appearance, capacity, and performance, is expressed as shame or as feelings of inferiority. It is not often that we can remedy ugliness, stupidity, or lack of social or economic power; nor can we easily hide those defects from others—and the more those defects are likely to be exposed, the most intense will our feelings of shame and inferiority be. One powerful source of self-esteem and pride, however, is work; for not only does work satisfy the superego, in addition it evokes admiration from other people and from the community (Ostow, 1965).

2. *Guilt feelings.* These represent an admonition from the critical portion of the superego that one has done wrong; as already noted, such a judgment is equally as harsh on unconscious thought as actual deed, and in practice we find that guilt feelings are particularly related to aggressive impulses toward other objects. Once the judgment of guilty has been leveled, the ego must make restitution; but this is easier said than done, when the ego does not know what crime has been committed, or what penitential measures will placate its intransigent judge.

3. *Moral masochism or Fate-neurosis.* The moral masochist has a need for punishment, and must act against his own interests, even to the point of destroying himself, in order to provoke punishment from authority figures as a way of undoing guilt feelings. Often the latter are related to forbidden oedipal impulses, and the moral masochist seeks his superego's forgiveness by demonstrating how much he suffers at others' hands.

4. *The criminal from a sense of guilt* is a special kind of moral masochist, whose antisocial activity provokes punishment from the community, a punishment that he hopes will satisfy his superego as adequate expiation for his unconscious crimes.

5. *Asceticism.* This is still another kind of moral masochism, in which

mortification, suffering, self-sacrifice, and self-injury are actively sought (instead of passively and seemingly accidentally endured, as in the moral masochist). In most such cases, mortification is sexualized and the self-injury is a distorted expression of the masked sexuality or aggressivity.

6. *Some types of delinquency,* already referred to, where defective parental superegos have produced gaps or lacunae in the child's superego. As Adelaide Johnson (1949) has pointed out, parental vacillation, ambiguity, or equivocation fosters antisocial behavior. The spurious admonition to proper behavior is rendered futile by parental permissiveness, and children sense the permission. Excessive parental concern for imagined future sexual misdeeds, suspicious questioning of the child about his behavior, and the phantasy that the child will get into sexual trouble—all serve to propel toward later sexual delinquencies.

7. *Distorted superego operations* are particularly evident in some of the neuroses and psychoses—obsessive–compulsive neurosis, depressive reactions, mania, paranoia, and schizophrenia. Space does not permit a discussion of these more specific psychiatric entities, but because of the frequency with which it expresses itself in questions of sin and morality, the obsessive–compulsive disorder ought to be mentioned. Symptomatically, the condition is characterized by spells of doubting and brooding, bouts of ritual-making and burdensome penitential measures, and fits of horrific temptation that may be expressed as confession-compulsions. The neurosis is rooted in the rage and defiance of the child during the period of toilet training, and many of his most distressing symptoms are distorted manifestations of aggression against all authority figures, including God. His endless broodings about what is right and wrong, his questions about how much of a sin is a sin, his obsequious compliance with each letter of the law and total disregard of its spirit are—at least at times—nothing more than disguised attempts to outsmart the lawmaker, to beat his parents at their own game, or to make a fool of his mentor or counselor, who is just one more representative of the authority he despises.

REFERENCES

Brenner, C. *An elementary textbook of psychoanalysis.* New York: International Universities Press, 1955.

Cameron, N. *Personality development and psychopathology.* Boston: Houghton Mifflin, 1963.

Fenichel, O. *The psychoanalytic theory of neurosis.* New York: Norton, 1945.

Freud, S. Further remarks on the defence neuro-psychoses (1896)–(trans. by J. Riviere). In *Collected papers.* Vol. I. London: Hogarth, 1948. Pp. 155–182.

Freud, S. *The interpretation of dreams* (1899)–(trans. by J. Strachey). New York: Basic Books, 1958.

Freud, S. *The ego and the id* (1923)–(trans. by J. Riviere). London: Hogarth, 1927.

Johnson, A. Sanctions for superego lacunae of adolescents. In K. Eissler (Ed.) *Searchlights on delinquency.* New York: International Universities Press, 1949. Pp. 225–245.

Klein, M. On the development of mental functioning. *International Journal of Psychoanalysis,* 1958, *39,* 84–90.

Knight, J. A. Adolescent development and religious values. *Voices,* 1968, *4,* 68–72.

Mowrer, O. H. Learning theory and behavior therapy. In B. B. Wolman (Ed.) *Handbook of clinical psychology.* New York: McGraw-Hill, 1965. Pp. 242–276.

Ostow, M. Psychic energies in health and disease. In N. S. Greenfield & W. C. Lewis (Eds.) *Psychoanalysis and current biological thought.* Madison: University of Wisconsin Press, 1965. Pp. 339–361.

Piaget, J. *Play, dreams and imitation.* New York: Norton, 1951.

Rubinstein, B. O., & Levitt, M. Some observations regarding the role of fathers in child analysis. *Bulletin of the Menninger Clinic,* 1957, *21,* 16–27.

Social Influences in the Development of Conscience

GERALD M. SHATTUCK

Gerald M. Shattuck received his A.B. degree (1953) from LeMoyne College, Syracuse, and his M.A. (1962) and Ph.D. (1964) degrees from Cornell University. He is a member of the American Sociological Association and the American Society for Criminology, and a contributor to professional journals in sociology. Dr. Shattuck is particularly active in sociological research, and is the Director of the Institute for Social Research at Fordham University, where he is an associate professor of sociology.

In approaching the question of conscience from the sociological viewpoint, three basic questions may be raised: *a*) what does conscience mean for society?; *b*) how does the societal view of conscience relate to the life of the individual member?; *c*) what is it about the condition of our present society that makes the function of conscience of particular concern?

CONSCIENCE AND SOCIETY

In response to the first question, it may be stated that sociologists attempt to understand social behavior on a scientific basis. A basic observation of sociology is that people behave predictably in their day-to-day experience.

The predictability of social behavior is dependent to a great degree upon fairly permanent social arrangements that are agreed upon by members of a society. Two of the most basic foundations of social predictability are culture and social institutions. The sociological meaning of conscience depends in part upon an understanding of these two concepts. The following definition of culture provides a useful starting point:

> Most inclusively, culture is social heredity—the total legacy of past human behavior effective in the present, representing the accumulation through generations of the artifacts, knowledge, beliefs, and values by which men deal with the world. It is the precipitate of *learned* human adjustments to the physical environment and to society [Williams, 1960, p. 22].

In a sense, culture acts as a storehouse of human experience. It emerges out of man's struggle for collective survival. What contributes to survival is remembered, stored up, and transmitted to new members. Thus, culture acts as a bridge between past and future. It is the social basis of human adaptation.

Fully developed cultural systems contain a normative aspect. That is, certain behavioral imperatives are defined and enforced, conformity to which supports the effectiveness of the group's survival capacity. These imperatives are couched in networks of mores, values, beliefs, and customs that articulate cultural expectations in the core areas of human social life, such as work, sexual behavior, the distribution of power, and the group's relation to the unknown.

The clustering of expectations, rules, and sanctions around these core areas of social life leads to what are called institutions. They activate cultural experience in ongoing social life. Religion as a social institution, for example, activates the cultural response to the unknown.

Social institutions are manned by policy makers, managers, and enforcers. Policy makers interpret the meaning of cultural values. Managers carry out the judgments of policy makers, and enforcers assure adherence to the rules. A problem regarding conscience arises in complex societies because institutions often do not or cannot represent the values of the total public in any given case.*

Thus, social institutions generate, perpetuate, and modify for members of society definitions of what their world *is,* and what it *ought to be.* The most elementary basis of institutional power is the assumption that it contains and is capable of validly delivering the cultural heritage of the society to its members for their collective survival and well-being.

To bridge the past and future, institutions must transmit cultural content, including the "rules of the game," to new members. This is achieved through the process of socialization. Normally, socialization occurs by transmitting

---

* This point will be discussed in more detail later.

cultural content to children so as to achieve their voluntary conformity to society's demands and needs. The outcome of this is the development of a built-in, self-monitoring set of rules and controls which, from a sociological viewpoint, could be called "conscience." At the societal level, conscience may be viewed as a culturally determined and institutionally transmitted mechanism that produces voluntary conformity on the part of the members.

CONSCIENCE AND THE INDIVIDUAL

Between the external institutional system and the internal self-monitoring system, society ideally could maintain a perfectly ordered relationship between cultural mandate and individual performance. In reality, however, this ideal balance is never achieved. First of all, no culture has all the answers to all the problems confronting it, and, secondly, no individual is ever perfectly socialized.

Furthermore, as previously noted, social institutions do not always clearly represent the will of all the members of society—either because institutions often become representative of limited vested interests, or because institutions do not always recognize the need for new solutions to problems, some members of the society may reject institutional demands. If such dissent becomes broad-based and tends to produce a threat to the maintenance of existing power distribution, and if institutional enforcers either *cannot* or would *rather not* enforce conformity, there are various strategies that may be used to establish a compromise situation. Such strategies may also be utilized if the gap between the rules of the culture and their institutional fulfillment generates more collective guilt than the society can bear.

Three such compromise strategies will be discussed here. The first is that of *patterned evasion* (Williams, 1960), in which a norm in question is periodically and ritualistically enforced, but generally evaded by the society. The American response to Prohibition would be a case in point. This was a case where the policy maker miscalculated the popular acceptance of the cultural norm and made an inappropriate policy.

The second strategy is called the *double standard*, wherein variable enforcement of rules is carried out depending upon the status of the parties involved. In American society, examples of this strategy can be seen in the variable enforcement of rules for rich and poor, black and white, male and female, or young and old. The double standard is often simply the practical application of the ancient axiom "might makes right."

As institutions develop a vested interest and a base of power, another strategy often comes into play. It may be called the *social myth*, which is defined as

> an unproved collective belief that is accepted and is used to justify a social institution [*Random House Dictionary*, 1967, p. 946].

In this case the institutional vested interest generates and perpetuates an inaccurate definition of the situation which tends to obfuscate the rift between the real and the ideal. For example, the ideal of equality of opportunity in American society is frequently accepted as an accomplished fact rather than as a goal.

The social myth is unworkable unless many people are willing to accept it. For instance there is a myth that says poor people are lazy, or immoral, or improvident, or perhaps all three. Thus, since the poor appear to violate the American value of getting ahead by hard work and saving, "why get excited about their problems—they brought it on themselves." This, of course, does not take into consideration the base of economic, social, political, educational, or psychological deprivation from which American poor people approach the world of work and opportunity.

Each of these strategies has as a goal the management of strains that may result from various weaknesses in the institutional network. As such, they may be necessary and reasonable in themselves. However, each strategy is marked by three intrinsic characteristics which, if not controlled, can lead to trouble. They are: expediency, the promotion of partisan advantage, and deception.

Expediency, while giving the normative system flexibility, is apt to foster arbitrariness. The promotion of partisan advantage, while allowing appropriate rewards in some cases, may lead to "pork-barrelism" on behalf of favored constituencies. Deception, which sometimes makes unavoidable situations bearable, is apt to lead to a complete lack of credibility.

If abuses in the enforcement of normative standards become routine in a society, individuals tend to lose respect for their institutional delivery systems. Arbitrary, inequitable, and deceptive application of norms then becomes self-defeating by effecting disillusionment, a polarization of interests, and, ultimately, the emergence of counter-systems (one of whose aims would be to remedy perceived abuses—at times by force).

In this kind of situation, the individual's sense of allegiance to social values is strained, not because he does not accept them in themselves, but because he does not accept the delivery system that is ostensibly their custodian. Thus, institutional leaders can, by abusing their authority, create problems of conscience and ultimately of order itself because under-represented groups may eventually comprise a dissenting numerical majority.

It is evident that the relationship between the individual and the institution is very complex. When the institution begins to fail in its task of influencing individual behavior in culturally productive ways, the society stands at the threshold of a breakdown in the normative order. Sociologists call such a breakdown *anomy*. Broadly defined, anomy means normlessness. More specifically, it means that social institutions in varying degrees lack the ability to function adequately as normative delivery systems. This may occur when there is confusion regarding the application of an accepted norm, or when there is conflict regarding the norm's validity, or when existing normative structures fail to meet adequately the demands of new problems. It may also occur when such strategies as patterned evasion, the double standard, and the social myth are abused to the point of making a mockery of the society's basic moral standards.

When the institutional basis of a society becomes intensely anomic, the individual suffers from it. He is like a man on a ship without a rudder. Without confidence in his previously accepted guiding principles and unable to find anything to replace them, he feels that he is no longer bound by the rules. Unless his internal control system is really entrenched, he may become alienated from his faltering institutions and even from himself.

At the point at which this condition becomes pervasive, the society begins to experience inability to cope with situations, and begins to drift from its culturally prescribed course into irrational conflict, social fragmentation, and eventually societal degeneration.

CONTEMPORARY CONCERN FOR CONSCIENCE

In contemporary American life, institutional leaders and citizens alike share a concern for the state of the society. The gap between what *is* and what *ought to be* appears to have widened and there also seems to be a basic lack of consensus regarding what *ought to be* in the first place. The society is experiencing *anomy* in varying degrees at both institutional and individual levels. There is a difference between pluralism and anarchy, between rational disagreement and purposeless violence—or, as one author (Schelling, 1960, p. 5) suggests, between distrusting partners and hated enemies. There are many recent cases in American society in which social behavior has been more destructive than useful in this sense.

Thus, for example, one of the most visible weaknesses in the society is its recently demonstrated inability effectively to manage dissent. It has been pointed out (Bernard, 1962, p. 46) that one basic function of an institution is the substitution of strategy for violence. That is to say, institutions provide a set of rules not only for conformity but also for disagreement. If a society's institutions cannot perform both functions adequately, then it is in danger of losing its coherence.

The present strains in American society spring from a very complicated network of causation. Three related causal factors will be mentioned here which are considered important but by no means inclusive. They are: *technological growth, urbanization,* and *increased complexity.*

Very simply stated, American society has a runaway technology. The innovation and social diffusion of a rapidly developing technological capacity is straining the society's adaptive capacity. The often arbitrary dispersion of new machines, new processes, and new uses cannot be tolerated by a society forever. There are hidden consequences of any innovation which may be harmful. The society must coordinate its technological progress with its human requirements or risk dangerous side-effects. The ecological basis of survival is being systematically whittled away by the technological juggernaut, and society appears unable to impose an effective control on this process. In another sector, the omnipresent mass media have exposed society's members to a relatively uncontrolled input of messages that carry a variety of normative messages, often confusing the public and generating unwarranted conflict, and often delivering outright deception. This, of course, has led to the well-known credibility gap between parent and child, between politician and constituent, between seller and buyer, and, in many ways, between culture and individual.

As the population has pressed into the cities and as small, visibly interdependent rural communities gradually disappear, institutional arrangements for families and individuals have changed dramatically. The intensity and diversity of the large city offer the family and the individual a sort of invisibility in which there is less immediate accountability for behavior and a far broader spectrum of moral choice. It would appear that physical proximity often leads to moral distance, and to the removal of a standard control-device present in a more simple society—namely, sheer visibility in terms of those to whom one is accountable. One is reminded of the question put to Christ: "and who *is* my neighbor?" It has been theorized (Greer, 1962) that urbanization has generated communities of "limited liability" in which people tend to develop a very circumscribed notion of their responsibility to their fellow men. This suggests the idea of a conscience of limited liability, i.e., one that ceases to function beyond one's class, color, or community boundaries.

A concomitant of technological growth and urbanization is increased complexity at every level. More innovation and more concentrated population create problems of how to deal with what has been added. The massive variety of choices, decisions, structures, and systems that have to be dealt with in an urban-technical society boggles the mind. The addition of more limiting rules, more labyrinthine organizational structures, and more obscure and inaccessible points of accountability is apt to push the individual member to the very periphery of social identity.

There can be little doubt that all the above has created for the society a critical problem regarding conscience. What is right or wrong, what is or ought to be, what is true or false are being defined differently by varying groups with varying stakes in a complex, urban, and rapidly changing society.

One challenge for those who are concerned with conscience, then, is to facilitate the resolution of the above problems in an integrative rather than a fragmenting way—to build strong bridges rather than high walls.

REFERENCES

Bernard, J. *American community behavior.* New York: Holt, Rinehart & Winston, 1962.
Greer, S. *The emerging city: Myth and reality.* New York: Free Press, 1962.
Random House Dictionary of the English Language. New York: Random House, 1967.
Schelling, T. *The strategy of conflict.* New York: Oxford University Press, 1960.
Williams, R. M., Jr. *American society: A sociological interpretation.* New York: Knopf, 1960.

III
FREEDOM OF CONSCIENCE IN MULTIDISCIPLINARY PERSPECTIVE

Freedom of Conscience in Philosophical Perspective

JOHN A. DINNEEN, s.j.

Father John A. Dinneen, S.J. received his A.B. (1952) and his M.A. (1955) degrees from Loyola University, Chicago, and his Ph.D. degree from the University of Louvain in 1965. He is a member of the American and the American Catholic Philosophical Associations, and he has contributed to several philosophical journals. Currently, Father Dinneen is assistant professor of philosophy at LeMoyne College, Syracuse. Previously, he was an instructor in philosophy at St. Peter's College, Jersey City, and then an assistant professor of philosophy in the College of Philosophy and Letters of Fordham University.

If philosophy is to shed some light on the problem before us, it is important to sort out the several philosophical problems bound up with the phrase "freedom of conscience." There is, first, the problem of freedom or of free will. Historically this problem has taken two distinct forms: the problem of freedom versus predestination, which is more a theological problem, and the problem of freedom versus determinism. The latter problem is properly philosophical and consists in reconciling belief in human freedom with determinism, which maintains that every event is fully determined in all its details by the sum of its preceding causes. It is an old problem, going back to the Stoics and Epicureans, and one rendered more acute today because of discoveries and advances in both the psychological and sociological sciences. I must presume a solution to this problem for purposes of this paper, for freedom is essential to moral life. Unless one could have done something other than what he did in fact do, then he cannot be held morally responsible for his action. And if one cannot be held morally responsible for his action, then no action is ever right or wrong.

In addition to this problem of freedom, there exists the problem of conscience itself. Does conscience exist, and, if so, what is its nature and function? Finally, we face the central problem of this Institute: freedom of conscience, i.e. moral as distinct from metaphysical or physical freedom of conscience. In order to view this problem in perspective, we shall first have to be clear about conscience itself.

VARIOUS MEANINGS OF CONSCIENCE

That man possesses a conscience, i.e. a moral approving and disapproving capacity, is clear from experience. What is far from clear is its exact nature. One modern writer summarizes the situation as follows:

> It has been said of conscience that it is fallible (Broad), that it is infallible (Butler), that its ultimate base is emotional (Mill), that its ultimate source is rational (Rashdall); that it is the voice of God (Hartmann), or the voice of custom (Paulsen); that it is merely advisory (Nowell-Smith), that it is a command internally imposed (Mayo); that it is conscious (Butler), that it is unconscious (Freud), that it is a faculty (Butler), that it is not (any contemporary moral philosopher); that it is the disposition to have certain beliefs, emotions, and conations, which, when operative, issue in conscientious action (Broad), and that it *is* conscientious action (Pyle) [Wand, 1961, p. 771].

What is conscience, then, and how does it function? On the one hand, if there is such a thing which tells us authoritatively what the right thing to do is, then it seems that the moral philosopher can simply repeat with Jiminy Cricket "always let your conscience be your guide." On the other hand, if there is no such thing, if ordinary men and women do not have consciences, it is hard to see how moral philosophers can have any subject matter. Conscience is important, but its exact nature needs definition.

Basically there are three positions about its nature: (1) that conscience is intelligence—the rational power of the mind exercised upon a particular subject matter; (2) that conscience is a distinct mode of perception—a moral sense; (3) that conscience is neither of these but rather a distinctive sentiment or mode of feeling and desiring. Briefly, these are the rational, the perceptual and the emotive conceptions of conscience (Duncan-Jones, 1955). Now, what we claim about the nature of conscience is crucial for our understanding of the freedom of conscience. What conscience is and how it works surely influence the place and scope of its freedom. Let us look, then, at these positions in more detail.

The second position, the "moral sense" view, likens conscience to sight or hearing. It sees into concrete situations and declares that here and now a certain person ought or ought not to act in a certain definite way (or that the act he performed was good or bad). Without wishing to deny all merit to this view, particularly as it may relate to connatural knowledge, I find the positing of a distinct moral sense or faculty unsupported by evidence and unnecessary for an explication of moral knowledge.

The third position, the emotive view, is connected with the emotive theory of value and differs radically from the other two views. Since the total person is engaged, emotions of one kind or another will surely accompany the exercise of conscience, and may frequently influence the exercise. But to reduce conscience to emotion is to make it essentially non-cognitive and to deny that its utterances could in any way be true or false. Moral relativism and subjectivism is the logical result. Just as there has been a reaction against logical positivism in recent years, so there has been a reaction against the irrationalism of the emotive theory of values. Men like Richard Hare (1961, 1965), Stephen Toulmin (1953), and Kurt Baier (1958) have sought to restore the place of reason in ethics, and in so doing have given at least implicit recognition to the view of conscience as rational activity. No other view, it seems to me, is warranted by evidence.

CONSCIENCE—AN EXERCISE OF PRACTICAL REASON

Conscience, I submit, is neither a distinct moral sense nor an emotion, but the exercise of practical reason on matter of moral values. Moral values and moral laws need to be applied to particular acts by particular persons, and such is the task of conscience. Certain expressions may tend to obscure this application as a work of reason, e.g., "I feel this is wrong." On inspection, however, "I feel this is wrong" is parallel to "I think this is inconsistent." * "I feel this is wrong" implies that reasons exist to show that it is wrong in much the same way as "I think this is inconsistent" implies that reasons exist to show that it is inconsistent. There is a difference between value judgments (whether moral or non-moral) and factual judgments, or, to use a common way of putting it, a difference between prescriptive and descriptive uses of language. I do not wish to deny this difference. Value judgments and factual judgments are distinct logical classes and should not be confounded. Nevertheless they are related in numerous ways and, in particular, the value judgment is warranted or unwarranted according to its relationship to facts, to what is the case. As with factual judgments, so

---

* Cf. M. C. McGuire (1963) for a cogent development of this parallel.

with judgments of conscience can I be called upon to defend my judgment, to give evidence, reasons, views of appropriate authorities, and so forth. Truth and falsity play not a small role in morality.

It may be helpful to spell out some of the implications of this view of conscience as rational. First, is conscience infallible? Is it an infallible judge of what is right and what is wrong in particular cases? No, it is not; as a human judgment and as a practical judgment it is subject to human error. Of course, this does not deny that a person is infallibly right in following his conscience, even an erroneous one. But conscience itself is fallible. Secondly, if conscience is not infallible, is it reliable? Is there not a great diversity of moral codes in different societies? Have not most men at some time or other been deceived in matters of conscience? If conscience was wrong once, how can we be sure that it is ever right? Basically this is the old argument of skepticism, and I believe that we know how to handle that. We do indeed make mistakes but we also recognize them and correct them. If conscience is an exercise of reason, it will come as no surprise that it fails to provide an automatic certain guide for many important and crucial issues, or even that it gives us little idea of the right alternative in complex cases.

At the same time, however, if conscience is the exercise of reason, we are able to face the challenge of the erroneous conscience: we can say why it is that, even if a murderer's conscience approves of his acts of murder, his conscience is nevertheless in the wrong. Eichmann's tragedy, according to Hannah Arendt (1964), was not that he was motivated by hatred of the Jews but that his conscience told him to obey orders. Again, if conscience is the exercise of reason, it enables one to suggest the true moral quality of intellectual honesty and openness to someone who says: "My conscience tells me so; that is the end of the matter." If conscience is the exercise of reason, finally, and granted that forty million Frenchmen could still be wrong, the fact that many others disagree with my judgment of conscience should at least give me pause.

CONSCIENCE—A RESPONSE TO VALUE

To focus as clearly as possible on the question of freedom, we should look more closely on the working of conscience as reason. Values and laws, we said, are applied to particular acts by conscience. Conscience, then, is the source of our response to value and the center of moral responsibility. But let us understand the kind of response involved. As Gilbert Ryle puts it, conscience is "a private monitor" (Ryle, 1940). We do not say "My conscience says that *you* ought to do this or ought not to have done that." Conscience is concerned with *my* acts. It is a personal response to value, then, a response by which I appropriate and assimilate (or not) a particular value and assume personal responsibility for my act. As individual persons differ, so too will this personal assimilation of values. But let me stress the process: conscience responds to value and shoulders responsibility for the particular response. The terms are three: conscience–value–responsibility; not merely two: conscience–responsibility. I alone am responsible for my acts of conscience—but it is not a vague kind of responsibility; rather one in terms of my response to value. This specific kind of responsibility makes all the difference when the question of moral freedom arises. It defines and limits that freedom.

Furthermore, since conscience is this response to value, the main philosophical problem in regard to freedom of conscience becomes clear—namely, the reality and objectivity of values. What is the "good" and how is it grounded? Does value possess some objective status or is it a matter of individual taste? The answer counts decisively in the question of freedom. If I respond to and actively receive values, then moral freedom has set boundaries; if on the other hand I simply create values, this freedom has few boundaries. The problem of the objective status of value is not new. Within the analytic tradition, David Hume (1961, Bk. III, Pt. 1, sec. 1, p. 423) separated radically values and facts and left no objective status to values; G. E. Moore (1903, pp. 1–21; 1912) took up the question again in the early part of this century, but left it fundamentally unresolved; Alfred Ayer (1956, ch. 6) and the positivists solved the problem by making values a matter of emotion alone; today, however, efforts are made to give value some objective standing. What is distinctive of moral laws, R. M. Hare for one argues, is that they are universalizable, i.e., they belong to man precisely as man (Hare, 1961, 1965).

Everyone will recognize the proportions of this problem of objectivity. Without pretending to have established an objective status for value, I would stress once again the nature of conscience as rational. To know is not to create but to assimilate actively; similarly to know values is not to create them but to receive them actively and personally. I can no more decide that one act is good and another bad than I can decide that one affirmation is true and another false.

SUMMARY

Let me summarize. Conscience is an exercise of practical reason by which man responds to value. The objective status of value is the main philosophical problem involved in the determination of the freedom of conscience, although the theological problem—i.e., the place of authority on the formation of conscience—is probably the more pressing contemporary problem.

Philosophically speaking, what can we say about freedom of conscience? As an exercise of practical reason, first of all, conscience is free in the metaphysical and physical sense. I may choose to appropriate a moral value in this way or in that way, or choose here and now to appropriate this and not that value. All practical judgments are free in this sense, since there are ordinarily a number of possible ways of achieving a certain goal and of assimilating a certain value. Ordinarily again, no one practical judgment exhausts the number of possibilities either of attaining a particular goal or of incarnating a particular value. In the metaphysical and physical sense I am even free to reject a certain moral value, just as I am free to contradict myself in speech or action. But—and this is the difference—I am not morally free to reject the good which I recognize as such. I am not morally free to do evil. I ought to do the good; I ought to follow my conscience.

But what about the number of cases in which the rightness or wrongness of an act is not clear? Since conscience is the exercise of reason, I am obliged before acting to investigate, to search out the evidence available, and to achieve a practical certitude concerning the morality of the act in question. Otherwise I am not acting morally. But after an honest and open search, if freedom of conscience means anything, it means that I am free to follow what I judge here and now to be good.

To sum up, conscience is morally free to choose this or that good, to incarnate a certain good in this or that way, and to follow what it judges to be good upon honest investigation. When all is said, perhaps it would be more accurate to speak of the rights and duties of conscience rather than of the freedom of conscience.

REFERENCES

Arendt, H. *Eichmann in Jerusalem: a report on the banality of evil.* New York: Viking Press, 1964.

Ayer, A. J. *Language, truth and logic.* New York: Dover Publications, 1956.

Baier, K. *The moral point of view: a rational basis of ethics.* Ithaca: Cornell University Press, 1958.

Duncan-Jones, A. The notion of conscience. *Philosophy,* 1955, *30,* 131–140.

Hare, R. M. *The language of morals.* Oxford: Clarendon Press, 1961.

Hare, R. M. *Freedom and reason.* New York: Oxford University Press, 1965.

Hume, D. *A treatise of human nature.* Garden City, N.Y.: Doubleday, 1961.

McGuire, M. C. On conscience. *Journal of Philosophy,* 1963, *60,* 253–263.

Moore, G. E. *Principia ethica* (1903). New York: Cambridge University Press, 1959.

Moore, G. E. *Ethics* (1912). New York: Oxford University Press, 1965.

Ryle, G. Conscience and moral convictions. *Analysis,* 1940, *7,* 31–39.

Toulmin, S. *An examination of the place of reason in ethics.* New York: Cambridge University Press, 1953.

Wand, B. The content and function of conscience. *Journal of Philosophy,* 1961, *58,* 765–772.

Freedom of Conscience in Theological Perspective

JOHN J. McNEILL, S.J.

*Father John J. McNeill, S.J. received his A.B.
degree from Canisius College, in his native city
of Buffalo, in 1948. Subsequently he earned a
master's degree in education from Bellarmine
College, Plattsburgh, in 1954, a licentiate in theology from Woodstock College in 1960, and finally
a doctorate in philosophy from Louvain University
in 1965. He joined the faculty of LeMoyne College,
Syracuse, in 1965, where he is currently assistant
professor of philosophy. He is the author of*
The Blondelian synthesis *(1966), and an award
from the American Council of Learned Societies
enabled him to spend the summer of 1966 in
Europe at work upon a projected volume in the
philosophy of religion. Father McNeill has lectured
on modern European philosophy at various universities, including Fordham, Cornell, Colgate, Syracuse, and the State University of New York at
Oswego and Cortland.*

Bishop G. Emmett Carter observed in his comments on the Declaration on
Christian Education that the theme of personal responsibility dominated
many of the deliberations of the Second Vatican Council (Carter, 1966, p.

640, footnote). One such example is found in the opening lines of the Declaration on Religious Freedom which reads as follows:

> A sense of the dignity of the human person has been impressing itself more and more deeply on the consciousness of contemporary man. And the demand is increasingly made that men should act on their own judgment, enjoying and making use of a responsible freedom, not driven by coercion but motivated by a sense of duty [Vatican Council II, 1966, n. 1, p. 675].

What is important to note here is that the document places this theme of personal responsibility within the context of a recent historical development of philosophical and theological understanding concerning the role that freedom must play in man's life. Certainly, one can use the suggestive negative wording of an *America* editorial to say of the Church's doctrine in this respect:

> No one can account to God for his talents simply by pleading that he acted as an agent for Peter. The abdication of personal moral responsibility has never been a doctrine of the Church [*America*, 1968, p. 94].

The Council fathers, however, see this increasing awareness of the dignity of the human person as a sign of the times and as a definite positive step in the progress of civilization. This progress carries with it a parallel need for the Church to stress positively the right and duty of every individual to arrive at a greater freedom of conscience:

> . . . every man has the duty, and therefore the right, to seek the truth in matters religious, in order that he may with prudence form for himself right and true judgments of conscience. . . . The inquiry is to be free, carried on with aid of teaching or instruction, communication, and dialogue [Vatican Council II, 1966, n. 3, pp. 680–681].

In practically the same words as the opening statement quoted above we read in Louis Monden's work *Sin, liberty and law*:

> The self-discovery experienced by man in the past century has given rise in him to an urgent need for mature autonomy in his existence, for a freedom from all bonds of dependence. There is a general feeling that for the first time in history man is being offered the chance to become fully himself [Monden, 1965, p. 75].

Monden sees a radically new historical context in which we must reconsider the relation that should exist between personal freedom and all forms of authority, including the authority exercised within the Church. He speaks of a universal phenomenon that sets modern man against all constraints on his personal moral decisions on the part of any outside agency whatsoever: "Before the sanctuary of his personal decisions of conscience every influence from without must come to a halt. Only his inner freedom decides what is good and what is bad" (Monden, 1965, p. 99).

Monden is inclined to see in this new spirit a call to man to achieve a new moral maturity. He speaks of the new morality as a reflection in the consciousness of believers of a crisis of growth through which mankind's collective consciousness is now passing.

> With all its exaggerations, it [the new morality] might represent an attempt, both human and Christian, to break out of the shelter of exterior safeguards and to coincide in a renewed and more complete self-possession with the deepest roots of one's own being and vocation. Then, all those exaggerations would only be the unavoidable ransom that youth must pay in breaking through to adulthood, not a phenomenon of decadence, but a sign of spring [Monden, 1965, p. 111].

Perhaps the single most important statement on conscience in the documents of Vatican II occurs in the Pastoral Constitution on the Church in the Modern World:

> . . . man has in his heart a law written by God. To obey it is the very dignity of man; according to it he will be judged. Conscience is the most secret core and sanctuary of man. There he is alone with God, whose voice echoes in his depths. In a wonderful manner conscience reveals that law which is fulfilled by love of God and neighbor. In fidelity to conscience, Christians are joined with the rest of men in the search for truth, and for the genuine solution to the numerous problems which arise in the life of individuals and from social relationships [Vatican Council II, 1966, n. 16, pp. 213–214].

Practically every major theme which will be treated in this paper can be found in this statement. Conscience is described here as the voice of God speaking to man immediately from within his own consciousness without the necessary aid of an external mediation. Man's freedom to follow his conscience is seen as the source of his true dignity. And this freedom is understood not as an anarchic principle but, on the contrary, as the only true foundation for real community and as the only valid ground for a solution to social problems.

Another example of the persistent theme of personal freedom and responsibility is to be found in the Declaration on Christian Education where it is applied to the formation of the conscience of the young: ". . . children and young people have a right to be encouraged to weigh moral values with an upright conscience, and to embrace them by personal choice . . ." (Vatican Council II, 1966, n. 1, pp. 639–640). The Council thus indicates a corresponding obligation on the part of educators to lead young people to a true and responsible freedom of conscience.

Again, the same theme is to be found throughout the Pastoral Constitution on the Church in the Modern World, where it is stressed that the layman is not to exaggerate authority, but to take personal responsibility for his choices and actions:

> Laymen should also know that it is generally the function of their well-formed Christian conscience to see that the divine law is inscribed in the life of the earthly city. From priests they may look for spiritual light and nourishment. Let the layman not imagine that his pastors are always such experts, that to every problem which arises, however complicated, they can readily give him a concrete solution, or even that such is their mission. Rather, enlightened by Christian wisdom and giving close attention to the teaching authority of the Church, let the layman take on his own distinctive role [Vatican Council II, 1966, n. 43, p. 244].

According to this document the layman's role is to be that of mediator between the Church and the world, having the responsibility and the corresponding right to determine how the message of the Gospel applies to the complicated problems in the field of his competence.

One example of the free moral responsibility which, the Council insists, belongs to the conscience of the individual layman is to be found in the teaching of the Council on modern warfare, where the right of the layman to reach the moral decision to be a conscientious objector is stressed, and the corresponding duty of the state to enact laws respecting that right is noted (Vatican Council II, 1966, n. 79, p. 292). The Council stresses further that each individual soldier can no longer justify his actions in time of war in terms of blind obedience to authority, but must bear personal responsibility for the morality of his actions.

The Council throws light on the moral freedom and responsibility of the individual both by what it says and by what it fails to say. As Daniel Maguire observes in his article Morality and the Magisterium, the consistent refusal of the Church to use its prerogative of infallibility in the past (and most recently in the birth-control issue) is "theologically instructive":

> It seems to me that in practice, despite its firm grasp of the moral vision of the Gospel, the Church seems to realize . . . that it does not enjoy an infallibly guaranteed competence to apply that moral vision of the Gospel to complex natural law questions such as medical ethics, genetics, business ethics, international law, social reconstruction and war and peace [Maguire, 1968, p. 41].

It is precisely by determining how the moral vision of the Gospel is to be incarnated in concrete decisions in these areas of his competence that the layman "plays his own decisive role."

In so acting, the Council and the magisterium acted in the spirit of the moral message of the New Testament. As Charles Curran points out in his article The Ethical Teaching of Jesus, that message is a constant reminder of the absolute claim which the presence of the reign of God makes on the follower of Jesus (Curran, 1967). Jesus does not proclaim universal norms of conduct which are obligatory on all Christians under all circumstances. Rather, He indicates the goal and the direction that should characterize the life and the actions of His followers. "Give to everyone who asks" would be an impossible command, if it were understood as an absolute ethical imperative. Rather, such a demand indicates the thrust that should characterize the life of the Christian. How such an imperative is to be implemented in his situation is left to the free judgment of each individual. Christ does promise, however, the help of the Spirit, who will enlighten and strengthen each individual who sincerely seeks out the divine will in his situation.

MORAL FREEDOM IN THE THOUGHT OF MAURICE BLONDEL

As the texts quoted above from Vatican II indicate, a new and stronger emphasis was placed by the Council Fathers on freedom of conscience, and that emphasis was understood as a response by the Council to an historical development within philosophy and theology concerning the role that freedom of conscience must play in man's life. The same insistence on freedom in moral life in practically the same terms is one of the most fundamental themes in the writings of a recent Catholic moral philosopher, Maurice Blondel, whose thoughts, perhaps more than that of any other single man, influenced the thinking of the fathers of the Council (*Le Monde* reported that Blondel's name was mentioned in the debates on the Council floor more than sixty times).

If there is anything new in the moral philosophy of Maurice Blondel, it is because that philosophy is based on a newer and deeper understanding, both psychological and metaphysical, of the nature and importance of human freedom.

> There is no being where there is only constraint. If I am not that which I will to be, I am not. At the very core of my being there is a will and a love of being, or there is nothing. If man's freedom is real, it is necessary that one have at present, or at least in the future, a knowledge and a will sufficient never to suffer any tyranny whatsoever [Blondel, 1893, p. vii].

The Nature of Human Freedom

For the objectifying intellect, man first is; then he acts: *agere sequitur esse*. This scholastic axiom is frequently misunderstood as implying that the existence of the subject is reduced to the passive being of an object. The only subject acknowledged in such a reduction is the logical subject understood as a center of attribution. In such an understanding the statement "I am free" can be reduced to the abstract statement "The category man to which I belong possesses the attribute of freedom." From this viewpoint, substance is understood as a static, unchanging reality. All actions are considered as functions which can only influence that unchanging reality on the phenomenal or accidental level of being. Thus, freedom is understood as limited to a choice of actions consequent on substantial determination.

The statement "I am free" means something radically different to Blondel. It implies that, for man, to be is to act, and in acting to mold freely his substantial reality. Man alone is capable of saying "I am," because in his actions he immediately seizes himself as free action. As a result, man is not totally or authentically human unless in the depths of his being and action he seizes himself as free source, *Ursprung,* action itself, a constant self-positing. Human freedom, then, cannot be adequately understood as a mode of action posterior to being. Man's freedom must be understood beyond all particular actions as the radical self-positing of his own reality. Man must exist at every moment as a consequence of his freedom. If in the depths of his own subjective being man meets with any determinism whatsoever— whether that be understood as biological, psychological, social, or even a determinism springing from the divine will, a determinism which lies radically outside the sphere of his free ability to determine himself—then, according to Blondel, one would be forced to accept Spinoza's conclusion that the existence of the free individual human person as such is an illusion (Somerville, 1968, pp. 43–53).

This insight into the nature of human freedom carries with it as a necessary consequence a radical change in the method of moral philosophy. All objectivized systems, especially the traditional idea of an ethics based on natural law, depend on the presupposition that man possesses a static, unchanging substantial nature as source of his actions. Such an idea has the advantage of rendering possible a moral philosophy of necessary, universal, and absolute principles. However, an overemphasis on these qualities of an objective system can lead and has led to a systematic misunderstanding of the existent person as such, and tends to deliver man from the ultimate risk of his freedom, which is his grandeur.

The entire movement of modern philosophy in Blondel's opinion has been a continual movement toward a deeper understanding of the role which the subject as such plays in human understanding and willing (McNeill, 1966). That movement began with the *Cogito* of Descartes, which found ultimate certitude in subjective self-awareness. The next step was the restructuring of ethics on the subjective a priori forms of knowledge and will in the *Critique of practical reason* of Kant. Fichte's effort to establish morality on the insight that the human subject is a pure act which cannot be object for itself followed. Hegel uncovered the dialectical laws which govern the dynamic development of the human subject. Schelling applied the same dialectical principles to a study of the development of the human will. Kierkegaard threw a powerful light on human choice as a creative power of self-actualization. According to Blondel, this movement has led to the conclusion that there is only one possible manner in which to attain the existing subject as such in its unique freedom in a legitimate philosophical manner: we must renounce all attempts to make the singular existing subject into an objective content of knowledge, and be content to seize it in our immediate experiential awareness of self in the deployment of our free activity.

If one accepts this insight into the nature of human freedom and the human subject, then one must accept a radically different understanding of the role that truth and value play in human life. According to the traditional concept, truth and value represent objective norms of action which impose their necessary clarity on the judgment. Classical realist philosophy conceived of its task as a search for abstract truth, an *adaequatio speculativa rei et intellectus*. For the contemporary philosopher of freedom, the human spirit in order to be true to itself cannot be totally passive before truth or value and totally determined by its object. Every affirmation, especially if it is closely linked with the problem of human destiny, must be an activity which has its source in man's radical freedom, in that self-positing which is the proper characteristic of a free being. It is necessary, then, in place of the problem of the harmony of thought with objective reality to substitute the equivalent but radically different problem of the adequation of ourselves with ourselves. To be true means to become that which one really is. It represents a search for all the necessary conditions of interior self-adequation, a search from within self-consciousness for the meaning and direction of man's freely willed activity. In this context, the moral self-fulfillment of man is understood as intrinsically connected with his ontological self-realization, rather than with his affective relation to reality understood as an object set off from himself.

Further, if freedom is at the source of all man's activities, my vision of the world can never be the result of a pure observation; it is necessarily also a commitment. Any discovery of meaning or absurdity is necessarily to some extent a simultaneous construction of that same meaning or absurdity. The point of view in which I am situated becomes *my* situation—that is, I make it my own, by the free attitude which I assume in regard to it. Nothing could be more hypocritical than to make believe that truths or values are imposed on me from without which are in fact to some extent at least the products of my own freedom.

The Principle of Immanence

It is this insight into the radical nature of human freedom that led Blondel to accept the principle of immanence as the fundamental methodological principle governing his moral philosophy of human action. Blondel thus formulates this principle of immanence: "Nothing can impose itself on a man; nothing can demand the assent of his intellect or the consent of his will which does not in some way find its source in man himself" (Blondel, 1964, pp. 60–61). All acknowledgment of value must in some sense also be an active and free valorization. To acknowledge truth or value remains an authentic human act only if at the same time there is a free, active construction of that same truth or value:

> That necessity which appears to me as a tyrannous constraint, that obligation which at first appears despotic, in the last analysis it is necessary that I understand it as manifesting and activating the most profound reality of my own will; otherwise it will be my destruction [Blondel, 1893, p. xxiii].

Blondel does not hesitate to apply this methodological principle of immanence to manifestations of the divine will. Although the divine will must manifest itself as in some way distinct from our finite will, yet that revelation, if it is not to destroy our freedom and integrity, must be made in some way from within our consciousness of self and prove capable of being assimilated into our free self-positing.

> If it is necessary to consider revelation itself as something which arrives completely from without as an entirely empirical given, then the very idea of a revealed dogma or precept would be totally unintelligible [Blondel, 1893, p. 394].

If God were to manifest His will exclusively from without man himself by means of extrinsic authority, He would involve Himself in the contradiction of creating man free and redeeming him in a way which would necessarily negate his freedom.

Having accepted the principle of immanence, Blondel was immediately aware of a dilemma to which that principle gives rise. Man in order to remain free must refuse any *purely* external and objective norm imposed on his actions. Yet, at the same time, unless one is willing to accept a totally irrational and amoral world of absurd and meaningless freedom, one must admit that freedom is dependent on a transcendent truth to which it must conform, that freedom is directed to values which, far from being man's exclusive creation, serve him as guide, norm, and sanction. The two most extreme positions have already been formulated into inadequate philosophical systems. Spinoza constructed a monism of deterministic rationalism in which the human subject and his freedom were completely absorbed. Sartre attempted to place truth totally in human hands, and proclaimed a totally irrational world. The problem that remains posed for our reflection is precisely that of understanding how one can maintain the unity in an act of affirmation, whether it be of truth or value, of the two necessary elements of free engagement and necessary adhesion.

Further, if a true moral science of right and wrong, free human actions is possible, it is necessary that real, concrete facts be capable of receiving an absolute qualification. One must be able to establish an absolute difference between right and wrong, true and false. Yet, if we are to discover these truths and values without being unfaithful to man's freedom and existential subjectivity, then we must discover the universality of truth and value from within our consciousness of our own existence. Thus, it is necessary to discern the absolute in the relative, the transcendent from within the immanent at the root itself of man's free action and existential subjectivity. As a result, the central problem posed for a philosopher of freedom is: Is it possible without going outside the subject and without being unfaithful to his freedom and existential uniqueness to discover within the subject an opening by means of which a transcendent can enter, a transcendent which perfects man's freedom without in any way negating it?

A Philosophy of Action

In Blondel's opinion only a philosophy of action can effectively respond to these problems, because only a philosophy of action, by revealing the dialectic of moral life itself, is capable of uncovering the necessary structures within human freedom without ceasing at the same time to recognize that life as a free and personal enterprise. Thus, only a philosophy of action permits one to discover the rational and determinate structures of life in reflection without in any way refusing to recognize the reciprocal transcendence of existence and freedom over thought.

Action, Blondel held, has its own a priori structure from which the whole of thought derives its meaning and direction. For this reason Blondel proposed his counter-Copernican revolution toward an even greater degree of subjectivity: Instead of assuming that it is thought which determines action, let us assume that it is action which determines thought. The center of perspective in philosophy should be transposed from the analytical element of thought into the synthetic element of action. What Blondel proposed was a study of *ideogenesis*—the process by which thought is derived from human action. This study would result in an understanding of the a priori structure implicit in the human will itself. Blondel's search for moral principles took the form of a search for the all-embracing dialectical law which governs immanently the evolution of human life. Underneath the most aberrant projects, beneath the strangest deviations of the human will, there always remains the necessary élan of the will—willing from which it is impossible to deviate. There is a necessary logic of freedom. Human actions can be illogical; they can never be alogical. Either one conforms freely to the law which one carries within oneself or one opposes it freely; one never escapes it.

The basic distinction underlying Blondel's understanding of the dialectic of evolving moral life is the distinction within thought itself between the plane of action or existence and the plane of thought or reflection. As act, thought participates in the spontaneity of the subject; it is commitment and freedom. As knowledge, thought reflects the given and ascertains its necessary relations. A necessary truth or value is, as a consequence, never purely passively acknowledged, but always freely recognized.

The first step in the moral dialectic of life, a step on the plane of action or existence, necessarily involves a direct or practical method of experimentation. For this step represents the pre-reflective unity of thought with existence. At this step the will aspect, the element of action, must take precedence over the intellectual element, the element of knowledge. The key presupposition of this step is an attitude of openness, of trust in life. One acts to achieve self-fulfillment; one must believe that by means of commitment one can achieve that self-fulfillment. One must be prepared never to accept a self-contradiction within the élan of one's will.

Natural Conscience

The criterion of certitude in the first step is to be found in the effects of the action undertaken on the individual's self-consciousness, the feeling of congruity or incongruity which the object of choice has with one's fundamental experience of self in consciousness. This feeling cannot become conscious until the will responds to a call from within itself. In this manner, freedom becomes interior to the most primitive stage of moral self-development.

At this stage one can speak of a natural conscience. Moral evil represents the refusal to be oneself; moral good, a sincere seeking of self-fulfillment. If this were the only step in moral life, one would be necessarily limited to a self-centered seeking of personal fulfillment on the part of an isolated and alienated existent. If one is faithful to the élan of life, however, the individual must move on. The initial pre-reflective unity of man must pass through the disjunction of thought and existence in order to find total fulfillment.

The Role of Thought

The second step of the moral dialectic occurs on the plane of thought or reflection. Here intellect takes precedence over will. It is on this level that one attempts an abstract, rational, universal, and, therefore, communicable understanding before one acts or commits oneself. In contrast to the trust presupposed in the first step, Blondel on this plane makes use of a method of total doubt. He systematically searches out all possible escapes from meaning or structure in freedom with the methodological assumption that the only means of proving necessity is to prove impossibility.

If in the process one discovers a necessity which governs man's free actions from within, one has succeeded in discovering an aspect of the intelligible law and rational regulation which governs free activity.

> If this indeterminate power [of our will] is defined by the fact *that* it wills, and not by that *which* it wills, further, if in the very activity itself of the will is revealed the end to which it necessarily tends and the series of means which it must use, then, that rigorous continuity contains a scientific determination; there is a necessary logic of freedom [Blondel, 1893, p. 127].

However, one must never conceive the rational structures of freedom as given a priori at the point of departure of one's philosophical quest. In order to be the truth of free action, rational structures, without ceasing to be necessary, must be engendered by that spontaneous source which is the reality of a free subject. In other words they must be engendered by the free commitment of the first moment.

Blondel speaks of the thought content of this second step as the "fruit of past action and the seed of consequent action." The instinctive role of thought is to project out all the unused potentialities of the human will as ideal goals for human commitment. He also locates the entire traditional concept of metaphysics within this moment of the moral dialectic:

> The metaphysical order is certainly not something which is outside the will as an extraneous end to be attained; it is contained within the will as a means to move beyond. It does not represent a truth already constituted in fact, but it places that which one wishes to will as an ideal object before thought. It does not express an absolute and universal reality; rather, it expresses the universal aspiration of a particular will [Blondel, 1893, p. 293].

The possibility of incorporating the transcendent ideals of a metaphysics into action leads to an awareness of that action as a properly free moral action and of self as a free moral agent. Man is, thus, freed from all pre-determinism; ". . . the will is led to place the center of its equilibrium beyond all factual realities, to live as it were on itself, to search in itself alone the purely formal reasons of its acts" (McNeill, 1966, p. 87). The creative power of the moral act is not to be found in the creation of a universal law; this is given in the metaphysical system of the second step. Rather, this creative power is to be found in the power of the will to synthesize that given set of ideals into the factual reality of its activity by free choice.

Because truth is founded on that which is within us and yet does not depend on us, on that which is the most intimate aspect of our subjectivity and yet common to the entire community of subjects, truth-in-us depends on the existential attitude we freely adopt in its regard. Or, to reverse the perspective and speak more properly, it is human existence itself which depends on the reception we freely give to truth or value. Consequent on the reflection of the second step, every free human agent is necessarily faced with the decision to accept or refuse the presence of transcendence within his will. Depending on the alternative chosen, that choice resolves itself either into the existential identity of lived truth or the real contradiction of lived error.

Synthetic Stage of Option

An option in the face of transcendence reveals itself in Blondel's system as the final synthetic step in the moral dialectic of life and the final necessary condition for the fulfillment of free human action. At this point in the dialectic, free affirmation reappears legitimately within the field of reflection. Option represents the necessary juncture in thought between the two planes of affirmation and reflection. From this point on, the free assent, which until now supported the dialectic of thought from without, is reflected from within in its turn. Reflective thought returns on its own existential reality.

The option of the third step has the function of existentializing reflection or thought itself. "The knowledge of being implies a necessity of option; the being which is within our knowledge is not before but after the liberty of choice" (Blondel, 1893, p. 436). Obviously there is at this synthetic moment a precedence once again of will or action over reflection. Freedom has the first and the last word in the moral dialectic of life.

Option's function is to render the unity of the abstract universal discovered in the second stage simultaneously experientially and rationally real. The two previous criteria, experiential and rational, are fused into one at the synthetic stage of option. However, just as will takes precedence over intellect at this stage, so the experiential criterion takes precedence over the rational criteria, using them as directives but finding ultimate certitude in the immediate and, therefore, absolutely certain experience of fulfillment or privation. Since this experience follows the second stage in the dialectic and is consequent on acceptance or refusal of transcendence, it is no longer necessarily an experience of the isolated self, as in the first stage of the dialectic. Rather, in its positive form of acceptance it is an experience of being existentially one with the other.

The ideal of a unity in existence with all men reveals itself in the second stage of the dialectic as a necessary aspiration of the human will. The very fact that man spontaneously thinks universally in the name of humanity, as though humanity were one, indicates that man's will necessarily aspires to exist universally at one with all men. This ideal is the primary example in Blondel's thought of the category of those commitments which man discovers as necessary, if he is to find his fulfillment, and simultaneously impossible to accomplish by his own unaided powers. Insofar as these commitments are necessary, they represent a possible immanent dimension of man's existential reality; insofar as they are impossible for man to realize by his own unaided freedom, they indicate the presence of a power within man that transcends man himself. This, in Blondel's opinion, is the key experience which leads man to project out an idea of God as the immanent–transcendent. Our idea of God, taking its genetic origin in the experience of the necessary and impossible, is a "projecting out of all the unused and unusable potentialities of the human will." Man finds it necessary in order to find the perfect identity of himself with himself in his voluntary actions to look within himself until he comes to that point where that which is of himself ceases. What we can know of God, Blondel argues, is precisely "that surplus of interior life which demands its employment."

Blondel is well aware that the possibility of an existential unity with one's fellow man would remain forever an abstraction unless man could somehow realize an existential unity with the divine will.

> At the very root of being, in the common practice of life, in the secret logic of consciousness, without God there is no fellow man for man. In order to be *one,* in order to exist, it is necessary that I do not rest *alone.* I have need for all the others. What is necessary, then, is to capture within myself the source of all unity (the divine will) and to transmit the truth of its intimate action [McNeill, 1966, p. 190].

To refuse to acknowledge the transcendent which manifests itself from within self carries with it as a necessary consequence the total isolation and alienation of the individual existent. Whereas to open to the transcendent, to recognize a truth, a value, a being which imposes itself from within man and is valid for all, is an absolutely necessary condition in order that man escape the isolated self and achieve unity with the real self in a community with others.

As the moral dialectic of life evolves, existence will always remain to some extent solitude, and truth and value will always remain to some extent at least abstract and external. The fusion of truth and value with existence, however, is always the result of man's free moral commitment and can be acquired by no other means. By his free choices man has the power to insert the absolute of being into the relativity of phenomena. Ultimately, man's knowledge of God is his immanent experiential awareness that "at the roots of his *ego* there is an *ego* that is no longer his *ego.*" However, it is only in the very act by which we would freely consent to such an intimate presence that we can achieve actual consciousness of it as an immanent dimension of our own existential reality. For it is only by free consent that we can change that presence from an abstract possibility to an experienced actuality. This, then, is the ultimate creative meaning of man's moral freedom—it lies in our power to make God exist or not exist *in our lives* by reason of our freely chosen style of existence.

The moral dialectic of action does not come to an end with Blondel's justification of the option for self-transcendence on the level of reflection. Philosophy, he believed, is necessarily false precisely when it tries to enclose life within reflective thought. Philosophy is capable of showing the necessity of a final option and clarifying its terms, but it cannot supply for option itself. Free commitment, then, has the last word, and philosophy must give way to a new dialectic of religious commitment and theological reflection based on the immediate certitude of the experience of religious life as a response in faith to revelation.

FREEDOM OF CONSCIENCE IN RELIGIOUS LIFE

Moral life, then, is evolutionary. It is a dynamic dialectic of fact and possibility, of the actual and the ideal. We must look for ideal human nature not in the past but in the future. And the key to that future is the creative moral freedom of man. In this evolutionary framework natural law should no longer be understood as based on a static structure or essence; rather, it represents a statement of conditions for man's own growth seen as a possibility and a task to be freely accomplished.

Conscience within this perspective is a developing form of self-awareness; it is to be understood as the deepest self-consciousness of man insofar as it acts as a power of discrimination, deciding in every choice what will promote authentic selfhood and what will stand in its way. Man on the moral level is characterized by self-development. He perceives every choice as a choice between authentic and inauthentic humanity. He sees his life as having a meaning only he can give it through his free choice. Moral obligations can only be accepted; they cannot be imposed. A psychologically mature adult can be called on to commit his freedom; he cannot be called on to submit it. For as long as a man is not directing his own activity on the moral level he is not to that extent a free agent. Consequently, to the degree that he is not a free agent, he is neither a responsible nor a moral person.

As Ignace Lepp notes, the evolution of moral conscience takes place according to the same general laws that govern the passage of individuals and social groups from infancy through adolescence to maturity (Lepp, 1965, p. 8). The growth of human psychic life will always proceed from instinct to rational self-development, and should culminate in a continuous process in religious self-donation. On the level of religious life, conscience is transposed into love itself. Sin on this level becomes the refusal to be for others. Freedom is a true moral value for religious life only when and to the degree that it promotes a superior form of personal and community life. The fullness of moral life is to be found precisely in that act by which one establishes oneself as person in a community of persons.

With a personal community, the false notion of conscience is the idea that we are each equipped with an exclusively private source of moral information, that we have a conscience in isolation. Today's identity crisis, its sense of alienation, and its crisis of faith are all related to the problem of the proper relation between person and institution. As John Sisk points out, modern man has been conditioned to think disjunctively of the relation of person to institution (Sisk, 1968). Institutions are the objective expressions of the communal and social aspects of ourselves. The institution tends to become the other, the enemy, only insofar as we are alienated from a part of ourselves. If a conscientious decision is really to be mine, I must make the effort of self-discovery; and I can do this only in communion with others. I cannot discover myself in isolation. Therefore, I cannot have a conscience in isolation.

If, as Vatican Council II declared, the Church in its essential reality ought to be an interpersonal community of love, then the achievement of true moral freedom and adult responsibility is a necessary condition for authentic religious life in the interpersonal community of the Church. Also, there can be no true moral authority unless a community is one of free persons. A community based upon power and subservience produces not authority but domination. Our call in Christ is a call to share in a community of love, a community in which each member retains his full personal responsibility and, consequently, his full personal freedom.

In the teachings of Paul, the negative aspect of the law was its inability to give life, precisely because it remained an external norm which did not contain in itself the δύναμις, the power of life (Fitzmeyer, 1967). The law schooled man in preparation for Christ, the end of the law. The law was a temporary disposition of God permitted until mankind reached the maturity in which it would be able without a pedagogue to respond to Christ with an adult and personal commitment. The principle of Christian activity is no longer merely in the external listing of "do's" and "don'ts" but, rather, in the internal whispering of the dynamic Spirit. Love in Paul's teaching is the fulfillment of the law because it is itself a dynamic force impelling man to seek the good of others. Ideal spiritual adulthood for the conscience would consist in this: that the compass of love would point the direction so unfalteringly that the external law is no longer needed. In such a man the law has been so fully assimilated, its deepest implications so much a matter of personal experience, that it has become a conscious instinct and an infallible power of discrimination. If we can assume that there has been a gradual assimilation of revelation within the community of the Church, then, what the Council seems to be telling us is that perhaps today the Christian community is in a position to begin to live out Paul's concept of the new freedom which should characterize a follower of Christ in a more perfect manner than ever before.

DISCERNMENT OF SPIRITS

Blondel's moral philosophy indicates a new appropriateness for Saint Ignatius' doctrine of the discernment of spirits as a means of pragmatically resolving our conscience in the process of making free moral choices. For that doctrine, as Karl Rahner points out, tacitly presupposes a philosophy of human existence in which a moral decision in its individuality is not merely an instance of general ethical normative principles but something positively individual and unique (Rahner, 1964, p. 110). Since man is positively an individual, and not just a negative or material instance of a general nature, as a spiritual personal being man is more than the point of intersection of general truths and maxims, more than the particular instance of a multipliable essence. This unique and special factor, the single human existence, can be summoned by an imperative prescription which is different in kind from any moral principle derived from general characteristics. Thus, the individuality of the person is the norm which the person must finally obey when pursuing his perfection by means of free choice.

The consequence of this understanding of man for moral life is that man's conscience has a function over and above the application of general norms to concrete circumstances. That function is that whereby the individual person recognizes an individual obligation in conscience which cannot be deduced from general principles (Gerken, 1963, pp. 141–152). The divine will is also a personal free will which is capable of entering into a personal dialogue with the individual as such and of exercising free initiative in that dialogue. Further, this personal divine will respects the free choices which the individual existent has made in the past and, thus, in the context of the dialogue respects the limits which those choices have established for future response. It belongs to the moral obligation of man to be and to become by free choice the individual that he is. In the discernment of spirits one seeks an intellectual knowledge which is incapable of being expressed in objective concepts. This knowledge is ultimately grounded in the simple presence to itself of the intrinsically intelligible subject, which in the very accomplishment of its acts has knowledge of itself through self-consciousness without the contrast of knower and things known.

In important decisions, Rahner maintains, practically every man chooses more or less in the manner which Ignatius had in mind. For, in such resolves, the person forms his choice nearly all the time from the basic experience of himself and from the feeling of congruity and incongruity that the object of election has with his fundamental experience of himself. He will make decisions, not only or finally from a rational analysis, but from the experience of whether or not something fits him. This experience is measured according to whether the thing makes him happy, satisfies him interiorly.

It is important to note the role that the creative imagination plays in making such a decision. One studies the choice to be made; one imagines the situation which such a choice would bring upon him; one tries to live in advance with such a choice. While doing this the person is constantly aware of what this choice causes in him. Saint Ignatius' doctrine presupposes that the individual morality of a proposed course of action is not discovered exclusively in the objective essence of the action. Rather, the morality of the course of action is also discovered from its effects on the individual's self-consciousness. Peace, joy, quiet, happiness: it is by using these as criteria that one learns whether the object of one's decision is good or not.

This doctrine is based on the theological presupposition that in every sincere believer the inner law of the Spirit is at work like a kind of connaturality with the God who speaks to him through Christ—a kind of power of discrimination, a spiritual sense of touch capable of discerning what is and what is not an authentic realization of God's invitation. Conscience is sacred because, when I get down to the real self in my search for self-fulfillment, I find a depth in myself which does not belong to me but to which I belong, a depth which theologians refer to as the Holy Spirit dwelling in me.

The use of the discernment of spirits as a practical means of resolving the individual conscience is based on one all-important presupposition. That presupposition is a basic option, not in terms of any particular object, but a basic option in favor of transcendence, in favor of openness. Man must open himself up to God, because his concrete nature is an openness to the infinite and transcendent God. Man must freely assent to this reality of his own being. If the inclination in any given decision concerning a particular good is really one which fits the individual, then this particular movement will necessarily support and deepen that basic openness and resulting peace. Granting that openness, the moral process of choice is a process of testing whether a particular commitment is compatible or incompatible with that openness which constitutes the innermost essence of man.

As Rahner points out, Ignatius' fundamental spiritual principle, the finding of God in all things, is only the habitual practice of that supernatural existential logic implied in the discernment of spirits, whereby one finds God's will by noting one's consolations and desolations (Rahner, 1964, p. 155). The individual reality which one meets, or which one must choose, or do, or suffer, is held up to one's fundamental openness to God.

The appropriateness of the discernment of spirits as a practical means of resolving conscience lies in the fact that it does respect the uniqueness of the existing subject and his liberty of conscience while, at the same time, it gives man a method whereby he can discover the will of God not as something totally outside himself, but as the deepest reality of his own will.

Further, this practice leads man not just to an abstract conceptual awareness of God, but to a vital experiential sense of the presence of the divine spirit within. As Thomas Sartory observes in his article Changes in Christian Spirituality:

> Tomorrow the devout man will be a "mystic," a man who has experienced something, or there will be no devout men. In the past any personal experience and decision always found its way prepared by the convictions of the public and by general religious customs taken for granted in which piety could find support. But this support is fading away. The personal religious experience of the individual, therefore, is going to be increasingly decisive [Sartory, 1968, p. 79].

REFERENCES

America. An editorial statement on "Human Life." *America,* 1968, *119,* 94–95.

Blondel, M. *L'Action.* Paris: Presses Universitaires de France, 1893.

Blondel, M. *The letter on apologetics and history and dogma* (trans. by A. Dru & I. Trethowan). New York: Holt, Rinehart & Winston, 1964.

Carter, G. E. In W. M. Abbott (s.J.) (Ed.) *The documents of Vatican II.* New York: Herder & Herder, 1966.

Curran, C. E. The ethical teaching of Jesus. *Commonweal,* 1967, *86,* 248–258.

Fitzmeyer, J. (s.J.) Saint Paul and the law. *Jurist,* 1967, *27,* 18–36.

Gerken, J. (s.J.) *Toward a theology of the layman.* New York: Herder & Herder, 1963.

Lepp, I. *The authentic morality.* New York: Macmillan, 1965.

Maguire, D. C. Morality and the magisterium. *Cross Currents,* 1968, *18,* 41–65.

McNeill, J. J. (s.J.) *The Blondelian synthesis.* Leiden: Brill, 1966.

Monden, L. (s.J.) *Sin, liberty, and law* (trans. by J. Donceel [s.J.]). New York: Sheed & Ward, 1965.

Rahner, K. (s.J.) *The dynamic element in the church* (trans. by W. J. O'Hara). New York: Herder & Herder, 1964.

Sartory, T. Changes in Christian spirituality. In H. Küng (Ed.) *Life in the Spirit.* New York: Sheed & Ward, 1968. Pp. 70–79.

Sisk, J. P. The escalation bends. *National Catholic Reporter,* 1968, *5* (8), 6. November 6, 1968.

Somerville, J. M. (s.J.) *Total commitment: Blondel's* L'ACTION. Washington: Corpus Books, 1968.

Vatican Council II. W. M. Abbott (s.J.) (Ed.) *The documents of Vatican II.* New York: Herder & Herder, 1966.

Freedom of Conscience from a Psychiatric Viewpoint

WILLIAM W. MEISSNER, s.j.

Father William W. Meissner, S.J. received his A.B., M.A., and Ph.L. degrees from St. Louis University, his S.T.L. from Woodstock College, and his M.D. from Harvard University. In addition to a number of articles, he is the author of three books: Annotated bibliography in religion and psychology *(1961),* Group dynamics in the religious life *(1965), and* Foundations for a psychology of grace *(1966). Currently, Father Meissner is resident psychiatrist at the Massachusetts Mental Health Center.*

It is advisable in approaching a subject as complex and difficult as that of human freedom and its implications that we be as explicit as possible about the intent and extent of what we have to say. This is particularly necessary in view of the fact that what we have to contribute from the vantage point of modern psychiatry is only one facet of a multifaceted problem, the intelligibility of which is not exhausted by the analysis of many disciplines. The concern of modern psychiatry reaches into the inner being of man, into the inner reaches of the conscious and unconscious mind. It grapples hand-to-hand, as it were, with the complexities of human freedom in its existential realization in the human psyche. It confronts the human mind as it struggles to achieve or to avoid its own freedom. The vantage point is very special. It is a therapeutic vantage point above all else. The basic concern about human freedom with which the psychiatrist involves himself is the intensely personal one of why this concrete, existing, living human being has not achieved a fullness of the freedom of mind and spirit which is his human heritage, why he cannot realize it in the ongoing current of his life and experience.

I would like to subdivide my remarks on this aspect of the problem of freedom by addressing myself first to the question of the nature of psychiatric understanding. I put this first on the agenda because I feel it is important to be clear in knowing what we can expect from any given discipline and how much weight we can give to its contributions. Then I would like to consider some of the clinical phenomenology that relates to the problem of freedom. Thereafter I would like to explore the complicated question of psychic determinism and its relation with the problem of freedom, since it is a basic and necessary postulate of psychiatry. Next, I will make an attempt to formulate a theoretical understanding of freedom in psychiatric terms. And lastly, but certainly not leastly, I want to consider the question of responsibility, which in a sense is the repository of freedom for the psychiatric approach.

NATURE OF PSYCHIATRIC EXPLANATION

The problem of human freedom has traditionally been the proper province of philosophy and theology. Psychiatry, however, comes to the problem by way of the psychic experience which is associated with the diminution or absence of freedom as well as the experience which is associated with its presence and exercise. Psychiatry is fundamentally a science, and its approach to any problem is generated from the evidence available to it. It attempts to formulate theory in such a way as to clarify, organize, and integrate in some intelligible fashion the mass of data that its practitioners are continually collecting. It is essentially an empirical enterprise.

Modern psychiatry has become a very complex and rapidly expanding field. Psychiatry as a science is less a methodologically pure scientific approach than an aggregate of scientific methods organized under the rubric of "psychiatry" and governed by a general interest in the understanding of the causes and complications of mental illness. Thus, modern psychiatry embraces the methods of biochemistry, neurophysiology, medicine, all the basic biological sciences, psychology, sociology, epidemiology, and more. What is distinctive, if one can speak of anything distinctive about the approach of psychiatry, is that all these contributions and methodological approaches are subsumed under the primary clinical orientation of the psychiatrist.

The domain which is peculiarly the psychiatrist's is the arena of the intrapsychic dynamics of the patient. The entire course of his medical training, while it is concerned with the acquisition of a certain amount of scientific information, is uniquely focused on the development of a caretaking person. It is directed to the shaping of a professional person who is committed to the patient in an intimate and concerned way which is shared by no other discipline. The psychiatrist shares this orientation with other physicians. It is an orientation which puts the concern for the patient in a primary place, above personal consideration. The medical student, the intern, and the resident learn that personal wish, personal inclination or need, physical fatigue, the hours of the day, or whatever, do not take precedence over the needs of the patient. This personal commitment and involvement with the patient is extended to the psychotherapeutic relationship. This does not mean that other disciplines do not share in this concern—as, for example, clinical psychologists. But it does not provide the primary focus of their training and professional commitment.

The vantage point of the psychiatrist, therefore, is a very special one. It is primarily from the inner experience of the patient, insofar as it can be communicated and shared in an intense personal relationship, that the psychiatrist works. If there is any methodology that he can claim as distinctive it is the methodology of personal interaction by which he reaches the inner core of the patient's feeling and experience. Psychiatry is, therefore, a science of interpersonal interaction and inner experience. But it is also necessarily an art—the two aspects cannot be divorced since they depend so intimately on each other. The psychiatrist is uniquely the instrument of his own science. It is through his own interaction with the patient that he gathers the data on which he bases his attempts at theoretical understanding. Psychiatric understanding therefore always contains a subjective element which contaminates even as it contributes the basic evidence of the science. The fundamentally introspective and intersubjective aspects of psychiatric evidence impose certain unavoidable limitations on the validity of psychiatric inference and make it necessary that the criteria for acceptance of evidence, formation of theories, and validation of constructs go forward in unique ways which do not fit the hypothetico-deductive and constructural models of physical or even rigidly behavioral sciences (Meissner, 1966).

The psychiatric approach to freedom is consequently governed by the perspective of the inner experience of freedom. Some years ago, Robert Waelder set down the problem of freedom for psychiatry in these terms:

. . . the problem to be investigated is the purely psychological one of freedom *from* something, for example, from affects or anxiety, or freedom *for* something, say freedom for coping with a task set before one. Anyone afflicted with an obsessional neurosis and acting under a compulsion is psychologically not free; if he is "freed" from his compulsion, he will have acquired a measure of freedom [Waelder, 1936, p. 89].

Freedom meant to Waelder that man was not tied down to his biological or social environment—to what he called "the *hic et nunc*" of his actual existence. In virtue of his freedom man was able to make himself an object of his own reflections and to abstract himself from his immediate situation. It was a form of transcendence, a capacity to rise above oneself and one's environment, which distinguished man from all other creatures. It was this transcending experience which Knight later called "the sense of inner freedom" (Knight, 1946).

It is important to remember that the psychiatric approach to freedom is generated out of a context of experience and is governed by that experience. The psychiatric interest is focused on the experience. The expression "a *sense* of inner freedom" underlines the experiential quality of it and limits the inquiry to that aspect. The further question whether man is indeed really free is left open and unanswered. Psychiatry limits itself to a theoretical understanding of the experience. The further question lies beyond the phenomenology and its understanding; it lies in the realm of metaphysics. The curiosity, of course, is that the metaphysical argument in part rests on the experience of self-imposition and self-determination as a self-originative act—the so-called experimental proof of freedom. Psychiatry and philosophy share a common datum and it would seem that their respective conclusions should not violate each other.

PHENOMENOLOGY

Psychiatry, therefore, concerns itself with the presence or absence of the sense of inner freedom. Psychiatrists work primarily with people who have experienced some disorganization and impairment in their intellectual and emotional functioning. With the objective of clarifying what it is that we mean by the sense of inner freedom, we might ask what kinds of clinical states are associated with the diminution or intensification of this psychic experience?

There are a number of clinical states which seem to be associated with a loss or diminution of the experience of freedom. States in which all experience is missing are obviously such. Death, coma in which there is a loss of consciousness, and phases of sleep in which there is no conscious dreaming activity would be conditions in which all conscious experience is absent. There are other states of mental confusion, disorientation, delirium from various causes, and states of clouding of consciousness which are associated with conscious experience but in which any sense of freedom is wanting. The subject feels incapable of self-directed and integrated activity.

States in which there is a breakthrough of instinctual, drive-dependent forces are also associated with a diminution of the sense of freedom. In acute schizophrenic episodes the patient feels as though he has lost control, as though his behavior is driven by forces over which he has no control. The loss of control over feelings and thought processes is often a feature intermittently of more chronic schizophrenic states as well. These conditions are strongly marked by a diminution of secondary-process kinds of mental organization and a predominance of primary-process organization. Along with this relative disorganization, there is a loss of a sense of mastery, and the ego feels inundated by unconscious forces. Similar phenomena are observable in other psychotic states. The manic-depressive in the manic phase feels as driven and incapable of control as the acute schizophrenic.

It might be useful to say a word here about the so-called borderline personalities. Such states of personality organization are characterized by presenting symptoms of the neuroses or character disorders but also having transient psychotic decompensations under the influence of stress or drugs. They have a chronic, diffuse, free-floating anxiety, usually present a variety of neurotic symptoms including obsessions, phobias, conversions, and dissociative states, hypochondriacal and paranoid trends. Sexuality is often what Freud described as "polymorphous perverse." The syndrome is characterized by a developmental inadequacy of the ego which lacks the capacity for impulse control and has never evolved appropriate channels of sublimation. The basic defensive mechanism is *splitting,* by which the good and bad aspects of the self and objects are actively kept separate. The use of splitting in conjunction with the use of primitive introjection and projection leads to a shifting between a clinging to an idealized "magical," all-powerful, and providing object, and the elaboration of fantasies and behavior of a primitive self-omnipotence. The fantasy of omnipotence is an infantile one, but it serves a restitutive function in that it protects the individual from the threat involved in the primitive need and fear of others. The borderline is threatened constantly by the fear of loss of control and the inner struggle of conflicting emotions. The sense of self-possession and inner trust so essential to a sense of inner freedom is quite impaired.

The depressive states are also characterized by a diminution of a sense of freedom. The psychotic depressions are associated with a complete loss of control in a kind of paroxysm of impending destruction. But even in the less acute and intense depressive states the patient often describes a feeling of lethargy, of being weighted down, burdened, and guilty. The simplest decisions or initiatives require more energy than they can muster. The patient has a sense of worthlessness and impoverishment. Rather than being out of control, the patient feels unable to assert control; he feels weak and deprived. The sense of inner capacity and control associated with freedom are lacking.

In other drive-dominated states the sense of inner freedom is impaired. Extreme hunger and thirst are examples, as well as extreme fatigue. Similarly in states of sexual or aggressive arousal the individual feels himself in the grip of forces which prevent him from deliberately choosing a course of action. Certain neurotic states are associated with a diminution of freedom. One thinks particularly of compulsions and phobias, but in fact all the neurotic manifestations are to some extent characterized by the struggle between repressed unconscious forces and the repressing and defensive functions of the ego. The diversion of ego-energies in this countercathectic fashion deprive the ego of energies that might be available for reinforcement of the ego's sense of mastery and control.

There are certainly artificial states as well which seem to reveal a lessening of the sense of freedom. Hypnosis and other states of increased suggestibility seem to be associated with a transient diminution in the sense of free will. It also seems that certain drug-induced states are associated with such a diminution. The hallucinogenic drugs often produce an experience of forced thinking or the experience of the passive modification of thoughts and feelings. Lysergic acid diethylamide (LSD) experiences are often of this quality, and even marijuana often produces a kind of dream-like euphoria. Amphetamines can produce a driven quality to the thought processes with associated loss of control and its concomitant anxieties. The amphetamine psychosis has been described which consists of an extreme form of this state and which presents the aspects of loss of control and ego-disorganization found in other psychotic states.

Organic syndromes should also be mentioned, since a variety of central-nervous-system pathologies can produce similar phenomena. Brain tumors, cerebro-vascular accidents, trauma, and other organic afflictions can produce ego-disorganization and impairment of the sense of inner freedom. Particularly noteworthy are temporal lobe syndromes of whatever etiology. Temporal lobe seizures, more accurately denominated as limbic seizures, are associated with impaired impulse control, amnesias, complex psychic experiences which are often illusory or hallucinatory in quality, bizarre experiences of derealization or depersonalization or of the déjà vu type, and forms of automatic behavior which are often quite complex and which are carried out in a kind of fugue state. Often the differential diagnosis between such seizure states and psychiatric disorders is quite difficult to make.

It has also been pointed out by E. Hartmann (1966) that the activity of dreaming in normal persons is one in which the sense of freedom and control is also diminished. There is a sense of the dream "happening" as though the dreamer were caught up in a process over which he had little direct control. The events of the dream happen to rather than are directed by the dreamer. There is a similar quality to daydreams when they steal upon us. We lapse into a revery in which our thoughts seem to run their own course for a time and then we "snap out of it" to assert once again our conscious control.

When we survey these various states of diminished freedom, and we have not attempted to present a complete catalogue, there are two aspects that stand out. These states represent forms of permanent or transient weakening of the ego. The ego loses control and becomes dominated by other intrapsychic forces which drive the ego one way or the other without its being able to direct the process—or at least with diminished capacity to do so. The other point is that all of these states represent a shift from a predominance of secondary-process thinking to a predominance of primary-process thinking. The predominance of primary process and the weakening of ego will give us a handle on these states for further considerations later on.

If there are states of diminished sense of freedom, there are also evidently states of increased or intensified freedom. It is difficult to denominate such states, and I suppose that it is best for every individual to consult his own experience. There are times when each of us feels more in control, more secure, more adequate, more confident. At such times the doubts and anxieties of our individual neuroses seem to fade into the background. It seems to me that such experiences are associated with an increase of basic self-esteem and trust. There is an inner feeling of worthfulness, trustworthiness, autonomy, and capability. I believe that this feeling is linked to what Robert White was talking about in using the term "competence" (White, 1959), and what other ego theorists have been calling "ego-strength." It is apparent that the sense of inner freedom presents itself phenomenologically across a broad spectrum from total disruption to a high degree of intensification. The experience of every individual, moreover, varies along this spectrum—moving back and forth between states of more or less diminished freedom to states of more or less increased freedom. It would be my feeling that in some rudimentary sense the inner sense of freedom, however diminished and compromised by pathological states, is never totally absent in the conscious person. Even in the most regressed and psychotic states, as Freud has observed, there is always a hidden psychic corner in which the ego preserves its nonpsychotic and observant capacity—and it is in this segment of preserved ego that the sense of freedom lies hidden.

PSYCHIC DETERMINISM

Before attempting a more theoretical approach to the sense of inner freedom, it is important that we deal with one of the basic issues in psychiatric thinking. How can psychiatrists talk about freedom and its correlative responsibility when psychiatry as a science rests upon the postulate of psychic determinism?

The conflict is well displayed in Freud himself. Freud was an uncompromising determinist, and relentlessly applied the principle to his analyses of behavior and experience. He made room, however, for the conviction of free will as a conscious experience, but maintained that strict determinism was operative at the unconscious level. In 1901 he commented:

> According to our analyses it is not necessary to dispute the right to the feeling of conviction of having a free will. If the distinction between conscious and unconscious motivation is taken into account, our feeling of conviction informs us that conscious motivation does not extend to all our motor decisions. *De minimis non curat lex.* But what is thus left free by the one side receives its motivation from the other side, from the unconscious; and in this way determination in the physical sphere is still carried out without any gap [Freud, 1901, p. 254].

He called "psychical freedom" an illusion which he categorically denied (Freud, 1915). He went on to say: "I ventured to tell you that you nourish a deeply rooted faith in undetermined psychical events and in free will, but that this is quite unscientific and must yield to the demand of a determinism whose rule extends over mental life" (Freud, 1915, p. 106). Yet in *The Ego and the Id* (1923) he wrote: ". . . analysis does not set out to make pathological reactions impossible, but to give the patient's ego freedom to decide one way or the other" (Freud, 1923, p. 50). Freud was able to speak comfortably on both sides of the issue of free will. He conceded an experience of freedom at a conscious level but insisted on a strict determinism at the unconscious level.

This view of the matter has dominated the post-Freudian era in psychiatry. But in most considerations of the matter, as in Freud, there is a presumption that "free will" and "psychic determinism" are mutually exclusive alternatives. The late Robert Knight was the first to see that this was not necessarily the case. He wrote:

> In the psychological and philosophical realm there is also no real alternative to psychic determinism. To defend "free will" as an alternative is to be guilty of semantic confusion. Determinism refers to the complex of causal factors, heredity and environment, internal and external, past and present, conscious and unconscious, which combine to produce a certain resultant in a given individual. Determinism is thus a theoretical construct which fits the observed data, as demonstrated by predictions which were fulfilled, and which is essential to any psychology which claims to be scientific. The antithesis to this construct is the construct, indeterminism—pure chance, chaos. "Free will," on the other hand, is not on the same conceptual level as are these constructs. It refers to a subjective psychological experience, and to compare it to determinism is like comparing the enjoyment of flying to the law of gravity [Knight, 1946, p. 255].

Knight was perfectly accurate in seeing that free will and determinism are not strictly opposites, but he really sidesteps the basic problem by recourse to a Freudian solution—freedom is reduced to a conscious experience while determinism is regarded as a matter of real causal influences.

It is not clear that either presumption is entirely valid. It is not clear that the sense of inner freedom is not in some real sense a determination of self on the part of the ego. Nor is it clear that unconscious factors are simple causal elements.

Granted the influence of the prior unconscious event, it alone could not satisfy the causal conditions required for the act itself. Action requires the activation of multiple integrated systems in the person: imaginative, emotional, motor, and so forth. Thus, the unconscious influence must be counted as part of a complex causal process which results in a particular segment of behavior. Moreover, a given behavioral segment can be overdetermined, i.e., subject to the influence of more than one unconscious determining influence. Consequently, this kind of determination is not exclusive, but is exercised conjointly with other determinants as well as with other efficient or motor causes.

It is on the level of efficient causality that free will enters the picture. Some clarifications are necessary here. No one would hold that all human activity involving the use of the will is free. The will is free only when it is not forced, when it has the opportunity to select among choices. Under circumstances in which a man appraises a certain object as unreservedly good and desirable, the activity of the will is not free but necessary. The conditions of such necessity, however, are very seldom realized, since the objects and activities to which men are drawn in this life are seldom unmixed goods. When a man is confronted with a non-necessary, but attractive object, he is capable of pursuing it or not. Under such conditions, the doctrine of free will maintains that there is nothing outside of a man or inside of him which forces him to choose, or to choose between available alternatives. His decision is therefore said to be free.

But what about psychic determinism? Let us suppose that I choose at this moment to stop writing and enjoy a cup of coffee. My decision is not forced; I could just as easily have gone on writing. That decision is undoubtedly determined by certain unconscious influences. Under extensive free association, it would be possible to explain why I posed the question at this time and not another, why I decided to drink coffee and not tea, and so on. The explanation would explain why I chose one set of alternatives over another, why I had available these alternatives and not others, and why I chose at all; but they would not explain the fact *that* I chose and committed myself to a particular course of action. They explain the what, not the *that*. They explain the determination of action, not its efficiency. They explain the content of my deliberation, not the fact of decision. There is nothing in the given alternatives which forces my decision. Unconscious determinants can explain why I made the decision I made, but they do not account for the decision itself. I myself am the cause of my own free activity.

Other approaches to the problem of determinism have focused on the meaning of "causality" in psychological science. It has been argued that the role of the causality principle in contemporary physics has been undermined, so that its application to mental events is no longer justifiable. Causality and determinism are therefore not coextensive (Angel, 1959). If determinism does not imply causal influence, what does it mean?

Some clarification in this matter has been provided by E. Hartmann (1966) through an analysis in terms of horizontal and vertical relationships. If we propose a stratified model of the mental organization, at the lowest level there are the basic physiological and biological events which constitute the ongoing life of the organism. Stimulus input sets off a series of complex causal interactions which result in behavioral output. The analysis at this level is causal and events are strictly determined by causal relations. At the highest level of organization of mental functioning, conscious psychological experiences take place with a certain sequence and organization. The relations between such states are not causal. Moreover, the relations between events at each stratum are not causally related. The relationship is rather one of concomitance or of what Hartmann calls "indicator" relations. Every psychic state indicates a correlative physiological state, but a given physiological state need not have a correlative psychic state. To understand the relationships between strata, psychological theorists interpose a system of mediating concepts. In psychoanalytic psychiatry, these intermediate concepts include a description of unconscious processes. The question involved in psychic determinism can be resolved into what kinds of relations obtain between psychic states at each level of the model—between conscious psychic states on one level and between intermediate states on another. It is clear that the relations are not simply causal as they are on the physiological level.

One of the contributions of the phenomenological movement has been to point out the role of meaning in such relationships. The determinism is not a determinism of third-person forces operating on and in the psyche, but it has to do with connections of meaning. Psychic determinism is a matter of the necessities of meaning. Freedom is not associated with a lack of determinism—rather that act is most fully free which is most fully determined. But it is a determination that the ego imposes on itself in deliberate consciousness of the necessities imposed by the inner and the outer world. Thus free association establishes a chain of meaningful necessities, but the necessity is retrospective and reconstructive. The best formulation of this aspect of analytic explanation has been provided by Freud himself:

> So long as we trace the development from its final outcome backwards, the chain of events appears continuous, and we feel we have gained an *insight* which is completely satisfactory or even exhaustive. But if we proceed the reverse way, if we start from the premises inferred from analysis and try to follow these up

to the final result, then we no longer get the impression of an inevitable sequence of events which could not have been otherwise determined. We notice at once that there might have been another result, and that we might have been just as well able to understand and explain the latter. The synthesis is thus not so satisfactory as the analysis; in other words, from a knowledge of the premises we could not have foretold the nature of the result [Freud, 1920, p. 167].

Thus what may be "freely" established at any point in the chain of events becomes in retrospect one of the "necessities of meaning" (Fisher, 1966).

It is my position that real freedom can coexist with such necessities of meaning. But it must be added that such necessities are not in themselves totally determinative of current behavior and experience. The experiences which they represent are imbedded in the personality and have not merely a past existence but a present reality. In the transference, for example, the infantile love and hate for the parent are directed to the analyst: that love-and-hate is an immediate, vital, present and active force. It is not just a meaning. Its necessity is a present and active force. As Freud has remarked, the ego is a precipitate of object relations. Thus relations to other persons are internalized and become more or less permanent structural acquisitions of the personality. The past lives on, transformed and unconscious, as a functional and dynamic aspect of the present life of the human organism. Thus the necessities of meaning, while they serve a necessary explanatory function, are at the same time caught up in a complex interaction of causal systems and psychic influences out of which the ongoing current of behavior issues. Thus the determinants of action are complex, partial, and multiple —the explanation is therefore never complete and the personality must be regarded as a truly open system. In such an open system there is room for the exercise of freedom, not without determination, but as an additional determinant interacting with other determinants of the course of action.

THE METAPSYCHOLOGY OF FREEDOM

In the light of what has been said above and in the face of a psychiatric tradition which clings to a narrow conception of psychic determinism—a conception which is based on a more or less mechanical notion of causality and leaves no room for free choice and leaves room for a merely subjective sense of freedom—I would like to pull together the elements of a theory of ego-functioning which does leave room for the exercise of free choice.

The emergence of a psychoanalytic ego-psychology has brought with it the growing realization that the earlier emphasis of the dependence of the ego on drive forces—and we might substitute the expression "determination by" here as well—did not present a complete picture. Rather, beginning with Hartmann's revolutionary introduction of concepts of autonomy and adaptation (H. Hartmann, 1958), published in German in 1939, an appreciation for the independence of the ego has grown. Rapaport (1967) speaks of the independence from drive forces as *autonomy of the ego from the id* and independence of behavior from external stimulation as *autonomy of the ego from external reality*. The ego is not merely a passive agent driven by influence outside itself. It maintains a relative autonomy and it is the implications of that autonomy that we wish to explore.

The autonomy of the ego is of more than one kind. H. Hartmann (1958) introduced the concepts of primary and secondary autonomy. The ego has certain apparatuses of primary autonomy—memory, motor systems, perceptual apparatuses—which are biologically derived and evolutionary given structures which provide the basis for the organism's capacity to fit in or adapt with its environment. The apparatuses of secondary autonomy, however, are not given but must be developed out of instinctual modes and vicissitudes. Thus structures are derived from instinctual sources or defenses are elaborated in dealing with conflicts, and these then acquire an adaptive function. Such structures undergo a "change of function"—a change from defensive to adaptive functions—in the course of which they acquire an autonomy from the instinctual or drive-dependent context in which they arose. The ego is then capable of applying them in the interest of other independent ends. Rapaport sees these forms of autonomy as related.

> Man's constitutionally given drive equipment appears to be the *ultimate* (primary) *guarantee* of the ego's autonomy from the environment, that is, its safeguard against stimulus-response slavery. But this autonomy too has *proximal* (secondary) *guarantees*: namely, higher order superego and ego structures as well as the motivations pertaining to them. Like the ego's autonomy from the id, its autonomy from the environment also is only relative [Rapaport, 1967, p. 727].

The maintenance of such relatively autonomous structures requires a measure of stimulus-nutriment. If stimulus-nutriment is decreased, as in sensory deprivation, the maximized autonomy from the environment produces a correlative minimizing of its autonomy from the id. Similarly, the maximizing of ego-autonomy from the id as a result of obsessive–compulsive defenses leads to a maximal dependence on environment. Only a relative autonomy of the ego from the id—within an optimal range—is compatible with a relatively optimal autonomy of ego from the environment. Reality relations are, therefore, the guarantee of autonomy from id, and, paradoxically, instinctual drives are the guarantee of autonomy from the environment.

Relative autonomy, its maintenance and effectiveness, depends in part on the elaboration of the structures of secondary autonomy. The structural organization of ego and superego provide the basis on which the developed independence from external and internal forces is attained. Freud long ago defined identification as the mechanism of structural formation. Through identification, the organism acquires an increasing internalization of controls so that what was originally required by way of external control becomes part of the inner resources for control and mastery. The process of structuralization provides a measure of independence from drive-derivatives and opens the way for the adaptative use of structural derivatives in the service of other needs of the organism. Thus what originated in the resolution of conflict can undergo a change of function and thus become part of the conflict-free sphere of the ego. Thus while relatively autonomous structures may derive from drive vicissitudes they never become absolutely autonomous. Under the influence of regression, these structures can once more fall under the influence of the instinctual drives.

Correlative to the development of secondary autonomy and psychic structure, Hartmann has advanced the notion of neutralization. Freud originally described neutralization in relation to identification and structure formation. Through identification, the object-libido originally directed to the object was turned toward the self and thereby desexualized. The libidinal energy was thereby neutralized. Hartmann extended this notion to aggressive energies as well. The evolution of structure was accompanied by an increasing availability of neutralized energies and an increasing capacity to neutralize. The development of structure made increasing amounts of energy available for the conflict-free interests of the ego (H. Hartmann, 1955). Other theorists have argued that one need not appeal to neutralization for the origin of such drive-independent energies, but that there are independent ego-energies which in no sense derive from instinctual drives (White, 1963).

The development of structure, secondary autonomy, and the capacity for free choice are correlative. The first analyst to formulate this principle was Waelder. He regarded freedom as the capacity to transcend the conditions of human existence. What enabled man to do this was his superego. He saw the formal function of the superego as the observation, the objectification of one's self, and the attainment of a position above one's own ego. He wrote:

> Freedom then in its most general sense is found in the existence of the superego, in that formal function of the superego in virtue of which man rises above himself and apprehends the world from without and beyond his immediate perceptions and his biological needs [Waelder, 1936, p. 92].

Man's capacity to transcend his instincts, to achieve some degree of autonomy from inner drives and outer environment, are not due simply to his superego. The optimal degree of functional autonomy and the balance of the forms of secondary autonomy rest in turn on the integral functioning of ego and superego. The capacity for freedom involves a degree of inner regulation which preserves a degree of optimal autonomy as described by Rapaport. The integration of ego and superego functions is essential for this to be achieved. The truth of Waelder's statement is that the optimal degree of superego development is an essential condition for the internalization of drive-independent controls which are the basis of ego-autonomy and freedom.

It is possible now to return to phenomenology with which we started this consideration. The states of diminished freedom which we described revealed a common set of characteristics. They were all states of diminished ego-capacity and weakness. Moreover, where consciousness was maintained they revealed a predominance of primary-process thought-organization. Primary-process thinking is dependent on and derivative from the influence of instinctual drives. It implies an increase of a drive-dependent organization of thought-processes and represents a diminution of that degree of secondary autonomy which is required for the maintenance of secondary-process thought-organization. It implies, therefore, a minimization of autonomy from the id and a correlative maximization of autonomy from reality.

The concept of real freedom of choice is a visible one in terms of psychoanalytic ego-theory. It need not be restricted to a merely subjective sense of freedom. It requires a degree of maturity of integral ego and superego functioning which insures some degree of autonomy from other determining forces which impinge on and influence the course of action. The act of free choice can thus be seen as derived from an executive function of the ego responding to a determining context of meaning and autonomously directing the course of action in one meaningful channel rather than another.

RESPONSIBILITY

The correlative of real freedom in the subjective world of intrapsychic realities is responsibility. The problem of responsibility arises in relation to the determination of legal responsibility as well as in the context of moral responsibility. These are complex areas, and I shall leave it to others more competent to discuss them. Responsibility remains, however, a central concern in psychiatry. It is one of the major goals of therapy and one of the cornerstones of mature and adult adjustment. I would like to explore briefly the meaning of responsibility, its relation to inner freedom, and its importance in the psychotherapeutic process.

To have a sense of responsibility is to have a sense of inner reality and identity. To be responsible is to assert one's sense of vitality and mastery. The responsibility we are concerned with is what Weisman calls subjective responsibility. He writes:

Subjective responsibility . . . accords primacy to man as the initiator of acts instead of man as an object acted upon. It recognizes the reality of choice, freedom, consciousness, motivation, and the capacity to control the consequences of purposeful action. These realities are a man's private property, and he cannot barter, share, or surrender them. Subjective responsibility corresponds closely with the sense of reality for what we are and what we do. Existentialists call this *authenticity*; psychoanalysts call it *identity* [Weisman, 1965, pp. 167–168].

Thus, in this psychoanalytic view of freedom and responsibility, man lives with his unconscious, not by it. He is capable of recognizing his own uniqueness and value even in the face of obligation and conformity. The sense of inner harmony and self-esteem which is linked with the sense of responsibility derives from a sense of trust and trustworthiness and implies an approximation of ego-functions to the implicit values of the ego-ideal. Thus superego-derived values serve as a system of internal regulation which stabilizes and reinforces the ego's capacity to choose freely and act responsibly. Superego-functions support responsible actions only insofar as they are harmoniously integrated with ego-operations. Without such integration they can evoke guilt, remorse, and depression, and in fact undermine the individual's capacity for freedom and responsibility.

To catch up the threads of the previous argument, the idea of a capricious or undetermined free will on one hand or the idea of rigid psychic determinism on the other— both leave little room for responsibility. Responsibility is the power to respond, to choose and carry out one path of conduct rather than another. Causal necessity without choice destroys responsibility. An indeterminism that makes choice a random selection from unlimited range of possible courses also evacuates responsibility. The reality of the person does not limit itself to an organization of processes. The unconscious belongs to the person, not the person to the unconscious. Man uses his psychic equipment, it does not use him. "There are unique dimensions of existence in which each person exists alone, not only influenced by his unconscious processes but committed to responsible activity and able to exercise a measure of control" (Weisman, 1965, p. 175).

The relationship between relative autonomy and responsibility has been noted by Lewy (1961). He recognizes that autonomy along with the adaptability of the ego are the foundations on which individual responsibility is built. Man cannot be held responsible or accountable for his actions unless those actions are attributable to him in some authentic sense. They must be *his* acts, directed, governed, and controlled by him in virtue of his own inner sense of direction and intention. Yet they are not completely autonomous and undetermined. They are a response born of the individual's capacity for responsiveness to a complex interplay of determining variables which supply a constantly developing framework of interaction and process within which the ego responds. The response which enables the ego to insert itself in relevant and realistic ways into this shifting framework is adaptive in that it achieves a "good fit" with the forces of reality, but it is at the same time responsible in that it is a response and not merely a reaction. It is an operation of the ego which is determined and at the same time determining; it is responding to a complex of inner and outer determinants while it asserts in the same act its autonomy and self-direction. The delicate balance is well expressed by Mendel:

> The healthy individual can assert his individuality and responsibility. He can choose his behavior to some extent; he can even choose the problems on which he intends to focus. Free will is limited in each of us by capacity, history, and biology. Yet when we are healthy we have the experience of choosing and we function as though we can choose. As we disorganize and become "ill" our choices become more limited. We are less able to take responsibility for the conduct of our lives and we become more helpless. Finally, the individual who suffers from an illness we call psychosis becomes a helpless victim of his inner world. He has abdicated all responsibility for his thoughts, his conduct, and his stand to reality and to himself [Mendel, 1968, p. 701].

Thus the capacity for free choice and responsible self-determination are primary objectives of the therapeutic process. To call psychotherapy a treatment process is a distortion. It is a collaboration, a cooperative venture, an alliance between patient and therapist. The therapeutic relation *presumes* in even the sickest patients a core of responsible ego which permits the patient to enter into the therapeutic process. Whatever builds that core of responsibility is therapeutic, whatever diminishes and undercuts it is antitherapeutic.

Therapy is a process of coming to grips in stark existential reality and human concreteness with the forces of psychic determinism and personal responsibility. The analytic process is in part a matter of bringing the determinants into focus and exploring how it is that they function as determinants. The patient so often emerges as a captive of the past, as a slave to his own unconscious and the forces of his own inner world. But therapy is more than a process of merely filling in the picture of determination. The determinants have a present reality and force. They are re-created as an imminent force within the transference. But the analytic relation is not restricted to transference. There is also a therapeutic alliance, based in mutual trust and respect between therapist and patient, and elaborated in and through the mechanism of an evolving identification of patient with therapist. The patient introjects the calm, objective, respectful, trusting and trustworthy aspects of the therapist and by this identification begins to build within his own ego the resources for increasing self-esteem, self-trust, and inner autonomy. Internalization and identification are the mechanisms of intrapsychic structuralization, and as inner psychic structure is built through the therapeutic interaction the basis for autonomy and responsibility is laid.

SUMMARY

It seems to me as I look back at the above formulations that they are very much of a single piece. Each part hangs on the others, and each presumes what the others have to offer. If I have left you with the impression that an authentic concept of human freedom is both a theoretical and a practical necessity for the primary enterprise of modern psychiatry, I shall not apologize for that. I have made some effort to bring into focus an argument and a related theoretical formulation which makes such a concept viable and relevant to the concerns of modern psychiatry. That is ambitious, I admit, and may not achieve much by way of success. But it may serve to extend a point of view that is in the process of evolution in contemporary psychiatric thinking. It recognizes the complexity, the dignity, the uniqueness, the inherent meaningfulness and transcendence of human psychology.

REFERENCES

Angel, R. W. The concept of psychic determinism. *American Journal of Psychiatry,* 1959, *116*, 405–408.

Fisher, A. Freud and the image of man. In W. W. Meissner (s.j.) *Foundations for a psychology of grace.* Glen Rock, N.J.: Paulist Press, 1966. Pp. 124–145.

Freud, S. *The psychopathology of everyday life* (1901). *Standard Edition,* Vol. vi. London: Hogarth Press, 1960.

Freud, S. *Introductory lectures on psycho-analysis* (1915). *Standard Edition,* Vol. xv. London: Hogarth Press, 1963.

Freud, S. *The psychogenesis of a case of homosexuality in a woman* (1920). *Standard Edition,* Vol. xviii. London: Hogarth Press, 1955. Pp. 145–172.

Freud, S. *The ego and the id* (1923). *Standard Edition,* Vol. vi. London: Hogarth Press, 1961. Pp. 1–66.

Hartmann, E. The psychophysiology of free will: An example of vertical research. In R. M. Lowenstein, L. M. Newman, M. Schur, & A. J. Solnit (Eds.) *Psychoanalysis—A general psychology.* New York: International Universities Press, 1966. Pp. 521–536.

Hartmann, H. *Ego psychology and the problem of adaptation.* New York: International Universities Press, 1958.

Hartmann, H. Notes on the theory of sublimation (1955). In H. Hartmann (Ed.) *Essays on ego psychology: Selected problems in psychoanalytic theory.* New York: International Universities Press, 1964. Pp. 215–240.

Knight, R. P. Determinism, "freedom," and psychotherapy. *Psychiatry,* 1946, *9*, 251–262.

Lewy, E. Responsibility, free will, and ego psychology. *International Journal of Psychoanalysis,* 1961, *42*, 260–270.

Meissner, W. W. (s.j.) The operational principle and meaning in psychoanalysis. *Psychoanalytic Quarterly,* 1966, *35*, 233–255.

Mendel, W. M. Responsibility in health, illness, and treatment. *Archives of General Psychiatry*, 1968, *18*, 697–705.

Rapaport, D. The theory of ego autonomy. In M. Gill (Ed.) *The collected papers of David Rapaport*. New York: Basic Books, 1967. Pp. 722–744.

Waelder, R. The problem of freedom in psychoanalysis and the problem of reality-testing. *International Journal of Psychoanalysis*, 1936, *17*, 89–108.

Weisman, A. D. *The existential core of psychoanalysis*. Boston: Little, Brown, 1965.

White, R. W. Motivation reconsidered: The concept of competence. *Psychological Review*, 1959, *66*, 297–333.

White, R. W. *Ego and reality in psychoanalytic theory*. New York: International Universities Press, 1963.

Freedom of Conscience in Legal Perspective

WILLIAM C. CUNNINGHAM, s.j.

Father William C. Cunningham, S.J. received his Ph.B. (1951) and his LL.B. (1953) degrees from Marquette University. He earned an M.A. degree from Loyola University, Chicago, in 1960, and an LL.M. degree from Georgetown University in 1961. He served in the Judge Advocate General's Corps of the U.S. Army from 1953 to 1955. Father Cunningham is a member of the Bar of the Supreme Courts of Illinois, Wisconsin, and the United States. At the present time, he is assistant professor of law at the Loyola (Chicago) University School of Law.

WHAT HAS GONE BEFORE

In the first section, conscience was discussed in a theological perspective. And it was clear from that discussion that in its Pastoral Constitution on the Church in the Modern World, the Second Vatican Council gave clear expression to the need for legal tolerance for conscientious objection. The relevant part of the Constitution reads as follows:

> Moreover, it seems right that laws make humane provisions for the case of those who for reasons of conscience refuse to bear arms, provided however, that

they accept some other form of service to the human community [Vatican Council II, 1966, n. 79, p. 292].

That was little enough to say about such an important topic, but it was not without significance. It showed that there was no inflexible or universal position on the part of the Church that favored the waging of war, to the point where a country could coerce its citizens to wage that war, even as against their conscientious objection to participation in combatant service. They did, however, call for, in lieu of that service, some other form of service to the human community. And the difficulties only begin when one tries to assess what that other service might consist in.

Let me push a bit farther on the conscientious-objector problem in our society. If it is clear that the Second Vatican Council's statement on con-scientious objection was rather carefully and narrowly drawn, it is equally clear that the Pastoral Letter of the American Hierarchy, issued November 15, 1968, was as carefully drawn to recommend a modification of the Selec-tive Service Act:

> We therefore recommend a modification of the Selective Service Act making it possible, although not easy, for so-called conscientious objectors to refuse— without fear of imprisonment or loss of citizenship—to serve in wars which they consider unjust or in branches of service (e.g., the strategic nuclear forces) which would subject them to the performance of actions contrary to deeply held moral convictions about indiscriminate killing. Some other form of service to the human community should be required of those so exempted [U.S. Bishops, 1968, p. 27].

What had been left in general terms by the Second Vatican Council was made specific by the American Hierarchy when they recommended that the Military Selective Service Act of 1967, as it amended the Universal Military Training and Service Act, be modified to allow for the legal accommodation of a selective conscientious objection to combatant service. It seems clear, too, from a reading of that statement that the American Hierarchy saw this letter as an extension of the limited scope of the statement on conscientious objection made by the Second Vatican Council. For the Second Vatican Council had spoken about the necessity for humane laws for conscientious objectors, and the American Hierarchy spoke specifically about our own Selective Service Act and the necessity for a legal accommodation of the *selective* conscientious objector.

We have, perhaps, some indication of the pastoral concern that prompted this statement from the American Hierarchy when they said:

> The war in Vietnam typifies the issues which present and future generations will be less willing to leave entirely to the normal political and bureaucratic processes of national decision-making [U.S. Bishops, 1968, pp. 25–26].

And dealing with the question of whether or not it might be cowardice that prompted those attitudes, the bishops said:

> But a blanket charge of this kind would be unfair to those young people who are clearly willing to suffer social ostracism and even prison terms because of their opposition to a particular war. One must conclude that for many of our youthful protesters, the motives spring honestly from a principled opposition to a given war as pointless and immoral [U.S. Bishops, 1968, p. 26].

With this I shall conclude the look backward at the earlier sessions of the Institute, but not before I call attention to one phrase in the last excerpt: ". . . principled opposition to a given war. . . ." For this, I believe, is roughly descriptive of a claim of conscientious objection, be it general or selective.

WHAT IS YET TO COME

This Institute has still to deal with such topics as Conscience and Civil Disobedience, Conscience and the Church, Conscience and the Encyclical *Humanae vitae,* and the Mature Conscience in Multidisciplinary Perspective.

So, it seems to me that to deal with the "Freedom of Conscience in Legal Perspective" I must keep the focus of my paper for discussion narrowed to the problem of providing a legal accommodation for selective conscientious objection. When you become aware from a reading of the U.S. Supreme Court's decisions in the area that freedom of conscience is often used interchangeably with freedom of religion, you realize that there are a host of First Amendment questions that are touched upon. But cases involving free speech, whether symbolic or oral or written, to whatever extent they may either manifest a "principled opposition to a given war as pointless and immoral," or embody an exercise of speech to petition the government for the redress of grievances, or a call to society peaceably to assemble to protest some definite policy of government—I cannot now deal with them. Nor can I deal now with the legal response to the burning of individual draft cards or the collective burning of Selective Service records as a manifestation of principled opposition. I want to deal with this phenomenon of selective conscientious objection which centers on so many of the problems this Institute deals with, and what our society, civil and ecclesial, has to say to those problems.

WAY OF PROCEEDING

Our concern at this Institute is pastoral. It should not be difficult for me, trained as a lawyer, to speak in a legal language all my own. And I might by some legerdemain lead you through the labyrinth of laws concerned with conscientious objection, and leave you exhausted if only somewhat enlightened at the end, but no closer to being able to cope with the pastoral problems that arise in dealing with the legal accommodation of freedom of conscience in the area of selective conscientious objection. At the risk of making law seem intelligible and practical, I want to present you with some specific laws, legal principles, and some of the facts, together with law in a recent case that focuses, I believe, on the problems that sooner or later all of us might face in any work that is pastoral.

I remember Cardinal Wolsey saying to Thomas More at one point in the play *A Man for all Seasons*: "You're a constant regret to me, Thomas. If you could just see facts flat on, without that horrible moral squint; with just a little common sense, you could have been a statesman" (Bolt, 1962, p. 19). Whether or not Wolsey's assessment was astute I leave you to decide, but I would and do insist that More's moral squint, or call it what you will, was a constant way of looking at things and the unwavering articulation of a "principled opposition to any law or act of government or sovereign which he perceived as pointless or immoral." I suppose that that phrase "moral squint" is as good a shorthand as any for "conscience." And I would hope that this legal perspective might somehow sharpen the "moral squint" of all of us who participate in this Institute.

HISTORICAL BACKGROUND OF LEGISLATION ON CONSCIENTIOUS OBJECTION

Act of 1864. There has been a lengthy and consistent governmental recognition in this country of the moral dilemma posed for members of certain religious faiths by the call to bear arms. This recognition came first from the Colonies and later in the states' statutes and constitutions. So there was a tradition in which Congress was acting when in 1864 it provided for an exemption from military service for conscientious objectors who were members of religious denominations "who shall by oath or affirmation declare that they are conscientiously opposed to the bearing of arms, and who are prohibited from doing so by the rules and articles of faith and practice of said religious denomination . . ." (Act of Feb. 24, 1864, Ch. 13, §17, 13 Stat. 9). Those who qualified under the Act were to be drafted as noncombatants, or they could pay a commutation fee of $300. It is clear from this legislation that the particular church had to be clearly on record, both as to its rules and articles of faith (what might be termed its "teaching") and as to its practice, as advocating pacifism. In other words, the particular belief and practice of conscientious objection had to be highly visible within that faith. And this had the effect of establishing various denominations as "peace churches," the Constitutional prohibition notwithstanding.

Draft Act of 1917. In the Draft Act of 1917, Congress again had the occasion to consider who might be exempted from the draft. They declared that exemption would be granted to members of "any well-recognized religious sect or organization . . . whose existing creed or principles forbid its members to participate in war in any form and whose religious convictions are against war . . ." (Act of May 18, 1917, Ch. 15, §4, 40 Stat. 76, at 78). The practical effect of this legislation was that it continued the practice of the 1864 statute which required membership in a "peace church" and personal adherence to its tenets, but it added the additional qualification that the objection had to be to war "in any form." In short it required that a conscientious objector had to be a total pacifist. In other words, he could not object to this or that particular war, but had to be opposed to all warfare, *i.e.,* to war "in any form."

Selective Service and Training Act of 1940. Congress again turned its attention to the qualifications for exemption from military service in 1940. And the exemption was broadened in the Selective Training and Service Act of 1940 to cover anyone "who, by reason of religious training and belief, is conscientiously opposed to war in any form" (Ch. 720, §5 [g], 54 Stat. 889). What Congress had done by this provision was to make it unnecessary to belong to a "peace church" and to be a practicing member of that church. But Congress refused to drop the requirement of an organized religious affiliation by the one claiming the exemption. At least that much affiliation was implicitly required in order to show that one's conscientious objection proceeded from "religious training and belief." And as the cases arose in World War II, the problem of interpreting Congress' intention centered on an understanding of the meaning of that phrase "religious training and belief."

In one of the first cases dealing with that language and its meaning, the Second Circuit Court of Appeals of the United States decided that an atheist whose scruples against participation in World War II stemmed primarily from acute distaste for President Roosevelt did not fall within the orbit of the exempting language (*U.S.* v. *Kauten,* 1943). But, said Judge Augustus Hand, the statute as he read it conferred an exemption on any person whose "conscientious scruples against war in any form [was] a response . . . to an inward mentor, call it conscience or God . . ." (*U.S.* v. *Kauten,* 1943, at 708).

Several years later, the Ninth Circuit had occasion to deal with the meaning of that same language. The objector in this case was Herman Berman, and neither his conscientiousness nor his sincerity was contested. But Berman did not believe in God, nor even in a god. Could his conscientious objection then be said to qualify as being "by reason of religious training and belief"? The court held that it could not, because "philosophy and morals and social policy without the concept of deity cannot be said to be religion . . ." (*Berman* v. *U.S.*, 1946, at 380). Between Judge Hand's remarks in the Second Circuit case and the Ninth Circuit there was an apparent conflict.

Now, you should know that, when there is an apparent conflict between circuits in the interpretations of a congressional law, that is one of the criteria for the United States Supreme Court to grant certiorari in a case. In this way, through the exercise of discretionary review, the court could presumably resolve any conflict in interpretation existing between the circuits. In 1946, however, the Supreme Court denied the petition for a writ of certiorari* in the Berman case, leaving the apparent conflict unresolved. But you should also know that there is a maxim among lawyers that since certiorari is a discretionary review, nothing can be inferred from its denial by the Supreme Court. That is to say, one cannot infer that the court agreed or disagreed with the Ninth Circuit's interpretation.

Draft Law Revision of 1948. Congress again revised the draft law in 1948, amending the language of the statute and declaring that "religious training and belief" was to be defined as "an individual's belief in a relation to a Supreme Being involving deities superior to those arising from any human relation, but [not including] essentially political, sociological, or philosophical views or a merely personal moral code" (50 U.S.C.A. Appendix, §456 [j]). So Congress, at least, was convinced that the Berman decision stated the best interpretation of the phrase "religious training and belief," and continued the definitions contained in the amended Draft Law of 1948. From subsequent decisions by the Second and Ninth Circuits it appeared that the 1948 Act had resolved the conflict between them, and that the courts and Congress were both in agreement that an individual's conscientious objection had to be based upon his belief "in his responsibility to an authority higher and beyond any worldly one" (*Berman* v. *U.S.*, 1946, at 380).

It is interesting to note whence Congress derived that definition of religion. And to trace its derivation one must go back to a case decided by the United States Supreme Court in 1931 (*U.S.* v. *Macintosh*, 1931). Macintosh was born in the Dominion of Canada, and came to the United States in 1916. In 1925 he declared his intention to become a citizen. His petition for naturalization was presented to the federal district court for Connecticut, and that court, after hearing and consideration, denied the application upon

---

* A writ issued by a superior to an inferior court of record, or other tribunal or officer, exercising a judicial function, requiring the certification and return to the former of some proceeding then pending, or the record and proceedings in some case already terminated, in cases where the procedure is not according to the course of the common law.—*Bouvier's Law Dictionary.*

the ground that, since Macintosh would not agree in advance to bear arms in defense of the United States unless he believed the war to be morally justified, he was not attached to the principles of the Constitution. The Circuit Court of Appeals reversed the decree and directed the district court to admit Macintosh to citizenship. From there the case went to the United States Supreme Court for final determination. And the Supreme Court, in a 5–4 vote, reversed the decree of the circuit court of appeals, denying citizenship to Macintosh. They held that Macintosh had no constitutional right to exemption from service as a conscientious objector, but that that right was dependent upon the will of Congress and not upon the scruples of the individual, except as Congress provides.

There was, I think, some questionable theology interwoven with the court's opinion. For the court had reasoned that even though we were a Christian people, according to one another religious freedom, acknowledging the duty of obedience to the will of God, our "government must go forward on the assumption . . . that unqualified allegiance to the Nation and submission and obedience to the laws of the land, as well those made for war as those made for peace, are not inconsistent with the will of God" (*U.S.* v. *Macintosh*, 1931, at 625). That leaves little room for the exercise of the individual conscience. And I think that Chief Justice Charles Evans Hughes' dissent (in which he was joined by Associate Justices Holmes, Brandeis, and Stone) has more tolerance for the individual conscience within the scope of "religious training and belief" when he describes the "essence of religion" as "belief in a relation to God involving duties superior to those arising from any human relation" (*U.S.* v. *Macintosh*, 1931, at 633–634). That is what Congress adopted as a definition of religion. But one must be careful to read the rest of that dissent to see that the Chief Justice spoke of religious liberty in terms of "freedom of conscience," "the supremacy of conscience within its proper field," and the "dictates of conscience" (*U.S.* v. *Macintosh*, 1931, at 634). The only point I want to make here is that if Congress wanted to use Hughes' dissent as stating a definition of religion, it should also have seen the part conscience played in that descriptive definition. At any rate, it is clear that Congress got its definition of religion, in its positive statement of what it is, from Hughes' dissent in *Macintosh*. And the lack of recognition by Congress and the courts for the part in religion played by the individual conscience was, to say the least, questionable theology.

But if Congress was satisfied that religion had been adequately defined for the purpose of determining whether a given conscientious objection was resultant from "religious training and belief," there were still those who had reservations and objections. Such a person was Daniel Seeger, who, unlike Kauten and Berman before him, was not an atheist. But on the form which he filled out to secure an exemption as a conscientious objector, he preferred to leave the question as to his belief in a Supreme Being open, rather than answer a flat "yes" or "no." His belief as he said was a "belief in and devotion to goodness and virtue for their own sakes, and a religious faith in a purely ethical creed" (*U.S.* v. *Seeger*, 1965, at 166). His claim was denied by the trial court because it was not based upon a "belief in a relation to a Supreme Being" as required by §6 (j) of the Universal Military Training and Service Act, 50 U.S.C. App. §456 (j) (1958 ed.). But, although his conviction for refusing to submit to induction was reversed by the Court of Appeals, the Supreme Court of the United States granted certiorari in his and two other companion cases, which raised constitutional questions under the First Amendment's Establishment and Free Exercise clauses and the Due Process clause of the Fifth Amendment. The Supreme Court took these cases because of their importance in the administration of the Act.

It is important to note here that some scholars of constitutional law contend that it is impossible for the Supreme Court to define religion. This is so, they argue, because, to the extent that that definition was more or less comprehensive of the total spectrum of religious beliefs, it would inevitably establish some religions and disestablish others. And to that extent it would, concomitantly, deny the free exercise of religion for some while guaranteeing it for others. If this be so, then for the Supreme Court to define religion would be at once a violation of the constitution. Whether or not this is a valid argument, I cannot say. Suffice it to say, however, that the Supreme Court has never really formally defined religion. (It goes almost without saying that theologians are presented with the same conceptual and practical difficulty.) But in Seeger's case, to get around that difficulty of deciding his and the companion cases on First and Fifth Amendment constitutional grounds, the court decided the cases by construing the statute to determine Congress' intent when they used the words "belief in relation to a Supreme Being." You should know, too, that it is a legitimate and time-honored limitation of judicial power to decide a case on non-constitutional grounds whenever it is possible to do so.

At any rate, the court concluded that:

> Congress, in using the expression "Supreme Being" rather than the designation "God," was merely clarifying the meaning of religious training and belief so as to embrace all religions and to exclude essentially political, sociological, or philosophical views. We believe that under this construction, the test of belief "in a relation to a Supreme Being" is whether a given belief that is sincere and meaningful occupies a place in the life of its possessor parallel to that filled by orthodox belief in God of one who clearly qualifies for the exemption [*U.S.* v. *Seeger*, 1965, at 165–166].

The court had avoided the thorny constitutional questions involved, but they had formulated a test that opened the door for the widest possible spectrum of religious beliefs. The court was careful to point out that none of the three objectors was professedly an atheist. But the test that the court sanctioned by its decision seemed to admit of such extension even to an atheist.

Revision of Draft Law in 1967. Be that as it may, Congress took the cue, and in 1967 it amended section 6 (j) of the Universal Military Training and Service Act to read as follows:

> Nothing contained in this title shall be construed to require any person to be subject to combatant training and service in the armed forces of the United States who, by reason of religious training and belief, is conscientiously opposed to participation in war in any form. As used in this subsection, the term "religious training and belief" does not include essentially political, sociological, or philosophical views, or a merely personal moral code [Public Law 90, 90th Congress, S. 1432, June, 1967].

The net effect of this amendment was that it dropped the requirement of a "belief in relation to a Supreme Being" as a requisite for exemption for conscientious objection, it retained the requirement of total pacifism, and it reiterated the negative norms of the Berman decision excluding essentially political, sociological, or philosophical views, or a merely personal moral code as a basis for conscientious objection. But it could not limit the application of the Seeger case's test for religious belief. And the stage was thus set for a case which might pose the problem of the constitutional validity of a non-formally-religiously-based conscientious objection to a *particular* war.

THE SISSON CASE

In the recent past the United States Supreme Court has avoided deciding the question of the constitutional validity of conscription at a time when war has not been declared. The court did this by denying petitions for writs of certiorari. And so the question remained open presumably until the court would decide to rule on it. But all this was changed by a ruling on April 1, 1969, from the U.S. District Court for the District of Massachusetts by Chief Judge Charles E. Wyzanski in *United States* v. *John Heffron Sisson, Jr.* (*U.S. v. Sisson,* 1969).

The facts briefly are these. On March 21, 1969, in the United States District Court sitting in Boston, a jury returned a verdict that John Heffron Sisson, Jr., was guilty of unlawfully, knowingly, and willfully having refused to comply with the order of local board No. 114 to submit to induction into the Armed Forces of the United States, in violation of the Military Selective Service Act of 1967 (Title 50, Appendix, United States Code, Section 462).

One week later the defendant filed an amended motion in arrest of judgment arguing that no offense is charged in the indictment because it is laid under a statute which, as applied to him, violates the provision of the First

Amendment that "Congress shall make no law respecting an establishment of religion, or prohibiting the free exercise thereof," and the "due process" clause of the Fifth Amendment.

The court in its opinion addressed itself to the issue "whether the government can constitutionally require combat service in Vietnam of a person who is conscientiously opposed to American military activities in Vietnam because he believes them immoral and unjust, that belief resting not upon formal religion but upon the deepest convictions and ethical commitments, apart from formal religion, of which man is capable" (*U.S.* v. *Sisson*, 1969, at 904).

Sisson, it should be noted, never did claim that he is or was in the narrow statutory sense a religious conscientious objector. The first indication that he had conscientious scruples was in a letter of February 29, 1968, in which he notified his local board that "I find myself to be conscientiously opposed to service in the Armed Forces. Would you please send me SSS Form No. 150 so that I might make my claim as a conscientious objector." But on receiving the form he concluded that his objection not being religious, within the administrative and statutory definitions incorporated in that form, he was not entitled to have the benefit of the form. He therefore did not execute it.

The opinion makes clear that, although there was no earlier formal indication of conscientious objection, his attitude as a non-religious conscientious objector had a long history. And at the trial Sisson himself referred to his moral development, his educational training, his extensive reading of reports about and comments on the Vietnam situation, and the degree to which he had familiarized himself with the United Nations' Charter, the charter and judgments of the Nuremberg Tribunal, and other domestic and international matters bearing upon the American involvement in Vietnam. In the end, the judge found that Sisson was courageous, not motivated by purely political considerations, and had borne the burden of proving by objective evidence that he was sincere in his beliefs. And the judge concluded that Sisson's views were not only sincere, but, without necessarily being right, reasonable. To support this conclusion, the judge pointed to the similar views of two reasonable men who are qualified experts, Professors Richard Falk of Princeton University and Howard Zinn of Boston University.

The court then dealt with the two issues presented by Sisson: (1) The broad contention, growing principally out of "the free exercise of" religion phrase, that no statute can require combat service of a conscientious objector whose principles are either religious or akin thereto, and (2) the narrower contention growing principally out of "the establishment" of religion phrase, that the 1967 draft act invalidly discriminates in favor of certain types of religious objectors to the prejudice of Sisson.

The court then held that, Sisson's case being limited to a claim of conscientious objection to service in a foreign campaign, the free-exercise-of-religion clause in the First Amendment and the due-process clause of the Fifth Amendment prohibit the application of the 1967 draft act to Sisson to require him to render combat service in Vietnam. And the chief reason for that, said the court, is apparent "after examining the competing interest in not killing in the Vietnam conflict as against the magnitude in the country's present need for him to be so employed" (*U.S.* v. *Sisson,* 1969, at 910). As to the narrower issue whether the 1967 Act invalidly discriminates against Sisson as a non-religious conscientious objector, the court held that in granting to the religious conscientious objector but not to Sisson a special conscientious-objector status, the Act, as applied to Sisson, violates the provision of the First Amendment that "Congress shall make no law respecting an establishment of religion or prohibiting the free exercise thereof."

But before I pose for you the problems I think are raised by these principles and laws I have given you, and the problems raised by the Sisson case. I want to call your attention to an important observation in Judge Wyzanski's opinion on the importance of conscience and the legal accommodation that must be made for it. You will remember that in the Seeger case the objection was not the result of "formal religious training and belief." And yet the court found that his belief was akin to religious belief and occupied a place in his life parallel to a belief in God for the orthodox religionist. Now Judge Wyzanski pushes that reasoning to its relation to the individual conscience:

> Duty once commonly appeared as the "stern daughter of the voice of God." Today to many she appears as the stern daughter of the voice of conscience. It is not the ancestry but the authenticity of the sense of duty which creates constitutional legitimacy [*U.S.* v. *Sisson,* 1969, at 909].

It seems that by this reasoning the freedom of religion guarantees are extended to guarantee a comparable freedom of conscience. And the Supreme Court is now squarely faced with the problem of deciding whether the meaning of "religion" can be stretched that far.

PASTORAL CONSIDERATIONS

I would now like to suggest that all these cases with their principles and their laws are relevant to the response that can be made to the Pastoral Letter of November 15, 1968, of the American Hierarchy. For the bishops were clear in their urging us to work for a change of our law to provide some sort of accommodation for selective conscientious objection. But with our law in its present posture this presents some of the difficulties that I have explained to you.

One of the problems, I think, is legal. And it could be stated in the form of a question: If the Supreme Court reverses the U.S. District Court in Massachusetts, and if it rejects the reasoning of the lower court opinion, how will we be able to protect the sincere, non-religious, selective conscientious objector? This question, in turn, presents another related question, in part theological, in part legal, which could be stated thus: How will we be able to define religion in order to protect it? Must the definition be in terms of conscience? It seems, curiously enough, that Judge Wyzanski has been in the vanguard of that attempt in his opinion in the Sisson case.

Finally, we must ask ourselves as members of this Institute how we shall respond to the American Hierarchy's recommendation to modify the law so as to provide some sort of legal accommodation for sincere, selective conscientious objectors. I cannot say what your response will or should be. But I suggest that some response must be made in order adequately to protect religion. Your pastoral response to the problem of selective conscientious objection may well redound to the benefit not only of religion but of law as well. For your attention to the problems of conscience is directed, I am sure, at strengthening the moral fabric of our society. And on this Judge Wyzanski was eloquent:

> The law grows from the deposits of morality. Law and morality are, in turn, debtors and creditors of each other. The law cannot be adequately enforced by the courts alone, or by the courts supported merely by the police and the military. The true secret of legal might lies in the habits of conscientious men disciplining themselves to obey the law they respect without the necessity of judicial and administrative orders. When the law treats a reasonable, conscientious act as a crime it subverts its own power. It invites civil disobedience. It impairs the very habits which nourish and preserve the law [*U.S.* v. *Sisson,* 1969, at 910–911].

Whatever effort you make, then, to strengthen the moral fabric of our society by your attention to the problems of conscience with which you deal in your work is an effort directed at the strengthening and preservation of law in its best sense. And if we are confronted with questions at the end of our reflection, that should not be cause for concern. For the answers to these questions may change, but the questions, if they are well-conceived, remain constant, and might lead us to continuing new answers. And these problems that we face together are, I believe, worthy of our most serious and studied consideration.

REFERENCES

Berman v. *U.S.*, 156 F. 2d. 377 (9th Cir.), *cert. denied,* 329 U.S. 795 (1946).

Bolt, R. *A man for all seasons.* New York: Random House, 1962.

Brodie, A., & Southerland, H. P. Conscience, the Constitution, and the Supreme Court: The riddle of *United States* v. *Seeger. Wisconsin Law Review,* 1966, *2,* 306–330.

Dodge, J. M., II. The free exercise of religion: A sociological approach. *Michigan Law Review,* 1969, *67,* 679–728.

Macgill, H. Selective conscientious objection: Divine will and legislative grace. *Virginia Law Review,* 1968, *54,* 1335–1394.

Rabin, R. L. Do you believe in a Supreme Being?—The administration of the conscientious objector exemption. *Wisconsin Law Review,* 1967, *3,* 642–684.

U.S. Bishops. Collective pastoral: Human life in our day. *Catholic Mind,* 1968, *66* (December, no. 1228), 1–28.

U.S. v. *Kauten,* 133 F. 2d. 703 (2nd Cir.) (1943).

U.S. v. *Macintosh,* 283 U.S. 605 (1931).

U.S. v. *Seeger,* 380 U.S. 163 (1965).

U.S. v. *Sisson,* 297 F. Supp. 902 (1969).

Vatican Council II. Pastoral Constitution on the Church in the modern world. In W. M. Abbott (s.j.) (Ed.) *The documents of Vatican II.* New York: Herder & Herder, 1966. Pp. 199–308.

IV
CONSCIENCE AND THE
CIVIL ORDER

Conscience and Civil Authority

JOHN H. HALLOWELL

*John H. Hallowell, who is professor of political
science and chairman of the department at Duke
University, received his A.B. degree from Harvard
in 1935, his M.A. from Duke in 1937, and his
Ph.D. from Princeton in 1939. He is a member of
the American Political Science Association, and of
the Society for Political and Legal Philosophy, as
well as a past president of the Southern Political
Science Association. Dr. Hallowell was a Guggen-
heim Fellow and at the same time a Fulbright
professor at the University of Munich, 1955–1956.
In 1963 he was the recipient of the honorary degree
of Litt.D. from the College of the Holy Cross,
Worcester, Massachusetts. He is the author of the
following books:* Decline of liberalism as an ideology *(1943),* Main currents in modern political
thought *(1950), and* The moral foundation of
democracy *(1954).*

Historically considered, there have been two kinds of democracy: one emerging from English political thought and experience and the other emerging
from the Jacobins at the time of the French Revolution. For brevity's sake
we may refer to the one form as Anglo-Saxon democracy and to the other
form as Jacobin democracy. Throughout American history there has been
some competition between these two conceptions of democracy, but, for the

most part and until recently, we have been committed to the Anglo-Saxon form.

TOTALITARIAN DEMOCRACY

The Jacobin or totalitarian form of democracy not only affirms its belief in the sovereignty of the people but tends to invest the majority of the people with absolute and unlimited power. Rousseau, the philosopher who justifies this form of democracy, speaks of the "general will" of the people as being always right and tending to the public advantage. The people can do no wrong, nor can they mistake their own best interest. The general will, moreover, is indivisible, inalienable, and infallible. The test of true law is not its conformity to reason or to the demands of justice, but its emanation from the will of the people. It can no longer, in fact, be asked if a law is just, for justice is what the people decree. Such a conception of democracy can tolerate no intermediate associations between the individual and the state or any limits to what the state may do. In fact, the whole of human existence becomes the proper domain of politics. The obsessive conviction that the "people" can and should rule—that the general will must prevail—leads easily to the rise of a dictator who claims to know and embody the general will better than any elective assembly. Such a conception of democracy leads to the peculiarly twentieth-century phenomenon of a dictatorship based upon mass support and enthusiasm. Mussolini, Hitler, Peron, Stalin, Castro, and Nkrumah represent but the end product of this kind of democratic thought. Talmon (1955) has provided an excellent historical account of this form of democracy:

> The Totalitarian democratic school . . . is based upon the assumption of a sole and exclusive truth in politics. It may be called political Messianism in the sense that it postulates a preordained, harmonious and perfect scheme of things, to which men are irresistibly driven, and at which they are bound to arrive. It recognizes ultimately only one plane of existence, the political. It widens the scope of politics to embrace the whole of human existence. It treats all human thought and action as having social significance, and therefore as falling within the orbit of political action. Its political ideas are not a set of pragmatic precepts or a body of devices applicable to a special branch of human endeavor. They are an integral part of an all-embracing and coherent philosophy. Politics is defined as the art of applying this philosophy to the organization of society, and the final purpose is only achieved when this philosophy reigns supreme over all fields of life [Talmon, 1955, p. 2].

TRADITIONAL AMERICAN DEMOCRACY

By contrast, Anglo-Saxon democracy has never invested the rule of the majority with any unusual sanctity or authority. While it has assigned the majority a legitimate and necessary role to play in politics, it has never equated the will of the majority with what is true or good. The framers of the American Constitution understood what Edmund Randolph called "the turbulence and follies of democracy," and all of them rejected setting up a government that somehow would involve direct rule of all the people. They rejected the Jacobin principle that the rule of the people is the voice of God. While the framers recognized the principle that government should rest upon the consent of the governed, they thought of majority rule as a check upon government—not as a substitute for government. They established accordingly a representative government by means of which the voice of the people would be filtered through many layers of mediating institutions. It is significant that no law can be adopted under our form of government by a direct vote of all those eligible to vote, nor is any officer of government elected by such a vote. There is no one majority that can act, but many majorities for different purposes. Power is divided and diffused. Through the system of checks and balances, legislative, judicial, and executive powers are entrusted to separate personnel, and through the federal system political power is widely diffused on a geographical basis.

The framers of our government did not think that politics should extend over all aspects of life or that politics could cure evils that spring from defects in human nature. They believed that they had provided a reasonably good framework of government within which men could work to find, in the words of Reinhold Niebuhr, "proximate solutions to insoluble problems." While they thought that politics could help to create the conditions for a good life, they did not think that this good life could, in the main, be achieved by political means.

MODERN POLITICAL THINKERS

It is in this sense that the framers differ so radically from many modern political thinkers. For many today, politics has become a kind of religion promising men nothing short of redemption from evil and suffering. Government can deal with the effects of evil, it can seek to restrain and punish those who would perpetuate injustice, it can seek to create a better environment for the unleashing of creative capacities for good; but it is not an institution that dispenses grace. It cannot heal spiritual sickness nor correct the human condition. Government must deal with men as it finds them, not as it would like them to be. And those who govern are, indeed, nothing but imperfect, fallible, and sometimes vicious men themselves. The Puritans once dreamed of establishing a kingdom upon earth that would be governed by the holy and regenerate. Though convinced that they had a proper title to holiness, they created a repressive dictatorship which proved that they were not, indeed, the saints they proclaimed themselves to be but petty, fallible, imper-

fect men. The revolutionary militants today who scorn words like holiness
and saintliness put themselves forward as men of perfect righteousness and
omniscience. History, if not introspection into our own lives, should make us
skeptical of such claims whether put forward by old-fashioned Puritans or
the Puritans of the New Left.

Eric Voegelin, drawing upon the original account of Richard Hooker,
describes the mentality of the Puritan in vivid terms:

> In the Preface of his *Ecclesiastical Polity* Hooker gave an astute type study
> of the Puritan, as well as of the psychological mechanism by which Gnostic
> mass movements operate. . . . In order to start a movement moving, there
> must in the first place be somebody who has a "cause." From the context in
> Hooker it appears that the term "cause" was of recent usage in politics and
> that probably the Puritans had invented this formidable weapon of the Gnostic
> revolutionaries. In order to advance his "cause," the man who has it will "in
> the hearing of the multitude," indulge in severe criticisms of social evils and in
> particular of the conduct of the upper classes. Frequent repetition of the per-
> formance will induce the opinion among his hearers that the speakers must be
> men of singular integrity, zeal, and holiness, for only men who are singularly
> good can be so deeply offended by evil. The next step will be the concentration
> of popular ill-will on the established government. This task can be psycholog-
> ically performed by attributing all fault and corruption, as it exists in the world
> because of human frailty, to the action or inaction of the government. By such
> imputation of evil to a specific institution the speakers prove their wisdom to
> the multitude of men who by themselves would never have thought of such a
> connection; and at the same time they show the point that must be attacked if
> evil shall be removed from this world. After such preparation, the time will be
> ripe for recommending a new form of government as the "sovereign remedy of
> all evils." For people who are "possessed with dislike and discontent at things
> present" are crazed enough to "imagine that any thing (the virtue whereof they
> here recommended) would help them; but the most, which they least have tried."
>
> If a movement, like the Puritan, relies on the authority of a literary source,
> the leaders will then have to fashion "the very notions and conceits of men's
> minds in such a sort" that the followers will automatically associate scriptural
> passages and terms with their doctrine, however ill-founded the association may
> be, and that with equal automatism they will be blind to the content of Scripture
> that is incompatible with their doctrine. Next comes the decisive step in con-
> solidating a Gnostic attitude, that is, "the persuading of men credulous and
> overcapable to such pleasing errors, that it is the special illumination of the
> Holy Ghost, whereby they discern those things in the word, which others reading
> yet discern them not." They will experience themselves as the elect; and this
> experience breeds "high terms of separation between such and the rest of the
> world"; so that, as a consequence, mankind will be divided into the "brethren"
> and the "worldings."
>
> Once a social environment of this type is organized, it will be difficult, if not
> impossible, to break it up by persuasion. "Let any man of contrary opinion

open his mouth to persuade them, they close up their ears, his reasons they weight not, all is answered with rehearsal of the words of John: 'We are of God; he that knoweth God heareth us': as for the rest ye are of the world: for this world's pomp and vanity it is that ye speak, and the world, whose ye are, heareth you." They are impermeable to argument and have their answers well drilled. Suggest to them that they are unable to judge in such matters, and they will answer, "God hath chosen the simple." Show them convincingly that they are talking nonsense, and you will hear "Christ's own apostle was accounted mad." Try the meekest warning of discipline, and they will be profuse on "the cruelty of bloodthirsty men" and cast themselves in the role of "innocency persecuted for the truth." In brief: the attitude is psychologically iron-clad and beyond shaking by argument [Voegelin, 1962, pp. 135–137].

Not all persons who invoke the name of conscience in protest against the action or inaction of government are of course gnostic revolutionaries in Voegelin's sense, but many are, and the prevalence in our contemporary society of the gnostic mentality is indicative of a deep crisis that threatens the continuation of that form of government we have called Anglo-Saxon democracy.

THE NATURAL-LAW TRADITION

Unlike the Jacobin form of democracy, Anglo-Saxon democracy is premised upon the natural-law tradition. It assumes that while the people are free to choose the form of government under which they want to live they are not free to choose the fact of government itself. Some form of government, some form of civil authority, is a human necessity. It arises out of the social nature of man, because man is not self-sufficient and requires the fellowship and services of other men. Government is necessary to adjudicate rival claims and interests, to decide how the material and spiritual resources of the community are to be shared, to restrain individuals from harming other individuals, to defend the community from external attack, to promote the common good. It is not only life that men desire but the good life; and government comes into being to help men to live that good life by removing obstacles to its enjoyment and by providing, as much as is within its power and capacity, the best possible environment for the growth of human potentiality. Since men have not only potentialities for leading the good life but inclinations to evil as well, the state has the function not only of helping to provide the social, economic, and educational conditions conducive to the proper development of human potentiality but also of restraining the evil propensities of men. The state has both positive and negative functions. These functions are inherent in the nature of government itself. While the *ends* of government are derived from the nature of man, the *form* of government is a matter of choice. In a democratic system, such as ours, as Simon observes,

> . . . deliberation is about means and presupposes that the problem of ends has been settled. In the order of action, propositions relative to ends have the character of principles; they are anterior to deliberation and presupposed by it. The freedom of expression which is required by the democratic process of persuasion concerns all subjects that have the character of means and are matters of deliberation. Under fully normal circumstances the propositions relative to the very ends of social life are above deliberation in democracy as well as in any other system. Circumstances which make it necessary to deliver the principles of society, its very soul, to the hazard of controversy are a fateful threat to any regime, democratic or not. . . . Preserving principles may be more difficult in a democracy than in nondemocratic societies. In democracy more than in any other regime it is a problem to assert principles in such a way as not to jeopardize the free discussion of means, and to insure free discussion of means without jeopardizing the principles without which social life no longer has end or form [Simon, 1951, pp. 123–124].

This does not mean that some forms of government—tyranny, for example—are not intrinsically bad, but it does mean that there are a variety of legitimate forms of government.

From the natural-law perspective, politics is not a form of social engineering but of moral endeavor. Good government is not a matter of providing the correct blueprint of a perfect society and of constructing, on the basis of that blueprint, a new society; rather, it is a matter of working with what are often recalcitrant individuals to secure that degree of order and of cooperation of which they are capable. Individuals are not like so many bricks or pieces of steel that have only to be laid in the right place according to a blueprint. They can cooperate or rebel. To enlist their cooperation is one of the principal tasks of politics. The statesman is not concerned with making anything, but rather with inspiring right action; his ability to enlist the cooperation of others in taking right action is the test of his ability as a statesman. As a consequence it is not theoretical knowledge that the statesman requires but practical wisdom or prudence.

The Western political tradition which has inspired Anglo-Saxon democracy is based upon the conviction that there are principles of natural justice to which all governments should conform if they are to be legitimate. The classic statement of that conviction is found in these words of Cicero:

> True law is right reason in agreement with nature; it is of universal application, unchanging and everlasting; it summons to duty by its commands, and averts from wrongdoing by its prohibitions. And it does not lay its commands or prohibitions upon good men in vain, though neither have any effect on the wicked. It is a sin to try to alter this law, nor is it allowable to attempt to

repeal any part of it, and it is impossible to abolish it entirely. We cannot be freed from its obligations by senate or people, and we need not look outside ourselves for an expounder or interpreter of it. And there will not be different laws at Rome and at Athens, or different laws now and in the future, but one eternal and unchangeable law will be valid for all nations and all times, and there will be one master and ruler, that is, God, over us all, for he is the author of this law, its promulgator, and its enforcing judge [Cicero, *Republic,* Bk. III, Ch. XXII, No. 33*].

THE CONTRIBUTIONS OF CHRISTIANITY

Constitutional government arises not only from the conviction that there are principles of natural justice binding upon ruler and citizen alike but also from the conviction introduced into the West by Christianity that man has a dual loyalty and a dual citizenship. The Christian is a citizen not only of the state in which he lives, but potentially at least a citizen of the kingdom of God. The allegiance which a Christian can give to any government is necessarily limited, and the jurisdiction which the state may claim over his life is likewise limited. This notion that man has dual citizenship and a dual loyalty was bound to create tension and even conflict, but it lies at the foundation of what we call constitutional government. It is the loss of this tension that creates a situation that makes the coming of totalitarian government almost inevitable. The principle has been violated on both sides—by some Christians who sought to unite church and state in a theocracy, and by some secularists who insist upon the absolute sovereignty and omnicompetence of the state. It is the recognition of a dual loyalty that gives freedom substantive meaning. An excellent discussion of the implications of the Gelasian doctrine and its application to contemporary political problems has been provided by Murray (1960).

Those who have been anxious to assert the absolute sovereignty of the state have always been critical of the Christian religion as a divisive force in society. Thus J. J. Rousseau complains:

> Jesus came to establish on earth a spiritual kingdom. By separating the theological system from the political system, he brought it about that the state ceased to be one, and caused internal divisions which have never ceased to agitate Christian peoples. From this twofold power there has resulted a perpetual conflict of jurisdiction, which has rendered all good politics impossible in Christian states. No one has ever been able to know which one to obey, priest or political ruler [Murray, 1960, p. 207].

And Thomas Hobbes registered his complaint by saying: "Temporal and

* Loeb Classical Library, Cicero, *De republica et de legibus* (trans. by C. W. Keyes), p. 211.

spiritual government are but words brought into the world to make men see double and mistake their sovereign which is Leviathan, the Mortal God" (Murray, 1960, p. 207). The modern totalitarian state claims, in effect, to be both church and state; it acknowledges no limitations to its competence, it claims to be the source of what is true and good and promises men nothing less than salvation. By contrast, the Western political tradition has insisted that while the state comes into being to promote the good of men, it is not competent to define that good. Though helpful to men in providing the conditions conducive to a good life in society, the state is not an instrument of spiritual salvation, nor can it bring into being the kingdom of God.

THE ROLE OF A PUBLIC PHILOSOPHY

Anglo-Saxon democracy which is premised upon the insights of the Western political tradition presupposes the existence of a public philosophy, a common universe of discourse. This public philosophy stems from three basic principles. The first is that "The world is made up of contingent substantial entities existing in an order of real relations, which is independent of human opinion and desire" (Wild, 1951, p. 26). The world in which we live is an orderly universe—a cosmos, not a chaos. A second conviction is that man is endowed with a faculty of reason which enables him, at least in part, to grasp the meaning of this reality. Knowledge does not involve the making or constructing of anything, but rather the discovery of what already exists.

A third principle is that being and goodness belong together. Through knowledge of what we are, we obtain knowledge of what we ought to do. Reality is not something we can manipulate to conform to our desires; it imposes obligations upon our will and limitations upon our desires. On the basis of these underlying principles or convictions, a public philosophy emerged which provided a context within which public discussion could fruitfully take place about matters of political policy. This public philosophy was not the same thing as majority opinion, but rather the reason of many generations of men reflecting upon historical experience (Murray, 1960, p. 105).

It is within this context of the public philosophy that civil authority operates. Civil authority, which is the rightful use of power to promote the common good, is necessitated, as said earlier, by the social nature of man. All authoritative commands have the potentiality of rational elaboration. This elaboration appeals to the principles embodied in the public philosophy. It is one of the functions of individual conscience in a democracy of the Anglo-Saxon form to prod civil authorities to elaborate the reasons for their commands and to justify their actions or inaction. The opportunity to express dissent from governmental policies is an essential aspect of such a democracy, but this dissent can never be dissent from the basic principles upon which the public philosophy is established. The purpose of dissent is not to alter basic convictions about the purposes of government but to call attention to policies which may be in need of change. The function of dissent is not to undermine the public consensus but to identify it, to make it more conscious and articulate. The dissent proper to this form of government is rational persuasion and the organization of political activity designed to effect change in policy through persuasion.

THE PRESENT TURMOIL

The turmoil in which we find ourselves today is in large part a result of the disintegration of the public philosophy. The political turmoil is not so much cause as symptom of the lack of any common universe of discourse. The intellectuals who in past centuries have been the custodians of the public philosophy have themselves revolted against the traditions of the West. They have proclaimed that reality is not something to which ultimately all of us must conform but rather something which we can change to accord more with our desires. They have insisted that there are no universal moral principles and that the scientific method is the only method for discovering truth. Questions that cannot be answered by that method are not genuine questions or meaningful ones. As a consequence, the public philosophy has given way to intellectual nihilism.

In such a climate there can be no fruitful public discussion. Dissent can no longer help to identify the public consensus, for there is none there to be found. Dissent, accordingly, frequently takes the form of private revelation founded upon individual desire seeking to replace other private revelations and other desires. Such conflicts cannot be resolved by reason but only by violence. Persuasion is replaced by hysterical, emotional appeals; arguments are replaced by non-negotiable demands; deliberation guided by reason reflecting upon experience is replaced by "thinking" with one's race, class, blood, or color. The essential unity of the human race and its attribute of rationality is denied.

Intellectual nihilism and political anarchy are the forerunners of totalitarian dictatorship. The fact that it has not happened here as yet is no assurance that it will not. Freedom was traditionally conceived as the opportunity and capacity to choose rationally between alternative courses of action on the basis of the choiceworthiness of the alternatives. It was conceived as a means to an end more ultimate than freedom itself. It presupposed the existence of universal moral principles accessible to human reason. Today freedom is conceived more and more as the opportunity to fulfill all one's desires. Driven by egocentricity to demand unlimited freedom to fulfill all desires, however, modern man frequently discovers that what he proclaimed as freedom is in reality slavery. He has actually placed himself under the arbitrary and unpredictable dictatorship of self. His freedom turns out to be a pseudo-freedom producing anxiety, fear, guilt, meaninglessness, and despair. What was once conceived to be man's greatest opportunity is felt to be an intolerable burden. In an effort to escape that burden, to escape from freedom, modern men have been tempted to give up their freedom to a dictatorship which will assume the function of defining truth and goodness for them.

Although sometimes described as authoritarian regimes, the modern totalitarian dictatorships are embodiments not of authority but of naked power. They are an effort to fill the void left by the repudiation of reason and of God by a will that is unguided by reason, unrestrained by considerations of justice, and unmindful of the commandments of God. They are not governments in the true sense of the word, but perverted attempts to employ the techniques of government when government fails. The total character of the dictatorship is necessitated by the *lack* of any common authority. Compulsion replaces consent in every sphere of life, because there is no longer any common agreement obliging consent in any sphere. Freedom of conscience is expressly denied, since no authority exists to which an appeal can be taken. Since all truth is political and the monopoly of the party apparatus or state, dissent becomes synonymous with treason. No longer are there two realms demanding man's loyalty, but one only—the political.

The freedom that was conceived as the freedom to alter reality in accordance with one's personal desires culminates in slavery. Walter Lippmann describes it in this way:

> The Jacobins and their successors made a political religion founded upon the reversal of civility. Instead of ruling the elemental impulses, they stimulated and armed them. Instead of treating the pretension to being a god as the mortal sin original, they proclaimed it to be the glory and destiny of man. Lenin, Hitler, and Stalin, the hard totalitarian Jacobins of the twentieth century, carried this movement and the logical implications of the gospel further and further toward the bitter end.
>
> And what is that bitter end? It is an everlasting war with the human condition: war with the finitude of man and with the moral ends of finite men, and, therefore, war against freedom, against justice, against the laws and against the order of the good society . . . [Lippmann, 1955, p. 71].

REFERENCES

Lippmann, W. *Essays in the public philosophy.* New York: New American Library, 1955.

Murray, J. C. (s.j.) *We hold three truths: Catholic reflections on the American proposition.* New York: Sheed & Ward, 1960.

Simon, Y. R. *Philosophy of democratic government.* Chicago: University of Chicago Press, 1951.

Talmon, J. L. *The origins of totalitarian democracy.* London: Secker & Warburg, 1955.

Voegelin, E. *The new science of politics.* Chicago: University of Chicago Press, 1962.

Wild, J. The present relevance of Catholic theology. In E. D. Myers (Ed.) *Christianity and reason.* New York: Oxford University Press, 1951. Pp. 18–35.

The Conscience of the Political Leader

WILLIAM V. O'BRIEN

William V. O'Brien has had thirty years of association with Georgetown University. He received his bachelor's and master's degrees in foreign service in 1946 and 1948 respectively, and his Ph.D. in government in 1953, all from Georgetown. Currently he is professor of government and chairman of the Institute of World Polity at Georgetown. Dr. O'Brien spent the year 1951 on a Fulbright Fellowship in the Faculty of Law, at the Sorbonne, Paris, and in 1963 he was at the Max Planck Institute in Heidelberg as a visiting research professor. He is a frequent contributor to periodical literature and is the editor of a significant series of volumes on world polity. In addition, he is the author of several books written in collaboration with others, and on his own of the following two books: Nuclear war, deterrence and morality *(1966), and* War and/or survival *(1969).*

I see three basic approaches that might be taken in dealing with the subject to which I am to address myself:

1. a comprehensive, systematic treatment of the guidelines and rules of the game which, according to the normative foundations on which it is grounded, *ought* to govern politics—e.g., the social teaching of the Catholic Church,

most recently refined in *Pacem in terris* (John XXIII, 1963) and in the Pastoral Constitution on the Church in the Modern World (Vatican Council II, 1966, pp. 199–308);

2. one or more case studies from which rules of the game, pragmatically but conscientiously arrived at, may be induced and "lessons learned"—e.g., John F. Kennedy's (1956) *Profiles in Courage*;

3. a survey of the functions, goals, and resources of the politician in terms of which he judges and is judged as a morally responsible decision-maker.

I choose to take the third approach, partly because of a preference for it on its merits, and partly because this manner of addressing the subject seems more appropriate to the magnitude and scope of the present Institute. Accordingly, I will attempt to outline briefly what Kenneth Thompson has termed "the nature and dynamics of the political process, its requirements, limits and laws" (Thompson, 1960, p. 70). My hope is to provide perspectives and insights, not answers or tidy sets of rules.

MORALITY AND POLITICS

The organizers of this Institute were well advised to select The Conscience of the Political *Leader*. It is difficult to overstate the need to "pierce the corporate veil" in discussions of political morality. Much debate over the morality of contemporary domestic and international politics has tended to proceed in formulations which are unrealistic and unhelpful. We have today another revival of the perennial Idealist–Realist debate over the nature of politics and its Clausewitzian extension by other means—war. "Dove–Hawk" confrontations have deepened the intensity of these debates. Beyond this, "pro- and anti-Establishment (or, System)" confrontations have spawned sweeping moral perspectives and judgments.

All these debates and confrontations have, in my judgment, tended to be conducted in excessively institutional, corporative, or societal terms. Proponents of the conflicting positions mentioned all share a tendency to ascribe a high degree of corporate or societal unity and, accordingly, of corporate or societal responsibility, guilt, prerogatives, or license to contemporary political entities. This is true with respect to political systems at the domestic, national, and international levels. All too often political criticism and defense is couched in terms of "The Community," "The White (or, Black) Community," "The Nation," "The Nation*s*," The "West," "East," "North," "South," "Rich," or "Poor" nations, and that unfortunate final destination of all insoluble problems, "the United Nations." These objects of political controversy have too often been treated in ways that encourage a vague belief in their comparatively independent existence and in moral judgments about them that tend readily to be divorced from the human beings who reside in them and who lead them.

Catholic social teaching, as well as much of liberal Protestant, Jewish, and humanistic thought, has quite frequently been marked by prescriptions, admonitions, and judgments directed to *bodies* rather than to the *politicians* who influence or control the dynamics of these bodies. Modern realist political thinkers, for their part, have appeared to ascribe responsibilities—indeed, destinies—to corporate entities, particularly powerful states. This has had its effect, notwithstanding the realists' concern with the individual decision-maker.

To be sure, both the idealist and realist prescriptions concerning political morality are also addressed to responsible individuals. Thus, for example, Catholic social thought, which falls decidedly in the idealist category (O'Brien, 1969, pp. 6–16), has reached down to individuals: in management and labor, government, soldiers and pacifists, scholars, and to responsible individual Christians. This is notably the case in the Pastoral Constitution on the Church in the Modern World (Vatican Council II, 1966, n. 79, pp. 291–293), where the Council fathers speak directly to conscientious objectors, government officials, experts on war and peace, and members of military establishments. The political realists lay great emphasis on the responsibilities and prerogatives of the "responsible decision-maker." But neither broad approach—political idealism or realism (or, in the even more imprecise terms of contemporary controversy, Doves and Hawks, the New Left, and the Establishment)—has penetrated sufficiently into the subject: The Conscience of the Political Leader. To the extent that this appears to be the case, I believe that the principal explanation lies in the picture that the idealist and realist (and their contemporary offshoots) have of the politician.

For the idealist, the politician is viewed as a *"statesman"* or as the "civil authority" (in the personal rather than in the corporate sense). He is a man with power as well as authority. This power is to be used in consonance with enlightened moral guidelines based on reason, love, and humanity. The task of the moralist is to explain to the statesman, or civil authority, the preferred or morally permissible goals and means relevant to his jurisdiction. Moreover, the moralist should seek to do more than guide. He should seek to elicit behavior responsive to his prescriptions. Further, the idealist viewpoint sees the problem of compliance with moral prescriptions as extending to the challenge of education and inspiration of the leader's constituency. This challenge is not left to the political leader alone, but is extended to educational, intellectual, and, importantly, religious institutions and leaders.

There is generally a note of concern over the past and projected responsiveness of the political figures in power to moral prescriptions. It is seldom the case that such prescriptions are accompanied by speculation over such basic questions as these: "How did the political leader gain power?"; "How much power does he have?"; "How well established is this power?"; "To what uses can this power be put?" Nor do moralists, or normatively informed political analysts, often find the occasion or need to dwell on the predicament of the "enlightened" political leader who is following the "right" path but lacks the support, or even the sympathy, of his colleagues and constituents. Suppose, as is the case more often than not, that the generality of the citizenry are not informed, educated, and sensitized to the political, economic, social—and moral—issues to any degree comparable to the political leader. What does the statesman do then? In short, what about the *politics* of morally informed political leadership in a morally deficient body politic?

The realist tends to assume that this problem has been adequately identified and dealt with in his pragmatic political-moral prescriptions, his emphasis on the importance of "power politics," his concern with the "dilemmas" of the "morally perceptive decision-makers," rather than in broad rules and politically unrealistic codes of political conduct. But, as has been repeatedly observed in the perennial Idealist–Realist debates, if the idealist viewpoint tends to be deficient in its appreciation of the political dimensions of political morality, the realists are in constant danger of absorbing morality into politics to the point that there is little or no tension between the two (Ramsey, 1968). This, in itself, is not fatal. Political morality, however permissive and marginal, is useful and meaningful only when it finds expression in the political process. What is dangerous is the equation of good politics—indeed, moral politics—with the political determinations made by selected politicians who have been dubbed with the characterization "responsible" or "morally perceptive" by realist admirers (Thompson, 1960, pp. 22–61).

Thus, there are complementary vulnerabilities to the two basic approaches to political morality. The idealist seems to take continued and effective political power for granted (indeed, to treat it with suspicion) and to see the political-moral problem almost exclusively in terms of channeling and regulating existing political power. The realist is always in danger of equating effective political power with "morally responsible" political power. Indeed, one is tempted to believe that the logical conclusion of the realist line of analysis lies in a pattern of normatively prescribed behavior derived by inductive reasoning from the actual record of behavior of selected "responsible decision-makers" who have, by some normative process of selection, been designated as the political-moral models of behavior.

Actually, the politician is not necessarily either an "authority" with sufficient durable power to effect moral policies within his jurisdiction or a power-manipulator whose political successes somehow gained for him a presumption for acceptance as a "morally responsible decision-maker." Let us, then, examine more closely the conscience of the politician in terms of two fundamental aspects of his office:

1. as a representative of a corporate entity (generally the sovereign state in this discussion) and as an individual with his own personal conscience;
2. as an official who must balance his own judgments about right and wrong —prudent or imprudent—in the life of the body politic against the constraints of the political system in which he operates.

I will limit this discussion to politics in the United States. Moreover, since the problems of conscience facing the judiciary are discussed in Justice Murtagh's paper,* I will only be concerned with the executive and legislative branches of the national government. Although the perspectives will be those of leading legislators and presidents, the political and moral issues raised are faced in varying degrees by politicians on all levels of public service.

THE POLITICIAN'S CHANGING HIERARCHY OF FUNCTIONS AND GOALS

In any analysis of the conscience of the politician it is important to distinguish—but then identify the interrelationships between—his official functions, the goals related to those functions, and the constraints, of power politics as well as of morality, which affect the politician's performance.

The President is endowed with executive powers that are generally listed under the headings chief executive, commander-in-chief, representative of the nation in foreign affairs, legislative leader and partner with the Congress in the process of enacting laws. He is, moreover, in a unique way, representative of "all the people" as well as the head of his political party. The Congress has legislative powers from which emerge deliberative and investigative powers. These expand from a focus on possible legislation and checks on the executive to a virtually limitless prerogative to discuss and probe into almost anything that can be said to concern the public interest. These powers must be exercised with a view to representation of constituents' views as well as to efficiency in their exercise.

These multiple functions obviously create shifting emphases as concerns responsibilities, priorities, goals, and moral issues, according to the subject matter and, importantly, the individual office-holder's concerns, concepts of roles, and the political and moral influences at work in concrete situations.

For both legislators and presidents, certain goals, goods, or values are pre-eminently important. They are:

1. representation of the will of the people;
2. pursuit of the political good;
3. education and leadership to the end that the people will increasingly recognize, support, and accept new and improved concrete formulations of the political good;
4. maintenance of political power necessary to the accomplishment of the first three goals, within the bounds of law and morality.

* See page 190.

Usually it is in the realm of the third function—education and leadership—that the conscience of the politician is tested. I take it that we are not concerned with routine acts of representation and the exercise of government. Nor need we linger over the basic fact of political life that all politicians must stand firm on certain issues that are viewed as essential by the voters who elect them, more or less regardless of the merits. Thus, in the United States, outstanding political leaders have managed to achieve greatness and general moral responsibility while still living with the inhibitions that their constituents place upon them with respect to such parochial issues as farm subsidies, oil depletion allowances, the preferences of labor or management, justice for the underprivileged elements of certain areas or elements of society, and the perennial problem of rewarding loyalty with appointments to public office, with locations of public facilities and the awarding of contracts, and other political plums. It has always been possible for a good politician to meet these responsibilities without excessively impairing his overall usefulness. Thus, a Southerner who is acceptable to voters on racial issues often enjoys considerable freedom with respect to foreign and defense policy—and even domestic reform problems outside predominantly racial concerns. A Midwesterner can be extremely "liberal" on almost anything if he is "sound" on agricultural policy or the industrial interests of his area.

This does not mean that there are no problems of conscience involved in "going along" with the electorate on issues that may well involve moral dimensions, as both race and farm- or business-support questions do. But it is not too much to say as a broad generalization that the moral issues raised on such issues concern the question whether the individual goes into politics at all. A promising politician may decide that it is disproportionately compromising to "go along" with the electorate. A possible politician may not be able to stomach this necessity in the first place. But, as emphasized at the outset, we are concerned with the conscience of the politician. In order to be a politician, the individual has to be elected to and maintained in office. No matter how enlightened the constituency, it has prevailing values and interests. If the politician has doubts about them he would do well to keep them to himself. A good recent example of this requirement is to be found in the tribulations of Mr. Nixon's Secretary of the Interior, Walter J. Hickel, at the time when his appointment was being considered by the Senate. Mr. Hickel may have been right, and had a right to believe privately, that the United States Government should not follow a policy of "conservation for the sake of conservation." But he could not long appear to act in accordance with such an attitude, much less to articulate it, and still expect to be a useful (or even incumbent) Secretary of the Interior in an age when concern over conservation of the nation's natural resources and beauty is high and the Secretary of the Interior is expected to be their first defender.

In like manner, it is well known that, in elections in such states as Mississippi, Alabama, and Georgia, the standard tactic of the real racists is to challenge the degree and honesty of the racial attitudes of moderate candidates. No matter what mental and moral reservations the moderate may have, he must somehow pass these loyalty tests. The price may be to affirm or acquiesce in attitudes and policies which he cannot condone in his own conscience. The price of remaining faithful to conscience may be twofold: loss of opportunity to ameliorate somewhat the racial policies of the constituency, and to make significant contributions with respect to problems not closely related to race. Further, the price of a clear conscience may well be either no moderate candidate or a defeated moderate candidate and the election of a vehement and effective racist who exacerbates bad situations and prolongs the life of wrong, misguided points of view. This problem-area can only be identified here, for its prudential complexities are a study in themselves. Suffice it to say that the perennial answer "Countenance some wrong so that more good may be done" cannot be brushed aside lightly. Of course it is a potential cover for hypocrisy and apathy, but it is also a challenge to good men in bad situations. Unless some good men pick up such challenges, the moral levels of politics decline.

Leaving, then, this difficult area of a priori compromise by the politician, consider the official, whether in the executive or legislative branch, who is relatively uninhibited by morally questionable commitments or understandings. Consider the President or member of Congress who is relatively free to balance his obligations of representation, pursuit of the political good as he sees it, and responsible performance as a leader of men and molder of enlightened opinion. This, I submit, is the most important point of examination for an analysis of the conscience of the politician. I say this particularly in view of the fact that there is a widespread tendency to assume that representation is the greatest responsibility of the politician, whereas political scientists in the United States increasingly stress the need for the politician to mark off and assume his part of the burden of furthering the political good and educating his constituents, rather than merely acting as the voice of the people. Exceptions to the latter viewpoint tend to be found among scholars, politicians, and voters who oppose change in the status quo and independent initiatives in government.

The reason is that it is now fairly well established that comparatively few voters retain a constant interest in and informed opinion on issues other than "bread and butter" parochial issues. Moreover, attitudes toward major issues are often of debatable value to the knowledgeable and morally concerned politician. Walter Lippmann has said:

> The unhappy truth is that the prevailing public opinion has been destructively wrong at the critical junctures. The people have imposed a veto upon the judgments of informed and responsible officials. They have compelled the governments, which usually knew what would have been wiser, or was necessary, or

was more expedient, to be too late with too little, or too long with too much, too pacifist in peace and too bellicose in war, too neutralist or appeasing in negotiation or too intransigent. Mass opinion has acquired mounting power in this country. It has shown itself to be a dangerous master of decisions when the stakes are life and death [Lippmann, 1955, pp. 23–24].

Moreover, it appears that a substantial portion of the members of the electorate are well aware of their limitations, not inclined to make the effort to improve their bases for judgment on great issues, and disposed to demand that both legislators and executives "take care of" them. There seems to be strong inclination to feel that politicians are "paid" to dispose of the complicated, endless, and often arcane matters which occupy "those people in Washington." In one of the best studies of American democracy in action, Bailey and Samuel recounted the experience of William Ayres (Republican–Ohio), then a new member of the House of Representatives. Congressman Ayres issued the following news release and advertisement to his constituents:

I have done my best to find out what the people in the 14th District want done regarding wage and price controls. I held a mass meeting to discuss the matter and have asked people to send me their opinions. To date there has been very little interest shown. Although I personally do not believe that price controls will bring on lower prices or stop inflation, I am certainly open to suggestions. . . .

Your opinions will be appreciated because as your duly elected representative it is my responsibility to vote your wishes and not my opinions [Bailey & Samuel, 1952, p. 115].

Instead of praise for his concern for the representative function and helpful indications of the will of the people, Ayres' appeal elicited the following reaction in the *Oberlin News-Tribune* which, in the experienced view of Bailey and Samuel, expressed a classic view of the responsibilities of the legislator. The newspaper's front-page editorial stated:

The idea expressed in your news release is that Congressmen should be not better than applause meters or poll takers. . . . As I see it, the people of a large nation can remain free only if they have the right to choose, and are reasonably successful in choosing, political representatives who are free to act according to their informed convictions and judgments, and who have the intestinal fortitude to act that way. . . . Any representative so fearful of losing his seat that he votes against his own best convictions in order to please what he thinks is majority opinion, deserves to be unseated. . . . Why should a Congressman be expected to hear hours of expert testimony and debate, and I assume, study and ponder and pray and wrestle with himself and finally come to his own conclusion as to what is best for his country . . . and then desert his own convictions in the face of an avalanche of letters from home expressing a contrary view? [Bailey & Samuel, 1952, pp. 115–116].

In addition to his great responsibilities as a participant in the legislative process and other Congressional functions, the leading Senator or Congressman also partakes importantly of the *symbolic* mission of the two houses. Participation in such a mission in itself engenders major moral responsibilities. Odegard and Baerwald write:

> Congress is at the same time a symbol of Government at the Grass Roots, and of Government at the Summit of the American Power Structure. It is also more than a symbol. For in it one can find living ties with virtually every phase and facet of the American nation [Odegard & Baerwald, 1964, p. 331].

Accordingly, each member of the Congress must strive to make this symbol a positive and inspiring one. When a Congress fails to do so, the disenchantment of the people and, in all likelihood, the decline of efficacious and enlightened government, will follow. Note that this facet of legislative responsibility carries with it a built-in propensity for conflict between the lofty symbolic role of the Congress, collectively and individually, and the grubby, sometimes downright dishonest exigencies of "politicking" without which even the best politician cannot stay in office.

At the highest and most crucial point in this business of symbolic representation and leadership is the President. Douglass Carter, an attentive observer of power and morals in American politics, is right in asserting that

> The paradox is that the growth of the President's role as the central agent of government is by no means the same thing as leadership. His role has grown largely because no one else—neither Congress nor the courts nor the bureaucracy—can supply the services he is called on to provide. The White House is the only place where the competing claims on government can be brought into some sort of adjustment [Carter, 1964, p. 74].

Given our concern with the conscience of the politician, in this case the American politician, it is fitting to ponder Carter's words (with which most American political scientists and politicians would agree). The President has the voter's mandate and the inherited symbolic power to represent the nation. As he calculates the political and moral implications of his policies he, in his official and private person, pierces the corporate veil of *raison d'état*. He commits his nation, his administration, and himself, as a human being. As Carter says, "the President's role as the central agent of the government is by no means the same thing as leadership." An *agent* acts for his principal and an agent binds normatively both his principal and himself.

ETHICAL ENDS AND POLITICAL MEANS: THE MORAL CALCULUS OF POLITICS

A review of the functions and goals of Presidents and Congressional leaders has shown the practical and symbolic responsibilities of each, as well as the

locus of leadership in the President. To meet these responsibilities, to mar-
shal these powers, the President must show leadership, and the men who
make the Congress move, and their constituents, must respond to that leadership. Woodrow Wilson was neither the last nor the first President to discover
painfully, and at considerable cost to the world, the impracticality of leadership directed to "the people" of the United States and of the world, but not
adequately to the other branches of the U.S. Government and the governments of foreign nations. Since it is widely acknowledged that the President
has the initiative in proposing and eliciting support for his programs, I will
put these general remarks on the ethical context of political decision-making
in terms of the President's perspective. This is more manageable than an
attempt embracing legislative decision-making. But it should be remembered
that the same ethical issues ought to be consciously considered by legislators.

To the modern mind, accustomed to highly complex formulations of
political-moral issues, and to normatively loaded "inputs" from contemporary social science and culture, the following ethical ends of the politician
at a high level of any national government—and especially of a great power
such as the United States—may seem simplistic. But, as in the case of currently "in" formulations which look more complex and may or may not be
more profound, the outcome depends upon definitions and applications as
worked out in practice.

The traditional formulation of these ends in Catholic thought remains
useful. The national executive must look to:

1. the national common good: a prudential calculation constrained by
adequate concern for all less-than-national corporate goods, as well as for
the good of each individual and family;

2. the international common good: the good of all nations, of all men of
the world, of which the national common good can never be more than a
part (Rommen, 1945, pp. 306–358). In the words of Suarez:

> The reason for the Law of Nations, under . . . [the concept of an inter-
> national society] is that the human race, though divided into no matter how
> many different peoples and nations, has for all that a certain unity, a unity
> not merely physical but also in a sense political and moral. This is shown by
> the natural precept of mutual love and mercy, which extends to all men, in-
> cluding foreigners of every way of thinking. Wherefore, though any one state,
> republic or kingdom be in itself a perfect community and constant in its mem-
> bers, nevertheless each of the states is also a member, in a certain manner, of
> the world, so far as the human race is concerned. For none of these communi-
> ties are ever sufficient unto themselves to such a degree that they do not require
> some mutual help, society or communication, either to their greater advantage
> or from moral necessity and need, as is evident from custom . . . [Suarez,
> *De legibus ac de Deo legislatore*, Lib. II, Cap. XIX, Par. 9; Eppstein, 1935, p.
> 265].

If the language and concepts of the Scholastics fail to elicit the interest of our contemporaries, substantially the same thoughts are to be found in some passages by Theodore Sorenson on The Powers of the President, in *Kennedy*:

> One of John Kennedy's most important contributions to the human spirit was his concept of the office of the Presidency. His philosophy of government was keyed to power, not as a matter of personal ambition but of *national obligation*: the primacy of the White House within the Executive Branch and of the Executive Branch within the Federal Government with the United States *and of the United States within the community of nations.*
>
> And yet he almost never spoke of "power." Power was not a goal he sought for its own sake. It was there, in the White House, to be used [emphasis added; Sorensen, 1965, p. 389].

In these passages from Sorenson's appraisal of Kennedy's understanding of political and ethical ends and means we find the concepts of both the legitimate national good and the ultimate international common good. We also find the element that is generally slighted in Catholic political ethics—less so in the late Scholastics than in contemporary papal and conciliar documents—namely, an appreciation of the role of power in pursuing the national and international common good (O'Brien, 1969, pp. 17–68).

Having remarked on this similarity between traditional theoretical and contemporary applied versions of the hierarchy of political goods, it is only fair to add that the same Kennedy who acknowledged this hierarchy and its ultimate guiding force was also an accomplished pragmatist who struck while the iron was hot and fought for the tactical openings without which strategic breakthroughs towards higher goods would not occur or would come too late. Moreover, it is fitting to recall that Suarez himself was a diplomat and arbiter as well as a priest, doctor, and scholar. Suarez' balancing of general and particular, immediate, mediate, and ultimate goals, must have been difficult for one possessed of an extraordinarily scrupulous conscience as well as a very high sense of duty.

In short, as is usually the case with moral prescriptions for political behavior, the rule is very general: "Seek the legitimate national good in the light of the international good." But even this general rule guides the politician in both negative and positive ways. Negatively, it prohibits pursuit of the national good, as concerns both ends and means, to the detriment of the international common good. Positively, it emphasizes that political morality is not limited to the negative act of avoiding policies harmful to the international common good, but rather requires conscious, positive efforts to advance that international good.

For example, let us give President Kennedy the benefit of doubts on a number of critical and controversial issues of his administration. Let us suppose that when he inaugurated the Alliance for Progress and the Peace Corps, when he pressed for the Kennedy Round of tariff negotiations, when he persevered in the difficult task of supporting United Nations peace-keeping in the Congo, he was at one and the same time pursuing the national good of the United States and the international common good. The point may seem obvious to some, but it is not even granted by many today in this era of discontent and self-criticism in the United States. The most enlightened measures are increasingly scrutinized for evidence of selfish—indeed, base —motives. Moreover, there seems to be something about the phenomenon of political power which inclines Americans, and many foreign critics, to assume that to raise questions of morality or conscience means identification of prohibitions, crimes, sins, and the assignment of guilt to politicians and, indeed, to nations.

To be sure, there are crimes and sins of which politicians and the polities they represent may be guilty. But the conscience of the politician should be at least as concerned with the responsibilities of power as with the moral limits on ends and means under which he ought to labor. For a powerful nation, abnegation of power may more properly be criticized than the frequently charged "arrogance of power." In judging the morality of the exercise of power by a politician such as an American President, we have little to guide us beyond the concepts developed with respect to that most extreme form of political power, recourse to armed force. Both with respect to occasions of use and choice of means, the exercise of political power has to be judged very much as the theory of the just war has been developed to judge war. In both instances the key concept is that of proportionality, of ends to both the national and international goods, and of means, in terms of both an ethic of means and an ethical analysis whereby the proportionality or appropriateness of particular means to particular ends is made. Like such general concepts as justice or due process of law, proportionality is something that must be judged on a case-by-case basis, unless moral doctrines and precedents have developed to the point at which a policy is rather evidently impermissible. There are few such clear-cut guidelines in political ethics, as a consideration of recent official documents emanating from popes and bishops will reveal. Thus, the Pastoral Constitution on the Church in the Modern World is actually very restrained insofar as it lays down specific prescriptions on modern war and deterrence, which it greatly decries (Vatican Council II, 1966, nn. 79–81, pp. 291–295), and places great emphasis on positive measures to avoid and curb war (Vatican Council II, 1966, nn. 82–83, pp. 295–298; nn. 91–93, pp. 305–308).

The point, then, is that the politician, especially the politician with great power, must search his conscience, not only to find whether he has done things—as a public figure and as an individual—which were wrong, but to determine whether he has done *enough* for the various goods he must serve.

Relativism, compromise, and hypocrisy are always at work in politics, and, as we have said, the man who wants to be a politician and to do the good things of which an effective politician is capable must learn to live with the dangers of his trade. In so doing he would benefit from the lesson on political ethics laid down by Bernard Shaw in commenting on the attitude of a labor candidate in Britain, one Joseph Burgess, whose refusal to compromise on principle cost him a seat in Parliament and the opportunity to help constituents who desperately needed help from and representation in Parliament. Shaw observed:

> When I think of my own unfortunate character, smirched with compromise, rotted with opportunism, mildewed by expediency . . . dragged through the mud of Borough Councils and Battersea elections, stretched out of shape with wire-pulling, putrefied by permeation, worn out by 25 years pushing to gain an inch here, or straining to stem a backrush, I do think Joe might have put up with just a speck or two on those white robes of his for the sake of the millions of poor devils who cannot afford any character at all because they have no friend in Parliament. Oh, these moral dandies! these spiritual toffs! these superior persons! Who is Joe anyhow that he should not risk his soul occasionally like the rest of us? [Pearson, 1942, p. 156].

REFERENCES

Bailey, S. K., & Samuel, H. D. *Congress at work*. New York: Holt, Rinehart & Winston, 1952.

Carter, D. *Power in Washington*. New York: Random House, 1964.

Eppstein, J. *The Catholic tradition of the law of nations*. Washington: Carnegie Endowment for International Peace and Catholic Association for International Peace, 1935.

John XXIII. *Pacem in terris*. Encyclical letter of April 11, 1963. *Acta Apostolicae Sedis*, 1963, *55*, 257–304. English translation: Peace on earth. *Catholic Mind*, 1963, *61* (September, No. 1175), 47–62, and 1963, *61* (October, No. 1176), 45–63.

Kennedy, J. F. *Profiles in courage*. New York: Harper & Row, 1956.

Lippmann, W. *Essays in the public philosophy*. New York: New American Library, 1955.

O'Brien, W. V. *War and/or survival*. New York: Doubleday, 1969.

Odegard, P. H., & Baerwald, H. H. *The American republic*. New York: Harper & Row, 1964.

Pearson, H. *G. B. S.* New York: Harper & Row, 1942.

Ramsey, P. *The just war: Force and political responsibility*. New York: Scribners, 1968.

Rommen, H. H. *The State in Catholic thought*. St. Louis: Herder, 1945.

Sorensen, T. C. *Kennedy*. New York: Harper & Row, 1965.

Thompson, K. W. *Political realism and the crisis of world politics*. Princeton, N.J.: Princeton University Press, 1960.

Vatican Council II, W. M. Abbott, (S.J.) (Ed.) *The documents of Vatican II*. New York: Herder & Herder, 1966.

The Conscience of the Civil Servant

HOWARD B. WHITE

Shortly after receiving his A.B. degree from Hamilton College in 1934, Howard B. White came to the New School for Social Research in New York City with which he has been associated ever since. He received his master's degree in 1938 and his doctorate in 1943, both in social science and both from the New School. He has held a succession of positions at the New School, including that of dean of the graduate faculty, and he is currently professor of political science. Dr. White has been a frequent contributor to such journals as Social Research *and the* American Political Science Review, *and is the author of* Peace among the willows: Study of the political philosophy of Francis Bacon, *published in 1968.*

In 1647 John Cotton, the antagonist of Roger Williams, wrote as follows:

> Oh the woeful perverseness and blindness of a conscience, when it is left of God, to be so far transported with prejudice, as to judge a cause of conscience and a cause against conscience to be all one [Cotton, 1963, p. 31].

It is fair to say today that Cotton's perverseness and blindness is widespread perverseness and blindness. I am glad to say that such is not the case here. Though my own frame of reference is classical, the Platonic tripartite soul is not so far from St. Thomas' συντήρησις as both are from the autonomous and subjective conscience so widespread in our time. Yet even here the conscience of some of the students and the conflicting conscience of the administration may show the difficulty of objectivity. Perhaps the best way to approach the problem of the conscience of the civil servant is to reflect on the rather terrifying fact that, had the bureaucracy indulged in nonsense for the cause of conscience, as did so many university students, we might not even be here.

So harrowing is that possibility, so well qualified to cause our fearful reflections, to touch upon our horror, that it seems a waste of time to talk of other matters: whether Senator Thomas Dodd's staff members were disloyal to Dodd or loyal to the Constitution; whether the formula of former Senator Paul Douglas to return every gift which appeared to be worth more than ten dollars might strengthen the backbone of the bureaucracy; whether the school-board president, who filled his station wagon with baskets of whiskey on Christmas morning and returned them to the over-generous architect who had presented them the evening before to board members and officials, had, by this courageous and imaginative action, found a formula for others—these questions pale into insignificance when faced with the simple formulation: if nonsense for the cause of conscience in the civil service had equalled or even approached that of the universities, who knows what would have happened even to this program?

For that reason, as well as others, it seems to make sense to talk about the conscience of the civil servant in terms of the soul-rending decisions which loyalty demands rather than questions of immunity to avarice and greed, important as those questions are.

THE MULTIPLE LOYALTIES OF THE CIVIL SERVANT

Perhaps we can help to understand the problem if we see that each civil servant has three or more loyalties: the loyalty to the civil service, the loyalty to country, and the loyalty to the regime. Under normal conditions, the three tend to fuse, but normal conditions are becoming abnormal today. In the Oppenheimer hearings, Thomas E. Murray, tracing the origins of the word "loyal" to the Latin *legalis,* suggested that loyalty to the regime was indicated because the regime was a rule of law (Curtis, 1955, pp. 267–272). Unfortunately this etymological hocus-pocus is not a formula. Part of the difficulty is that there is no formula.

Let me give a few illustrations of the tension in the conscience of a civil servant because of the three loyalties. About two months before the German invasion of Russia in 1941, the first secretary of the American embassy in Berlin invited his Russian colleague to cocktails, that he might meet a German air force officer, who was to tell him that his squadron was being transferred to the east (Salisbury, 1969). The German officer wanted to avoid war between Germany and the Soviet Union. The American first secretary wanted, presumably, to strengthen the Russian defenses. The German officer acted on the authority of his conscience or his judgment, but he was not a civil servant. How far his private or autonomous conscience dictated the action of the American first secretary I do not know.

Revolutionary governments are, to a certain extent, governments of upstarts. Thucydides knew that the higher bureaucracy is usually composed of quite different people. Both in Germany and in Russia, it is quite possible that the upper civil service regarded Hitler and Stalin respectively as men with insufficient historical insight successfully to conduct foreign policy. It is not easy to say whether public servants, whether civil or military, were right in playing their private games according to their autonomous consciences. Even we, with the judgment of hindsight, may find it hard to weigh the suffering in Leningrad against the relief in London, and find the balance.

"The civil servant," wrote Kurt Riezler, "serves no regime; he serves the 'order' in any regime—everyone in his tiny place. This amounts in practice to serving the regime in power—yet within certain limits" (Riezler, 1943, p. 332).

Where the civil service had a tradition of perfect integrity and full efficiency, as in Germany before Hitler, and as in Great Britain before World War II, the civil service developed a conscience of its own. A revolutionary regime could forestall opposition by the civil service by leaving it to do its own work, and appealing, explicitly or implicitly, to the conscience of the civil servant. The civil service under the Nazis might discover that a Jewish professor had been underpaid, or that a Jewish business man had made an overpayment of his taxes (Riezler, 1943). The civil servant who made the discovery might make a reimbursement or a credit, and the fact that the Jew was regarded as the enemy of the regime would not have stopped him. How long the civil service retains its own conscience, implemented by reason, is an open question. The bureaucracy may be destroyed or replaced. Yet it is not inconceivable that any bureaucracy would sooner or later develop its own non-partisan conscience.

I once heard Harold Laski speak in New York. When asked whether the British civil service would be loyal to a government under Sir Stafford Cripps, he answered that if Sir Stafford Cripps came with a bill of particulars, yes. If he merely said he wanted to bring in socialism, no. It seems clear that the conscience of the civil service will permit a change in the regime, provided that there is mutual respect for the prudence of the regime and that of the bureaucracy. The urgent problem that confronts us is not the relation of the civil servant to a change in regimes, but to a retention. No one can write a formula for the transformation of conscience from civil obedience to civil disobedience. All that one can say is that such a transformation must not be undertaken "for light and transient causes." The maturity, the integrity, and the traditional loyalty of the civil service will go far to insure the parallelism between the civil servant's conscience and what the political man interprets as the needs of his country. Yet there are factors which make this parallel less likely than it once was, and we have to turn to some of those factors.

SINCERITY AND THE CIVIL SERVANT

Among those factors, probably the most important is the development of sincerity as the highest good, elevated above thought, conscience, or commandment. The pathos of sincerity and the irreducibility of sincerity to any other measurement of conduct are usually associated with Jean Jacques Rousseau. However, the problem arises with modern political philosophy. It arose when the soul developed into the self, to the extent that the self became the mark of personal identity, and the soul became abandoned. The substitution of the self for the soul may originate in Machiavelli, Bacon, or Descartes, or perhaps even Rembrandt. It reaches clear and emphatic treatment in Locke.

> . . . consciousness always accompanies thinking, and it is that which makes everyone to be what he calls self, and thereby distinguishes himself from all other thinking things . . . [Locke, 1894, I, p. 449].

It is true, however, that Rousseau modified the problem of the self-conscious, because he took it out of the city and made it the way of life of the solitary. In so doing, he glorified throughout his confessional works his own passionate sincerity and the passionate sincerity he bequeathed to others (Rousseau, 1962). The civil servant is not a *promeneur solitaire,* and, in many cases, he will not have heard of Rousseau. But he may be under the influence of teaching which holds sincerity higher than thought or discipline (Strauss, 1968, pp. 260–272). In fact, where subversive activities have actually existed and have been established, they are usually less traceable to corruption than to the pathos of sincerity.

Needless to say the sincere adherence to the subjective conscience is not the traditional hallmark of the civil service. A top German civil servant left Germany when the Nazis came to power. Returning to Germany as an American official during the occupation, he refused to speak German at meetings with German officials, for he felt that that would be incorrect for an American official. His integrity was unquestioned. The conscience of a civil servant was the conscience of a patriot, and even the inconvenience of speaking English to German-speaking officials had to be accepted. I mentioned Commissioner Murray's identification of loyal and *legalis.* The application Murray used was, I believe, far-fetched. But it is fair to say that the traditional conscience of the civil servant holds strictly to the law. Not perhaps the only alternative, but the only alternative to nonsense for the sake of conscience widely available in our time is constitutional democracy.

The only way which, as far as I know, can insure that the conscience of the civil servant be also the conscience of the law, and adhere fully to the νόμοι of constitutional government, is education. Again, there is no formula, but there are intellectual disciplines, and there is the growth of reason. The study of ethology, the study of history, in particular, may encourage the future civil servant to the same rigid regard for the law that once characterized the bureaucracies of Great Britain and Prussia. If, on the other hand, the student is taught, as he sometimes is taught, that "the time is out of joint," which may be true, but also that he must play Hamlet's role and set it right, our hope must rest only on the possibility that such badly educated students may not enter the civil service. Thousands, tens of thousands of Hamlets, setting the time to rights, could certainly wreck the bureaucracy.

There is another problem which must face the civil service of the future. It will have enormous power. It will have enormous power, first, because modern government has enormous power, because it has enormous wealth. Yet that is not all. We, a nation which distrusts experts, are beginning—just beginning—to face what may well be the greatest rule of experts in history. It is a tradition of writers on British government that it is more difficult for cabinets to cut the budgets for the armed forces than any others which may come from the respective departments. Each of us knows that he is not an expert on missiles. Every parent, on the other hand, claims to be an expert on schools. The complexity of the problems of tomorrow, the vast changes in technology, the need for long-range planning, the fact that lay control is increasingly difficult mean that perhaps today and almost certainly tomorrow the conscience of the civil servant will be challenged, and something more than the loyalty to the law, the absolute integrity which has marked the civil service at its best, will be required.

Recently the State of Michigan outlawed DDT. So did the town of Huntington on Long Island. No layman can seriously weigh the toxic effects of DDT against the depredations of the borer. The knowledge of the conservationist and that of the nurseryman will have to be combined, and, in this case, they tend to be on different sides. Joined to both these kinds of knowledge must be the botanically educated conscience of the civil servant, and he must be allowed a great deal of freedom to conduct long-range planning. Control, of course, must be had, but there are mechanisms of control (Kirchheimer,

1969). The difficulty is that the politician does not know how to use them. However, I do not think that long-range planning is the primary problem for the foreseeable future. With the exception of great statesmen, politicians tend to think in terms of short-range problems and short-range solutions. In other words, they split up their political decisions. Yalta was a short-range conference, as was Versailles.

Civil servants must be permitted to think of long-range problems, not only in foreign policy, but also in the ever-increasing ecological problems of our time. Many of these are problems for our grandchildren. Great independence must be permitted for thought. When a civil servant may take, and even must take, independent action is a question which no institution can determine. Such occasions must be rare, but no one can say, I believe, that they never exist.

As Plato well knew, the only really lasting institution of a regime is its education. Increasing power, increasing pressure demand that the civil service be educated not only for expertise, but also for conscience. It is not my task to talk about the universities, but a few remarks are necessary for us to understand the dark problems of the future. I have said some harsh things about nonsense for the cause of conscience, and I do not retract them. But there is in student protests a plea, not always clearly understood, for relevance that should be heeded. Even humanistic education should not be disembodied. The British civil service of the nineteenth century, for example, was educated in the classics, but their teachers, not necessarily good philologists, were good historians, and they forced the civil service into relevance.

One must be blunt and admit that our chances are not good. The problems are too complex; the dangers are too imminent; the alternatives are too grave. "And reason kens he herits in a haunted house." It will take the education of conscience, the education of expertise, the education of reason. And it will take the efforts of all of us. I have no formula. I can only plead that those who attack the anonymous and amorphous establishment eschew the puerile violence, and turn to the real world where they can make the establishment relevant, can help us to assure, for our children's children, that future we care so much about.

REFERENCES

Cotton, J. A reply to Mr. Williams. In R. Williams. *Complete writings* (7 vols.) New York: Russell & Russell, 1963. Vol. 2, pp. 9–237.

Curtis, C. P. *The Oppenheimer case.* New York: Simon & Schuster, 1955.

Kirchheimer, O. Expertise and politics in the administration. In F. S. Burin & K. L. Shell (Eds.) *Politics, law and social change: Otto Kirchheimer's selected essays.* New York: Columbia University Press, 1969. Pp. 372–382.

Locke, J. *Essay concerning human understanding* (2 vols.). Oxford: Clarendon Press, 1894.

Riezler, K. On the psychology of modern revolution. *Social Research,* 1943, *10,* 320–336.

Rousseau, J. J. Les rêveries du promeneur solitaire. In *Oeuvres complètes.* Bruges: Pléiade, 1962. Vol. 1, pp. 995–1099.

Salisbury, H. E. *The 900 days: The siege of Leningrad.* New York: Harper & Row, 1969.

Strauss, L. *Liberalism ancient and modern.* New York: Basic Books, 1968.

The Conscience of the Jurist

JOHN M. MURTAGH

John M. Murtagh received his A.B. degree from the College of the City of New York in 1931, and his LL.B. from the Harvard Law School in 1934. He was awarded an honorary LL.D. degree by LeMoyne College, Syracuse, in 1956. From 1938 to 1941 he was assistant attorney general of the State of New York, and from 1946 to 1950 he was commissioner of investigations for the City of New York. Justice Murtagh has filled a distinguished series of court appointments which include: Chief Magistrate, City of New York, 1950–1960; Chief Justice, Court of Special Sessions, City of New York, 1960–1962; Administrative Judge, Criminal Court, City of New York, 1962–1966; and finally Justice of the Supreme Court of the State of New York, 1967 to the present. It was in the latter capacity that Justice Murtagh came to national attention as the judge in the pre-trial hearing of the thirteen Black Panthers charged with conspiring to murder policemen and bomb buildings in New York City.

In April, 1969, a judicial proceeding was conducted in Philadelphia relating to the 1963 obscenity conviction of the publisher Ralph Ginzburg (*New York Times*, 1969a, p. 44). It was a hearing ordered by the United

States Court of Appeals for the Third Circuit to determine whether Ginzburg's five-year sentence should be reduced or suspended. The hearing took place before Federal Judge E. Mac Trautman. It followed a 5–4 decision of the Supreme Court affirming Ginzburg's conviction.

A New York Judge, Irving Younger, testified at the hearing as a character witness for the defendant. While not having been counsel for Ginzburg in the criminal proceeding, Judge Younger was well acquainted with Ginzburg, having represented him in other capacities before his recent ascension to the bench.

After praising Ginzburg's "exemplary" moral character, Judge Younger said:

> "I am proud to be a lawyer. But in this case, and this case only, I feel that if the defendant goes to prison then I would, for the first time in my career, be ashamed of the legal profession."
>
> "Why this and no other?" Judge Trautman asked.
>
> "Because," Judge Younger said, "I believe that there are four conceivable justifications for imprisoning a fellow human being: rehabilitation, the protection of the public, vengeance, and deterrence. By any rational process I cannot see that any of these purposes would be served by jailing Ralph Ginzburg."

The Judge replied by pointing out that five Supreme Court Justices and three Circuit Court Judges had affirmed the conviction.

Judge Younger then observed that "inevitably" judges were forced to "play God" but that the Ginzburg sentence could in no way be justified.

This prompted Judge Trautman to state:

> "There has been delegated to us a rather burdensome and distasteful task made necessary because there are those who violate the law. If this is playing God, then God must be unhappy a lot of the time."
>
> "I suspect He is, your honor," Judge Younger replied.

THE JUDGE'S DILEMMAS

Perhaps you may wonder why Judge Trautman refers to the judicial role as "a rather burdensome and distasteful task." The task of the judge appears to be pleasant, and not too strenuous. The public sees relatively short hours on the bench, respect for the robe, deference for the jurist's opinions, awe of his power over people's lives. Why then is it burdensome and distasteful? Would you not feel harassed if your mind and heart always carried at least two sides of several cases? How could you be sure that the side you call right is truly right? Can any person trust himself so fully as to be always positive of his judgments? Who knows so much about the complicated ills that beset the people who came into a courtroom that he can deprive them of their liberty and rest secure in his judgments?

The judge's inner life can never be quite tranquil. His peace of mind is shattered by a vision of justice from which the reality always falls short. The conscientious judge is an incredibly harassed and busy man. The Judge who is a Catholic does not bear his responsibility any the more lightly when he reflects on the nature and origin of his authority. We, as Catholics, trace the right to rule back to God as its natural and necessary source. Because God ordains men to live in civil society, He also commands them to obey duly constituted authority. Whether or not we refer to the judicial role as "playing God," it is God alone who can commit to a man power over his fellow man. And, it is to God and His norm of justice, to Christ and His norm of charity, that the judge is ultimately responsible.

What does the judge know, when we come right down to it, about the special ills and inner conflicts that make people into murderers, rapists, muggers, burglars, thieves, confidence men, drug addicts, pickpockets, or shoplifters? What does anybody know? But other people are not called upon to make daily judgments about these people. The judge is! He must plunge headlong into this whirlpool of tragedy and farce and try to probe for real understanding.

Why are the young men and women who come into our courts criminals? Who failed them?—the home?; the school?; society-at-large? The judge needs to know the whys and wherefores of those young people and of their strife-torn mothers and fathers. It is not easy to get the answers to these questions.

THE HARDENED CRIMINAL

Obviously, there are criminals beyond our help. In the spring of 1969, in Manhattan, two defendants were tried and convicted before me, after trial by jury, of robbery in the first degree, grand larceny in the first degree, assault in the second degree, sodomy in the first degree, and burglary in the first degree. These individuals had terrorized an area of Greenwich Village by accosting respectable couples as they entered their apartments. Having forcibly gained entrance, they bound the males and literally ravished the females. It is difficult to believe that any human beings could be guilty of the atrocities they committed.

Shortly thereafter, in the Bronx, a defendant was tried and convicted before me, again after trial by jury, of rape in the first degree, sodomy in the first degree, grand larceny in the first degree, robbery in the second degree, and assault in the second and third degrees. He was six-feet-four-inches tall and twenty-seven years of age. His crime consisted of seizing a fifty-five-year-old widow who was entering her building on the Grand Concourse, dragging her into an alleyway and into a storage room where he attacked her. Again his crimes defy human understanding. He began his criminal career twelve years before with a charge of attempted rape in North Carolina.

More recently, again in the Bronx, two men and a woman were convicted before me, after trial by jury, of robbery in the first degree, grand larceny in the third degree, possessing a weapon as a felony, possessing a weapon as a misdemeanor, and assault in the second degree. This prosecution arose out of a mugging that took place on April 10, 1968, at 165th Street between Gerard and River Avenues. The same trio had killed another mugging victim days before, a crime for which I had no alternative but to absolve them because of constitutional difficulties. One of the defendants took the stand, and on cross-examination claimed that he could not estimate whether the number of his previous muggings was 50, 100, or 200.

In May, 1969, after trial before me without a jury—it was evident that the defendant and counsel feared the inescapable wrath of a jury, and, therefore, waived trial by jury—a defendant was convicted of murder, rape, and sodomy. He was twenty years of age; the victim was his eleven-year-old sister.

The judge needs little guidance in passing sentence on defendants such as these. It is not for the human judge to attempt to assess their subjective responsibility—this is a matter reserved for the Lord Himself. The protection of society demands long-term segregation based on their objective responsibility. I will not detail the sentences imposed on these particular individuals except to observe that they reflected justice rather than charity.

THE JUDGE AND THE RECLAIMABLE DEFENDANT

Much greater interest must be developed, however, in the restorative possibilities of our courts to deal with other defendants not beyond our help, and here the judge needs help and guidance.

With Judge Younger, we must inquire in increasing degree what the function of a judge in a criminal court is. Is it merely to segregate and punish? Or is it not also to try to understand and help? While the judge on his bench has the obligation to reflect the justice of God, must he not also be the dispenser of the charity of Christ? Life for the judge who believes the latter is infinitely more complicated.

The heaviest burden of crime is not imposed by the hardened, incurably vicious criminal, the clear candidate for long-term segregation. The real problem is the also-ran in the competitive struggle, the man or woman who entered the race ill-equipped. The unhappy people who are in serious conflict with our criminal courts have, for the most part, nothing against decent society. Many, if not most, would like to be a part of it if they could find a way. But their mental states range all the way from normal through mere superficial confusion to deep psychosis and feeble-mindedness. Some are congenitally lazy. Most of them have grown up in shocking circumstances of crowding, mistreatment, and neglect. Relatively few are really vicious, and each has tried in his own poor stumbling way to find a place in life. We cannot help all of them, but we can help more than we do, transforming them from burdens to helpers.

Many of them indeed do not belong in a criminal court. I refer particularly to the thousands of hapless drug-addicts and alcoholics who are currently paraded before the bench in an endless revolving-door proceeding. This drama could be the inspiration for another *Erewhon,* the book in which Samuel Butler satirized the cruelty of punishing the sick. You may recall that one victim of the practice was convicted of "pulmonary consumption" and sentenced to "imprisonment, with hard labor, for the rest of your miserable existence." The judge reproached him:

> It is intolerable that an example of such terrible enormity should be allowed to go at large unpunished. Your presence in the society of respectable people would lead the less able-bodied to think more lightly of all forms of illness; neither can it be permitted that you should have the chance of corrupting unborn beings who might hereafter pester you. . . . But I will enlarge no further upon things that are themselves so obvious. But you may say that it is not your fault. . . . I answer that whether your being in a consumption is your fault or no, it is a fault in you, and it is my duty to see that against such faults as this the commonwealth shall be protected. You may say that it is your misfortune to be a criminal; I answer that it is your crime to be unfortunate [Butler, 1917, pp. 112–117].

THE ROLE OF CONSCIENCE IN JUDICIAL DECISION

How many times do we judges, in our sincere desire to be just, overlook our obligation of charity? Think for a moment of the frightening responsibility which is the judge's as he sits there on his bench. Who is sane and who is crazy, and should the issue hang on a judge's last-minute uninformed whim? These issues face the judge daily. Do the maladjustments frequently associated with offenses against society, yet short of lunacy, deserve consideration? The judge in a criminal court judges the guilty; it is his job. And, if he is sincerely trying not merely to reflect the justice of God but also to dispense the charity of Christ, he cannot assign sole guilt for their wretchedness to the bewildered defendants appearing before him. Many of them need help, not judgment; charity, not justice. Whether they will ever get it is, in the last analysis, up to the judge—and his conscience.

Up to the judge—and his conscience? One may well say that conscience applies to one's perception and judgment of the moral qualities of his *own* conduct. It does; but, in a wider sense, it also denotes a similar application of the standards of morality to the acts *of others.*

The Honorable John Dean, a distinguished Justice of the Pennsylvania Supreme Court, referred to this meaning of the word "conscience" when he observed:

> Every man of ordinary intelligence understands, in whatever other words we may express it, that conscience is that moral sense which dictates to him right and wrong. True, this sense differs in degree in individual members of society; but no reasonable being, whether controlled by it or not in his conduct, is wholly destitute of it. Greatly enlightened it is in some by reason of superior education, quickened in others because of settled religious belief in future accountability, dulled in others by vicious habits, but never altogether absent in any . . . ; *every decision pronounced by a court* . . . is professedly based on a moral sense, prescribing what is right and prohibiting what is wrong. . . . [Some one may say] "It is simply a difference in judgment, and no question of conscience whatever in the case." But judgment is only the result or conclusion of *conscience,* after the latter has performed its office in the different steps leading up to the conclusion; and this conclusion, then, is the very truth to him who has arrived at it by conscientious preparation and reasoning [emphasis added; *Miller* v. *Miller,* 1898].

The good judge recognizes God as the source of his authority, and humbly exercises that authority only after listening to his conscience—to "the voice of God in man." Unless it is inspired by the gift of the Holy Spirit, the judgment of mere man is, at best, limited.

Mr. Justice Felix Frankfurter acknowledged this judicial dependence on conscience in *Rochin* v. *California* (1952). This was a case in which the defendant was charged with possessing "a preparation of morphine" in violation of the California Health and Safety Code. The evidence established that three deputy sheriffs of the County of Los Angeles entered the defendant's bedroom. On a "night stand" beside the bed the deputies spied two capsules. When asked "Whose stuff is this?" the defendant seized the capsules and put them in his mouth. A struggle ensued, in the course of which the three officers "jumped upon him" and attempted to extract the capsules. The force they applied proved unavailing against the defendant's resistance. He was handcuffed and taken to a hospital. At the direction of one of the officers, a doctor forced an emetic solution through a tube into the defendant's stomach against his will. This "stomach pumping" produced vomiting. In the vomited matter were found two capsules which proved to contain morphine. After trial, the defendant was found guilty. On appeal to the Supreme Court of the United States the conviction was reversed on the ground that the police conduct in using a stomach pump violated the due-process clause of the Fourteenth Amendment of the United States Constitution. In holding that the due-process clause was violated, Mr. Justice Frankfurter observed: "This is conduct that shocks the *conscience*" (emphasis added).

In amplifying his judgment that the due-process clause was violated, Mr. Justice Frankfurter stated:

> The vague contours of the Due Process Clause do not leave judges at large. We may not draw on our merely personal and private notions and disregard the limits that bind judges in their judicial function. Even though the concept of due process of law is not final and fixed, these limits are derived from considerations that are fused in the whole nature of our judicial process. . . . These are considerations deeply rooted in reason and in the compelling traditions of the legal profession. The Due Process Clause places upon this Court the duty of exercising a judgment, within the narrow confines of judicial power in reviewing State convictions, upon interests of society pushing in opposite directions. Due process of law thus conceived is not to be derided as resort to a revival of "natural law" [*Rochin* v. *California*, 1952].

In a rather critical analysis of this philosophy, Professor Livingston Hall of the Harvard Law School and Professor Yale Kamisar of the University of Michigan ask these rhetorical questions:

> *How does a judge escape from the "idiosyncrasy of a personal judgment"?* If, as Justice Frankfurter insists, the . . . test is not based upon "the idiosyncrasies of a merely personal judgment," *whose* moral judgments furnish the answer? And *where* and *how* are they discoverable? The opinions of the progenitors and architects of our institutions? The opinions of the policy-making organs of state governments? Of state courts? The opinions of other countries? Of other countries in the Anglo-Saxon tradition? [Hall & Kamisar, 1966, p. 15].

An answer to these rhetorical questions (although the professors and, indeed, many judges would probably reject it as a resort to "natural law") is that *conscience* will furnish the answer.

The judge who acknowledges his dependence on God, who recognizes God as the ultimate source of his authority, and who prays for the grace to be truly wise—who listens to his conscience, the voice of God—before rendering judgment, can escape from the "idiosyncrasy of a personal judgment." Indeed, only the judge who has the humility to seek divine guidance can truly render justice.

Those who believe in a philosophy that acknowledges the role of conscience in the judicial process can take encouragement from the fact that President Richard M. Nixon in announcing his appointment of a new Chief Justice took occasion to commend the philosophy of Mr. Justice Frankfurter (*New York Times*, 1969b).

REFERENCES

Butler, S. *Erewhon.* (Rev. ed.) New York: Dutton, 1917.

Hall, L., & Kamisar, Y. *Basic criminal procedure.* St. Paul: West Publishing Co., 1966.

Miller v. *Miller,* 187 Pa. 572, 41 Atl. 277, 280 (1898).

New York Times. April 10, 1969. (a)

New York Times. May 23, 1969. (b)

Rochin v. *California,* 342 U.S. 165, 170–172, 177–178 (1952).

V
CONSCIENCE AND CIVIL DISOBEDIENCE

Conscience and Civil Disobedience

WILLIAM C. CUNNINGHAM, S.J.

Father William C. Cunningham, S.J. received his Ph.B. (1951) and his LL.B. (1953) degrees from Marquette University. He earned an M.A. degree from Loyola University, Chicago, in 1960, and an LL.M. degree from Georgetown University in 1961. He served in the Judge Advocate General's Corps of the U.S. Army from 1953 to 1955. Father Cunningham is a member of the Bar of the Supreme Courts of Illinois, of Wisconsin, and of the United States. At the present time, he is assistant professor of law at the Loyola (Chicago) University School of Law. Since the writing of this paper in which he describes his experience as one of the defense counsel for the "Catonsville Nine," Father Cunningham has had a similar experience as one of the defense lawyers for the "Chicago Fifteen," who on May 25, 1969, allegedly ransacked the Selective Service Center in Chicago and took out records and burned them.

In discussing Freedom of Conscience in Legal Perspective, I wrote that I would limit myself in developing that topic to selective conscientious objection and that I would refrain from discussing civil disobedience, since the latter was scheduled to receive formal treatment in the Institute program. When it developed that the scheduled speaker on civil disobedience was unable to appear, I agreed * to fill the breach with some reflections on several dimensions of problems of conscience that I had seen recently in my work as one of the defense counsel for the "Catonsville Nine." I had not brought with me to New York my files and notes on this case; nor did I have time to prepare a paper on this subject. What follows, then, came more from a full heart than from a prepared mind.

I should say, however, that I used to give talks on civil disobedience before the Catonsville experience. They were heavy on theory since, until that time, I had no practical experience with civil disobedience, either as a disobedient or as a lawyer for one. I usually began with Sophocles' *Antigone* and worked my way forward to the present day. By way of bibliographical interest, I should say that anyone reading on the matter would do well to include the paper on dissent and civil disobedience of former Justice Abe Fortas (1968), and the reply to that essay by Howard Zinn (1968). One more writing that you would do well to consider is an occasional paper published by the Center for the Study of Democratic Institutions (1966), which contains its own bibliography on the subject of civil disobedience. But to get back to Antigone. Faced with the problem of what her response would be to a law that ran counter to what she felt impelled in conscience to do, her plight is classic: whether to defy Creon's law forbidding burial of her own brother and his son, or to obey his law and go against what she felt impelled to do in response to her conscience and a higher law.

The problem Antigone was faced with was placed thus at the juncture between law and morality—a juncture which has been aptly called the "Cape Horn of Jurisprudence." But as Harry W. Jones, the Cardozo Professor of Jurisprudence at Columbia University School of Law, observed in an address before the American Philosophical Society, if "the civil rights movement, seriously examined, does not establish either the theoretical legitimacy or the political efficacy of civil disobedience as an across-the-board tactic of social action," then perhaps we must deal with the second theorem he proposed, at least for examination, that "the civil rights movement cannot, with any semblance of reason, be appropriated on behalf of . . . the draft card burners and other civil disobedients generally" (Jones, 1967, pp. 197–198). The point he makes is that in the former case with the civil rights movement, especially in the South, obligation to follow law in a democracy is premised on the assumption that the citizen has a right to participate in the law-making process, and that, if the citizen was systematically excluded from any participation in the political order against

---

* This request was made by the Chairman of the Institute Committee in view of Father Cunningham's theoretical knowledge of the question as well as his practical acquaintance with it as one of the attorneys for the "Catonsville Nine," a group tried in the Federal District Court in Baltimore, Maryland, October 7–10, 1968, for the destruction of Selective Service records. The paper, delivered extemporaneously at the Institute, was subsequently prepared by its author for inclusion in the present volume.—Ed.

which he rebelled, his act of civil disobedience was far less a challenge to law than an appeal to law. These are interesting observations, and they challenged me in my own reflecting on the conscience problems that I saw surface in my own work as defense counsel for the "Catonsville Nine."

Before I begin to outline some of those conscience problems that I observed, however, let me tell you how it came about that I returned to the practice of the law in this particular case. In the summer of 1966, shortly after I was ordained, and one year after I had met Father Daniel Berrigan, s.j. personally, I had occasion to offer him some help with a misunderstanding that had developed between him, his friends, and the New York City Police over a demonstration that took place at the United Nations. I offered to contact a friend of mine who had since become a high-ranking police officer in New York City. My friend was more than willing to meet with Dan to discuss the matter, but the press of Dan's own plans that summer made a meeting practicably impossible. So, later that summer I wrote to Dan to tell him that I had not intended to try to foist legal help on him if he did not want it, but that if it ever were unnecessary for him to go to jail that I would go a long way as his brother in Christ, and as a lawyer, to prevent his going. I also told him that if it ever became necessary for him to go to jail, I would, perhaps, be able to understand that, and still would like to be able to help in whatever way possible.

I think this is my only and last adventure as a minor prophet. For almost two years later, in June, 1968, I received a letter from Dan asking whether, as Jesuit lawyer and brother, I would join the defense team for the "Catonsville Nine." I agreed to do this and went to the first meeting of the lawyers and the "Nine" on July 9, 1968, in New York City. I will return later to speak of my own reaction to this request, for it seems proper that I speak first of what Dan outlined in his first letter to me. The letter was written approximately one month after May 17, 1968, the date on which the "Catonsville Nine" (Daniel Berrigan, s.j., Philip Berrigan, s.s.j., David Darsh, John Hogan, Thomas Lewis, Marjorie Melville, Thomas Melville, George Mische, and Mary Moylan) entered Local Board No. 33 at Catonsville, Maryland, and seized and burned some 300 or more Selective Service records with homemade napalm manufactured from a recipe in the *Special Forces Handbook*.

THE CONSCIENCES OF THE NINE

But to return to Dan's letter. He had said in that letter that among the issues they hoped to raise were those of conscience and man's law, non-violence, free speech, and the morality of modern war, and of the Vietnam War in particular. They had, in a statement issued on the occasion of their arrest on May 17, 1968, declared their belief that in their judgment some property had no right to exist, and among such property they included the files of conscription for the war in Vietnam. Believing as they did that this war was not only immoral but illegal, they felt impelled in conscience to express their opposition to our country's waging of it, to raise an outcry that would call us to a sense of our responsibility and our purpose as a responsible and a most powerful nation.

Each of the "Nine," as I was later to find out, had come to this act as an ultimate step on a ladder of escalation of his own concern. Having tried so many other and such varied ways to call this war and all its starkness to the attention of the people in whose hands, at least theoretically, the responsibility for continuing it rests, it became necessary for them to take this action, at once symbolic and real, to bring us to our senses. So they thought and think, and in witness to this belief they acted together on May 17, 1968, at Catonsville. I did not see them as they agonized over the formation of conscience that preceded those judgments, but, having seen and known them since, I cannot say they were not the sincerest people in arriving at that conscience-judgment that led to their action.

One thing to point out was their insistence that their action was the destruction of paper—not lives. It goes without saying, but I have told the "Nine" this as well, that they are wonderful human beings, but tough to defend. They do not fit into any of the categories of the ordinary criminal defendant. As defense counsel one does not often find defendants (much less nine of them) who wait at the scene of the alleged crime in broad daylight while they are being photographed by sound camera equipment, pass out statements explaining their action, mail them out to those who could not avail themselves of the opportunity to be there, admit the act on the witness stand in court, and then confer with their lawyers about the issues that might be raised in the defense! That is not the ordinary defendant; but, then, this was not an ordinary trial.

CONSCIENCE AND THE JUDGE

Since they wanted to raise the issue of conscience *vs.* man's law, it was, of course, necessary for them to tell the court and the jury precisely why they had done what they had done. And it was this whole issue over testimony regarding their motivation that occasioned, I believe, one of the most severe legal problems for the judge in the case.

The trial of the "Catonsville Nine" took place October 7–10, 1968, in Baltimore, Maryland, in the Federal District Court before Judge Roszel C. Thomsen. Since all nine of the defendants took the witness stand to testify in his own behalf, the issue of the motivation was raised as to each defendant. All nine were tried for mutilation of government property, destruction of government property, and willful interference by force with the administration of the Selective Service System. The government took the position that only their intent was relevant, and that that could best be revealed by the nature of the act itself. Accordingly, the government argued that their motives for so acting, or the events and thinking that led to their motivation, were irrelevant. The judge then had the difficult task of deciding whether or not, and under which restrictions, to allow testimony from the defendants dealing with the whole matter of motivation.

In the end, the judge did allow the defendants to testify concerning the gradual formation of the belief that led them to the action of May 17, but he carefully warned the jurors each time that the motives of the defendants were immaterial—that their intent was the only relevant factor to be judged. He conceded that the defendants' motives might have been noble—indeed, even religious—but that at the end of the trial he would instruct the jurors to decide only whether the defendants in fact did the acts charged in the indictment with the requisite intent. He was trying, I believe, to allow them some opportunity to tell how and why they formed their beliefs. At the same time he was trying to keep the issues of the legality and morality of our country's waging war in Vietnam out of the case. And if this caused him some agony of conscience, it was best revealed in the remarks he made at the end of the trial when he held a forty-five-minute colloquy with the nine defendants in open court. I will tell you at the end of this paper some of the things he said, but here I want merely to note that their acts of civil disobedience had caused, in their own way, some problems of conscience for the judge who heard their case.

PROBLEMS OF CONSCIENCE FOR JESUIT SUPERIORS

Another crisis of conscience appeared when the Jesuit pastor of St. Ignatius Church in Baltimore, Father William Michelman, s.j. agreed to allow the defendants and their associates the use of the premises at St. Ignatius Parish to prepare for and discuss the trial as it progressed in Baltimore. Many people had come to Baltimore for the trial, and some of the marches and vigils had, at times, several thousand people in them. In the past Fr. Michelman had never denied any reasonable request when the location was needed for a forum to give expression to assent or dissent in the debatable issues of the time. Certainly many peace groups in Baltimore saw the need for such a forum. To be sure, Fr. Michelman's charity was not greeted with open enthusiasm by the religious and Catholic communities of Baltimore—indeed, of his own community at St. Ignatius. But to Bill Michelman it would have been impossible in conscience to fail to extend the charity of the use of the hall to the defendants and their supporters. So he drew up a statement on October 4, 1968, in which he set out his reasons for arriving at that decision. He was, of course, sensitive to those who opposed his action, and he carefully explained that neither the people of the parish nor the Jesuit community sponsored or espoused any specific demonstration. A letter written by the Jesuit Provincial of the Maryland Province accompanied this statement, and in it, Father James L. O'Connor, the Provincial, made the point that until the trial was over the issue of the guilt of those who were going on trial was still in question. He pointed out that the court would rule on the legal aspects of the case and that the people would then have the difficult task of forming their own consciences about the moral aspects of the case. In the end, he asked that the people use the same care and effort at objectivity which Father Michelman and he accorded to the many protests they received over the planned use of the hall. And so there were still other dimensions of conscience-problems revealed in the action of the local Jesuit pastor's dealing with protests from the local communities for his allowing the defendants and their friends and supporters to use the hall at St. Ignatius to prepare for and to discuss the trial of the "Catonsville Nine."

CONSCIENCE AND THE PROSECUTING ATTORNEYS

Could the trial also have caused problems of conscience for the two United States Attorneys who prosecuted the case? One was black and the other Jewish. Certainly the possibility of this was in the minds of the defendants, for at several points in the trial one or another of them speculated about how difficult it must be for members of minority groups to prosecute nine people who had given so much of their adult lives to working to help minority groups. But if it caused some sort of a conscience-problem to prosecute the government's case, the U.S. Attorneys did not acknowledge it to us during the course of the trial.

CONSCIENCE AND THE DEFENSE COUNSEL

In addition to myself, the other three lawyers comprising the defense counsel were William Kunstler, the famous civil-rights lawyer from New York City,* Harrop Freeman, Professor of Law at Cornell University and a personal friend of Dan Berrigan's, and Harald Buchman, a practitioner of law in Baltimore, Maryland. They were, respectively, Jew, Quaker, and Jew. We made a curious defense team, then, with two Jews, a Quaker, and a Catholic priest. And I must say that they all won my admiration and respect.

* William Kunstler gained considerable publicity since the writing of this paper by reason of his role as the chief defense attorney for the "Chicago 7," tried for conspiracy to incite to riot during the 1968 Democratic Convention. Mr. Kunstler was himself sentenced to four years in jail for contempt of court as a result of the trial proceedings.—Ed.

For myself, as one of the defense counsel, I saw no problems in conscience raised by my participation in the trial of the "Catonsville Nine." I believe that as a teacher of law in a law school one's vocation is at least fourfold. I see a need first and foremost to prepare and teach the subjects assigned to me to present. But I see additional demands to engage in research and to write for the larger scholarly community of the legal profession, to participate in and work on committees for legislative and judicial reform and other related aspects of civic concern, and finally, to take civil cases for, and to defend, the poor.

I believe I have a legitimate demand made upon me to take civil cases for, and to defend, the poor by dint of being a lawyer. But I have come to believe that as teacher and as a member of a Christian religious order this is one creative way for me to serve the poor who, the Gospel assures us, we will have always with us. At this trial the request had come for my services initially from Father Daniel Berrigan, who was my personal friend, my brother Jesuit, and who was poor by virtue of his religious vow of poverty. As I told my own Provincial, *to have had to refuse* this help he asked of me would have created a problem in conscience for me as lawyer, as teacher, as Jesuit, and as Christian. But my Provincial's understanding obviated any problem. I went with his permission to participate in the trial.

One small problem I did have was whether or not to wear my clerical attire at the trial. Since I was only one of four lawyers present throughout the trial, I decided to wear it. I thought that had I been by myself in court it might have looked like an obvious appeal to the sympathy and emotions of the jury. But I asked for no special treatment, nor did I expect it at the trial. And since my brother Jesuit had asked me to participate in the defense, and since I knew he would be wearing his clericals himself, I thought that it would be inappropriate for me to come in anything but clericals. Right or wrong, I had to make my own decision, and this was what I decided to do. We all learned as we went through the experience that there were many things that happened for which there certainly was no precedent. I suppose that that indicates some degree of originality in the whole action of the "Catonsville Nine." It had simply never been done before, and it called on everyone connected with the trial of this case to reflect on the action and to take some stand in respect to what he was trying to say by it.

CONSCIENCE AND THE JURY

Finally, I should outline the problem of conscience that this action and our defense attempted to raise for the jury. I say "attempted to raise" advisedly, because the judge in the last instance refused to allow Bill Kunstler to argue to the jury their right to nullify by their verdict the effect of the law. There was a time when one could argue to a jury that it had a right to ignore the judge's charge, to find a verdict according to its conscience, and by its verdict to nullify unjust laws, and to repudiate unjust governmental policies.

This was not the first time such an argument had been attempted or used. Following the Spock trial several legal scholars made that very point. In a brilliant article, Professor Joseph L. Sax (1968a) of the University of Michigan School of Law argued from English and American legal history to substantiate this right on the part of the jury to nullify by their verdict laws or policies they deem unjust. He points to Fox's Libel Law in England which gave that right to the defendant to appeal to the jury for acquittal on a principle which no formal law-maker, whether legislator or judge, would accept, and by their act recognize the propriety of what we would call civil disobedience. He pointed also to John Peter Zenger's trial for seditious libel in 1735 in America—a trial at which Andrew Hamilton successfully argued that same right to a jury that acquitted Zenger and established one of the most important precedents for freedom of the press in this country. He pointed, too, to the juries and the other people who steadfastly refused to enforce Congress' Fugitive Slave Law. I had that article, as well as another by Joseph L. Sax (1968b) when I went to Baltimore for the trial—the former by dint of Professor Sax's courtesy in sending a reprint to me at the trial.

I had also seen, as did my fellow counsel, an interview with Professor Paul A. Freund, written by Israel Shenker (1968). In his discussion as presented in this interview, Freund urged that leeway should be allowed for juries in conscience cases. He speculated that there should be some new doctrine which would permit a judge to tell a jury that they were to decide in the light of all the circumstances. And after the judge had explained the law to them, the judge could add that the defendants could be acquitted and that the jury did not have to give reasons. Such an instruction by the judge would have allowed us to argue to the jury that they could pardon by their verdict if they felt so inclined. But this became a question only for appeal later, because the judge refused instructions drawn up along that line, and he also prohibited any final argument to the jury that would have told the jury they had the right to nullify with their verdict the law as given to them by the judge.

THE CONCLUSION OF THE TRIAL

Before I close, let me tell you a bit about the ending of this curious trial. The nine defendants had indicated to us on Thursday, October 10, at lunch, that they wanted to address the court. Perhaps each of them wanted to say something. For they felt and feel that the judge and the whole legal machinery of the trial had failed to come to grips with the real issues of law and life that met in the trial of this case. And so, after the jury had been charged the judge sent them to the jury room, but he instructed the bailiff not to let them begin their deliberations before they were told. The judge, I think, believed that what the defendants were going to say to him would be in the nature of exceptions to his charge to the jury. And if he had found them meritorious, perhaps he would have modified his charge. It became clear, however, after the first defendant, Tom Melville, spoke that their remarks were more in the nature of a reservation or an abiding discontent with the whole legal process and the way it had been used to deal with the issues of life presented at the trial. The nine defendants were standing behind their counsels' table. The courtroom was packed with spectators. The judge's bench was ringed in front by U.S. Marshals (I rather think they expected some outburst). And the judge, having heard the first remarks, sent instructions to the bailiff to tell the jury to begin their deliberations. But the judge stayed on the bench and engaged in a forty-five-minute colloquy with the nine defendants.

They were trying desperately to understand the judge and his view of the issues. And he was trying desperately to understand their view of the issues. Dan Berrigan speaks, of course, a poet's language. And he told Judge Thomsen that the trial had made him feel like a cadaver, as though his body were there in the court, but his soul somewhere else. Their acts, he said, had seemed to be drained in this legal process of all their moral passion. And the legal process seemed to create a sharp division between issues of law and of life.

The judge said to Dan Berrigan that history might prove someday that he (the judge) was wrong and Father Berrigan right. He also told the nine that he wanted to see the war in Vietnam halted, perhaps for not entirely unselfish reasons. He had a grandson coming up to draft age, he told them, and he did not relish the idea of his going if it were unnecessary. What the judge did stress was that what the "Nine" wanted him to decide was a political, not a legal, question. He said that if the issue were ever presented as a legal one, no judge worth his salt as a judge would duck the question. Then they asked the judge why not decide the question of the legality and constitutionality of the war in this court, here and now. And back and forth they went for about forty-five minutes of a most probing and sensitive exchange. The judge told how, as a man, he had been deeply moved by Father Daniel Berrigan's testimony, but he said that he had to decide questions as a judge. And as a judge he was bound to follow the law as it is.

Finally, Father Daniel Berrigan told the judge that he was sure he spoke for all of them when he thanked him for doing what he had done at the trial within the context of the legal process as he saw it. But he said that he did not want it to appear by anything that had been said or left unsaid at the trial that they believed that the sharp edge of division between law and life had been dulled or blunted or honed down in any way. They did not feel that this had been accomplished; nevertheless they wanted to thank the judge for doing what he thought he could.

Then, as casually as the exchange had begun, Father Daniel Berrigan asked whether they might end the trial with a prayer. To say we were somewhat surprised is an understatement. There was a pause while the judge pondered the request in silence. Then he said, as I remember, that he saw present in the back of the courtroom the U.S. Attorney, Steve Sachs, who had something to say about how government property could be used, so he would like to hear whether or not there were any objections by the government. But, the judge added, as long as he sat in that room it was his court, and he would reserve the right to overrule the U.S. Attorney. The U.S. Attorney said that on behalf of the government there was no objection, and speaking as an individual he thought it would be a good way to end the trial. As though we had been given a cue by some invisible commentator, everyone in the court room stood up. And Dan began, slowly, the Lord's Prayer. How many joined, I cannot say. I know that it was reverently and loudly prayed, and that it was one of the most moving prayer experiences I have ever had. When it ended I looked up and I saw Federal Marshals crying. I do not know whether the judge was crying, because I am a trifle near-sighted, and I was crying myself.

The verdict came 45 minutes later—all nine guilty on all the charges. They have since been sentenced to from two to three-and-a-half years, and all are, at this writing, free on bond pending appeal of the case to the Fourth Circuit Court of Appeals of the United States.* It was the most unusual ending for the most unusual trial I had ever been in in my life. And it revealed all these dimensions of problems of conscience that I have singled out to reflect on with you.

REFERENCES

Center for the Study of Democratic Institutions. *Civil disobedience: An occasional paper on the free society.* Santa Barbara, Cal.: Center for the Study of Democratic Institutions, 1966.

Fortas, A. *Concerning dissent and civil disobedience.* New York: New American Library, 1968.

Jones, H. W. Civil disobedience. *Proceedings of the American Philosophical Society,* 1967, *3* (4), 195–198.

Sax, J. L. Conscience and anarchy: The prosecution of war resisters. *Yale Review,* 1968, *57,* 481–494. (a)

Sax, J. L. Civil disobedience: The law is never blind. *Saturday Review,* 1968, *51,* 22–25. (b)

* This court in October, 1969, upheld the convictions. The appeal was then carried to the United States Supreme Court, which on February 25, 1970, refused to hear the appeal.—Ed.

Shenker, I. Interview with Professor Paul A. Freund. *New York Times,* September 19, 1968.

Zinn, H. *Disobedience and democracy: Nine fallacies on law and order.* New York: Random House, 1968.

Conscience and the Soldier

GORDON C. ZAHN

Gordon C. Zahn received his A.B. degree from the College of St. Thomas, St. Paul, Minnesota, in 1949, and his M.A. degree in 1950 and Ph.D. degree in 1952 from the Catholic University of America. Dr. Zahn has had a series of post-doc-toral fellowships including a Social Science Research Council Post-doctoral Fellowship, which he took at Harvard University; a Fulbright Research Fellowship in Germany; and a Simon Research Fellowship in England. In addition to numerous articles, he is the author of the following four books, among others: German Catholics and Hitler's wars: A study in social control (*1962*); In solitary witness: The life and death of Franz Jägerstätter (*1964*); War, conscience and dissent (*1967*); and The military chaplaincy: A study of role tension in the Royal Air Force (*1969*). *At present, Dr. Zahn is professor of sociology at the University of Massachusetts at Boston.*

THE REVOLT OF JULY 20 AGAINST HITLER

July 20, 1969, marked the twenty-fifth anniversary of the nearly successful attempt to assassinate Adolf Hitler. What makes the commemoration of that event particularly relevant to this paper, however, is not the fact that the attempt was made or that it failed after coming so close to success; rather, that in its planning and execution it was the work of a high-ranking military hero, and represented a far-flung conspiracy involving men at the highest level of military authority. The tributes paid to Colonel Claus von Stauffenberg, Colonel-General Ludwig Beck, retired Chief of the German General Staff, and the almost two hundred others who paid with their lives for their involvement in the conspiracy (Fitzgibbon, 1956; Gollwitzer, *et al.*, 1956; Zeller, 1969), however much they focus on the heroism of the effort and the tragedy of the failure, will be wanting in the true lesson to be taken if they do not reflect the fact that, objectively speaking, these men were guilty of treason. For it is precisely because men of this stature and rank did knowingly and willingly assume the role of traitor that the events of that July 20 hold meaning for us and for the future.

The military *Putsch* is not a particularly rare occurrence. Had this effort succeeded, the commemorations would take on a somewhat different character and "treason" would probably be rejected as an altogether inappropriate term. Success has a way of justifying such actions, as our own history and the record of our foreign policy over the years amply illustrates. The United States has experienced no particular difficulty in extending recognition and support to an embarrassingly large number of military dictatorships that have come to power in Latin America, Greece, and elsewhere by means similar to those employed unsuccessfully in Berlin a quarter-century ago.

Nor is it altogether unique that coups have failed and have been followed by bloody reprisals. The thing that does set July 20 apart is the extent to which this particular show of treason has become recognized and almost universally applauded as an act of conscience. To Stauffenberg and his associates, the attempt to overthrow the Nazi regime and to kill the nation's *Führer* was "a command of moral purification and of honor that had to be obeyed" (Zeller, 1969, p. 289), and it has been accepted as such. Even Winston Churchill, who had been neither particularly receptive to the advance feelers put out by the conspirators nor overly impressed by the attempt when it finally came off, was to change his mind after the war and speak admiringly of the German Opposition "which was among the greatest and most noble groups in the political history of all times. These men fought without help from inside or outside—*driven solely by their uneasy conscience* . . ." (emphasis added; Zeller, 1969, p. 394).

To call this treason may seem unduly harsh and unfeeling, but in the strictest sense that is what it was. Not only did these men, again military officers most of them, organize not one but a series of attempts to assassinate the Supreme Commander to whom each and every one had sworn a personal oath of loyalty and unquestioning obedience, but they used the power available to them because of their positions of trust to shift military units about to suit the advantage of their plans; they ignored and disobeyed orders issued by their immediate superiors; they deceived those same superiors and, where prospects seemed favorable, attempted to persuade them to join in their conspiracy; they established and maintained contacts with the enemy to discuss possible surrender arrangements and consequences; and, at the end, they were prepared to order a complete and unilateral cessation of hostilities on one of the two major fronts, thereby inviting the invasion of the homeland they were commissioned to defend. One general went so far as to furnish a foreign power with complete and specific details in advance of the scheduled invasion of its territory (Zeller, 1969, p. 21). In all these actions, they gave and knew *they were giving* "aid and comfort to the enemy." In addition, they must have known that by their actions— and this is particularly true in General Oster's case—they were placing the lives of men in the armed forces in serious jeopardy. If all these acts were routinely documented and put into a set of formal charges, there is little doubt that these men could have been indicted for treason, sentenced, and condemned in any court, martial or civilian, including our own.

That Hitler and his henchmen saw fit to take their vengeance in a series of show trials, conducted in an atmosphere of hysteria and vindictiveness so that they were reduced to a perversion of the very idea of justice, was characteristic of his regime, but it was as unnecessary as it was barbaric. There would have been more than enough eminently responsible and respectable officers in the military itself to try to convict the unfortunate culprits according to established procedures.

The July 20 *Attentat* can serve as a classic case for any discussion of the relationship between the personal conscience and the duties and obligations associated with the military calling. These officers decided among themselves that the government they were serving and the war it was waging were unjust and immoral. Some of them, it should be remembered, placed their emphasis upon the first issue, giving little or no thought to the morality of the war; but, even so, each had come to a personal judgment that he could no longer honor the oath he had sworn without sacrificing all respect for himself and his nation. As events turned out, Nazi Germany was defeated, and what was for them an individual act of conscience was confirmed in the name of all humanity by the victor court at Nuremberg. But even had Hitler won, and, it goes without saying, the plotters fixed forever in their nation's history as betrayers of a sacred trust and defilers of German honor, their tragic history would still serve to illustrate the problem of defining the rights and limits of the individual conscience when the individual happens to be a member of the armed forces.

SOME PARALLELS TO OUR OWN COUNTRY

How, one might ask, does all of this relate to us in the United States today? The answer should be obvious enough. An increasingly unpopular war in Southeast Asia has brought this nation to the point where a growing number of its men in uniform have reached decisions similar in direction, if not yet in content, to those reached by Stauffenberg and his co-conspirators. Thus, although we are not likely to witness any concerted attempt to overthrow the established government (and certainly not to assassinate the nation's leaders), we can no longer ignore the great upsurge of individual disaffiliation, first with the war and the military and then, when it is deemed unavoidable to the man in uniform, with the nation itself. There is another important difference that must be noted too. The patterns of dissent, disobedience, and desertion are not found—except for a very few widely publicized cases—at the officer level. The military "resistance," such as it is, seems to be concentrated in the ranks. This may, of course, be a function of the assignment and reporting procedures within the military establishment itself which make it easy to cushion and hide officer defections. Another, and perhaps more likely, explanation would suggest that the Westmorelands, the Maxwell Taylors, and the others in our upper echelons of military command are cast more in the Jodl and Keitel mold and lack the sensitivity and commitment to humanistic values that seem to have played so large a part in bringing Stauffenberg and the others to their fateful decision.

It will be objected at once that a much better explanation lies in the difference between a closed totalitarian system like Hitler's Third Reich and even the Johnson/Nixon variants of a democratic government in which legitimate channels for opposition, however restricted, still exist. Also, it will be argued further, the nature and conduct of the war in Vietnam are not at all comparable to the wars unleashed by Hitler and the strategies and means he employed. Both objections have merit, though the first, I would hold, is clearly the stronger of the two. To the extent that there are mechanisms, electoral and other, to influence decisions and, where necessary, to change the men who make the decisions, a military *Putsch* would be both unnecessary and unjustifiable. This is not to say, of course, that these other mechanisms work as well or as surely as we like to think. After all, the electoral "overthrow" of the Johnson administration does not seem to have had any substantial impact upon the policies and war programs which brought it about. If anything, the Nixon administration promises to be even more devoted to the continuation of a "warfare state" and, though it scarcely seems possible, even less responsive to those who seek an immediate end to a war they consider unjust and immoral in both purposes and conduct.

If they are right, the second objection to my application of the July 20 model loses much of its force. No one would deny that the two wars are vastly different in scope. Hitler unleashed a war he had been warned would engage all the major nations of the world: Vietnam has remained localized in intention and, for the most part, in fact. True, our military operations in neighboring countries (and those of the North Vietnamese as well) together with our sometimes desperate efforts to dragoon our SEATO allies into more active involvement (matched, again, on the other side by the opponents' reliance upon supplies from the Soviet Union and Communist China) could set off a broader, ultimately a world, conflagration; but, to this point at least, the danger has not been acute. It becomes quite another question when we consider the scale and intensity of our military operations within the happily still limited scope. Our leaders announce with pride statistics which show bombing tonnages far in excess of levels attained in World War II—evidence that, in this respect at least, we have outdone Hitler since Germany's defeat has been attributed in large part to her inability then to match Allied aerial bombardments. "Search and destroy" missions were undoubtedly a part of the overall Nazi operations potential and practice, but they were seldom crude enough to proclaim this as a military objective. Morally indefensible tactics, including the use, or at least complicity in the use, of torture in interrogation are a matter of grim record (Melman & Falk, 1968), as are the frankly racist overtones that mark the attitude of substantial segments of our military forces toward Vietnamese ally and foe alike. The punitive destruction of entire villages, often in declared reprisal for shots allegedly fired at American fighting personnel, has already provoked the disquieting suggestion—from a German writer at that!—that Lidice and Oradour are today villages in Vietnam. Finally, on a broader scale, the glowing accounts of successes registered for "pacification" and "Phoenix" operations sometimes suggest troubling echoes of the accomplishments of the infamous *Einsatzkommando* operations which set forth to "pacify" the newly conquered territories of Eastern Europe.

It is not my purpose, nor is it necessary for this discussion, to argue that this nation has matched or surpassed the evil excesses committed by the Nazi forces. I, for one, would deny that we have even approached that level of atrocity just as I am convinced that atrocities have been committed in our name in Vietnam. If the "us=ss" legend that graces so many walls in friendly foreign capitals has any justification at all, it lies in the quality and not in the extent of the acts which have given rise to that accusation. What is important, however, is the fact that many in our own nation, including in particular men in the armed forces, have been troubled by these things and have been forced to much the same conclusion reached by the men of July 20. Once one is convinced that the war, or even a specific military operation, is immoral, it is a small and altogether natural step to wish to dissociate oneself from it and to consider ways of actively opposing it so that the nation's "ultimate dignity before the judgment of world history" might yet be preserved.

There are different levels of active opposition, and we are familiar enough with most of them as they apply in the civilian context. There is, first of all, the simple expression of personal disapproval or disfavor. These tend, in time, to develop into more organized expressions of dissent: letters to one's elected representatives become letters to the public press, petitions to be circulated and signed, advertisements to be published, rallies to be organized and attended. From there it is a simple matter to move into more demonstrative forms of dissent, to the picketing and the vigils and the protest marches. Most of these actions have become so much a part of the normal expression of opinion that we sometimes despair of their having any real impact any more. However, as the dramatic and sometimes spontaneous mobilization of opposition to recent anti-ballistic-missile (ABM) proposals —and the impact it seems to have had upon Congress and, to some extent, upon the President as well—have shown, it is perhaps too early to write them off altogether as ineffective vehicles of dissent.

For civilians subject to call for military service there is a more direct and explicit form of rejection of a war in conscientious objection. Those who for reasons of age, sex, or some other deferrable characteristic are not draft-eligible do not have this option, except vicariously in that they can provide support for the conscientious objector and publicly associate themselves with him and his witness. Conscientious objection, it should be noted, is still dissent—that is, opposition within the law. Indeed, it might be said to be "under the law" in that the law (in this case, obviously, the conscription law) not only gives recognition to this form of opposition to a war effort but goes further to specify the conditions and the qualifications which will entitle one to recognition as a conscientious objector. Increasingly this fact has been held by many to invalidate the position, for, as they see it, by submitting to classification and exemption by the war-making authority, the conscientious objector (CO) has, in effect, "opted out" and permitted himself and his protest to be "channelled" into a pre-established slot to the interest and benefit of the war effort. That there is a strong element of logic and consistency to this argument cannot be denied, and many conscientious objectors find it persuasive enough to be a source of personal strain and dissatisfaction. This is unfortunate. For what it is worth—and this opinion is undoubtedly colored by the writer's own background as a wartime CO —I would insist that conscientious objection remains a valid and effective expression of opposition to war and deserves the fullest respect as such. The mere provision for this classification under the conscription program should not be taken as a sign of official "support" or even indifference to the stand; indeed, it is reasonable to suggest that any sudden increase in applications for this classification would cause every bit as much, perhaps more, consternation and disapproval on the part of the authorities as might a comparable number of draft-card burnings.

The latter action, of course, is one of the more publicized tactics employed by the movement which has come to be known as "the Resistance." Though the opponents of war gathered together under the omega symbol include conscientious objectors and others who limit their opposition to dissent within the law, the major thrust of the Resistance is toward activism and civil disobedience. Open violation of the law, sometimes to win a specific objective but more frequently as an exercise in "symbolic speech," is not only taken as permissible where necessary but, increasingly, as essential to any meaningful confrontation with "the system." The principal actors in the Resistance, again, are men subject to the draft—though many of them, it should be noted, have intentionally rejected deferments to which they would have been entitled. Strongly "New Left" in orientation, it sets as its primary objective the disruption and ultimately the destruction of conscription itself, so that the prime focus of their efforts is the formal refusal of induction and programs to persuade others to join them in making that refusal. The Resistance has its supporters and fellow-travellers who, in addition to furnishing moral and financial assistance, usually accept some responsibility to engage in acts of civil disobedience so that they may share the risks borne by the young men who are more directly involved. By merely encouraging men to resist, these supporters are subject to legal prosecution (witness the Spock case); some go further, to such acts as "receiving" draft cards turned in by Resistance "converts," providing sanctuary, participating in obstructive demonstrations at induction centers, and the like.

Beyond the programs of the Resistance and its support auxiliaries, there are other forms of civil disobedience, more individual in conception and execution, engaged in by persons not eligible for the draft. Tax refusal, for example, has had a long and respected history as a device for expressing opposition to war and military expenditures. More recent and much more dramatic are the acts of "creative destruction" initiated by the Fathers Berrigan* and their associates in two Maryland draft-board raids, and taken

---

* On October 27, 1967, Rev. Philip Berrigan, s.s.j. and three companions entered a Baltimore draft-board office and, after diverting the attention of the clerks on duty, pulled open the file drawers and poured blood on the records of men scheduled for induction into the armed forces. The following May, a week before "the Baltimore Four" were scheduled for sentencing, Fr. Berrigan and Thomas Lewis of the original raiding party together with seven others, including Rev. Daniel Berrigan, s.j., invaded another draft-board office at Catonsville, Md. They filled several wire baskets with draft files and took them to the adjoining parking lot where they proceeded to burn them with home-made napalm. These actions served as models for a series of similar raids in Milwaukee ("the Milwaukee 14"), Chicago ("the Chicago 15"), Indianapolis

as a model for even larger actions in Milwaukee, Chicago, Los Angeles, and Washington, D.C. These "peace partisans" have taken the refusal of the conscientious objector to accept military service and the refusal of the resister to cooperate with the demands of the conscription program one step, and a very significant step, further in their direct attacks upon the operations of Selective Service or, as in the case of the "D.C. Nine," Dow Chemical.

This is at best a superficial summary of the variety of ways in which the ordinary citizen can express his rejection of an immoral war. The point of introducing it in the present context is to make it possible for the reader to place these different forms of dissent and disobedience in a meaningful context that will permit him to understand and respect each in the terms set for them by the individuals who chose one or the other. That the Berrigan-type activity is the most daring and involves a more severe (and certain) risk cannot be denied; that the resister's stand is purer and more consistent than that of the conscientious objector can be argued quite persuasively; that the conscientious objector, in turn, is "putting more on the line" than the individual who is able to limit his expression of opposition to petitions and the picket line must be acknowledged—what is important is to realize that none of these can be dismissed as completely meaningless or ineffective or unworthy of recognition and respect.

THE DIFFICULTY OF CONSCIENTIOUS DISSENT FOR THE SOLDIER

This conclusion takes on added force when the focus is shifted from the civilian to the soldier. In the soldier's "world," the mere expression of personal doubt or disapproval of the war effort is enough to lay the offender open to harassment and punitive discipline. Evidence of such abuse may break into the general news-media from time to time, but it is safe to assume that the bulk of such suppressive and reprisal actions are conducted "by the book" so that they never see the light of day. Even so shocking a case as that involving Sgt. Michael Sanders,* the member of the Arlington honor guard who suddenly found himself assigned to Vietnam duty after voicing criticism of the war, was permitted to run its course as the Army willed.

("the Beaver 55"), Philadelphia ("the East-Coast Conspiracy") as well as in Boston, Minneapolis–St. Paul, San Francisco, New York City, and Washington, D.C. In some cases—"the D.C. Nine" being one example—the objectives were the offices of corporations engaged in essential war production, but most have been directed against draft boards. The rationale behind these raids is set forth in most telling fashion in Daniel Berrigan's account, *The trial of the Catonsville nine* (Berrigan, 1970).

* Sgt. Michael Sanders was a member of the "Old Guard"—the 3rd Infantry unit assigned to guard duty at the Tomb of the Unknown Soldier in Arlington National Cemetery. After expressing a personal opinion critical of the war in Vietnam, he was abruptly transferred to duty in Vietnam. The official explanation, needless to say, was that the reassignment was "routine" and had nothing to do with the opinions attributed to Sgt. Sanders.

After all, who was there to prove that it was not, as was claimed, a normal and routine reassignment? The October 1968 assurance on the part of the Continental Army Command that the soldier enjoys the same right as any other citizen to peaceable assembly as guaranteed under the First Amendment is encouraging enough; but the absence of suitable protective procedures still leaves the serviceman completely vulnerable to arbitrary decisions by his military superiors, decisions he would have slight chance of showing were related to his exercise of that proclaimed right.

This vulnerability is evident at every level of opposition to war discussed in the preceding section. Private expression of opinion, as the Sanders case demonstrates; participation in "outside" anti-war marches and other demonstrations; organization of "inside" discussion groups and meetings; and the publication and distribution of the newly emerged underground G.I. press —all these parallel the dissent activities conducted "within the law" by civilians. But in the military they become almost heroic gestures carried on at the gravest risk and sacrifice. So, too, with the second level of opposition. There are established procedures for obtaining discharge for reasons of service-initiated conscientious objection, but, as will be seen, chances are exceedingly slight that one will win separation from the service on such grounds. The resister has his counterpart, too, if we recognize desertion as a kind of "post-induction refusal" to serve. Whether one can go beyond this and speak of more direct action assaults on the military establishment that would be comparable to the draft-board raids is difficult to say; one does hear of occasional disturbances in disciplinary barracks and some rather fantastic rumors do circulate concerning the high casualty rates for combat officers in actual engagements, both of which might offer some food for thought in this connection.

Military structures and the authority system being what they are, there is really no way of knowing how much opposition to the war effort exists, or how serious it is within our armed forces at home or in the actual theaters of war. Enough is known, however, to justify the suspicion that it is substantial. And while it would be naïve to assume that all the dissent—or, for that matter, the desertions—can be attributed to a conscientious conviction that the war is immoral, it would be blind stupidity to deny that a good share must be traceable to something more fundamental than the usual run of servicemen's gripes or avoidances of duty based on self-interest alone.

A recent count provided by the Fellowship of Reconciliation (FOR) speaks of "at least 16 harshly irreverent underground newspapers produced in varying degrees of secrecy by enlisted men." That these represent a significant new phenomenon on the military scene is indicated by two lengthy reports carried by Associated Press. In one of them an Army officer is quoted as saying, "It's still a small problem in terms of numbers, but it's getting more attention at the Pentagon. We still have no solution." Later, speaking of possible effects, the same officer declared, "They can range from a clear danger by getting more people to commit disloyal acts, down to being a source of embarrassment and irritation to the Army—which is where we are now." *

Along with the appearance of this underground press, and admittedly linked with it both as cause and effect, is the rapid proliferation of off-base radical coffeehouses—sort of a U.S.O. "morale" facility in reverse—where servicemen are encouraged to meet and discuss their opposition to the war with like-minded others, thereby spreading and at the same time deepening their anti-war convictions. No systematic efforts seem to have been made to suppress the newspapers or declare the coffeehouses off-limits, though there have been reports of occasional harassment of both.

This is a game, of course, in which the military authorities hold all the trump cards. Leaves can always be canceled (for military reasons of one sort or another) for weekends on which major anti-war parades (in which military personnel had been invited to participate) are scheduled—just one illustration of how the game is played. The vulnerability of the serviceman, demonstrated most clearly perhaps in the quite unwarranted mutiny charges brought against the "Presidio 27" † and the patent unfairness of the subsequent court-martial proceedings, operates to keep all but the most courageous from putting their dissent on open record. The reported fact that there are now more than 10,000 men in the 25 U.S. Army confinement centers in this country (more than 7 of every 1,000 men in the Army!)‡ may not be the most reliable measure of conscience-related opposition to the war; but it is a telling demonstration of the vulnerability of the man in the ranks.

Most of the 10,000 are lost in anonymity, but occasionally a case is "special" enough to bring military procedures under public scrutiny. The celebrated courts martial of Captains Levy§ (U.S.A.) and Noyd ‖ (U.S.A.F.)

---

* Taken from an unpublished report prepared by Ron Young for the Fellowship of Reconciliation, May, 1969. The latter is an interdenominational, although predominantly Christian, peace organization founded in 1916. It has long been active in civil-rights areas as well, and CORE was founded under its auspices in 1942.

† The "Presidio 27" refers to a group of prisoners at the San Francisco stockade who attempted to petition the officers in charge for a correction of abuses. A "sitdown" on the grass was met with charges of extreme severity against the prisoners. A full-scale treatment of the case is given by Gardner (1970).

‡ Cited by Young in his report prepared for the Fellowship of Reconciliation. The author gives as his sources the April 20 and April 28, 1969 issues of the *New York Times.*

§ Captain Howard Levy, M.D. gained national notice (and a court martial and sentence) for refusing to instruct Green Berets bound for Vietnam service in medical techniques and practices, basing his refusal in part on his personal responsibility as a member of the medical profession. A report of his case is given in an article entitled: The conviction of Captain Levy (von Hoffman, 1967).

‖ Like Captain Levy, Captain Dale Noyd, U.S.A.F., refused to train pilots destined for service in Vietnam. The Noyd case is particularly important for the issue of "selective objection." Helpful sources of information on the case are articles by Larner (1968) and Trillin (1968).

involved officers who refused to obey orders which, in their opinion, constituted a violation of conscience. Levy is already serving his sentence while Noyd is still working his way through the appeals process—a particularly involved process in his case since the strands of interlocking civil and military justice cannot be easily unraveled. In both cases the issue was not the personal and direct commission of some immoral act but, of far greater significance, a refusal to help prepare others for duty which would involve commission of such acts. In this both Noyd and Levy come close to the kind of motivation that brought so many high-ranking desk officers into the Stauffenberg conspiracy. The Noyd case is further complicated by his placing the issue in the context of a selective conscientious objection, affirming a willingness to perform all other duties consistent with his rank and training but refusing to instruct trainees destined for service in Vietnam.

As a selective objector, Noyd comes up against the same legal obstacles faced by civilian objectors who do not meet the test of being opposed in conscience "to participation in war in any form." Even were this not at issue, however, Noyd, like every other serviceman, would face special problems and obstacles written into the Army Regulation concerning personnel separation on grounds of conscientious objection. For one thing, the serviceman must show that his objection developed "subsequent to entry into the active military service." This means that any previous effort to gain recognition by his draft board on these grounds would render him ineligible; even more to the point, any such objection which existed *but was not claimed prior to induction* is not to be "entertained" by the military authorities. One can see some justification, perhaps, in a policy which seeks to prevent the military from becoming a review body for decisions already reached by civilian draft boards (though why it would be to the Army's advantage to be stuck with draft-board errors in judgment in such cases is difficult to understand); but that a sincere objection which for some reason or other—and let us not overlook the youth of the individuals most likely to be involved or the pressure of family and peer controls in this connection—was not previously claimed should now be dismissed as unworthy of consideration is both unreasonable and unjust.

The copy of the Regulation in my possession follows the pattern set in the earlier version of the Selective Service System's Form 150. That "special form for conscientious objectors" has been revised and significantly improved. Among other things it has eliminated the question dealing with the applicant's attitude toward the use of force and much of the emphasis formerly placed upon formal religious sources and associations. If the Army Regulation has not been similarly revised, and I suspect it has not, the continuance of these questions would represent a distinct discrimination against the man in service.

There are other procedural touches that add considerably to the soldier's disadvantage in this respect. Immediately upon receipt of a request for discharge, the commanding officer is to instruct the claimant that such discharge would bar him from all rights, except government insurance, "under laws administered by the Veterans Administration based upon the period of service from which discharged or dismissed." If, as it appears, this withdraws privileges and rights already accrued through the individual's service up to the time of his "conversion" to conscientious objection, this can only be read as a punitive gesture on the part of the military intended to pressure the applicant into taking second thought. This impression gains added force when one notes that the only exception to be allowed is the case in which it is established to the satisfaction of the Administrator that the man is insane.

The implication that insanity is likely to be linked with conscientious objection finds more definite expression elsewhere in the Regulation. A serviceman requesting separation on these grounds is required to undergo a counseling interview by a chaplain and a psychiatric interview by a psychiatrist (or medical officer if a psychiatrist is not available). The chaplain's involvement makes some sense and will be discussed at a later point. As for the psychiatric interview—it can be taken as an intrusion upon the rights of the individual which is not forced upon the civilian in the comparable situation. That such an interview could be helpful is not denied, but to make it a specified part of the application procedure is quite another matter.

Nor does this exhaust the list of discriminations suffered by military personnel. Once the application has been completed and considered by the Adjutant General "in coordination" with the Selective Service System, the decision reached is not open to appeal. The commanding officer is specifically authorized "to return to an applicant, without action, any second and subsequent application for discharge under the regulation when review reveals that it is substantially the same as a previous application." The civilian applicant has at least one appeal, and usually two, from an adverse decision by his local board; in the case of his serviceman counterpart, the very looseness of the terminology leaves him helpless. Who is to determine whether a second application is "substantially the same," and by what measure? The answer is clear enough: someone higher in the military establishment who is almost certain to be biased against conscientious objection and conscientious objectors and who will have free and unchallengeable rein in using his prejudice as the guide for his decision.

It would be extremely interesting to know (a) how many applications are actually received and processed by the military in the course of a year, and (b) what proportion of these applications win favorable action. Both figures, I am confident, will be small indeed. In the first place, it is unlikely that men in the armed forces are at all aware that they have the right to apply for such discharge; those who do know and who decide to put it to the test will soon learn that they are playing against a stacked deck. The civilian seeking recognition as a conscientious objector from a suspicious and all too often openly antagonistic draft board has a difficult time enough. The serviceman, it should be obvious to all, has a far slimmer chance of getting any kind of a fair hearing.

With the route to authorized discharge on grounds of conscience so effectively blocked, it should be no surprise that many men become resigned to desertion as the only alternative to violation of their conscience or the severe penalties associated with direct refusal to obey some morally offensive order. Not all desertions arise from this dreadful forced choice, of course. There will always be men who find the burdens of military service personally inconvenient or too dangerous and decide to "go over the hill." But when we are suddenly faced with a significant increase in such decisions—and the recent reports of a one-year total in excess of 50,000 would lead one to believe this is the case today—it should be a fairly safe assumption that the men in uniform are, to use John F. Kennedy's telling phrase, "voting with their feet" on the justice and morality of the war. The FOR summary cited earlier reports that the desertion rate has now passed the Korean War peak of 28 per thousand men in uniform; the Swedish "colony" of American deserters alone numbers 300 or more; others are to be found in Canada, England, and France. In his report to the House Defense Appropriations Subcommittee, Lt. Gen. A. O. Connor estimated the total desertions for the year ending June 30, 1969, at 50,000—an increase of nearly 30 per cent over 1968 (Connor, 1969). Even in the United States, one is beginning to encounter men who have been AWOL long enough to be classified as deserters and who have no clear intention of returning to duty.

Desertion of any kind for any reason carries distasteful overtones for most Americans, yet it may be well for us to recognize that a program of national conscription, coupled with a war of questionable morality waged by an unresponsive government, can under certain circumstances give rise to a kind of justifiable "conscientious desertion." As I have already suggested, these are the serviceman counterparts of the draft resister who refuses to take that all-important step forward at the induction center. If the comparison breaks down at any point, it is in the fact that a larger proportion of the deserters may consist of men who would have been more than willing to accept classification as conscientious objectors. Whatever else we may think of them and their action,* we should always bear in mind that it cannot be an easy thing for a young man to tear himself away, perhaps permanently, from his country, his family, and friends. Some, we know, have already decided to come back and take the penalty for their actions; more undoubtedly would

* General Connor's explanation of the increase may be satisfying to the military, but it seems much too superficial: "Getting more kooks into the army, for one thing. We are getting more young men who are coming in undisciplined, the product of a society that trains them to resist authority" (Connor, 1969).

do so were it not for the fact that the military with its usual short-sightedness and inflexibility chose to "make an example" of those who did by handing down unnecessarily severe punishments.

Between the minimal level of simple expression of dissent and the more thoroughgoing refusals represented by both conscientious objection and desertion, there is the category of individual and isolated refusals to obey specific orders on grounds of conscience. This is the course of action proposed by the more traditional interpretations of the moral theology of war and peace. The individual citizen, so the argument goes, does not have all the facts at his command; it follows that he is not really competent to decide upon the justice or injustice of a given war and the overall strategy of the war; therefore, he is to be advised to accept his military service as a civil duty but to govern all his acts in the performance of his duty according to the established principles of morality. There is nothing wrong with the argument in the abstract. Unfortunately, it fails to take account of the dynamics of individual psychology, especially the influence of a situation of stress upon the individual's behavior. One very important element in the soldier's existential situation (even apart from the emotional involvement that may be his as an effect of the "conditioning" he had undergone in the training camp) is the knowledge that disobedience of an order in a combat situation is certain to carry drastic penalties and that these can, and probably would, be applied in an arbitrary manner. It is less than realistic to expect that the ordinary man in uniform will be able to display either the sophistication in judgment or the degree of moral commitment this course of action would require. However, to the extent that some will be driven by their conscience to such acts of selective disobedience, they deserve respect and support and the recommendations to be offered below for a reform of military procedures dealing with the more general manifestations of dissent, conscientious objection, and desertion would apply, with perhaps even greater force, to them as well.

NEEDED RESTRUCTURING OF MILITARY JUDICIAL PROCEDURES

General William Westmoreland, in a Vermont speech, described dissent within Army ranks as something which goes against the concept of discipline which, in turn, is "essential" to an efficient fighting force. Discussing the present situation in the armed forces, he described the level of dissent as not a major problem but more "a matter of concern" since, as the news report quotes him, "to have a military force you must have discipline. Otherwise you will have a mob and a mob is not responsible." Here, as in other statements he has issued in the past, Westmoreland seems to have missed a crucial point. What does one do when he decides that the responsible and well-disciplined fighting force of which he is a part is engaged in prosecuting an immoral and completely *irresponsible* war? To answer this it is well to return again to July 20, 1944. Claus von Stauffenberg and the high-ranking career officers who joined his conspiracy certainly knew the value of military discipline fully as well as Westmoreland— possibly even better, when we put these men in the perspective of their "Prussian militarist" traditions and values. It was precisely because they believed in those traditions and accepted the ideals that they were led first to dissent against the established authority, and ultimately to revolution.

Men in American uniforms have found good reason to reach the same judgment. The process probably begins in something like Frank Harvey's troubling observations about the B-52 crews and the mission assigned to them in Vietnam, a mission he describes as "to blast or burn large areas of jungle (also roads, buildings, and fields) containing living things, animals and men, some innocent and unaware, without warning." Reflecting further on this he writes:

> It is not a mission of their choosing. It's just the way the ball happened to bounce. But one can't help but wonder what a man thinks about, after he's set fire to 50 square miles of jungle from high altitude with a rain of fire bombs, and wakes up in his room in the darkness—and lies awake watching the shadows on the ceiling . . . [Harvey, 1967, p. 127].

Some of them, sooner or later, will begin thinking about the same questions of justice and morality that troubled German officers in World War II. Indeed, if they happen to be Catholic and know that the Vatican Council has specifically condemned area bombings as a "crime against God and man himself," their thoughts are even more likely to turn in the direction of dissent, refusal, and, for some at least, desertion. Americans who are willing to join in honoring the memory of the men of July 20 for the conclusions they reached and the consequences they drew from them should be able at least to understand the men in our armed forces who have chosen to dissociate themselves from the war effort in Vietnam.

For American Catholics this should not be much of a problem at all. After all, the whole issue revolves about the recognition and application of two familiar and fundamental moral principles. Every man, it has always been taught, has a personal moral obligation to form a right conscience on all actions he is asked to support or ordered to perform. The second follows from this: having formed his conscience, he is obliged to act according to its dictates—even, if we may revert to the much abused phrase in the moral-theology handbooks, when he is the victim of an "erroneous conscience." The Archdiocese of Detroit has spelled this out in the context most immediately relevant to this discussion; in the words of one of its synodal documents, it is "each man's burden in conscience to decide the rectitude of his country's policies as a world power, or its involvement in the armament race, or of its participation in wars against other men" (*Milwaukee Journal,* 1969).

If this is true as a general rule, it must be true in particular application to the men in the armed services, and that for two reasons. First, they are in the best position to judge from their own experience the nature, the scope, and the effects of their nation's policies relating to "participation in wars against other men." Second, they know that it is they who bear the immediate and direct responsibility for performing the actions determined by those policies, a knowledge that makes what is "each man's burden in conscience to decide" an inescapable obligation for them.

This is easy enough to say, but if we return to the special vulnerability of the serviceman trapped in an authority structure which has the power and the means to punish and even destroy him, it must not stop at that. Those of us who are "on the outside" have a responsibility to furnish him with the support and, wherever possible, the protection he needs. At the very least, really to assure the man in uniform of his basic rights under the First Amendment, we must strive to establish and maintain contact with the dissent (and the dissenters) who are causing the military establishment the "concern" of which General Westmoreland spoke. The civilian Resistance has made an important and valuable beginning in helping to establish the coffee houses mentioned earlier and in aiding the production and distribution of the underground service papers. The more "respectable" segments of American society ought to take it from there and exert what influence they can to make sure that the man in the armed forces is able to exercise freely the rights for which he is supposedly fighting. So that when the military authorities move to "crack down" on dissent as they did (but with slight success) at Fort Jackson or when they set out to punish (with complete success) a Sgt. Sanders for speaking his mind, these actions must not go unprotested.

But protest, as we have learned to our dismay in the case of the "Presidio 27," may not be enough. A major restructuring of military judicial procedures is probably required. At the very least, it is essential that the civilian judiciary be opened to appeals from the overly harsh and arbitrary exercise of military authority. There has been for far too long a disposition on the part of our courts, including the Supreme Court, to maintain a hands-off policy in the area of military "justice" (actually a judicial "cop-out" that extends for the most part to Selective Service procedures and decisions as well). This policy should be reversed. Whatever inconvenience it may cause the military to have its courts martial made subject to judicial review would be a small price to pay for assuring men in service, most of them there through no choice of their own, of their basic rights as American citizens.

The protection of the soldier's right to simple dissent must be expanded to provide for less restrictive procedures for granting discharge on grounds of service-associated (not merely *initiated*) conscientious objection. The most pressing need is for recognition of selective conscientious objection, a change that should be adopted with respect to the civilian objector as well. Other changes should be introduced to remove the special disabilities placed upon the soldier whose conscience tells him he may no longer serve. The psychiatric interview must be eliminated as a specified part of the procedures. If, after due consultation with chaplain or commanding officer, an individual elects to discuss his stand with a psychiatrist (assuming, needless to say, that the "agreement" is not imposed by undue pressure), this would be quite proper; but neither the conference protocols nor its results should be linked to the substance of his conscientious objection. By the same token, the individual claimant should suffer no threatened or actual loss of rights he may have earned up to the time of his discharge. Elementary justice would require that even the time that elapses while his application is "in the works" should be counted as time spent as a full-fledged serviceman with all the rights and privileges this would imply.

The most important procedural change, however, involves the redefinition of the role of the chaplain. Here, too, whatever consultation takes place should be at the soldier's option and not a required part of the process. After all, civilian objectors are no longer obliged to establish a formal religious basis for their claim; they never were required to have prior consultation with a clergyman of any kind, much less a "hostile" clergyman such as the military chaplain is very likely to be.

Hostility or, if this is too strong a term, a lack of receptivity toward the conscientious objector and his stand will probably constitute a serious block to rapport in those cases, presumably the majority, in which the applicant does choose to request a consultation. It is of utmost importance, then, both to the soldier and to the military itself, that the chaplaincy institute special training for its men to provide them with the theological grasp and the emotional detachment this extremely sensitive situation requires. The writer's study of the RAF chaplaincy revealed a broad discrepancy in attitudes toward service-originating conscientious objection. Almost all respondents described the chaplain's responsibility in terms of determining the sincerity of the applicant, and fully 80 per cent assured me that, once convinced of a man's sincerity, most chaplains could be expected to help him gain release from the service or, at the very least, a transfer to other duties. Some, however, would be prepared to "advise" the sincere claimant, but would not go so far as to "assist" him. Others would try to persuade him to continue his service even in cases where they felt the man was sincere in his objection and, where this advice is not followed, would refer him to a psychiatrist or do what they could to prepare him to take whatever penalty he would have to face. An occasional padre would leave the whole matter in the hands of the military, and there were even one or two whose minds were so closed on this issue that they were literally unable to discuss it in any other context than the old, familiar "lack of moral fibre." Common to all the responses, however, was the unmistakable assumption that the investigation of the applicant's "sincerity" would have to take the form of the chaplain's arguing against the position taken and "correcting" him with respect to whatever theological arguments or interpretations he might advance in its favor (Zahn, 1969, pp. 124–131).

There is no reason to assume it would be different with the American chaplaincy. A recent handbook sets forth a rather extensive, though super-ficial, summary of the chaplain's ministry. A chapter devoted to conscien-tious objection, predictably enough, is devoted almost entirely to the civilian objector. The situation of the men who become CO's after induction into the armed forces is described as "discouraging," the author going so far as to note that an applicant whose request for *non-combat-duty* has been denied and who refuses to obey subsequent orders "will be arrested, court-martialled and imprisoned." As far as procedures for seeking *discharge* are concerned, "the prospects are dismal. Since the Spring of 1966 virtually all applications have been denied" (Swanson, 1968, p. 47). Significantly enough, the question of what the chaplain could, or should, be prepared to do to assist these men is ignored completely.

Two cases which have come to my attention provide something of an answer. Both reveal a shocking lack of concern and, to make matters worse, a gross incompetence on the part of the chaplains involved. The first involves a young man who was seeking discharge from one of the major army camps in the West. Included in the file he submitted for my information was a letter from a chaplain to the commanding officer reporting upon the inter-view conducted pursuant to the Army regulations in which he concluded, "I feel he is sincere in his feelings toward the morality of war, however he cannot cite any official doctrine of the Catholic Church to support his personal position." The finding is disturbing on two counts. First, the young man's application *did* cite a number of scriptural references, and these were supplemented by quotations from the speeches and writings of popes, theologians, and saints as well as from the official documents of the Second Vatican Council. A judgment that none of these may be taken to represent "official doctrine" of the Church is perhaps true enough in the strictest sense of formally defined dogma; but this was not what seems to have been meant. The second serious fault follows from this in that any judgment con-cerning the theological correctness or validity of the applicant's position was distinctly out of place. The only question with which the Army or any of its functionaries (including the chaplain) could legitimately be concerned is the question of the individual's sincerity. In that event, then, this chaplain's gratuitous intrusion of his own theological opinion was unnecessary and improper (not to mention unsound in the bargain), and could only serve to jeopardize the young man's chances for favorable action on his application.

In the hope of correcting this injustice and possibly avoiding its duplication elsewhere, I wrote to the Catholic Military Vicar, Terence Cardinal Cooke, requesting that he issue a general instruction to his chaplains clarifying this point. In reply, the Chancellor of the Military Ordinariate not only failed to address himself to the problem I had sought to raise but revealed a surprising level of unfamiliarity with the Army regulations as they apply to such cases. "I can understand the viewpoint of the Army," he wrote, "which wonders why a young man did not ask his draft board to change his status to 'Conscientious Objector.'" As he saw it, "this is more a problem for the draft board rather than for the Army." Certainly so highly placed an official of the military establishment should have known that once a man is inducted into the armed services, the draft board has no further jurisdiction in such matters; furthermore, according to the Army regulation quoted earlier, any pre-induction conscientious objection, whether stated or not, would be excluded from consideration in this case. Ignorance of these rather basic items of procedure is troubling enough. Much more serious, however, is the prevailing note of disinterest arising from the over-eager readiness to give such weight to the "viewpoint of the Army" that the possibility of serious injustice being done is passed over without comment. A second letter to Cardinal Cooke, reminding him of the limitations spelled out in the Army regulations and repeating my original request, was not even acknowledged. Fortunately, as things worked out, the young man's application for discharge was ultimately approved.

The second case tells much the same story without the happy ending. This application, too, was denied because someone in the military hierarchy decided that conscientious objection was not compatible with membership in the Roman Catholic Church—although, once again, the application included an impressive array of scriptural and conciliar citations. Since the documents that came into my possession did not include a chaplain's report or recommendation, I addressed a letter to the Senior Catholic chaplain at the base involved requesting additional information and assistance for the young man who was already serving a *second* sentence in the stockade. The overall sequence of events is illuminating. His first application for discharge was denied in June 1968 for the reason noted; a second application two months later was rejected because it was deemed not "substantially" different from the first. As he described his situation in a letter published in his diocesan paper three months after that decision,

> . . . I am now faced with a choice—to follow my conscience and refuse to comply with the Army thereby ending up in jail or compromise my conscience and serve. I had this same "choice" after my first application was refused. I disobeyed an order and spent 19 days in the Stockade. I believe this is the only course I can follow to avoid offending the Lord. I have, therefore, recently

disobeyed another order and now await Court Martial and the possibility of a substantially stiffer Stockade sentence [Goguen, 1968].

At the time I wrote to the chaplain, the young man had already entered upon his second sentence and I suggested that his willingness to undergo repeated punishment could be taken as evidence of his sincerity, which, I noted again, was the only legitimate basis on which the military authorities are to decide cases of this kind. There was no response at all to this letter—and as this is being written, several months later, the serviceman is still in the stockade.

One might prefer to idealize the chaplain as a moral guide, ever alert to those elements and temptations in the military situation that might constitute a threat to the spiritual welfare of his charges. This could even imply, under certain circumstances, counseling the men to dissent or, when a clear issue of morality is at stake, disobedience. As these two cases indicate, the reverse is far more likely to be true: when questions of conscience arise, the chaplain and his superiors in the Ordinariate become the advocates of the military establishment and its point of view. If this attitude is general, as I suspect it is, the serviceman is deprived of moral support which should be his, and his vulnerability is greatly increased. It would be well, therefore, to make provision for some disinterested civilian ecclesiastical authority (which, sad to say, will be hard enough to find!) to review all such cases to make certain that men who are sincerely troubled by the moral implications of their military service receive a fair hearing and competent consideration of their claims. Only when this is done can we even begin to hope for any significant improvement in the prospects for separation from service on grounds of conscientious objection.

And unless and until such improvement is forthcoming, we must be prepared to contend with a continuing leakage from the services in the form of what I have called "conscientious desertion." Men who desert because they can no longer take part in a morally repugnant war, and who are, at the same time, realistic enough to "know the score" as far as their chances of winning discharge as conscientious objectors are concerned, are really more the victim than the offender. To the extent that procedures can be liberalized along the lines suggested here, the problem will diminish and, in time perhaps, disappear altogether. For the moment, however, we are still left with the thousands of "unauthorized separations" from the military service. It would seem entirely appropriate to introduce a general policy under which all charges arising out of the act of desertion are dismissed for those men who can establish the moral foundation of their original decision. What I am proposing is not simply a matter of granting amnesty; rather it would be an attempt to redress the balance by giving these men the honorable discharge that would have been theirs under a fairer system of granting recognition and respect for the rights of conscience. This proposal should not be taken to imply that the writer would be equally in support of amnesty for the others as well. It is to be hoped that, once the war in Vietnam has come to an end, there will be a general amnesty for all who have violated the draft laws or who have been imprisoned for other forms of opposition to the war effort. This is not, however, strictly relevant to the thesis presented in this paper.

These are not really such radical proposals if we put them in the perspective of the human rights and values we so regularly proclaim. The conscience of the soldier, whether draftee or volunteer, is just as sacred as the conscience of the civilian. One of the essential marks of a democratic order is the recognition it gives to the widest range of beliefs and opinions consistent with the common good and the special protection it provides to a diversity of religious commitments. Our conscription laws, imperfect as they are, go part of the way toward meeting this test. Our military regulations and procedures, on the other hand, provide few or no guarantees of the basic rights of the individual subject to them; and this is complicated even further in the case of the military dissenter and conscientious objector by the spirit of resentment and indignation in which those regulations and procedures are most likely to be applied.

However much justification they may have had in other places or at other times, the time has come for us to abandon the old models of a military order based upon the arbitrary exercise of authority coupled with unquestioning obedience. If the wars of recent history have taught us nothing else, we should know now that a man can no longer be permitted to suspend his conscience merely because he has put on the military uniform. This is what the men of July 20 taught us when they converted treason into an act deserving highest honor. The Nuremberg Tribunal made it a matter of declared principle carrying the weight of international law.

> Principle III. The fact that a person who committed an act which constitutes a crime under international law acted as Head of State or responsible government official does not relieve him from responsibility under international law.

> Principle IV. The fact that a person acted pursuant to order of his Government or of a superior does not relieve him from responsibility under international law, provided a moral choice was in fact possible for him [Melman & Falk, 1968, p. 43].

With weapons of world-destroying potential already at hand, it is imperative that we reaffirm the responsibility and protect the right of each individual to form a personal moral judgment concerning the military programs and policies of his nation's rulers. The day may yet come when the conscience of some disobedient soldier may be the last remaining hope for the survival of man.

REFERENCES

Berrigan, D. J. (s.J.) *The trial of the Catonsville nine.* Boston: Beacon, 1970.
Connor, A. O. *Milwaukee Journal,* June 20, 1969.
Fitzgibbon, C. *20 July.* New York: Norton, 1956.
Gardner, F. *Unlawful concert: An account of the Presidio mutiny case.* New York: Viking, 1970.
Goguen, P. W. Letter. *Catholic Free Press* (Worcester, Mass.), October 25, 1968.
Gollwitzer, H., *et al. Dying we live: the final messages and records of the resistance* (trans. by R. C. Kuhn). New York: Pantheon, 1956.
Harvey, F. *Air war—Vietnam.* New York: Bantam, 1967.
Larner, J. Courtmartial of Captain Noyd. *Harper's Magazine,* 1968, *236* (6), 78–80 (June, 1968).
Melman, S., & Falk, R. *In the name of America.* New York: Clergy and Laymen Concerned about Vietnam, 1968.
Milwaukee Journal. March 30, 1969.
Swanson, E. I. *Ministry to the armed forces.* Washington, D.C.: General Commission on Chaplains and Armed Forces Personnel, 1968.
Trillin, C. U.S. Journal: Clovis. *New Yorker,* 1968, *44* (6), 106–113 (March 30, 1968).
von Hoffman, N. The conviction of Captain Levy. *New Republic,* 1967, *156* (24), 9–11 (June 17, 1967).
Zahn, G. C. *The military chaplaincy: A study of role tension in the RAF.* Toronto: University of Toronto Press, 1969.
Zeller, E. *The flame of freedom: The German struggle against Hitler.* Coral Gables: University of Miami Press, 1969.

Conscience and the Civil-Rights Worker

JOHN A. MORSELL

John A. Morsell received his bachelor's degree from the City College of New York in 1934, his master's degree in social legislation from Columbia University in 1938, and his doctoral degree in sociology, also from Columbia, in 1951. In 1956 he joined the staff of the National Association for the Advancement of Colored People (NAACP), where he is currently the assistant executive director. For the previous five years he was a study director with International Research Associates, and in this capacity he participated in research assignments taking him to the Far East, Europe, and South America. Other previous work by Dr. Morsell includes: Study Director, Bureau of Applied Research, Columbia University; Director, Institute of Community Relations, Sydenham Hospital; member, research staff, Mayor's Commission on Conditions in Harlem; member, field staff, studying effects of racial integration in the U.S. Army; and Chairman, Citizens Advisory Committee, New York City Housing and Development Administration. Dr. Morsell is the author of an impressive number of articles in technical journals, in symposia, and in magazines.

When I first considered the subject of Conscience and the Civil Rights Worker, it seemed to me that no issue of consequence could possibly be posed, since civil-rights work is an example *par excellence* of a good work and, hence, in unquestioned conformity with the dictates of conscience. One might argue, to be sure, that support of *apartheid* in South Africa is presumably an exercise of conscience, given the assumptions on which it rests; but this is an invitation to explore moral relativity and calls for an entirely different class of argument from that with which we are concerned in this Institute.

CONSCIENCE IN GENERAL

However little I may know of conscience, I am nevertheless certainly conscientious, and having accepted the assignment I had no choice but to wrestle with it. I examined the *Random House Dictionary of the English Language* (1966) and found the following definitions of conscience:

1. The sense of what is right or wrong in one's conduct or motives, impelling one toward right action.
2. The complex of ethical and moral principles that controls or inhibits the actions or thoughts of an individual.
3. An inhibiting sense of what is prudent.

The first of these—"the sense of what is right or wrong"—connotes an instinctual, internal, unstructured guiding impulse. It is an impulse, moreover, "toward right action." It does not reject rationality, but it is certainly not dependent upon rational process.

The second—"the complex of ethical and moral principles"—is much more formal. It clearly assumes that a reasoned process, invoking belief and principle in a systematic way, provides the guidance to conduct. Further, the guidance seeks to "control or inhibit" our actions or thoughts. This second definition moves away from unstructured freedom, from emotion and intuition, and imposes restrictions of a philosophic nature. Its thrust is not toward release but toward discipline.

The third definition is the narrowest of all: it is "an inhibiting sense of what is prudent," which means that the moral component is not essential to it. Its purpose is chiefly to keep one out of trouble, to avoid unpleasant or demanding consequences by a policy of avoidance.

One could extend this kind of amateur exegesis on and on, ending eventually with typologies which any one of us could recognize within his own acquaintance without any difficulty. The comparisons are relevant to virtually all pursuits, including that of civil-rights worker. It requires very little effort, and not too much exaggeration, to distinguish on the American race-relations scene individuals and groups whose commitments and programs are either impulsive, idealistic, and little affected by practicality, or disciplined, rationally organized—and maybe a bit hidebound; or, thirdly, cautious and prudent, reluctant to assume risks, anxious not to offend.

The strong temptation for me would be to hope fervently that my dispositions would combine the best elements of all three, but this is probably asking for too much. Which road one travels—or, more accurately, approximates—depends partly, of course, upon his temperament and partly upon how adequate is his understanding of the cause he serves and the circumstances affecting success or failure. But surely it is a service to "conscience," however that is experienced, to seek as much knowledge and understanding as possible as a foundation for planning and action. Anything less abdicates responsibility, and to be conscientious in the purest sense is impossible without responsibility.

HISTORY OF THE CIVIL-RIGHTS MOVEMENT

What, for example, do we mean by "civil rights" and the "civil rights movement"? It would appear from much of what one reads and hears today that the civil-rights movement began somewhere in the last fifteen years. Ancient veterans will go back as far as the Montgomery, Alabama, bus boycott of 1955–56, and a few of the most grizzled are willing to include May 17, 1954, when the U.S. Supreme Court outlawed racial segregation in the public schools. Most cannot look farther back than to the student sit-in wave of 1960. A great many conceive of the "movement" as starting (and very nearly finishing) with the "Mississippi Freedom Summer" of 1964, when some hundreds of northern white students joined southern Negroes under the aegis of COFO (Council of Federated Organizations)* for two months of exposure and work in behalf of voter registration, poverty reduction, and various other goals.

The Freedom Rides of 1961, the Mississippi and Birmingham, Alabama, demonstrations of 1963, the slayings of Medgar Evers, of Schwerner, Goodman and Chaney, of Viola Liuzzo and others meld in the memory into an imprecise image of action, high-minded dedication, sacrifice, blood and adventure—pervaded by an overwhelming sense of personal involvement—all adding up to the remembered glory of "The Civil Rights Movement." This is so for thousands and thousands of people, especially young people, even though for most it is entirely vicarious.

Now that objective conditions have changed, now that many of the prominent actors have moved off the scene, now that the requirements are

---

* COFO was sponsored by the following organizations: SNCC (Student Nonviolent Coordinating Committee), CORE (Congress of Racial Equality), the NAACP, the SCLC (Southern Christian Leadership Conference), and the National Council of Churches.—Ed.

different, the strategies revised, shifted or supplanted, many have a sense of the end of an era. Since reporters for the mass media, commentators, and intellectuals are as subject to all these effects as are the laity, it is not surprising that a myth of major magnitude has been sold to the public at large: namely, that the civil-rights movement, after its brief, dazzling fling, is over and done with.

Even the most modest and elementary knowledge of the experience of Negroes in America, or of their actions and movements in this century alone, would prevent a serious-minded observer from coming to such a fallacious conclusion. It would become apparent, given this knowledge, that the cult of recency has grown because so many people assume that it all began at about the time they themselves became aware that there was a problem. For example, no one who knew anything about the dark and bloody record of thousands of Negro lynchings, often conducted in incredibly barbarous and savage fashion; about the iron control maintained over southern Negroes by the combination of economic stranglehold and unbridled police power; about the systematic cheating of black children in segregated southern school systems; about the dual system of criminal and civil justice applied to Negroes in the states of the old Confederacy—could have been astonished to find that southern resistance to the youthful reformers would be obdurate, harsh, and deadly, even into the 1960s.

Not knowing these things, such contemporary judges were also, and inevitably, ignorant of what it had taken to make headway of any kind against these barriers. The consequence has been a denigration of the toil and sacrifice (including many, many lives) of black men and women who somehow went up against these monstrous opponents and won toeholds; then footholds; and then beachheads across which the multiplied forces could then advance in relative security.

Surely, the civil-rights movement has to include the boycotts protesting segregated trolley cars in more than twenty-five southern cities (including Montgomery) between 1900 and 1906. It has to include DuBois and Trotter, forming the Niagara Movement in 1905; and the founding of the NAACP in 1909, launching therewith a continuing fight against racism which has completed its sixth decade. The NAACP's 1917 anti-lynching protest march of 20,000 persons down New York's Fifth Avenue; the "Don't Buy Where You Can't Work" campaigns of the 1920s; the one-vote margin by which Judge Parker's nomination to the U.S. Supreme Court was rejected in 1930 following a nationwide fight based on his racial views; the original March on Washington of 1942, leading to a Presidential order directing fair-employment practices in war plants; the abolition of military segregation in 1951; the ordeals at Little Rock, Arkansas, at Clinton, Tennessee, at Mansfield, Texas, and at Clay, Kentucky, when Negro schoolchildren ran the gauntlet of enraged white mobs en route to their classrooms—all these events and many more, involving the active participation of many thousands of people, are part of the civil-rights movement.

Since it is axiomatic that every social development rests in large measure upon those that went before, it is quite certain that no achievement of 1960 or 1965 or 1969 could have come about had not equally significant things happened in 1909 and 1923 and 1954.

THE CIVIL-RIGHTS MOVEMENT TODAY

To be sure, defining the civil-rights movement in its historic fullness does not dispose of the assertion that it is now dead; although it may cause one to question whether such a vital, vigorous, and successful effort of such endurance could be put out of action so abruptly. The truth is that it is only the unique and compellingly dramatic events of a few years—a dozen at the outside and more accurately about half that—which have come to an end. These pregnant years had their historical function to perform and, once done with it, they and their memorable qualities moved on. But they were segments of a continuing sequence, not the start and end of something previously unknown.

For the battles go on, with or without the drama, with or without the glare of publicity. It was about three years ago that we first began to hear the civil-rights death-knell sounded. In those three years, we have enrolled a million-and-a-half black voters in the South, thanks to the 1965 voting-rights act and to the persistent and costly campaigning carried on by the NAACP and others. We have elected Negro mayors in cities ranging from the size of Fayette, Mississippi, and Chapel Hill, North Carolina, to Cleveland, Ohio, and Gary, Indiana; and a Negro won 44 per cent of the Los Angeles vote, where Negroes comprise only 18 per cent of the electorate. There are more than 400 elected Negro officials in the Old South, almost 30 of them in the State of Mississippi.

It continues to be crucial to wage the fight for ending job discrimination and for the massive programs needed to take up the employment slack and to retrain and rehabilitate those left behind in the technological sweep. Equal representation at all levels of government and in every phase of public activity remains an essential goal. Demonstrating and boycotting for jobs and services cannot be abandoned. Negroes are still under pressure to refrain from seeking the ballot; they are still excluded from proper representation in political party organizations. The federal machinery of compliance with existing anti-discrimination law could use twenty times the forces now deployed by the volunteer groups like the NAACP, the Urban League, and the Leadership Conference on Civil Rights, which maintain the continuing effort to see that the guarantees are enforced.

The catalogue could be extended at great length, but I need say only that the NAACP, bigger than ever, with more staff than ever, finds itself more overwhelmed than ever by the volume of demand for its help and by the load of work which this produces. There has been, in a word, no livelier corpse since the beginning of time.

CONSCIENCE AND THE CIVIL-RIGHTS WORKER

The need for civil-rights workers thus continues unabated. Now, as at every stage along the road, they must be dedicated and they must be idealistic. The issue of conscience for them may seem to be resolved by their commitment to the proposition that all men are brothers and that anything that stultifies or represses their God-given right to fulfillment is an evil to be rooted out. But they must also, I believe, serve conscience by performing in a *conscientious* manner. In general, this ought to mean lawfully and peacefully, and it certainly means with compassion. (I do not wish to deal here with the issue of civil disobedience, other than to assert that, if ever justified, it should be used on terms which ensure that it is never anything but a final and desperate resort.)

But acting in a conscientious manner also requires that the civil-rights worker—or, indeed, any kind of worker—live up to some canon of responsibility. This means that every important decision is made with care and with serious regard for fact and reason. It means the avoidance of "easy" choices, particularly those which cater to the popular notions of the moment. No one, to choose a contemporary example, will embrace segregated curricula or segregated dormitories because they are loudly demanded by confused and alienated young Negroes, so long as he has genuine convictions about the evils of segregation based on knowledge and thought.

The civil-rights worker may at times feel that he is a lonely figure maintaining a solitary outpost, and not without some danger. But this is part of his burden, and he cannot forego it as long as he claims a commitment. He is in this fight because he hates injustice and racism; and he identifies racism whether it emanates from a black mind or from a white mind. He believes that, while the odds do not appear any too promising for achievement of the integrated society, they are still far better than for any other visible course of action. And he will preach this gospel to all who will listen; his conscience will permit him to do no less.

REFERENCE

Random House dictionary of the English language (unabridged). New York: Random House, 1966.

Conscience and Student Protest

PATRICK H. RATTERMAN, s.j.

Father Patrick H. Ratterman, S.J. received his bachelor's degree from Xavier University, Cincinnati, in 1941 and licentiates, first in philosophy in 1944, and then in theology in 1951, from Loyola University, Chicago. From 1952 to 1966 he was Dean of Men at Xavier University, Cincinnati, and from 1966 until 1970 he was Vice President of Student Affairs at the same institution. He is currently at the University of Santa Clara. Father Ratterman is a member of the National Association of Student Personnel Administrators, and a member of the Commission on Students and Faculty of the Association of American Colleges, as well as the representative of the latter organization on the Joint Commission on Rights and Freedoms of Students. He has published various articles on the question of student rights and authority on campus, and is the author of The emerging Catholic university *(1968).*

The commencement oratory for 1969 repeated itself over and over at graduation exercises throughout the country: no nation can advance or even survive unless it cultivates idealism in its youth. Student idealism in the United States which protests the injustices and inequities that have become all but institutionalized in our American way of life is to be commended. Universities must not only allow but encourage free expression of student opinion however critical that expression might be of American society. On the other hand, student criticism and protest cannot be tolerated when it becomes violent and seeks its fulfillment through force rather than reason. Student violence not only destroys reasonableness, which should find its sanctuary on the university campus, but invites a corresponding unreasonable reaction such as will inevitably destroy the university itself. So spoke several thousand commencement speakers in early June, 1969.

So many thousand wise men cannot be, nor should they be, contradicted. This paper merely attempts to estimate *some* of the forces behind the movement on U.S. campuses which has excited such univocal commencement oratory. It asks but three questions: First, where does the balance of power lie in the current campus movements as students seek a set of social values with which *in good conscience* they can face the problems which confront American society? Second, how prepared are American colleges and universities to teach students to think with "moral clarity" as they address themselves to social problems? Third, what factors affecting the student movement are likely to obscure "moral clarity"?

CAMPUS PROTEST: AN EXPRESSION OF MORAL JUDGMENT

The current student protest movements on American campuses present many confused and complicated problems. The most radical, nihilistic student groups would maintain that the prevailing socio-economic and educational American systems generate and perpetuate such injustices and inequities that their complete overthrow constitutes a moral imperative. According to their thinking, therefore, any protest or campus disruption which helps to undermine the existing socio-economic system is justified. Whatever comes from the ashes of the resulting conflagration, the radical-nihilist reasons, will necessarily be an improvement. At the opposite extreme, the more moderate student protesters feel that the existing American socio-economic and educational systems, granted the injustices and inequalities they have spawned and currently tolerate, provide the most realistic possibility for overcoming economic and social inequities. The moderate student protesters, therefore, feel that it is morally imperative to work within the system for change and reform. Both groups—the radical-nihilists and the moderates—agree that change is imperative. Both groups agree on the ultimate objective—an order of equal opportunity for all men. They disagree on the manner of change and the proximate values they must currently respect in order to achieve that change.

It is sometimes argued that disturbances on American campuses, instead of reflecting social moral judgments, are clear manifestations of an underlying "plan" or "plot" which is being implanted in student minds and financially supported by outside sources. Without doubt, many campus disorders are planned, and there certainly does exist an overall "plot" in the minds of some radical students to use campus disruptions as a springboard to overthrow the national socio-economic order. Radical student groups have openly proclaimed such a program. Moreover, it would be ridiculous to think that some outside sources are not anxious and willing to contribute generously to the accomplishment of the radical-nihilist goal. However, such opinions fall far short of explaining total campus problems. Campus disorders would by no means be eliminated if all outside sources were somehow prevented from influencing and supporting the nation's radical student movements. American campus problems are basically home-grown. They reflect the problems of conscience which confront loyal American students as they perceive the injustices and inequalities of our present American way of life.

Consolation is sometimes taken in the fact that after all such a very small percentage of students are actually so very radical. It is further felt that if somehow this small percentage could be eliminated from the nation's campuses all problems would vanish overnight. Again, this is to overlook the fact that the problems which the small percentage of radicals bring so forcefully to the attention of the campus community are truly *community* problems. This became so very evident in the Harvard experience where very efficient (and needlessly harsh) efforts to eliminate a small percentage of campus radicals only served to trigger an all-but-universal campus reaction. What began as basically three radical Students for a Democratic Society (SDS) demands—discontinuance of all ROTC programs, an end to ruthless university expansion into poverty areas, and control of a black studies program—escalated overnight into matters of total university concern. Quite evidently, the SDS demands at Harvard were already underlying problems of conscience for a majority of the campus community. The small radical minority was speaking the majority mind probably more than they themselves ever dared dream. The consciences of an alerted center majority were forced to face problems they might otherwise have preferred to ignore.

It is easy enough to identify the small minorities which represent the extremes in today's student movements. Difficulties arise in attempting to describe the ideological positions of the large center majority of American students. For while there are very few confirmed radical-nihilists, as well as very few active moderates, the vast majority of seemingly unconcerned students spread themselves over a spectrum which extends between these two extremes. Moreover, for so many students their precise position on the spectrum shifts considerably depending on the particular issue and circumstances immediately at hand. The phenomena of "lashes" and "backlashes" is characteristic not only of people over thirty but of students as well. The indeterminate center majority, therefore, constitutes in reality a swing group which can be aroused to support a more radical or a more moderate cause depending on their immediate judgment of a current problem and its circumstances.

This is not to argue that the majority of American students endorse a situation-ethic philosophy. Most of them at any particular time have very determined ultimate values according to which they judge right and wrong. However, students who constitute the middle majority are constantly re-examining their values, and as a result are very hesitant to judge others in the light of whatever values they at present hold. They reject all authority in the determination of ultimate values. They are not inclined to accept as established and finalized the traditional dictates of religion, society, or family with respect to right and wrong. "It's a whole new world," they argue against their elders. "You yourselves are questioning and with good reason rejecting many of the social values which for so long you simply took for granted. We have no confidence in the judgments and values you *now* proclaim as sacred in what is obviously a rapidly changing society."

Perhaps such statements tell us more than anything else about the social moral judgments which underlie today's student protest movements. Campus protests constitute an effort on the part of youth to challenge traditional societal values and to establish in their place a set of new values with which they in their lifetimes will be able to live *in good conscience*. They are seeking to determine more proximate norms for the one and only basic principle they universally accept—that men must live together in a world of justice, friendship, and love. Until an order of subordinate values appears which convincingly and realistically complements this ultimate ideal, their own subordinate values will continue to be determined more as a sum of their immediate judgments than by "reasonings from eternal principles." If this is considered a quite pragmatic approach to the ideal of justice, friendship, and love, the students argue, so be it.

It seems apparent that the ultimate problem confronting youth today—a continuously unresolved problem—is one of moral decision, and this in the context of youth's rejection of traditional, authoritarian moral judgments. Young people are determined to reach their own moral decisions on the problems which confront mankind. Ultimately, therefore, the problem of youth today is one of conscience. To underestimate this fact is to miss the issue at hand with sometimes dreadful consequences. Police methods might provide an immediate and necessary answer to one or the other more preposterous and violent campus disturbance, but they provide no ultimate answer. Unwisely used, police methods only complicate the moral judgments which the center majority of students must ultimately face.

STUDENT CONSCIENCE IS SELF-DETERMINING

The college and university campus is becoming more and more the place where the center majority of students make their decisions with respect to the great moral issues which confront American society. It is, therefore, becoming the place where the moral consciences of young people are being determined. Once again it is important to stress that the consciences of young people are for the most part being *self*-determined since students are not disposed today to accept uncritically the moral judgments of their elders. They insist on making their own judgments. If this is true, a very key question must logically be asked: does the modern American campus provide a situation in which students can be helped to make honest and objective moral judgments with respect to the problems which confront the American society?

In a paper* prepared for the 1969 Conference of the National Association of Student Personnel Administrators, Dr. Lloyd J. Averill, Distinguished Professor of Sociology at Ottawa University, gives considerable attention to the problem faced by American colleges and universities in aiding students to develop a capacity for what he terms "moral clarity" in their thinking. Basic to his whole consideration, Dr. Averill insists, must be a willingness to discuss *in the classroom* ("not only in the counseling office and in dormitory bull sessions, not only in deans' offices and in occasional conversations with teachers in the coffee shop, but precisely at the heart of the educational enterprise, the academic classroom") what he terms "the pre-moral dimensions of experience." "The question, Who am I?," Dr. Averill points out, "is existentially prior to, What shall I do?" and must be discussed as the heart of the educational effort if the college is to impart a significant moral dimension to student thinking. A college can contribute to "moral clarity" in student thinking, Dr. Averill maintains, only if it is prepared to deal openly and honestly with the questions men ask about themselves. "When that which is most human is evaded and avoided," he warns, "moral clarity is subverted."

Let there be no misunderstanding. Dr. Averill does not suggest the imposition of moral views by any arbitrary university authority. On the contrary, he insists upon a clear exposition of moral implications and alternatives by faculty and administrators who, nevertheless, are not afraid to make their own moral commitments visible. Moreover, he maintains, this must be done in an institutional framework where "values which are held in common by the community of scholars" are clearly enunciated.

* This paper, entitled: Student value development: Whose concern? was presented at the 51st Annual Conference of the National Association of Student Personnel Administrators (NASPA), held at the Jung Hotel, New Orleans, Louisiana, April 13–16, 1969. It is contained in a special volume circulated among NASPA members prior to the Conference, but as far as can be ascertained, has not appeared elsewhere.—Ed.

Whether or not one agrees with Dr. Averill's precise prescription for teaching students to think with "moral clarity," the urgency for colleges and universities to address themselves to this overall student need cannot be minimized. Once again, let it be said that the university campus is more and more the place where students make, and will be making, their moral decisions with respect to the great moral issues which confront American society. Either American universities adapt themselves to teaching students how to make these decisions rationally and intelligently or they will fail miserably in their responsibility to the American society and perhaps suffer the loss of their independence and even their identity in the process.

How prepared is the American university "to deal openly and honestly with the questions men ask about themselves"? Rightly or wrongly, education has developed as a problem-solving agent in American society. America has always regarded education as the ultimate solution to all its problems. Education has been used to solve the nation's agricultural and manufacturing problems. America has used its colleges and universities to prepare young men for professional and business careers and in doing so has developed the most tremendous economic potential ever known in the history of the world. However, in using education to achieve these material gains, America may well have disqualified its educational system as an agent which is adaptable to teaching students to think with "moral clarity."

Why is it that the educational system itself does not call the attention of students to the social ills of the nation, rather than leaving it to radical student movements to do so? Are the nation's campuses so committed to the vocational preparation of young people for the "American economic dream" that its colleges and universities form a partnership with business and professional interests which blinds them to the problems created by the nation's ever-increasing material productivity?

The phenomenon of American college and university education's being so closely associated by vocational training with American economic productivity presents further problems. An educational system which is committed to such an extent to the service of the American economy is not likely to attract or develop a significant number of faculty members who are dedicated to a consideration of the larger problems confronted by society. Moreover, large numbers of students entering such an educational system are likely to be motivated only by the material advantages which such an education promises. Were it not for the current student protest movements, a vast majority of both faculty members and students on American campuses could very easily constitute a self-perpetuating community whose interests and insights would not extend to the basic social issues of the day.

If this analysis is in any part true, American colleges and universities are ill-prepared to deal with the criticism of American society which radical students are fomenting. In the years ahead it will develop as a major university responsibility to guide the center majority of students to judge the social issues of the day with "moral clarity." It is not at all certain that university faculty members (and administrators) are prepared in large numbers, by either training or inclination, to assume this responsibility. In this sense American campuses seem ill-prepared to provide a situation in which students will be helped in the years immediately ahead to make honest and objective moral judgments with respect to the serious problems which will increasingly confront American society.

THE UNIVERSITY'S ROLE IN STUDENT STRIVING FOR MORAL CLARITY

A number of factors, all indirectly affecting the "moral clarity" of student social-value judgments, will become increasingly important in the years ahead. All these factors indicate that student movements on the nation's campuses will become a great deal more forceful and self-righteous. Self-righteousness and forcefulness constitute a truly frightening combination. These are the elements which, wrongly directed, can twist sane and wholesome idealism into a blind and fateful fanaticism. There is no guarantee against such a twisting except that colleges and universities accept as a primary responsibility in the years immediately ahead the task of teaching students to think with "moral clarity."

The *first* factor is that of sheer numbers. Population statistics indicate that within very few years the average age of the American citizen will have dropped to twenty-five years while college and university enrollments will have risen from the present figure of near 7.0 million to 8.5 and possibly even 9.0 million. These figures indicate that a tremendous amount of youthful idealism will find forceful expression (in numbers if in nothing else) in the decade ahead. No nation in history has ever attempted to make a university education available to such a large number or to such a large percentage of its population. What must not be overlooked is that while a good education teaches students to be critical, students are most likely to criticize that which is nearest at hand—the American society. Whether or not American society, and its universities, will be able to accept, absorb, and benefit by such an avalanche of idealistic social criticism is question enough. But even more crucial will be the problem of preventing this massive idealistic criticism from degenerating in large part into blind, ill-conceived, and self-destroying fanaticism.

A *second* factor which is already increasingly affecting student movements is the instant communication which students possess. It is already taken for granted in campus demonstrations that the news media, in particular the television cameras, are always notified to be on hand. The full effect of such complete student news-coverage is still to be felt. The United States has not yet experienced a united student movement which simultaneously arouses the moral indignation of millions of students throughout the land in support of a common cause. Such a movement in France all but brought an immediate collapse of the French government. American student movements will certainly become more unified and effective as a result of instantaneous and more complete news-coverage. Bigness and unity beget a sense of self-righteousness which in turn serves to confuse the "moral clarity" with which students view either the issues at hand or the consequences of their actions.

An important *third* factor with respect to student movements on American campuses is the force which is generated by success. It cannot be overlooked that to date student protests and demonstrations have been remarkably effective. It was only three or four years ago that the few students who raised their voices in protest against the war in Vietnam were considered a small clique of crackpots. That small clique has just about carried its day as the movement has swelled throughout the nation's campuses. In other areas, too, such as the reform of university government, the student voice is having an increasing impact. Success, however, like unified numbers, breeds its own sense of being right and lessens the likelihood of a calm, critical appraisal of the full implications of programs which excite an emotional, sometimes violent, student support.

A *fourth* key factor in student movements is frustration. Oddly enough, frustration not only is compatible with success but is generated by it if the success in question is only partial. Partial success generates a further expectancy which can be unrealistic—at least for a time. Students have already manifested their impatience with "law and order" solutions which must be worked out through "established channels," suspecting that law and order and channels are being used, as indeed they can be used, to obstruct change and prevent reform. Youth is driven by a "now" imperative for which an immediate, total solution provides the only satisfying answer. Anything short of this can easily result in a mounting frustration which generates its own blind violence.

The four factors—numbers, unity through communications, success, and frustration—are important to the present consideration of "Conscience and Student Protest" because in combination they breed an unreasoned righteousness and minimize the likelihood of "moral clarity" in student thinking. Such self-righteousness can make it very difficult for students not to accommodate conscience to the cause and its immediate accomplishment, rather than the other way around. Even now, the many "non-negotiable demands" with which universities are confronted exemplify the type of accommodation of conscience to cause which can be expected to increase as a larger, more unified student movement asserts itself, reinforced by the simultaneous experience of both success and frustration.

CONCLUSION

The considerations proposed in this paper perhaps seem ominous. The student movement can be expected to gather momentum through a combination of numbers, unity, success, and frustration. At the same time, there appears little likelihood that American colleges and universities are prepared to teach the middle majority of students to judge with "moral clarity" the full implications of the issues behind which the movement will attempt to rally student support. Many long, dark winters appear in the offing. However, a longer-range view may prove more encouraging. Two initial factors are important.

The first encouraging factor is the growing conviction of the student majority that "The university must remain open." During the 1968–69 winter the official shibboleth at the University of California at Berkeley was that the university must remain open to guarantee the silent majority their rights to attend classes. The motivation may have reflected an over-solicitous self-concern, but Berkeley did remain open. The silent majority did prevail. The second encouraging factor is the ever-growing insistence by the same center majority, and this without self-concern, that free speech, however critical of American society and its educational system, must be allowed on the campus. These are growing student stands on United States campuses. The university must remain open and free. However vocational its orientation, it must provide a public forum where those who wish to call attention to the injustices and inequities of the American socio-economic and educational systems can be heard.

University campuses on which the center majority refuses to surrender to the ultimate aims of the radical-nihilists to close the university, but simultaneously insists on the right of the most radical students to express their apprehensions with respect to the American way of life, have already taken the *first steps* toward producing a situation where "moral clarity" can develop. Where values which are held in common by the community of scholars are clearly enunciated, where faculty members (and administrators) are not afraid to make their own moral commitments visible—on such campuses there is a reasonable hope that students will learn to ask the pre-moral question "Who am I?" before determining "What shall I do?"

VI
CONSCIENCE AND THE CHURCH

Conscience and Church Authority

AVERY R. DULLES, s.j.

Father Avery Dulles, S.J. received his A.B. degree from Harvard College in 1940, Ph.L. and S.T.L. degrees from Woodstock College, and an S.T.D. from the Gregorian University, Rome, in 1960. As a writer, Father Dulles' works include numerous articles on such subjects as ecumenism, revelation, and apologetics in the standard theological journals, and seven full-length books in-cluding: A testimonial to grace *(1946);* Apologetics and the biblical Christ *(1963);* The dimensions of the Church *(1967); and* Revelation and the quest for unity *(1968). He serves on the Catholic Commission on Intellectual and Cultural Affairs, the Advisory Council for the United States Catholic Conference, and is a consultant to the Papal Secretariat for Dialogue with Non-Believers. Father Dulles is associate professor of systematic theology at Woodstock College.*

From my own area of specialization, I intend to address this topic not from the point of view of the moralist but from that of the systematic theologian. Accordingly, I shall understand the term "conscience" not as a judgment regarding the rightness or wrongness of a particular course of external behavior but as a man's personal judgment regarding what he should believe. Freedom of conscience obtains when a man is able to make this decision sincerely and spontaneously, without undue moral or psychological pressures. By "authority" I shall understand not the Church's power to command or to forbid certain external actions but rather its claim to teach in a way that calls for internal assent. Limiting my topic yet further, I shall omit all consideration of the unofficial authority of the scholar, the man of experience, and the charismatic, important though their role in the Church is. I shall confine my attention to the official magisterium, which claims to issue binding doctrinal pronouncements. How can the imposition of official doctrine be reconciled with the freedom of the individual believer?

THE FREEDOM OF CHRISTIAN FAITH

The conflict between freedom and authority, which arises in one form or another in all societies, is particularly poignant in the Church. For the Church is a society of faith, and faith, by its nature, is a free act. According to Vatican Council II, in its Declaration on Religious Freedom, "it is one of the major tenets of Catholic doctrine that man's response to God in faith must be free" (Vatican Council II, 1966, n. 9, p. 689). Christian faith, moreover, claims to enhance man's freedom. In the New Testament, Paul exultantly declares that Christ has set us free "from the law of sin and death" (Rom 8:2). "For freedom," he declares, "Christ has set us free. . . . Do not submit again to a yoke of slavery" (Gal 5:1). Christian freedom rests upon the gift of the Holy Spirit. "For you did not receive the spirit of slavery to fall back into fear, but you have received the spirit of sonship" (Rom 8:21). The faithful are called to "the glorious liberty of the children of God" (Rom 8:21), for, as Paul declares elsewhere, "where the Spirit of the Lord is, there is freedom" (2 Cor 3:17). The fourth Gospel likewise stresses freedom as one of the most precious fruits of Christian faith. "If you continue in my word," says Jesus, "you are truly my disciples, and you will know the truth, and the truth will make you free" (Jn 8:32). "If the Son makes you free you will be free indeed" (Jn 8:36).

That these assertions are not empty words is verified by the experience of countless Christians. Those who take the gospel seriously, and commit themselves to it, are wonderfully liberated from servitude to passion in its various forms and are emancipated from earthly attachments which could inhibit their self-mastery. Faith gives men courage to renounce all things, and to stand up unflinchingly against the threats of persecutors.

THE CHURCH'S FAILURE TO LIBERATE

In our own day, however, many Catholics complain that their faith seems to subject them to a new legalism of doctrine, not less burdensome in its way than the Old Law had been to Paul before his conversion. This malaise is clearly articulated by Charles Davis in his thoughtful testament, *A Question of Conscience.* After referring to some of the New Testament texts just quoted, he remarks that, whereas the early Christians experienced their entry into the Church as a liberation, today the reverse is true.

> A sense of narrowness and restriction pervades the Church. We meet with a suspicion of individual initiative, an anxious fear of new ideas even before they have been examined, a reluctance to discuss reasonably and a pressure to conform. Where is the joy and confidence in the truth which should be the mark of those freed by Christ? . . . Is it surprising that men have thrown off the yoke of the Church as an unbearable oppression? They are looking for freedom; they want to be themselves. They find no signs of a liberation in a life within the Church [Davis, 1967, p. 106].

Many Catholics would reply that the teaching of the Church is in no way contrary to true freedom, but that it fosters this by rescuing men from the slavery of error. Set up by Christ as teacher of all nations, the Church must staunchly adhere to its deposit of faith. Far from changing its doctrine in the light of shifting human opinions, the Church should judge the wisdom of the world in the light of God's revelation. Relying on Christ's assurance "he who hears you hears me" (Lk 10:16), Church authorities may rightfully exact a religious submission of mind and heart, even though there will always be some who "will not endure sound doctrine" (2 Tim 4:3).

This argument, however, is too authoritarian in character to meet the objections of theologians such as Davis. If we think of the magisterium as if it functioned automatically without dependence on human inquiry and debate, we can easily become victims of a myth of our own making. Modern psychology and theology are at one in pointing out that man likes to prostrate himself masochistically before an imaginary omniscient Church, thereby relieving himself of responsibility for his own religious convictions. With reference to such believers, Hans Küng rightly asks: "Do we not very often find hidden here a flight from personal responsibility disguising itself as loyalty to the Church, a timid lack of self-reliance pretending to be subordination, a misplaced waiting for ecclesiastical direction masked as obedience?" (Küng, 1966, p. 60). Where this mentality prevails, the Church becomes a haven for persons who cannot endure the strains of freedom rather than a place where freedom is achieved. Dostoevsky's parable of the Grand Inquisitor gives classical expression to the Church's perennial temptation to become the enemy of human freedom.

THE MAGISTERIUM IS NOT OMNISCIENT

The myth of an omniscient magisterium with a "direct wire" to heaven is an illusion based on dark psychological tendencies. Certain pastors and religion teachers foster this illusion by exaggerating the authority of ecclesiastical documents and by acting as though conformity with the pope were the essence of religion. Vatican II, in several of its finest documents, cautioned against such extreme authoritarianism, and sought to emphasize the responsibility of the faithful for forming the mind of the Church. The Pastoral Constitution on the Church in the Modern World, for example, declares frankly that the pastors of the Church do not always have solutions to every problem which arises, and acknowledges that, in the complicated and rapidly changing world of our day, the Church needs special help from experts in various sciences in order to "hear, distinguish and interpret the many voices of our age, and to judge them in the light of the divine Word" (Vatican Council II, 1966, nn. 43–44, pp. 243–247). In general, the Pastoral Constitution, following sound theological principles, greatly helped to dealienate and humanize the Catholic understanding of religious knowledge.

To make further progress in overcoming the dilemma of freedom vs. conformity in the Church, several practical steps may be proposed. For one thing, we need a more realistic theology of the magisterium. As already noted, the magisterium is not omniscient; it has no power to pass judgment on questions that belong properly to human sciences such as history, physics, and philosophy. Even in the religious area, its task can be little more than to find new ways of expressing the gospel of Jesus Christ. In working out new formulas of faith, the magisterium has to cooperate closely with the theologians and the faithful. In so doing it will not avoid all error, but it will minimize the number and seriousness of its mistakes.

In this connection, there is need of a theology of the Church's fallibility. While everyone knows that the Church sometimes makes mistakes, we still treat this too much as a theologically embarrassing anomaly, thus betraying our own failure to grasp the consequences of the Church's pilgrim state. Connected with this is an all-too-common concept of faith as a "blank check" by which we commit ourselves to whatever the Church teaches—as though the content really made no difference. In some juridicizing theories, the motive for the assent of faith would seem to be the will of the magisterium rather than God Himself in His truthfulness. Once we eliminate this confusion between God's authority and that of the Church, we can begin to develop a theology of conscientious dissent within the Church. Assent should never be automatic. Every Christian has the right and duty to use critical good sense. The authority of the magisterium should be prudently weighed against the evidence of reason and against other authorities, such as the consent of the theologians and the sense of the faithful.

IMPROVED ATMOSPHERE OF FREEDOM NEEDED IN THE CHURCH

Occasionally, of course, the Church claims to make use of its power to teach infallibly the revelation committed to it by Christ. Assuming that he has satisfied himself that the magisterium has not exceeded its mandate, the Catholic will of course wish to assent to such teaching. But even here, one should be on guard against feeling obligated to believe too many things. The Decree on Ecumenism acknowledged a hierarchical order of doctrines, varying in their relationship to the fundamental Christian faith (Vatican Council II, 1966, n. 11, p. 356). Primary emphasis should always be given to the gospel, the good news of God's saving action in Jesus Christ. Some secondary doctrines, even though they may once have been defined, are to-day of only peripheral significance, and need not be urged as if they were still crucial. Perhaps one may apply to dogmatic theology the principle which, in moral theology, has been called "parvitas materiae." Matters of trivial moment should not be treated as if they were all-important.

To draw a sharp line between fundamental and non-fundamental truths of faith is of course impossible, as the Fundamentalists of every generation have discovered. But for men of a given era living in a given sociocultural situation, we can sometimes say that a certain doctrine is clearly not decisive. For most of our contemporaries, for example, it is inconsequential what the shape of the glorified body is to be. For this reason I believe they should not be anathematized, as the Origenists were, for holding that the risen body would be spherical (Denzinger-Schönmetzer, 1963, n. 407). To give another example, I might add that I see no reason for demanding that men of our day should affirm that Cornelius Jansen understood his condemned propositions in the very same sense in which they have been condemned. If the Jansenists in the seventeenth century were required to accept this view, that is no reason why men of the twentieth century should be similarly obliged (cf. Denzinger-Schönmetzer, 1963, n. 2012). One might even ask whether the doctrine of indulgences, as defined against Luther, is so central in our day that anyone should be ejected from the Church for denying it (cf. Denzinger-Schönmetzer, 1963, n. 1449). Just as new anathemas can from time to time be imposed, as circumstances require, so too, it would seem, old anathemas can, in principle, be lifted.

To avoid misunderstanding, let me hasten to add that I am not advocating indifference to truth or historical relativism. I recognize that truth is a value in itself, and that what was once true remains true. But propositional truth assumes its true meaning and importance within a historical and spiritual context, and as the context changes, there may be reasons for relaxing certain prescriptions. To deny matters that are no longer central to anyone's concerns should not be considered tantamount to making "shipwreck of the faith" (cf. Denzinger-Schönmetzer, 1963, n. 2804).

I should like to mention just one more measure which I think might improve the atmosphere of freedom in the Church. In the present situation of doctrinal fluidity, the magisterium should be very reluctant to issue definitive pronouncements which purport to settle controverted questions. Vatican II, guided by the sure instinct of Pope John XXIII, already followed this policy. It recognized that doctrinal leadership for today must consist in giving light and in persuading, rather than in demanding submission under pain of canonical or other penalties. As a matter of fact, any attempt to settle controversies by decree is almost foredoomed to failure in the pluralistic Church of our time. The response given to recent papal pronouncements on transubstantiation, on clerical celibacy, and on artificial contraception proves that the attempt to use the authority of office to terminate the discussion often merely fans the flames of controversy.

THE CHURCH REMAINS A VOLUNTARY SOCIETY

I recognize, of course, that the Church must draw the line somewhere. Being essentially a community of faith and witness, it must stand by its original commitment to the gospel and firmly reject positions evidently incompatible with this commitment. But the obligation to belong to a voluntary society, such as the Church, is not unconditional. If anyone feels in conscience that he cannot accept the Church's basic stance, he should not be made to feel guilty about leaving. Catholic pastors and educators should not so inhibit the psychological freedom of the faithful that they can no longer take any responsible attitude, either for or against the Church. At such a price, it would not be worth while trying to keep people within the fold. We must have enough faith to believe that in the long run it is better for mature people to follow their conscience in full freedom than to be kept in servile dependence, even though we may regret the immediate consequences of a particular conscientious decision.

The tragedy today is that so many leave the Church not because they reject Christ but because the Church does not seem to be Christian enough. Perhaps if we can make the Church appear once more as a place of freedom, this phenomenon will be less widespread. In any case, the power of Christian witness never came chiefly from numbers. A few thousand free and committed believers, enthusiastic for the faith, can do more than many millions, if the majority of these millions are sullen, bored, unhappy, and oppressed. The more vividly the Church can recapture the exhilarating sense of freedom that characterized it in New Testament times, the more effectively it will bear witness to Christ in the world, and the more powerfully it will attract those who are drawn by the grace of Christ.

REFERENCES

Davis, C. *A question of conscience.* New York: Harper & Row, 1967.
Denzinger, H., & Schönmetzer, A. (s.J.) *Enchiridion symbolorum definitionum et declarationum de rebus fidei et morum.* (32nd ed.) Freiburg: Herder, 1963.
Küng, H. *Freedom today* (trans. by C. Hastings). New York: Sheed & Ward, 1966.
Vatican Council II. W. M. Abbott (s.J.) (Ed.) *The documents of Vatican II.* New York: Herder & Herder, 1966.

The Conscience of the Religious Leader

JOHN V. O'CONNOR, S.J.

*Father John V. O'Connor, S.J. received an A.B.
degree in 1939 and an M.A. in 1942 from Boston
College. He then earned an S.T.L. from Weston
College in 1946 and finally an S.T.D. from the
Gregorian University, Rome, in 1949. His career
as professor of theology was interrupted by his
appointment in 1949 as Rector of Weston College, the theologate of the New England Province
of the Society of Jesus, and his subsequent appointment in 1962 as Provincial of the New England Province. Currently, Father O'Connor is
Executive Secretary of the Conference of Major
Superiors of Jesuits with an office in Washington,
D.C. There he serves also as a consultant for the
Conference of Major Superiors of Men.*

Our considerations on conscience move now into the atmosphere of the
religious leader where today the pressures and problems seem to change
with each passing half-hour. While major superiors of religious communities
certainly merit the title of religious leaders, for our present purposes attention is directed chiefly to our bishops who in their daily task are brought
into contact with large and varied segments of the people of God. Our concern is about the conscience of a bishop as it is exercised in the area of his
dealings with all those whom he is appointed to lead.

While perhaps no special pleading is needed to dramatize his heavy burden, since each role in life has its own soul-searing cares, we should appreciate the fact that in a particular way a bishop today must daily face pressing difficulties. Now more than ever when someone knocks at his office door or when his phone rings he can presume that the business or the news coming his way will be challenging and may not be too cheerful. In the midst of rapidly changing scenes, with all his strength and weakness he must ask himself, in the presence of God, "What in conscience should I be doing as a leader of the people of God? How should I form my conscience with regard to action in areas directly affecting them, not only in this diocese but in the Church throughout the world?"

GUIDELINES FROM VATICAN II

For guidelines he can read and meditate the Vatican II Decree on the Bishops' Pastoral Office in the Church (Vatican Council II, 1966, pp. 396–429), which spells out his role in terms of service. He is to serve the community as the teacher of doctrine, the priest of sacred worship, and the officer of good order. In virtue of his power, he has the sacred right and duty before the Lord to make laws for his subjects, to pass judgment on them, and to moderate everything pertaining to the proper conduct of worship and the apostolate. With wisdom and prudence he is to guide the people of the New Testament in their pilgrimage towards eternal happiness; he has been enriched by Christ with a special outpouring of the Holy Spirit; and he carries out his function by counsel, exhortation, example.

Moreover, in view of the new emphasis on episcopal collegiality, he is to be aware of the role he plays not only on a local scene but in the universal Church. Hence his vision is to be as wide as the Mystical Body of Christ. He remembers Pope Paul vi's remarks that this whole doctrine of episcopal collegiality is so extremely large that we are not able to penetrate it fully even now and that as the years pass this doctrine will bring on an unheard-of transformation in the life of the Church. In short, the bishop hears the Church telling him in stentorian tones that he stands at the head of the people of God on the threshold of a new era in the history of the Church when long-pent-up energies are being released and rich spiritual resources are being tapped, and the degree to which the potential in his local Church and the universal Kingdom of God will be realized depends in no small measure upon him and the decisions which in good conscience he will make.

He may feel that Vatican II paints an ideal picture of the bishop as religious leader, and that cold realism can shock with the sight of a very different image. A prelate can be conscious of the powers which have been given to him by God, but he can remember also that he is taken from among men and is beset with weaknesses. He knows that bishops in humility have acknowledged how over the years in spite of much good that has been done in the Church there are instances of powers wasted, frittered away by folly, subjected to attrition by selfishness, stubbornness, ignorance, ill temper, and laziness, and all the other sorts of human shortcomings which have clogged up the salutary functioning of the Church.

So, it is with a realistic assessment of his own powers and his limitations that a religious leader approaches his task to decide how he should create an atmosphere which will help all for whom he is responsible to grow steadily in Christ.

THE BISHOP'S OWN SPIRITUAL REFLECTIONS

How is he to do it? I would submit that in the proper formation of his conscience the first exercise for the religious leader is prayer. This may sound somewhat simplistic and even pietistic, but for proper decision-making the religious leader above all others must be one who possesses true spiritual liberty. All of us can subtly and subconsciously design intricate prisons for ourselves and can be bound down by what John Gardner (1965, p. 43) calls "mind-forged manacles." We can be caught in a trap of fixed relationships and set ways of viewing all situations. To lead others, a prelate must extricate himself from such bonds. While there may be various ways to cut the knots and gain freedom and liberty, the main help for the religious leader is prayer. His desire should be liberation from self-seeking prejudice and all personal insecure fixations so that he may be truly open to the Holy Spirit and bent only on the greater apostolic service of the Church. He prays for light, not primarily about the content of a decision to be made but rather about himself, to see what motivation is impelling him, to discern with the help of God's grace the orientation of his thoughts and feelings so that he may truly operate as an instrument in the hands of God.

As a living instrument in the hands of God and free of many hobbling, narrow views, a religious leader will be characterized first of all by an attitude of peacefulness. This is the fruit of a realization that divine providence is disposing all things sweetly and that if God is asking him to face some particular crisis He will always supply the necessary grace to meet the situation well. Hence through his prayer there is developed a quiet trust in God— a calmness. Without this a religious leader could move into a decision-making process tense, over-anxious, and even panic-stricken in the face of persons or situations which seem a threat to him. Instead of being the ambassador of Christ, pondering in quiet prayer the words and wisdom of Christ, he could react frantically and endeavor to settle all his problems with a self-assertive and unnecessary display of power which eventually would create more difficulties than it solves.

Through prayer the religious leader who is truly an instrument in God's hands gains, in addition to calmness, clarity of vision so that he is well-positioned to distinguish goals from means. Unless he is properly oriented, he could even with the best of intentions project himself as a prime example of one who has fallen victim to "Churchianity" instead of being a promoter of Christianity. He could spend himself tirelessly in administering an empire of paper instead of feeding souls. His office files could grow thicker, but the spirit of his people could be running thin; or he could be building the Church and killing the creed. A religious leader at all times must realize that he is exposed to the risk of spending much of his time serving the machinery of the Church instead of serving its members: keeping the ark of salvation afloat and in good running order while the people of God drown in the flood.

Besides calmness and clarity, the religious leader should in prayer seek also, as a third disposition for decision-making, courage to make his way through a maze of obstacles to a high plateau on which he will be well-situated to see the decisions which he must make. The obstacles which I have in mind here are external to the man, but they can pierce to the very marrow of his being. This is particularly true today when it seems to be a popular sport to indulge in bishop-bashing and to promote assaults on authority.

Often the religious leader is subjected to swift, slashing attacks from individuals, which can be discouraging. While the communications media can be his great allies, they can also crucify him. Even within the community of the people of God some of the conversation can become harsh and brutal. There are some who feel that before the Council it seemed as though a bishop could do nothing wrong; since the Council it appears as though no bishop can do anything right. There is a growing concern about the lack of ordinary courtesy and respect in the way even people within the Church deal with one another. But, while this process is working itself out, the religious leader must try to steel his soul with courage and strength derived from prayer so that he may resist any temptation to become petulant or over-timid or fearful.

DATA-GATHERING FOR DECISION

With such dispositions, a religious leader takes a second step in the formation of conscience and moves into the area which is concerned with the process for decision-making—the gathering of data to serve as bases for a decision to be made, for the determination of a course to be followed.

The Vatican Council has noted that the Church brings to the world a deep faith in the divine plan for mankind. But the Council has also noted that the Church has no pat answers to every immediate human problem.

Unshakable confidence of faith may still leave untouched many intractable human problems. In pointing out the method of dealing with such problems the Council in its Pastoral Constitution on the Church in the Modern World stressed the need for competence, the danger of incompetence, and the illusion of omnicompetence: "Let not the layman imagine that his particular pastors are experts, that to every problem that arises, however complicated, they can readily give him a concrete solution, or even that such is their mission" (Vatican Council II, 1966, n. 43, p. 244). Hence to exercise leadership the religious leader must often place himself in the position of a learner. It is his task to read the signs of the times and to amass necessary knowledge and information in order to perceive what problems he should take up and what meaningful and apostolically effective decisions he should make.

The first source of assistance should be found in the themes which the Church is emphasizing today in all its pronouncements—on theology, on the priesthood, on the poor, on developing countries. Everything should be heard and a tendency to view life as compartmentalized should be avoided.

All creation is groaning for God. As St. Paul says, "The whole creation is eagerly waiting for God to reveal his sons . . . ; creation still retains the hope of being freed like us, from its slavery to decadence, to enjoy the same freedom and glory as the children of God" (Rom 8:19, 21).

There should be no picking and choosing in this process of listening to the Church so that one would hear only what one wants to hear. To the extent that one does not hear with exactness and in its entirety what the Church is saying, decisions will be defective.

Assistance from Theologians. Since the understanding of many pronouncements of the Church and the solution of so many problems facing the religious leader require a basis of correct theology, one of the main sources of assistance which exist for the religious leader is the community of first-rate Catholic theologians. I purposely mention *first-rate* theologians because the task of the religious leader is not made easier by the naïve tendency on the part of some to publish theological ideas which have not been sufficiently worked out, to promote them as revelations, and to disseminate them as quickly as possible to people who are not able to understand, to assimilate, or to assess them. Such unbalanced information recklessly broadcast is of little help to anyone and does much harm. In the face of such immaturity on the part of some, a religious leader could be tempted to fight shy of even many excellent theologians and thereby block even a solid internal Church renewal in his diocese. But his attitude should rather be to encourage a corps of sound theologians in their willingness to assist him.

It could be noted that in the past a bishop might have had the practice of turning to only one or two theologians for assistance in the solution of particular problems which faced him. But now a bishop can be better helped if he realizes that he can find in this country a resource group of theologians who are able to present a variety of significant judgments on many-sided problems. Many fine things stand a chance of emerging and developing as never before if such assistance is sought and if the full theological resources of the country are tapped and if all the intellectual talent in a diocese is encouraged for the benefit of both prelate and people.

Happily, communications between theologians and the bishops in recent years have been more and more fostered in various parts of the country. The occasions for greater communication should continue to multiply and the breadth of consultation should be widened.

Assistance from the People of God. In the process for decision-making, the religious leader must turn also to his people for assistance and must learn to listen to all of them. The signs of the time indicate that the Catholic community will regulate its affairs much more by discussion than it did in the past. No longer is it possible in any field—religious, political, or industrial —for a rugged individual leader to employ the intuitive trial-and-error methods which could be tolerated in an era when the pace of change was slower. The decision-making required today demands a much more profound and more rapid grasp of a multiplicity of details in a given situation which a leader cannot hope to search out on his own. So there must be wide consultation to appreciate the full dimensions of the problem with which a leader is dealing—otherwise he could be busying himself with everything but the point at issue.

In this discussion stage, the religious leader must make sure that he himself does not become a victim of "the system." It is amazing to hear today some members of religious congregations remark that their observations and suggestions never seem to reach the ears of their major superiors. The impression is given that the major superior is talking to a star chamber and that he is listening solely to the advice of those closest to him. A religious leader cannot work effectively in such close quarters; in such a confined circle his vision can very easily become narrow. As far as circumstances will permit, the bishop should try to consult directly with people at all levels.

As a listener he must endeavor to understand the proposal of another person as the other intends it, and to comprehend not only what the other person is saying but also the spirit in which his proposal is made and the overtones which it carries. The bishop's presupposition should be that the proposals from his people are based upon true dedication to and love for the Church. In acting in this way, the bishop fulfills the directives of the

Vatican Council, upholds the sense of dignity of the human person, and shows by his example how the Church in his person is coming to the modern world to learn as well as to teach.

In order that discussions with those who are anxious to assist may be fruitful, the religious leader must have a skill with regard to proper planning techniques. He should be able to create an atmosphere for an orderly and intelligent approach to the resolution of Church problems.

He should know how to pry beneath the surface of a problem and to probe its root cause, since not infrequently many people can spend their energies in dealing with a detail which is only a symptom of a much more deep-seated and far-reaching question.

At the same time he must know how to deal with individuals who have not learned the art of proper conversation. There are instances of well-intentioned groups' mapping out programs of action but brooking no opposition. Most people who encounter them react violently because they feel that such people have lost the attribute of Christian charity which is so vital to all. But, a religious leader must know the proper manner of dealing with such groups and individuals, and, even though he may not agree with their methods, he will not be deaf to their message.

It is essential also that the bishop have knowledge of all movements which are taking place within the boundaries of his jurisdiction. This is true even with regard to so-called "underground" projects, because he should have an opportunity to assess these movements so that in his role as the symbol of unity in his diocese he will be able to judge whether or not over the long run these movements will contribute to true edification, to the building-up of the community.

Having garnered with help and assistance from so many sources the data for decision, the religious leader who enjoys the special assistance of the Holy Spirit must now assess them. He must reflect on what the Church tells him, what people have told him, what groups have said, what ideals motivate them. This reflection should take place in a prayerful, meditative way because a bishop is endeavoring to come to a decision which he feels is in accord with the will of God for him and his people.

In some instances in the past, religious leaders have been at pains to publicize their desire to hear from the laity, but their subsequent actions indicated that all the fanfare was merely a façade to give the people a chance to air their grievances: no large amount of attention was given to their suggestions. But a prelate should be prepared to move to a decision.

THE CARRYING-OUT OF DECISIONS

When one passes to a consideration of the execution phase in the decision-making process, the words of John Francis Cardinal Dearden at the opening session of the April 1969 meeting of the hierarchy in Houston, Texas, come to mind. He remarked: "It is not authority that is questioned but the way in which authority is exercised, and it is one of the basic realities of our time that in the Church, as in other institutions, if authority is to retain its credibility it must function in a manner different from that of the past" (Dearden, 1969, p. 2).

The religious leader has the responsibility of exercising extreme delicacy in the carrying-out of the decisions which he has reached. He must know how to balance ever so carefully firmness and gentleness and take steps to protect those whom he is guiding from becoming victims of "the system." It can happen that individuals become caught in a bureaucratic maze even in the Church, and, while their hearts are filled with anguish and suffering, those to whom they turn for help seem to treat them just as numbers instead of as persons.

His method of dealing with people should be one which inspires trust. Vatican Council II (1966, n. 18, p. 37) in its Dogmatic Constitution on the Church recalls the New Testament theme of Christ as the Good Shepherd, the "pattern of authority in the flock" (1 Pet 5:2–4). There is no substitute for the personal relationship of pastor to people. One thinks of St. Augustine's words about St. Ambrose:

> He received me "episcopaliter" and I began to love him first of all not as the teacher of the truth—because I had despaired of finding such in your Church— but as a man who was kindly disposed to me [*Confessions,* 5.13.23].

As a good teacher he will deal with people and will realize that he should prepare his people for the lesson which he is teaching. He must be aware of their capabilities for accepting a certain teaching at a particular time. Otherwise he runs the risk of not being properly understood and of not being heeded.

If those whom he is teaching seem to have become entrenched in certain attitudes and positions, the religious leader must like a talented teacher try to guide such individuals by resorting not to mere authority but to the teaching authority of the Church. Simple condemnation of a certain position can be ineffective, whereas an effort to explain better its opposite in such a way that it is seen not only to be true but also finds its way to the hearts and intellects of the people will often be more effective in rooting out error. Since the religious leader aims to uphold and to bear witness to the truth, he should remember that, if truth is under attack, what ultimately will overcome its foe is not repression but refutation of the opposing falsehood when compared with the truth. He should be mindful of the fact that if a truth is questioned it may be a symptom that we do not yet understand enough a particular aspect of the truth. Again, the proper approach to this situation is not repression but deeper and more painstaking study. Moreover, in exercising his teaching authority, the religious leader must be sure that he makes clear distinction between the body of revelation and defined doctrine of the Church, and what might be termed "peripheral orthodoxy."

The bishop makes laws as the officer of good order. But he must guide with love and patience, letting others do their best, even when he can see better, because it is useless to try to force people into certain molds for which they are not fitted.

When others for whom he may be responsible see a situation in a way different from his own—even in ways which seem to be seriously wrong—he must endeavor to harmonize his responsibilities for the individual with respect for the individual's responsibility for the truth as he sees it. One of the most important functions of a religious leader, and particularly a bishop, is to help people to think—to help them to deepen their consciousness of what it means to be a Catholic and to make a genuine, personal exploration of what the scriptures and the Church are teaching us. It is in this way that the religious leader endeavors to exercise authority in an edifying manner after the example of St. Paul, who said that he did not wish to be severe in his use of the authority which the Lord had given him for building up and not for tearing down.

It may be that, when he reaches a decision-making stage in his thinking, a religious leader will be able to come to only a tentative conclusion; but he should not be afraid to experiment, realizing that experimentation can be a form of sound planning. By nature, an experiment proceeds with a view to the acquisition of a new insight, and yet does not anticipate the outcome. Change is foreseen but the nature of the change is not predicted. Experimentation involves creative risk-taking and must allow for the possibility of failure. A religious leader should not give grounds for the belief in some circles that there are no official mistakes because there are no official ventures. At the same time, experimentation should have controls and make provisions for proper assessment so that one is able to minimize the danger of costly, wide-scale adoption of trial-and-error formulas based on untested assumptions and promoted solely by popular enthusiasm.

NEED FOR CONFIDENCE IN GOD

Such, then, are some considerations on the formation of a religious leader's conscience. I would observe as a final note that the decisions and the positions of the religious leader should exemplify strong confidence in God. He should remember that he will receive from God only as much as he expects God to give him.

Sometimes we can talk a great deal about the Holy Spirit's presence in the Church, but we can act as if we were not sure of this presence and that we have to count more on human resources and efficiency than on the power of God. A religious leader does well to meditate long on the example of John XXIII for whom the fire of Pentecost was not a consuming fire but an inspiring one, not at all destroying but creating.

We have more than enough prophets of gloom who never weary of telling us how bad things are in the Church and why they are not likely to get better for a long while. The negative approach—the litany of all the things done badly or not done at all (the over-emphasis on words like "anguish," "discontent," "reaction," "tension," "rebellion," "bewilderment")—is more dramatic and more stirring than the careful weighing of successes and failures; but in the total view it is a distortion and it is dishonest. Christ came on this earth to give life, and hence His Church is essentially creative, growing, vigorous, endowed with all the wonderful characteristics of new life. Its image cannot be depicted in dark lines of negation and frustration. Such an unbalanced view would be a simple caricature. The Church leader must be sure that this does not happen. He must remember that the characteristic of leadership—as distinct from government, administration, and management —is that it encourages and reinforces followers, motivates them, and generates enthusiasm. By his actions, as well as by his words, he must serve the whole truth.

Prudence and humility, mingled with all the other qualities which we have mentioned, will be his familiar virtues. He will realize full well that not in every instance will he exercise his office in perfect conformity with reality, because his grasp of it, his understanding of it, will always be partial and imperfect. He will be quite aware that there will come times when he will fail to recognize the real, even when it is actually staring him in the face. Yet, in his diocese, for his people, for his local Church, for the world, he is a teacher, a sanctifier, and a ruler. If his teaching is cabined by his own imperfect understanding of the ultimate reality of God's word, if his sanctifying is hampered to some extent by the imperfect image he himself projects of the holiness of God, if his rule is made difficult by his inability to weigh all rights and duties in a perfectly balanced scale, yet he realizes that by the decision of God, expressed through the authority of the Church, it is his duty to lead. In humility he should continue his courageous efforts to fulfill his office well with the help of all the people of God, convinced of the mysterious ways of grace among God's people, and knowing that while the Church is always made up of men it can never be viewed only in human terms. He for one must rise to the challenge and demonstrate by his life day in and day out the miracle of the new Pentecost and the fresh approach of the Holy Spirit so that all under him, because of his sincere efforts to lead, will see clearly, brightly, and totally the wonderful ways of God.

REFERENCES

Dearden, J. F. On directions in the Church in the United States. Documentary
    Service, Press Department, U.S. Catholic Conference, Washington, D.C. April
    18, 1969, pp. 1–3.
Gardner, J. *Self-renewal*. New York: Harper & Row, 1965.
Vatican Council II. W. M. Abbott (s.J.) (Ed.) *The documents of Vatican II*.
    New York: Herder & Herder, 1966.

The Conscience of the Religious Subject

GERALD A. McCOOL, s.j.

Father Gerald A. McCool, S.J. has two degrees from Fordham University, an A.B. (1940) and a Ph.D. (1956), and three degrees from Woodstock College, Maryland, a Ph.L. (1946), an M.A. (1947), and an S.T.L. (1953). He has published articles in such journals as Theological Studies, Thought, International Philosophical Quarterly, Continuum, *and the* Modern Schoolman. *Father McCool is associate professor of philosophy at Fordham University. In view of the topic of his paper it may be observed that, in addition to his work at the University, Father McCool has had considerable experience in working with religious and in giving retreats to religious.*

The conscience of the religious subject is an extremely wide topic. Clearly some limits must be imposed on our discussion, if it is to be kept within manageable bounds. It has also become a very difficult topic on which to speak definitively. I have no great hope of offering clear-cut solutions to the problems which perplex the religious who is endeavoring to form his conscience today. Nevertheless, I am convinced that clear-cut solutions cannot be postponed indefinitely without serious danger to our religious life. Neither do I expect that what I say today will meet with universal satisfaction. If, however, some order and clarity can be achieved in specifying the problems which trouble the conscience of the religious in a rapidly evolving Church, our time will not have been wasted.

By "conscience" I understand the proximate practical judgment concerning the moral goodness or evil of an action or series of actions which the moral agent must make before an action is performed (Jone & Adelman, 1951, p. 109; Arregui, 1944, p. 125). The problems which are specific to the conscience of a religious arise from his membership in an institute to which he has committed himself by the three vows of religion. There is some dispute among theologians whether members of a secular institute should be considered religious (Rahner, 1963, pp. 319–352; 1964a, pp. 147–183; 1966, pp. 263–276). In any event, their life and their apostolate are sufficiently distinct from those of other institutes to warrant separate consideration. Consequently, leaving secular institutes aside, we will take "religious subject" to mean a member of an order, congregation, or society in which the life of the evangelical counsels is lived in common under the three vows in the specific form determined by its constitutions.

In the course of this paper I will endeavor to outline the progressive development of the moral problem presented to the religious subject by the obligation of his vowed commitment to a religious institute during the post-Vatican-Council period of adaptation and renewal. The problem has confronted the religious in different form at three successive stages in the contemporary evolution of religious life. The first stage was a period of general reconsideration of the moral and supernatural value of the life of the counsels. In Europe this period was roughly contemporaneous with the beginning of the Council and its impact upon America was not profound. The second stage might be called the war upon superiors for the implementation of the Vatican II reforms. During this period directors of conscience were largely concerned with subjects whose institutes or superiors continued to govern them in a manner which contravened their rights as religious and the theology of the religious life approved by the Council. The third stage, in which we are still living, is a period in which religious institutes have begun to change with great rapidity and in which subjects have been called to take an active part in a radical movement of religious and apostolic reform.

With these three stages, which cannot be neatly divided chronologically, we can associate a parallel evolution of post-Vatican-II theology of the religious life. In this theological development, the religious subject could find the principles which justified his commitment as an expression of the Church's sanctity, supplied the norms to which it must conform, and furnished the subordinate principles through which he could form his conscience as he was progressively confronted with the specific demands placed upon him by the successive stages of the post-Vatican-II religious renewal.

Today, however, the religious subject is reaching a crisis. It is becoming increasingly difficult for him to determine what in fact the demands are which are placed on him by the concrete institute in which he actually lives. Whether it be well-founded or not, the question whether his institute, as it concretely exists, has any longer the right to bind his conscience as a specifically religious community to which he is committed by vow, is no longer a rhetorical one in the mind of many a religious subject. Furthermore, directors of conscience are finding that the principles of post-Vatican-II theology which proved so useful in forming consciences during the earlier periods of institutional renewal are no longer as effective as they were. The problem which confronts the religious subject today is an ambiguity concerning the extent, nature, and duration of the commitment which the diverse members of his institute are willing to accept as the moral and religious consequence of the vows they have pronounced. The cause of this ambiguity is at least two-fold: the diverse understanding entertained by different subjects at a time of rapid change concerning the essential nature of their institute, and the rapid evolution of theology during the past few years.

The crisis in which the religious subject finds himself today is very grave. If he is to understand his obligations, he and his institute must be clear about their identity, their goals, their way of life. If he is to entertain the expectations of his fellow religious without which their institute cannot survive as a religious community, he must be sure that they are bound to him and it by a common commitment. Religious, old and young, are very much aware of this and they are troubled by the present ambiguity. To understand the cause of their present troubled state and to appreciate the help which they must receive from their institutes and from theologians if they are to survive as religious, we need to reflect a little on this history of the religious conscience and its problems during the past few years.

RECONSIDERATION OF MORAL AND SUPERNATURAL VALUE OF THE RELIGIOUS LIFE

In the history of the Church, periods of revolutionary change have been accompanied by attacks on the life of the three vows on the score that it is immoral of its very nature. Their ground has usually been the deleterious personal and social consequences of the vows, the abdication of personal responsibility which they entail, and the transmission to human intermediaries of moral choices which must be made by the individual alone in direct confrontation with Christ. Saint Thomas replied to an attack of this sort in his *Summa contra Gentiles* (Book III, Part II, cc. 130–138; Pieper, 1964, pp. 62–71). Suarez produced a similar defense at the time of the Counter-Reformation in his *Religio Societatis Jesu* (Suarez, 1857; Humphrey, 1884). Vatican II rehearsed once more in the light of more recent theology the reasons which support the human and supernatural value of religious life in the Dogmatic Constitution on the Church (Vatican Council II, 1966, pp. 14–101) and in the Decree on the Appropriate Renewal of Religious Life (Vatican Council II, 1966, pp. 466–482).

Post-conciliar theology (Rahner, 1966, pp. 404–479; 1967, pp. 58–104; Örsy, 1968) has defended the value of the counsels as an integral part of the Church's eschatological witness and indicated the role which religious institutions play as visible signs of her holiness. In doing so it has clarified the reasons which justify the renunciation of fundamental human goods through the three vows. It has also explained the ecclesial basis for the authoritative specification of the religious life in institutes in which a life of rule is lived under the direction of religious superiors.

Religious belong to what Karl Rahner has called the charismatic element in the Church. Their conviction that God has called them to follow Christ in the religious life is based on a non-formal process of inference which Saint Ignatius has called the discernment of spirits. Their decision to follow the divine invitation is freely taken. Its motive is growth in service of God and their neighbor and in the intimate union with God which Christian writers from patristic times have called holiness. The renunciation of earthly goods which the vows entail is justified because it is a manifestation of the Church's eschatological faith and hope. Through it, religious institutes give living public witness to the Church's certitude that life's significance does not rest exclusively on the encounter with God in the use of His creation, but on the lived hope of an encounter beyond the limits of space and time (Rahner, 1966, pp. 404–434).

A religious community in the visible Church is a response to a common charismatic call in which its members participate and which is the supernatural bond of their union. Since that call is given in the Church as a summons to give stable social witness to her holiness and hope, communal life of the counsels acquires permanent visible form in the diverse religious institutes. Thus, the interior charism unique to each institute finds the external expression through which it can be thematized and communicated, and the interior bond of charity which binds its members to God, to the Church, and to each other receives verbal expression in its constitutions.

Consequently religious vows are not taken *in vacuo*. They are always taken in a specific institute whose constitutions thematize the charismatic vocation to which each religious commits himself. Through her approval of the constitutions the visible Church commits herself to the religious as an authentic witness of her life and hope.

On the basis of this theological justification of the nature and value of the religious life, the religious subject at the beginning of the post-Vatican-II renewal was able to set down some general principles for the formation of his conscience in relation to his institute and its demands on him.

1. The decision to follow the religious life is morally justified through its public eschatological witness and through its service to God in the life of His Church. Its nature is distorted and its moral value compromised if it degenerates into an irresponsible flight from participation in the world through fear or dislike of God's creation. From the theology of the free person in the Church it follows that an individual call to manifest her sanctity through the public witness of the counsels should come in every generation to a number of generous Christians. Not only may Christians be religious —some of them should be.

2. Although the constitutions of a religious institute are not identified with its common charismatic call, its inner spirit, and its internal bond of charity, the constitutions cannot be separated from them either—a fact which Saint Ignatius saw most clearly. The constitutions of an institute are not purely juridical regulations with little or no relation to its interior spirit. They are the medium through which the religious vows can specify and maintain a perduring commitment to a common way of life. Consequently superiors, in fidelity to God and to the Church, have an obligation to see that the constitutions are observed. For, if a way of life is allowed to grow up within an institute which is at variance with the specific manifestation of the Church's holiness which it has been called to manifest, that institute has lost the supernatural justification for its existence. Thus complete freedom to follow individual decisions cannot be permitted to a subject in a religious institute. A Christian called to the religious life is called to accept a limitation on his freedom through obedience to his institute and its superiors.

3. Furthermore, since he shares in a common charismatic call which is incorporated in a specific institute, indications of the divine will should ordinarily come to him through his institute and its superiors. Although there can be legitimate conflicts at times, it is hard to reconcile a religious vocation with the conviction that the subject must make every important decision on his own responsibility and that the moral authority of a religious superior is restricted to his right to offer counsel. As one religious order recently expressed it, "a man who, time after time, is unable to obey with good conscience, should take thought regarding some other path of life in which he can serve God with greater tranquility" (Society of Jesus, 1967, p. 55).

THE IMPLEMENTATION OF THE VATICAN II REFORMS

The theology of the religious life which flourished after the Council not only gave the religious subject a clearer picture of the nature and value of the religious life than he had previously possessed. It also provided him with the principles through which a number of the problems arising from the conflict between obedience and his moral conscience could find an answer. A proper understanding of the theology of religious institutes made it clear that the constitutions of an institute specified not only the obligation of the subject. They also specified and restricted the legitimate authority of his superior. Superiors may rule only in accordance with the Constitutions and, in an institute whose reason for existence is to manifest the Church's sanctity and supernatural hope, they must rule religiously. Through his vows the subject has acquired a claim upon the conscience of his superior. For he has received a personal call from God to a life of individual witness and service within a specific community. Not all the demands which God makes on him can be determined by following uncritically in a quasi-automatic way the general orders of superiors. A number must be determined individually by the discernment of spirits. Since the subject's vocation has been entrusted to his institute, he has the right to the personal direction and understanding of his superior in his efforts to discover God's personal will for him. The superior in turn has the inescapable obligation to provide it, and to provide it as a religious superior and not as the director of a secular enterprise. Furthermore, a religious institute is a community of free individuals within a visible Church to which they have a definite responsibility. God will inspire them through thoughts and desires to move their institute to greater service of His Mystical Body. As they are bound to communicate these thoughts and desires to their superiors, so are superiors, because of their responsibility to their institute and to the Church, bound to hear their subjects and to consult them individually and collectively.

In the period immediately after Vatican II, these principles, which have now become clichés, were not commonplaces in American religious communities. Government often left much to be desired in a religious institute. Superiors, who were often quite ignorant of the theology of the religious life, ruled impersonally at times and at others gave the impression of a political mode of action which did not show the proper regard for the rights of the subject and the true interest of the universal Church. The problems of conscience which this mode of government created for intelligent, sensitive, and farseeing religious are too well-known to call for repetition here (Gleason, 1968).

At this period, however, the informed religious subject or his spiritual director felt that he could see a reasonably clear course of action for the religious subject to follow. Many of the subject's problems of conscience were the result of his living in an institute whose mode of life and government were not in accord with the approved theology of the religious life. Those who could would work for the reform of religious institutes through personal action, books, and institutes. Others, while waiting for the coming reform of their institute, could frequently solve their problems by using the ordinary principles which govern the reaction of subjects suffering under unjust commands. Difficult as this period was psychologically, it was not a period in which the religious subject needed to feel discouraged about a sound moral solution to his difficulties within the framework of the approved theology of the religious life.

This period in the history of religious institutes, despite considerable rearguard action here and there, has now come to its end. Reform and adaptation to the modern world have now become the goal of a general movement to which each institute is asked to contribute through a revision of its constitutions. Individual consultation with one's superior is now accepted, in theory at least, as a legitimate way of reaching important decisions. Group and community dialogue have become accepted instruments through which, in theory at least, each group endeavors to discern God's will concerning its future life and work. Immobile institutes have now begun to move with extreme rapidity. Post-Vatican-II religious renewal has entered a third stage and this stage too has its peculiar problems for the religious subject, many of them more agonizing than the problems he confronted in the past.

PERIOD OF RAPID EVOLUTION AND RENEWAL

No one expected that the communal effort of religious communities to discover God's will in regard to their future life and work would be an easy task. As it has proceeded, however, it has proven to be even more difficult than most religious anticipated that it would be. Once a movement of evolution and reform gets under way, commitment to the existing constitutions of an institute becomes provisional. It is assumed that in their revised form the constitutions will be a more exact expression of the present charismatic call which God is now addressing to the institute. Yet, since the constitutions specify the common commitment of the subjects to the institute and to each other, their sudden mobility, after a long period of stability, has affected the bond of union in the evolving communities. Problems now arise in the conscience of the religious concerning his relation to his community and his fellow religious which were not there before.

When the post-Vatican-II reform began, it was rather generally assumed that the period of communal discernment of spirits would reach its consummation in a renewed institute to whose revised constitutions the individual subjects could commit themselves with peace of soul. But in a changing Church and in a changing world, who can tell when a period of evolution will come to even relative rest? And does that not make any set of constitutions extremely provisory and relative? Furthermore, discernment of spirits is not an automatic process, the success of which is guaranteed. It is a delicate work of grace. Human resistance, human weakness and obtuseness can prevent it or delay it until the καιρός, the providential time allowed by God, has passed. Religious, both subjects and superiors, who are concerned with

changes in the life and work of their institute know very well that the movement of renewal, like every human movement, is not the outcome of a
simple impulse of the Holy Spirit but the resultant vector of multiple and
complicated forces. Secular ideas and desires are in the heart of every man.
Worldliness and spiritual blindness will make their contribution to the movement too. That is why the process is called discernment of spirits, and that
is why, like every discernment of spirits, it is a risky business.

In the process of discernment of spirits whose term is still undefined, an
ambiguous situation is created concerning the very nature of the life to which
the members of the institute have given their vowed commitment. If the
present constitutions are to undergo revision, perhaps indefinitely, what is
the subject's commitment to them in their present form? If the institute
should take a wrong turn, or miss its καιρός, what will be the subject's commitment to the constitutions in the future? It would appear that the religious
subject is invited to enter an indefinite process of judging his institute in its
fidelity to the call of grace, and his individual judgment will have a radical
effect on his commitment.

Thus uncertainty about their future commitment to their institute has begun to trouble the consciences of many religious, and divergent hopes and
fears concerning the form of its future life and work make them perplexed
over the attitude which they are called to take in relation to their superiors
and fellow subjects. At a time when the future of his institute is undefined,
when should a superior or a fellow subject be deferred to as a religious who
is exercising under grace his authentic call as a prophetic leader, and when
must he be resolutely and uncompromisingly opposed as a traitor to the
institute? In what does loyalty to one's institute consist at the present time?
What is charity, and what is selfish cowardly silence for the sake of peace
and personal survival? These are hard questions, but they are questions
which the religious subject cannot avoid today.

The effort of the religious subject to discern the movement of the Spirit
in his institute from the distorting influences of human infidelity and weakness has been complicated by the rapid evolution of theology in the post-
conciliar Church. The theology of the Church, of revelation, of grace, and
of nature has been the subject of considerable and sometimes turbulent
debate during the past few years (Curran, 1966, 1968). The consequence
has been a renewed discussion concerning the nature of Christian holiness,
the force and the duration of the vows, and the value of the witness of the
counsels in its traditional institutional form. The differences which are emerging have been great enough to raise in the minds of some religious subjects
the question whether in some communities there is no longer a common
understanding of the nature and role of a religious institute within the
Church. Should that be true, the consequences would be very grave indeed.
The fundamental theological presuppositions which sustain the process of

communal discernment of spirits could no longer be taken for granted, and there would no longer be common agreement about the nature of the supernatural end which justifies one's commitment to the religious life.

The religious subject, however, has not been left without guidelines to form his conscience during this difficult period of evolution and renewal. Since the Church has invited religious institutes to reform their constitutions, it is a safe assumption that many of them are no longer adequate expressions of the community's charismatic call. Furthermore, since communal discussion on various levels is the recommended means, there are good *prima facie* grounds for the assumption that the interplay of different points of view will be the means employed by the Holy Spirit to manifest the form of life and work to which the institute should now commit itself. Classical post-Vatican-II theology has also given the reasons why this communal reflection can be expected to lead to radical changes in some institutes (Örsy, 1968, pp. 255–286). The type of religious life suited to monastic-contemplative communities is very different from that demanded by an active-apostolic group. The order and form of life and prayer, the religious virtues required of subjects, the relationship between subject and superior differ widely in these two types of institute. In the past this essential difference was not sufficiently appreciated, and active congregations, especially of women, received a set of constitutions which were not suited to their active life. In such groups we could anticipate great changes. Likewise at a period in which the secular institute is coming into its own, we could expect that some institutes, or some groups within existing institutes, would be moved by the Holy Spirit to adopt this form of life for their active apostolate.

From the history of the Church, the religious subject can learn that movements of reform within religious groups have usually had their origin in the witness of charismatic leaders. On occasion these leaders have carried their whole institute along with them. More often, however, the movements which they have set on foot have led to divisions accompanied by suffering and bitterness. This was true of the divisions among the Franciscans and the Carmelites. It was true in the United States when the Paulists seceded from the Redemptorists to form a new congregation. The work of the Holy Spirit can be accomplished through bitter disagreement and ultimate division of groups which were once united. It would appear as well from the practice of the Church in releasing subjects from their vows after earlier reforms that a genuine possibility exists that the new form of life in a reformed institute may no longer correspond to the subject's personal call, and that his vocation for the future is to follow God in the lay state.

On the basis of those theological reflections, the religious subject was able to derive a few principles which, until fairly recently, were adequate norms to guide his conscience in relation to his dealings with his institute and his fellow religious during this period of change.

1. Since it is not inconceivable that the interplay of conflicting hopes and fears which divide an institute may be destined by God to lead either to a painful but providentially destined division or to a clearer understanding of the future form of life to which a united institute can commit itself, the individual religious subject cannot deny in an *a priori* way that in the same congregation loyalty to the institute and correspondence with their special grace may reveal itself in different subjects through fundamentally different orientations. Whatever may be the consequence which God ultimately intends, these diverse hopes and fears can be a faithful answer to a charismatic call which, for the moment, remains a common one. If they should lead to an intended division, the new institutes will be related in their origin in grace. They will be filial or sister institutes.

2. Therefore the individual religious subjects who find themselves in such an evolving situation are still united by the bond of fraternal charity and justice. Each is still called upon to contribute in the measure of his ability to the clarification of the future options which are emerging now.

3. Meanwhile the subject remains under the obedience of the institute through whose constitutions his vocation is specified at the present time. Its rule, its superiors, and his fellow subjects retain the claim on him conceded to them by his vows. Since its members are being led to their future vocation through their present institute, ways of acting or of withdrawal from common activity which violate the justice and the charity he owes them are not permitted to him. As long as they remain united, religious subjects must move forward on their path of sanctity and service in the manner which their institute permits.

THE PRESENT CONFUSION

Today, however, the religious subject is beginning to question whether these guidelines are any longer valid norms for him to follow in his relations with his institute. They are based, after all, on the theology of the religious life which is associated with the Constitution on the Church and the Decree on the Renewal of Religious Life. In terms of that theology, religious life is justified on the basis of its witness to the Church's sanctity and to her eschatological hope. On the same basis, the dialectic of obedience and initiative, personal sanctity, and service to the Church which underlay the struggle for the implementation of the Vatican-II reforms could make its claim for universal acceptance. Likewise the relationship between the common charismatic call of an institute and its formulation in its constitutions enabled a religious subject to chart a reasonable course of action during the earlier period of evolution and renewal. The religious was always in a position to assume that he was bound to his fellow subjects and to his superiors through a genuine supernatural bond and that through their vows, specified by the constitutions, each one of them had given a stable commitment to the others. They were a family, a society within the Church with all the rights and expectations which membership within such a family entailed.

It is becoming increasingly difficult for the religious subject to make this assumption as confidently as he did in the past. There are many reasons for his present difficulty.

In the first place, it is no secret that the movement of renewal is not going well. The defection figures are becoming alarming. Many religious, rightly or wrongly, have reached the conclusion that in the movement of reform their institute has missed its καιρός. Either it has failed to yield in time to the movement of the Spirit or it has yielded too much to the spirit of the world. In any event, these religious have decided that the form of life and work prescribed by their institute is no longer the way in which they can do the most for God. Other religious have withdrawn interiorly and made no secret of their withdrawal. Even though they remain within the institute, they are alienated from it and leave their fellow subjects uncertain about the depth, extent, and duration of their commitment to it. The longer the present "unhappy stage" of renewal continues with its increasing number of defections and interior withdrawals, the greater will be the uncertainty of the religious subject concerning the commitment of his fellow subjects and even of his superiors. And, if he can no longer be certain that their actions are proceeding from commitment to the institute, how should he behave toward them? Should he still deal with them as fellow religious? Or should he be prudent and follow the ordinary rules of political morality?

Ambiguity about commitment can be the result not only of the subject's judgment about the factual state of his institute. It can result also from ambiguity about the norm through which the spiritual health of the institute is measured. Such ambiguity might simply be the failure to distinguish whether the norm for a given institute should be the norm of contemplative prayer or apostolic action. But it may also be caused by increasing theological diversity within religious groups concerning the nature and end of religious life, the virtues which should characterize religious, the hope to which they witness, and the extent and duration of the commitment which they make to the community through the three vows. That such diversity exists today is clear to anyone who has been engaged in the work of religious renewal. It crops up in retreats, in discussions about community life-styles, and in reflections on the education of younger religious. More often, however, it lies beneath the surface and divides religious who are not fully conscious of the extent of their division.

For the religious subject today, his institute has often become a very unstable community. He is unsure how his fellow religious judge it in its present form and he is uncertain concerning their hope for its future. He is conscious that there is today a diversity among religious subjects concerning the extent and duration of the commitment which a subject makes to his institute by the vows of religion, although this diversity may not have been explicitly voiced in his group. He feels that the rapid evolution of theology in its scholarly and popular expression has led to a diversity of viewpoints among his fellow subjects concerning the nature of Christian sanctity and apostolic witness, and the relation of a religious institute to the visible Church and to the secular community.

Of one thing he is sure. His institute's constitutions in their present form, even after their revision, do not accurately express the nature, extent, and duration of the commitment which many of his fellow subjects are making in reality to his institute today. Yet the commitment of his fellow subjects creates the bond which makes the institute a living reality. Its duration makes the community a stable family; the area of its extent and the primacy which it occupies in a subject's life determines the depth and breadth of his association with his community and the priority which that association holds among the other commitments, professional and social, in his life. A serious change in the commitment of a notable number of religious subjects cannot fail to modify the nature of their institute. Thus, after a certain limit, ambiguity about the object, depth, and duration of the subjects' present commitment places the real nature of their institute in doubt. This doubt in turn creates in the subject's mind a second doubt about his present obligation to it which affects his own commitment. Obviously this is an escalating process and at the limit, when it leads to an increasing number of defections, it spells the death of a religious institute.

This agonizing doubt about the nature of his institute is tormenting many a religious subject today. It is a doubt which he cannot resolve himself. Since he cannot read hearts, he must be able to assume with reasonable probability that the vows as they are specified in his institute accurately express a genuine and stable union of minds and wills. If he cannot make that assumption, he does not know what it is to which he has pledged himself through his commitment to the community. Neither does he know what communal support, natural and supernatural, he may expect in return.

That is why today, as the movement of renewal proceeds, more religious are asking that their institutes state more clearly in word and deed what they really stand for. Some institutes are being asked to examine more honestly their present state. Does their religious life as it is actually lived conform to the ideal which their institute proclaims? Prolonged compromise and delay of genuine renewal, even for apostolic and economic reasons, inevitably leads to ambiguity concerning the commitment required of a subject in the institute, and can lead easily today to discouraged alienation among the young and generous.

Other communities are being asked to examine more carefully whether they are called to lead a contemplative or an active-apostolic life. These are different vocations in their demands, virtues, and styles of life. Yet both are viable, though not compatible. Is it not possible that in some existing institutes a division into separate groups following each of these vocations might be a healthy and perhaps a necessary thing? (Cardegna, 1968) Religious subjects might then be given the opportunity to live under constitutions which express more accurately their genuine vocation. Certainly spiritual directors working with these communities would be greatly assisted in their task.

Institutes also need to clarify the theological presuppositions which justify their basic choice of life and work. Not every understanding of the relation of the sacred and the secular, of eschatological hope, of the visible Church and its salvific role will ground religious life, in its present form at least, as a work and witness significant enough to justify the renunciation of fundamental human goods which the vows demand. Possibly there may exist within the Church in future a greater range of free theological positions than existed in the past. Yet acceptance of some of these positions might undercut the religious beliefs which justify the life of witness in a traditional religious institute. The Church of England is aware of this. Anglicans enjoy a far wider latitude than Catholics have heretofore enjoyed in their beliefs about the future life, the sacraments, the Church, and penance. Their religious communities, however, do not extend the same indulgence to candidates who wish to join their ranks. There is good reason for this refusal on their part. A man cannot live a contradiction. If he does not accept the theological affirmations on the basis of which an institute's work and life style are justified as meaningful and moral enterprises, he must either live a frustrated life or work to change the institute.

Today in a freer theological climate Catholic communities should examine the theological presuppositions which ground their way of life. If some of them are no longer tenable, they must be given up and the practices which rest on them should be abandoned. The others which remain sound theological positions should be recognized as such, even if they have become free positions which can be controverted by contemporary theologians, and their relation to the life and work of the institute should be made clear. The benefit of this clarification to the religious subject and to the director of his conscience would be very great. A subject would understand whether his total theological understanding of the Church and of the world moved him to commit himself to the life demanded by this institute as his answer to God's call to him, or whether on the basis of his beliefs he must in all honesty commit himself to a style of life which represents a break with the theological and spiritual tradition of his congregation. The result might be a beneficial clearing of the air from which all the subjects of the institute would benefit. Certainly spiritual directors would be once more in a position to present a clear, coherent theological exposition of the reason and value of an institute's commitment and to locate its witness in the larger spectrum of the witness of the Church. Novices and young religious would have the opportunity to see their commitment as a whole, to understand what it entails and why, and to realize how and why it must differ from other forms of Catholic and religious life.

For the peace of conscience of their subjects, institutes must define themselves more clearly and more thoroughly. They must be willing to make their choice of life style, goals, and ideals of sanctity and service. And they must explain the theology of the Church and of religious life which grounds their choice. They must come to a reasonable and communicable decision concerning the significance of the vows within their institute so that the religious subject may know with reasonable clarity where he and his fellow religious stand, and what meaningful anticipation he can have about his future association with them in this institute.

Will the religious subject receive this clarity in time? Will his institute be able to define itself sufficiently in an evolutionary world to give him the knowledge and the confidence he requires to sustain an enduring commitment? That is not an easy question to answer. It is already too late for some religious and perhaps for some institutes. So much must be done and time is pressing. Yet for many, religious faith and hope remain alive, and we can surmise that the ambiguity about the commitment of the vows within his institute which troubles the conscience of the religious subject today will be cleared up as the Church and her religious institutes move on into the next stage in the movement of renewal and reform.

REFERENCES

Arregui, A. M. (s.j.) *Summarium theologiae moralis.* Westminster, Md.: Newman, 1944.

Cardegna, F. F. (s.j.) The forms of religious life in the future. *Catholic Mind,* 1968, *66* (September, no. 1225), 9–13.

Curran, C. E. *Christian morality today.* Notre Dame, Ind.: Fides, 1966.

Curran, C. E. (Ed.) *Absolutes in moral theology?* Washington: Corpus Books, 1968.

Gleason, R. W. (s.j.) *The restless religious.* Dayton: Pflaum, 1968.

Humphrey, W. (s.j.) (Ed.) *Francisco Suarez, 1548–1617. The religious state: A digest of the doctrine contained in his treatise "De statu religionis."* London: Burns & Oates, 1884.

Jone, H. (o.f.m. cap.), & Adelman, U. (o.f.m. cap.) *Moral theology.* Westminister, Md.: Newman, 1951.

Örsy, L. M. (s.j.) *Open to the Spirit.* Washington: Corpus Books, 1968.

Pieper, J. *A guide to Thomas Aquinas.* New York: Mentor-Omega, 1964.

Rahner, K. (s.j.) *Theological investigations II.* Baltimore: Helicon, 1963.

Rahner, K. (s.j.) *Theology for renewal.* New York: Sheed & Ward, 1964. (a)

Rahner, K. (s.j.) *The dynamic element in the Church.* New York: Herder & Herder, 1964. (b)
Rahner, K. (s.j.) *Schriften zur Theologie VII.* Einsiedeln: Benziger, 1966.
Rahner, K. (s.j.) *Theological investigations III.* Baltimore: Helicon, 1967.
Society of Jesus. *Documents of the thirty-first general congregation.* Woodstock, Md.: Woodstock College Press, 1967.
Suarez, F. (s.j.) *Tractatus de religione Societatis Jesu.* Brussels: Geuse, 1857.
Vatican Council II. W. M. Abbott (s.j.) (Ed.) *The documents of Vatican II.* New York: Herder & Herder, 1966.

The Conscience of the
Roman Catholic Layman

WILLIAM BIRMINGHAM

William Birmingham was educated at St. Peter's College (A.B., 1946) and Fordham University (M.A., 1952). He has taught at Fordham University and is currently Coordinator of Operation EXCEL, at Queens College. It is, however, for his editorial work that Mr. Birmingham is best known: as general editor of Mentor–Omega Books, and as an associate editor of Cross Currents. *He has also edited (jointly with Joseph E. Cunneen)* Cross currents of psychiatry and Catholic morality *(1964) and* What modern Catholics think about birth control *(1964). Mr. Birmingham is also a contributor to such publications as the* National Catholic Reporter *and* Commonweal, *among others.*

Let me describe what I mean by the terms in the title of my paper:

———By conscience I mean the healthy and effective process of making decisions in significant matters. Though I shall develop the point later, I shall now simply state that the process is relational. That is, decisions are made not by man the isolated monad but, if they are healthy, by the person within the constellation of relationship that are constitutive of his self.*

——By Roman Catholic I do not mean a member of the ecclesiological construct or organization we designate Roman Catholicism. Within this paper, Roman Catholic stands for a Christian who makes his decisions within a particular life style—the Roman Catholic life style.

——By layman I mean the person aware of the death and resurrection to a new life which is the process of his baptism into the Christian community. This presupposes that both orders and monastic life are functions of the community and that those commissioned by the community to exercise those functions do not cease to be laymen. The bishop, in other words, is no less a layman than I am; there is no decrease of the mission conferred by baptism and confirmation because he has accepted holy orders.† The bishop's conscience, on the other hand, will differ from mine because of his different relationships, which spring from his having chosen religion as an occupation.

And now my purpose: to describe the decision-making process that I realistically hope will characterize the Roman Catholic Christian.

ROMAN CATHOLIC LIFE STYLE

I shall for the most part describe the Roman Catholic life style in terms of its strengths, and leave it to those who so wish to hold those strengths up to a mirror in which they may appear as weaknesses. The description is not meant to be exhaustive but suggestive.

1. *Roman Catholicism is institutional.* It is, in other words, a religion of book and tradition—the latter understood as evolution which changes from but resists denial of the past. As an institutional religion, Roman Catholicism preserves both sacrament and sacramentality, partly by permitting both to change through historical process in order to meet the needs of the day.‡

* Fontinell (1966 and 1967) develops a metaphysics of process and relationships within the Roman Catholic context. This paper is written from the metaphysical standpoint he describes. The discussion of the role played by the New Testament and tradition in decision-making by the Roman Catholic layman is an attempt to test the validity of his radical reconstruction of religious truth (Fontinell, 1967) by applying it to the question of conscience.

† O'Brien (1964) is the theological source of this view. The reader should note that it is counter to the central conclusion of the most developed theological work in the area, Congar's *Lay people in the Church* (1959), which defines the layman in negative terms as neither monk nor priest. It is unfortunate that O'Brien has not further developed his functional view of the priesthood, since it could provide a theological foundation for the restructuring of priesthood and ministry that is now under way.

‡ The conventional distinction between the institutional and charismatic Church is not fully satisfactory, since the term *institution* in this sense embraces everything from the Eucharist to the local parish school. For this reason, I shall distinguish between the Church institutional and the Church organizational. Underlying this distinction is my conviction that the Church organizational is more desperately in need of reform

2. *Roman Catholicism is multiform.* It has, in William James's phrase, "many cells . . . with many different kinds of honey" (1902, p. 359). It is ascetic and mystic, dogmatic and anti-ideological, primitive and rational, worldly and transcendental, universal and locked into particular cultures. It speaks of one faith but does not assume identity between the faith of a French housewife and that of a factory worker in Honolulu.

3. *Roman Catholicism resists elitism.* In the paragraph from which I have already quoted, James speaks of Catholicism's being

> indulgent in its multiform appeals to human nature. . . . To intellectual Catholics many of the antiquated beliefs to which the Church gives countenance are, if taken literally, as childish as they are to Protestants. But they are childish in the pleasing sense of "childlike"—innocent and amiable, and worthy to be smiled on . . . [James, 1902, p. 359].

Note that James says smiled on, not smiled at.

4. *Roman Catholicism celebrates.* Perhaps because it has not lost touch with the childlike, Roman Catholicism celebrates. It celebrates birth, and life, and death. It celebrates man in the saints. It celebrates God in Jesus Christ. It celebrates God in Himself. It does these things at Irish wakes and Italian street festivals, as well as at Eucharistic gatherings in a Harlem apartment or the Yankee Stadium.

5. *Roman Catholicism resists trespass upon personal autonomy.* With admittedly major exceptions—notably today in the area of sex and in the life of the religious professional—the Roman Catholic life style resists trespass by the organizational Church upon personal autonomy. Reflection on the book and tradition along with participation in worship and celebration may give energy and purpose. But the Roman Catholic life style does not presume that these things give competence. Even at the height of papocentrism, for example, few American Catholics other than the editors of the *American Ecclesiastical Review* took seriously the dominant papal theology of Church and state. Long before the late John Courtney Murray began to write, the implicit judgment had been made (and tacitly accepted) that the Vatican lacked competence to understand, let alone pass judgment on, United States practice in separation of Church and state.

6. *Roman Catholicism tries to organize the unorganizable.* Roman Catholicism tries within its life style to organize the unorganizable—an activity of great merit so long as the task is recognized as impossible. In the past it has transformed Paul's comprehensive notion of the Body of Christ into the

---

—in part because it tends to slow down or oppose the organic development of institutions. I give one view of the problem in the discussion below of the Church as Holy Mother. Presthus' *The organizational society* (1962) illuminates the entire problem of big organizations. Warwick (1967) gives a fine professional analysis of organizational effectiveness in the Roman Catholic Church.

harsh lines of the papal pyramid, the principle of order into canon law, the genius of Assisi into a monastic order wearing brown instead of black, and the mercy of God into that celestial bookkeeper's nightmare, the system of indulgences. At the same time—and more often than not through these and similar vain attempts to organize the unorganizable—Roman Catholicism has more than any other branch of Western Christianity socialized religious habit. Through organization, the Roman Catholic life style is part of the fabric of daily life.

These positive elements in the Roman Catholic life style enhance the decision-making process. An institutional religion provides a framework of value and worship. Multiformity makes action possible without fear of psychological excommunication from the community. Rejection of elitism locates the values of democracy at the center of religious existence, since it places full religious value on the work and worship of every layman who works and worships well. Celebration encourages that faith and hope in reality without which decisions are burdensome, if not impossible. Respect for autonomy contributes to personal confidence in judging experience and in making decisions that grow out of that experience. The socialization of religious habit—even in such forms now considered bizarre as wearing the green scapular—provides a religious foundation shared by the total community, including its saints and mystics.

These strengths of the Roman Catholic life style are diminished by an image that counters the ability to make decisions.

7. *Roman Catholicism and Holy Mother Church.* The poetic metaphor of the Church as mother has become, in sociological fact, a principle of the organizational Church that can be better understood in psychological than theological terms.

——Holy Mother Church sees her motherhood in a limited and dangerous sense of the word: she conceives herself the mother of religious infants and children. She is intolerant of adolescence and unaware that the goal of parenthood is, or should be in modern society, a relationship between adults: that is, not the vertical relationship imposed by the needs of early childhood but a horizontal relationship best described as friendship. Mother Church tries to keep her children infantile and her adults childish.

——Holy Mother Church sees herself as the perfect—and only—source of religious gratification. Within the family, of course, a mother's image of herself as perfect hinders the psychological growth of the child. Learning that the good mother and the bad mother of his experience are one and the same person is among the most important tasks the infant faces; if, once he makes the discovery, mother is ready to disown him because he now threatens with reality her self-fantasy, the child is in severe trouble. Much the same is true of the relationship of the layman or community of laymen with the organizational Church: it is difficult to avoid either becoming fixated on Mother Church as perfect source of religious milk or disowning her, as so many have of late, with violence.

——Holy Mother Church is skilled in the technique of the double-bind, the simultaneous issuance of contradictory orders.* The bishop is told to be the spiritual father of his diocese, yet is forced to spend his time in administration and finance. The ordained priest is advised that he is a catalyst for parishioners seeking spiritual maturity, but must himself obey rules that would demean the adolescent. The nun is told to give herself to a life of needed service and is then forbidden to meet needs she perceives, because to do so would demand her breaking the "Rule." The married couple are informed that their sexual intercourse is no longer tinged with sin but is indeed sacramental, provided it be in the service of life—the life not of their marriage or of their existing children but of children not yet conceived. The theologian is told to think creatively about the mysteries of faith so long as he limits his creativity to thoughts that will not disturb the tranquility of elderly Italian gentlemen living on a few acres in a corner of Rome. The double-bind is vicious: it breaks decision-making power by making every alternative wrong.

——Holy Mother Church plays the religious Mom. She "is the unquestioned authority in matters of morals in her home, and . . . in the community; yet she permits herself to remain, in her own way, vain in her appearance, egotistical in her demands. . . . In any situation in which this discrepancy clashes with the respect which she demands from the children, she blames her children; she never blames herself." The description is excerpted from Erik Erikson's analysis of the American Mom (Erikson, 1963, p. 290); but it fits Holy Mother Church as well.

A common strategy for refusing blame is the maintenance of extreme disjunction between the empiric and the true self. The empiric defects are disjoined from the mystery, experience is divorced from truth: the layman can trust what Holy Mother Church tells him but not his experience of her, unless it conforms to what he has been told.

Let me warn against making the notion of Holy Motherhood the controlling image in a description of the Roman Catholic life style. The organizational Church is only one element in the life style, and the image of Holy Mother designates only part of the organization. One result of this is the fact that the closer a person is or has been to the organizational Church the more the Church's mothering instincts seem to affect his decision-making; many priests who reject the Roman Catholic Church, for example, seem to do so because she is not an omnicompetent mother—if she were perfect, they would stay. Another result, however, is that the layman who is only tangentially related to the organization has his decision-making power in-

---

* For technical discussion of the double-bind, see Weakland (1960). Lynch suggests that the double-bind is a special temptation of religious groups (Lynch, 1965, p. 100).

creased by the positive elements without suffering so much from having his conscience weakened by the Church as Holy Mother.

My first hope for the conscience of the Roman Catholic layman is that he be freed from fixation on the Church as Holy Mother of her infant children. This debased transmutation of the patristic metaphor fosters unfreedom in laymen, especially in those for whom religion is an occupation, while it saps strength from those elements in the Roman Catholic life style that increase ability to make sound decisions.

ROMAN CATHOLIC CHRISTIAN

The Roman Catholic lives out the life style of his Church as a member of the people of Christ. The layman's Christianity offers a context and a vision in terms of which he exercises his conscience. The context is twofold: the moral teaching and example of the New Testament, and of Christian tradition. The vision is that of Jesus as the Christ. The context might be described as well by the term *call,* and is the manner in which the past relates to present decisions. The vision might be described as *promise* and is the intersection of future possibility with present reality.

Because it is a context, the moral teaching of the New Testament is not prescriptive. It does not tell me what to do. Thus, when the letter to the Hebrews (12:7ff) takes authority and strict discipline to be a sign of parental love, it does not tell me what to do—how to act—in relationship to my own children. It proves nothing to me as a decision-maker. In the same way, the New Testament passages advising slaves to reconcile themselves to their lot tell the Christian community nothing in regard to Black Power. But these examples are obvious: most thoughtful Christians long ago silently rejected the modern validity of the prescriptions of the early Church. I wish to go a step further: the New Testament at its best—the Sermon on the Mount, say—does not prescribe the content of the modern layman's moral decisions. It remains, however, a context within which he or his community determines the content of decisions.

The New Testament context for decision-making is love: a call to make decisions within the context of love for others. (To retain the gospel term "commandment" is difficult today, since we are aware that we cannot, in the sense that we understand *command,* make an act of love out of obedience.) The goal of love—and the faith that incarnated love reveals God —does not tell the Christian layman what to do in a specific circumstance. It makes no automatic decisions for him. But it is an orientation: a hope that fills his significant actions. And, when that hope is missing, he is aware that he is acting out of context.

The second New Testament element of the Christian moral context is Jesus Himself—the historical figure whom we discern through the veil of preaching. He embodies His own call to love, so far as the Christian is concerned. His is the plain humanity of the cosmic process of divinization. And His humanity—the harmonies of His life as perceived through faith— provides an even more important part of the New Testament moral context than the call to love. Here, we have something more solid than words. The traditional rubric under which decision-making from the context of Jesus' life as seen through faith takes place is *imitatio*. The Christian decides through, though not solely through, the imitation of Christ.

This imitation takes various forms throughout history. I would suggest that today this context derives its most useful shape from application to Jesus as man of the traditional dogmatic understanding of Him as word incarnate, flesh suffering, and body triumphant. The Christian sees in decisions that he makes the possibility that what he does will incarnate a word; but he acknowledges, too, that this genesis of the word in act will in all likelihood bring a crucifixion of self, a crucifixion he can accept because in faith he sees as well the hope of a resurrection.

Now, this *imitatio* provides no answers, no custom-made content for my decisions. (I assume that many significant decisions—not to rape my neighbor's wife, for example—are made within a context other than the religious.) Imitation of Christ does not even suggest that the way to make a decision is to ask what Jesus would do under similar circumstances. There is no indication whether He would burn His draft card—to take a current distortion of Jesus as a norm. Rather, the person of Jesus is the context for decision-making for the person who believes. Nothing more: but that is a great deal.

Tradition, as well as the Gospel, is part of the context of Christian decision-making. Like the Gospel, I suggest, tradition does not tell me what to do in a specific instance. It does not tell me how to discipline my children—or whether in my own life or in the life of a community (a developing nation, say) it would be good or evil for contraceptives to be used. It tells me, rather, what values have been central through the ages of Christianity and how in practice those values have been realized in society.

Let me briefly apply this to the question of abortion. In practice, Christian tradition has until recently condemned abortion (now that total condemnation is not expressed by the Protestant community, we cannot take the condemnation of abortion as so uniform in Christian tradition as we once did). This does not of itself tell me that abortion is to be universally condemned in our own day. It is not even my primary consideration when facing the question of abortion.

My primary consideration is the wisdom behind the tradition, which provides a context within which as a Christian I will attempt to make my conscientious decision. The wisdom, of course, is a reverence for life. The sanctity of human life is the context within which abortion has until recently been condemned. It is one area—unlike the questions of war and inquisitorial torture—in which respect for life has been applied with great rigor.

When the Christian makes a decision concerning abortion today, he will do so within the triple context I have just described: the call to love; an imitation of Christ that sees in decisions the possibility of a word, the likelihood of suffering, and the hope that out of creative suffering will come fullness of life; and the wisdom offered by tradition. This is not the whole of the context, but a part of great importance.

Finally the Christian layman, when he makes his decisions, has a vision: the vision of the coming of the Kingdom, of the cosmic Christ, of the Spirit filling the world. The metaphors through which we describe the vision could be multiplied, and would still be inadequate to the reality of hope, a hope that is implied by the context of Christian decision-making.

Let me offer another: the Christian vision is one of the world—the total cosmos, if you will—journeying toward Bethlehem in order to be born—born through pain and suffering, but born into a new life in which the limitless infuses the limited, the spirit swells the flesh, God in all fullness becomes man. The world, in Christian hope, can become another Palestine—the city of man can become the city of God.

This vision, it seems clear, does not tell the layman what to do in a specific situation. It suggests instead that, from a Christian point of view, life is experimental and that decisions must be made experimentally. Do my actions—do my community's actions—at least seem right now to make the ultimate vision clearer, and closer? Decisions that obscure the vision might then be reversed, and a new experiment begun.

THE RELATIONAL CONSCIENCE AND THE MODERN WORLD

So far, my rhetoric concerning conscience has been insufficiently different from the conventional. The conscience of which I have spoken could as well be the monad of traditional writing in the area as the relational conscience that I would maintain is the healthy reality.

Perhaps a counter-image to the monadic conscience will destroy that idol more quickly than argument. Some years ago, while he was teaching at Fordham University, Robert Pollock suggested to a friend of mine that he spend a week contemplating the fact that the person is closer to society than the body is to the soul. There is the presupposition behind any discussion of the relational conscience: the person who makes healthy decisions is not lonely, existentially cut-off; the act of conscience takes place in a moment of unity with the world; it is an act of relationship, and in an at least obscure way takes into account the totality of the person's being.

On another level the theology of the Trinity may be useful. Though we ascribe different "acts" to each member—the Father "creates"—theology insists that the Father does not make this "decision" alone: an act of the Father is relational, that is, an act of all three persons. Further, given the world, the Trinity cannot act as if the world did not exist: God's "decisions" are in relationship to creation. The world is within the field of the divine: God is more closely related to the world than is man.

If, indeed, the task of man is cooperation in the process of divinization (to use the Orthodox term), then the task of man is to become more related, to make his own relationships as intimate as those attributed to the Trinity.

This has several implications for the conscience of the Roman Catholic layman. I shall discuss but some of them.

———All his relationships come into play in decision-making, not just some of them. The Roman Catholic does not ignore even the organizational Church when he makes a decision: it is one relationship among the many that enter the process. The organizational Church does not determine the content of a decision, on the other hand, any more than does the far more compelling context of the New Testament.

———Though all decisions will be made in relation to the totality of the layman's life, each decision will best be made primarily in terms of its own reality. The Vietnam war gives one example: it is not a gospel reality, but a political reality. If opposition to it is not framed in terms of political reality—the increasing awareness that for a major power war is no longer a political option—the decision will be faulty. When observers at the Berrigan trial call out that the judge and jury have crucified Christ once more, they are confusing religious reality with a political one. If Berrigan's decision to destroy draft records was not political, it may well have been nothing at all.

———A decision can be free only to the extent that its necessary unfreedom is accepted. In making a decision to divorce and remarry, the Roman Catholic layman can act well only if he has come to terms with every element of unfreedom that will remain part of that decision—the Roman Catholic prohibition of divorce and the force of his own sexual instincts are two possible sources of unfreedom here. In making a decision to resist the Vietnam war, the United States Roman Catholic layman will not be free unless he understands that he can resist only as an American.

———No decision the layman makes will be made with certitude. There are no guarantees: neither God, nor Christ, nor life itself will act as an insurance company certifying a happy outcome—giving warrant that the decision being made is the best possible. Decisions are an experiment in relationships.

———The relational decision is a decision made in the midst of process, because relations are in process. This means that the Roman Catholic layman may make his decisions absolutely—but his decisions are not absolutes. (The same would be true of the community in its exercise of conscience.) The decision, in other words, places the person in a stream of life. He remains in that stream if the consequences lead toward fuller life throughout his relationships.

——Last, though faith does not supply decisions, the layman's decisions will not be divorced from his faith. If this is so, the significant decision is a prayerful decision. Part of its context is the faith that to him who prays is given the Spirit. This gift of the Spirit, however, does not render decisions infallibly right: rather, perhaps, it is an assurance that even a mistaken decision can, through the graciousness of the Spirit, have ultimate meaning. Prayer is not man's end in a contract signed by God to the effect that he will move mountains or undertake other construction work. It is, instead, a way in which the man of Christian faith becomes more fully himself and so in his decisions can transcend himself. Like grace, prayer changes everything—and nothing.

REFERENCES

Congar, Y. M. (o.p.) *Lay people in the church.* London: Geoffrey Chapman, 1959.

Erikson, E. H. *Childhood and society.* (Rev. ed.) New York: Norton, 1963.

Fontinell, E. Reflections on faith and metaphysics. *Cross Currents,* 1966, *16,* 15–40.

Fontinell, E. Religious truth in a relational and processive world. *Cross Currents,* 1967, *17,* 283–315.

Henry, P. (s.j.) *Saint Augustine on personality.* New York: Macmillan, 1960.

James, W. *The varieties of religious experience.* New York: Longmans, Green, 1902. Citations are from the paperback edition, New York: Collier Books, 1961.

Lynch, W. F. (s.j.) *Images of hope.* Baltimore: Helicon, 1965.

O'Brien, E. (s.j.) The role of the priest in the lay apostolate. In C. H. Henkey (Ed.) *Loyola quodlibets.* Montreal: Palm Publishers, 1964. Pp. 11–23.

Presthus, R. *The organizational society.* New York: Knopf, 1962.

Warwick, D. P. Personal and organizational effectiveness in the church. *Cross Currents,* 1967, *17,* 401–417.

Weakland, J. H. The "double-bind" hypothesis of schizophrenia and three-party interaction. In D. D. Jackson (Ed.) *The etiology of schizophrenia.* New York: Basic Books, 1960. Pp. 375–392.

VII
CONSCIENCE AND THE ENCYCLICAL *HUMANAE VITAE*

Conscience, the National Hierarchies, and the Encyclical

PAUL F. PALMER, s.j.

Father Paul F. Palmer, S.J. obtained his advanced education at Woodstock College, earning his bachelor's degree in 1931, his master's in 1932, and finally his doctorate in sacred theology in 1942. He taught dogmatic theology for almost twenty years at his alma mater, with a brief interlude from 1951 to 1954 at the Jesuit Theologate in Toronto, finally in 1963 joining the Fordham University faculty, where he is currently associate professor of theology. Father Palmer, in addition to numerous articles in representative journals, is the author of four books: Mary in the documents of the Church *(1952);* Sources of Christian theology: I. Sacraments and worship *(1955);* Sources of Christian theology: II. Sacraments and forgiveness *(1959); and* Sacraments of healing and of vocation *(1963).*

"How can you, a seemingly intelligent man, hold your Church's position on birth control?" That was the question asked of me some years ago during a discussion following a talk on the Christian attitude toward sex. By way of reply I said that as an intelligent person I could see reasons both for and against contraceptive intercourse, and that if I were engaged in debate I would be perfectly willing to defend either side. But as an intelligent person I was convinced that there could be but one side that would reflect God's will in the matter. I personally could not arrive at an answer, and since the position of the Catholic Church at the time did no violence to my intellect, I had no difficulty in subscribing to the traditional and general teaching of the Church.

In the intervening years I have read more than the average Catholic theologian on the problem of contraceptive intercourse, and I have mulled over the problem for a longer period than most theologians who are my juniors. But I am still unable to offer a convincing argument either for or against the practice. I do not subscribe to the arguments used by Pope Paul VI in reaching the conclusion that contraceptive intercourse is wrong —nor need I. But I must confess that I cannot understand, much less agree with, the position of dissident theologians who unhesitatingly and categorically assert that the pope is wrong in the conclusion at which he arrived in his encyclical *Humanae Vitae* (Paul VI, 1968).

ASSENT AND DISSENT

In handling the problem of assent and dissent, most statements of the various national hierarchies, in their pastoral response to *Humanae Vitae*, take as their point of departure the declaration of Vatican II as found in the Dogmatic Constitution on the Church. Speaking in this document of the "religious assent of the soul" which is due to the teaching of bishops on matters of faith and morals when they teach in communion with the Roman Pontiff, the Fathers of Vatican II continue as follows:

> This religious submission of will and mind must be shown in a special way to the authentic teaching authority of the Roman Pontiff, even when he is not speaking ex cathedra. That is, it must be shown in such a way that his supreme magisterium is acknowledged with reverence, the judgments made by him are sincerely adhered to, according to his manifest mind and will [Vatican Council II, 1966, n. 25, p. 48].

In applying this general norm of Vatican II to the encyclical *Humanae Vitae*, most of the national hierarchies seem aware of the qualification (Modus #159) of the doctrinal commission of Vatican II, which was prompted by three bishops who "invoke the particular case, at least theoretically possible, in which an educated person, confronted with a teaching proposed non-infallibly, cannot for solid reasons give his internal assent." The response of the Commission was: "For this case approved theological explanations should be consulted" (cf. Kommonchak, 1969, p. 104).

Following the varying explanations of approved authors (*auctores probati*), most of the national hierarchies admit that it is permissible for one who is competent in the matter to deviate in his private theory and practice from non-infallible teaching. The German bishops regard "such a case" as "conceivable in principle," but warn that a person "must question his conscience soberly and critically as to whether he can justify this before God" (German Bishops, 1968, p. 48).

The Belgian bishops limit dissent to one who is competent in the matter, but add:

> In such a case, he must remain sincerely disposed to continue his enquiry and beware of compromising the common good and the salvation of his brothers by creating an unhealthy unrest or, *a fortiori,* by questioning the very principle of authority [Belgian Bishops, 1968, p. 55].

The reluctance of the German bishops to allow private dissent and the qualifications of the Belgian bishops, which would limit dissent to experts in the matter, are not found in the pastoral statement of the Scandinavian bishops, the pertinent portion of which reads as follows:

> Should someone, however, for grave and carefully considered reasons, not feel able to subscribe to the arguments of the Encyclical, he is entitled, as has been constantly acknowledged, to entertain other views than those put forward in a non-infallible declaration of the Church. No one should, therefore, on account of such divergent opinions alone, be regarded as an inferior Catholic [Scandinavian Bishops, 1968, p. 51].

None of the pastoral responses of the national hierarchies takes up the question of public dissent. The bishops of the United States, however, do exclude the pulpit as a legitimate forum for such public dissent: "Even responsible dissent does not excuse one from faithful presentation of the authentic doctrine of the Church when one is performing a pastoral ministry in her name" (United States Bishops, 1968, p. 10). To exclude all public dissent would, perhaps, be unrealistic in an age of instant communication, when the opinions of individual theologians or groups of theologians are either ferreted out or simply overheard.

ASSENT TO WHAT?

More important from the pastoral point of view than the character of the assent to be given to *Humanae Vitae* is the object of the assent itself. The problem of assent and dissent has overshadowed and obscured the question rarely raised: assent to what? I am convinced that many dissenting theologians believed that Paul VI taught that contraceptive intercourse was of itself a serious sin, and that failure on their part to challenge such teaching would engender a crisis of faith in the minds of many Catholics. If the teaching of the encyclical, they argued, were unopposed by knowledgeable Catholic theologians, the laity would be faced with a number of intolerable options. These options have been spelled out briefly but cogently by Robert McAfee Brown. Writing of Catholics who have been using contraceptives, and who "have been participating in the sacramental life of the Church and have been sustained by it," Brown continues:

> And now they face hard choices. They must either (a) forsake the sacraments because of their convictions, or (b) forsake their convictions at what may bring harm to their marriage relationship, or (c) walk the disturbing tight rope of giving formal allegiance to the teaching office of the church but failing to apply its specific teachings to their own lives. I imagine many will quietly drift away from the church. Those who stay will increasingly wonder about the integrity of a situation in which church membership necessitates a disregard of church teaching. Whatever they do, their anguish will be great [Brown, 1969, p. 208].

Seemingly unaware that there might be an option other than rejection of the Church's teaching, many dissenting theologians stated quite categorically that the pope was wrong, and that the laity were free to form their own consciences and to receive the sacraments. Had they been less precipitous, had they attempted to determine the "manifest mind and will" of Paul VI on the gravity of contraceptive intercourse, as many national hierarchies have done, they could have counseled the laity to continue to receive the sacraments without rejecting the substantive teaching of *Humanae Vitae*.

At first reading it would appear that it is the manifest mind of Paul VI that contraceptive intercourse is objectively a grave sin, and that it is his manifest will that the sin must be confessed before receiving the Eucharist. Unquestionably, *Humanae Vitae* states that contraceptive intercourse is illicit, that such actions are "intrinsically disordered" and "intrinsically improper," and, as evil, they cannot be performed that good might come of them, nor can they "be made proper and right by the ensemble of a fertile conjugal life" (Paul VI, 1968, p. 40). Some would see in the expression "intrinsically disordered" the equivalent of "objectively grave." But lying and stealing are also intrinsically evil—forbidden because wrong, not simply wrong because forbidden—and yet allow of light matter. Again, Paul VI says: "And if sin should still keep its hold over them, let them not be discouraged, but rather have recourse with humble perseverance to the mercy of God, which is poured forth in the sacrament of penance" (Paul VI, 1968, p. 45). Paul, then, definitely regards contraceptive intercourse as a sin and strongly encourages frequent confession, but he does not say that such confession is mandatory. In fact the tone of his advice is hardly that which would be employed in counselling those over whom *grave* sin "keeps its hold." Finally, if Paul VI wanted to brand contraceptive intercourse as a grave sin, he could simply have repeated the teaching of his predecessor Pius XI, who clearly stated that contraceptive intercourse "is an offense against the law of God, and those who indulge in such are branded with the guilt of a grave sin" (Pius XI, 1931, p. 38).

All this is, perhaps, too benign an interpretation of the Pontiff's teaching, and does not reflect the real mind of Paul VI, but rather the wish which has fathered the thought of the present writer. And yet there are many statements of the national hierarchies which are equally benign in the interpretation of the encyclical. All admit that contraceptive intercourse is wrong, that it is an evil, although not always culpable, and that it is a failure to live up to the high ideal of marriage proposed by Paul VI. But no pastoral statement of the various hierarchies brands contraceptive intercourse as a serious sin. In fact, the statements which we shall now consider either explicitly or implicitly rule out serious sin except where extreme selfishness is the motivating factor. The Austrian bishops state quite categorically:

> The Holy Father does not speak of grave sin in his encyclical. Therefore, if someone should err against the teaching of the encyclical, he must not feel cut off from God's love in every case, and may then receive Holy Communion without first going to confession [Austrian Bishops, 1968, p. 59].

The statement of the British bishops is a bit ambiguous in its use of the word "sacraments," but they would seem to agree with their Austrian colleagues that the encyclical does not speak of grave sin. "There is no threat of damnation. Far from being excluded from the sacraments those in difficulties are invited to receive them more frequently" (British Bishops, 1968, p. 60).

THE TEACHING OF THE ENCYCLICAL SEEN AS AN IDEAL

No one would question the complete "religious submission of mind and will" of the Italian hierarchy to the teaching of *Humanae Vitae*. On the crucial question whether contraceptive intercourse is a serious sin, the Italian bishops seem to speak of the Pontiff's teaching as an ideal to be attained, rather than as a command binding under serious sin. Thus, the whole encyclical is regarded as the Church's courageous expression of "what is ideal," and what it must propose integrally to mankind. On the specific question of contraceptive intercourse, the bishops exhort the faithful not to be disheartened because of possible failures, and offer as a reason:

> The Church, whose task it is to declare the total and perfect goodness, is not unaware that there are laws of growth in goodness, and that at times one passes through stages still imperfect, although with the aim of loyalty overcoming them in a constant effort towards the ideal [Italian Bishops, 1969, 64].

The most benign, permissive, and progressive of all the pastorals in its interpretation of *Humanae Vitae*—and it is the latest that has come to my knowledge—is that of the Swiss bishops. In admitting the principle of "totality," the Swiss hierarchy seemingly is of the opinion that Paul's judgment that contraceptive intercourse cannot be made "proper and right by the ensemble of a fertile conjugal life" is not substantive to his teaching, but only supportive to his conclusion that contraceptive intercourse is "intrinsically improper." And it is the teaching of *Humanae Vitae* and not the arguments in support of that teaching to which an assent must be given. The Swiss hierarchy speaks as follows:

> Couples who have decided to confer life on children and who live a human and Christian conjugal love are responding to the *fundamental demands* of the divine will. If, in any particular case, they are unable to respond to all the directives of the encyclical on the regulation of births, and meanwhile act not from egotistical motives or from unalloyed desire for worldly goods, but strive with total sincerity to carry out the will of God ever more perfectly, they should not consider themselves guilty before God [emphasis added; Swiss Bishops, 1969, p. 6].

As in the statement of the Italian hierarchy, we find in the Swiss pastoral a tendency to distinguish between the fundamental demands of God's will, which bind under serious sin, and the perfect realization of God's will for married couples, as expressed in the encyclical. Failure to realize the ideal in every instance is not a serious sin, but such failures introduce into married life a disorder, a declination from the order of things willed by God. In this sense we can speak of the disorder as an evil, but since the disorder is at times all but necessitated by the disordered society in which we live, the disorder is not necessarily an evil which is culpable. This is essentially the position adopted by the Canadian bishops (1968, p. 56), as well as by the French bishops in their pastoral response to *Humanae Vitae*. The French bishops spoke as follows:

> Contraception can never be a good. It is always a disorder, but this disorder is not always culpable. It happens, indeed, that spouses see themselves confronted with veritable conflicts of duties. . . . On the one hand, they are aware of the duty of respecting the openness to life of every conjugal act; they also judge in conscience that they have to avoid or put off until later a new birth, and they are deprived of the resource of relying on biological rhythms. On the other hand, in what concerns them, they do not see how to renounce at present the physical expression of their love without menacing the stability of their home.
> On this subject we shall simply recall the constant teaching of morality: when one has an alternative choice of duties and, whatever may be the decision, evil cannot be avoided, traditional wisdom makes provision for seeking before God which duty, under the circumstances, is the greater. Husband and wife will make this decision at the end of a common reflection carried on with all the care that the greatness of their conjugal vocation requires [French Bishops, 1969, p. 52].

Paul VI in his encyclical rules out the principle of the "lesser of two evils" as applicable to the problem of contraception. And since the principle of a "conflict of duties" is but another way of stating more positively the principle of the "lesser of two evils," it would seem that the French bishops either regard Paul's reasoning as non-substantive to his conclusion that contraception is a disorder, or believe that their own understanding of the principle is not the same as that ruled out by the Holy Father. Paul VI—or, better, the theologian who lent his hand to this section of the encyclical— seems to confuse the principle of the lesser of two evils with the principle, rejected by all moralists, that "the end justifies the means." This section of *Humanae Vitae* deserves citation in full and further comment. It reads:

> In truth, if it is sometimes licit to tolerate a lesser evil in order to avoid a greater evil or to promote a greater good, it is not licit to do evil so that good may follow therefrom, that is, to make into the object of a positive act of the will something which is intrinsically disordered and hence unworthy of the human person, even when the intention is to safeguard or promote individual, family, or social well-being [Paul VI, 1968, p. 40].

The operative clause in the above passage is "to make into the object of a positive act of the will something which is intrinsically disordered." My own opinion is that there is a difference between intending an action which is recognized as evil and in which the evil accompaniment is tolerated, and willing as a positive good an action which has evil effects. The first is an application of the principle of the "lesser of two evils," or a "conflict of duties." The second is an application of the principle that "the end justifies the means" in the sense of canonizing the means as a good which can be positively willed. I believe that it is this distinction which underlies the parallel drawn by Bishop Pierre Boillon of Verdun, the spokesman for the French assembly of bishops, who gave this example:

> I killed four Germans. I try to justify myself before God, but I did not accuse myself at confession of a sin. I had a conflict of duties, between the duty of defending my country and that of respecting human life. Killing those Germans was evil but not a sin [Boillon, 1968, p. 3].

I suspect that Bishop Boillon is using the same principle that many moralists apply with respect to killing in self-defense. All killing is evil, a disorder, whether it be in a just war or in self-defense. It can never be justified as a good; it can never become, in the words of Paul VI, "the object of a positive act of the will." So, too, contraception must be recognized as an evil, as a disorder. And this the French bishops assert. But where there is a genuine conflict of duties, the evil can be tolerated. It cannot be willed as a good.

To inject a personal note, I have spoken with a number of married couples who have been forced by circumstances to invoke the principle of the lesser of two evils. All admitted that contraceptive intercourse left much to be desired as an expression and symbol of their married love, and that they would much prefer normal intercourse which is open both to life and to love, if the circumstances allowed. To my mind, this is an implicit admission that contraceptive intercourse is a disorder ("evil" is perhaps for many too strong a word)—a disorder, however, that is brought on by the disorder of human society.

CONCLUSION

To conclude, from the pastoral responses of the Austrian, British, Canadian, French, Italian, and Swiss hierarchies to *Humanae Vitae*, it is at least questionable whether it is the "manifest mind and will" of Paul VI, as expressed in his encyclical, that contraceptive intercourse is objectively a grave sin, to be confessed before receiving the Eucharist.

Up to the present, discussion of *Humanae Vitae* has been focused on the quality and the obligatory character of the assent that must be given to papal but non-infallible pronouncements. Of more pastoral concern is the question: assent to what? Personally I find no difficulty in assenting to the papal teaching that contraceptive intercourse is intrinsically disordered. But in the exercise of my pastoral office, as counselor and confessor, I do not regard the evil as grave or, where there is a real conflict of duties, as culpable. I do, however, regard openness to life and to love as the ideal of marriage and of the act which is most expressive of marriage. I am convinced, as the Austrian bishops say by way of summary, that "this image of marriage drawn by the Holy Father represents a lofty aim for all couples, and its attainment could bring forth happiness and contentment" (Austrian Bishops, 1969, p. 58).

REFERENCES

Austrian Bishops. Austrian bishops on *Humanae Vitae*. *Catholic Mind,* 1969, *67* (April, no. 1232), 57–60.

Belgian Bishops. Belgian bishops on *Humanae Vitae*. *Catholic Mind,* 1968, *66* (October, no. 1226), 53–56.

Boillon, P. *National Catholic Reporter,* November 20, 1968.

British Bishops. British bishops on *Humanae Vitae*. *Catholic Mind,* 1968, *66* (November, no. 1227), 58–62.

Brown, R. M. *Humanae Vitae*: A Protestant reaction. In C. A. Curran (Ed.) *Contraception: Authority and dissent.* New York: Herder & Herder, 1969. Pp. 193–215.

Canadian Bishops. Canadian bishops on *Humanae Vitae*. *Catholic Mind,* 1968, *66* (November, no. 1227), 52–57.

French Bishops. French bishops on *Humanae Vitae*. *Catholic Mind,* 1969, *67* (January, no. 1229), 47–54.

German Bishops. German bishops on *Humanae Vitae*. *Catholic Mind,* 1968, *66* (October, no. 1226), 47–53.

Italian Bishops. Italian bishops on *Humanae Vitae. Catholic Mind,* 1969, *67* (April, no. 1232), 60–64.

Kommonchak, J. A. Ordinary papal magisterium and religious assent. In C. A. Curran (Ed.) *Contraception: Authority and dissent.* New York: Herder & Herder, 1969. Pp. 101–126.

Paul VI. *Humanae Vitae.* Encyclical letter of July 25, 1968. *Acta Apostolicae Sedis,* 1968, *60,* 481–503. English translation: Human life. *Catholic Mind,* 1968, *66* (September, no. 1225), 35–48.

Pius XI. *Casti Connubii.* Encyclical letter of December 31, 1930. *Acta Apostolicae Sedis,* 1930, *22,* 539–592. English translation: On Christian marriage. *Catholic Mind,* 1931, *29,* 21–64.

Scandinavian Bishops. Scandinavian bishops on *Humanae Vitae. Catholic Mind,* 1968, *66* (December, no. 1228), 49–54.

Swiss Bishops. Swiss bishops on *Humanae Vitae. Documentary Service.* United States Catholic Conference, Press Department. February 10, 1969.

United States Bishops. Collective pastoral: Human life in our day. *Catholic Mind,* 1968, *66* (December, no. 1228), 1–28.

Vatican Council II. Dogmatic constitution on the church. In W. M. Abbott (S.J.) (Ed.) *The documents of Vatican II.* New York: Herder & Herder, 1966. Pp. 14–96.

The Encyclical from the Standpoint of a Biblical Theologian

CHARLES H. GIBLIN, s.j.

Father Charles Homer Giblin, S.J. has his A.B. (1950) and M.A. (1952) degrees from Loyola University (Chicago); his S.T.L. (1959) from West Baden University; and his S.S.L. (1962) and S.S.D. (1967) degrees from the Biblical Institute, Rome. He is a member of the Studiorum Novi Testamenti Societas, *the Society of Biblical Literature, and the Catholic Biblical Association. He is the author of* The threat to faith: An exegetical and theological re-examination of 2 Thessalonians 2 *(1967) and articles in* Theological Studies *and the* Catholic Biblical Quarterly. *Previously assistant professor at Bellarmine School of Theology, North Aurora, Illinois, Father Giblin is currently associate professor of theology at Fordham University.*

Reactions to Pope Paul's *Humanae Vitae* (Paul vi, 1968) have been stated from various standpoints, both theological and non-theological. Ultimately, the scope of the document requires a theological and pastoral standpoint on the part of the one who reacts, for the encyclical is ostensibly written to communicate a further understanding of Christian human life with reference to a pressing, practical problem. The general tenor even of theological response has been strongly negative, at least in Anglo-Saxon areas of the world. With the aim of clarifying a proper theologico-pastoral standpoint within the narrower scope of my own theological competence, but in consideration of this widespread, negative reaction to the encyclical, I pose the following question: Could a Catholic Biblical theologian, of all people in the modern Church, react favorably to Pope Paul's *Humanae Vitae*? I think that, to some degree, he could—loyally but discerningly.

His own vicissitudes at the hands of Roman documents have taught the Biblical theologian in the Church today to see larger issues and to seek out and clarify basic common perspectives. From his ecclesial and pastoral experience, he has also learned to contribute in the spirit of his métier some positive understanding in faith ($\pi\alpha\rho\acute{\alpha}\kappa\lambda\eta\sigma\iota s$) concerning what many major spokesmen in the Church try to do but fail to do effectively. Precisely because he professes to understand a shared faith, this Biblical theologian cannot avoid noting in *Humanae Vitae* certain dismaying deficiencies in the pope's way of proclaiming God's law. For the same reason, however, he cannot fail to try to understand the pope in the total perspective of their common faith in Christ's law.

DISTINCTION BETWEEN GOSPEL LAW AND POLITICAL LAW

Surely the pope *intends* nothing but what is adequately God's law. In spite of his disturbing statement, then, that the teaching of the Church is founded on the natural law illumined by divine revelation (Paul vi, 1968, n. 4, p. 36), he must at heart mean that it is founded on revelation (viz., on the revealed law of Christ's gospel) which illumines the natural law. A day or so after publishing his encyclical, according to a report in *The New York Times,* the pope averred that he had wished nothing but to proclaim the divine law, Christ's law of love. But Christ's law is a law of faith; revelation founding faith never plays second violin to reason (cf. 1 Cor 1:18–2:16). What is more, as St. Paul made clear to St. Peter at Antioch (Gal 2:11–21), there is no divine law to be followed or divine justice to which we are to aspire but that which we have in Christ. The "divine law" contains no "natural law" in *addition* to the law of Christ, any more than God Himself is "more" than Christ. Accordingly, let us judge the encyclical of Pope Paul vi—the Vicar of Christ and the successor of Saints Peter and Paul— as we may feel sure that he himself, in line with his charismatic *office,* would want us ultimately to judge it, viz., in the perspective of the evangelical law of Christ.

Gospel law is radically "no prohibition"—basically the German phrase which Paul vi used on July 31, 1968, of his own encyclical: *"kein <blosses> Verbot"* (there is some question whether or not the pope used the word *"blosses,"* but the hurried Vatican interpretation of "no pure prohibition" as *"not only* prohibition" was certainly in error; the latter would have been unmistakably different: *"nicht nur Verbot"*). In any event, the pope's encyclical must be tested against the gospel law, for the Church accepts the gospel as "canonical" or basically prescriptive for Christian life. Now, to understand the gospel law, one must take a theological perspective which justifies its name—a perspective which goes beyond biology or demography (as the pope himself notes [Paul VI, 1968, n. 7, p. 37]), but which also transcends a modern understanding of political law (as, unfortunately, he does not note). To communicate the gospel law to the modern world, especially to the non-Mediterranean world, it is of primary importance to distinguish gospel law from political law. Otherwise, the gospel law, which is what we want to hear from the Vicar of Christ, will not be seen for what it really is. It will be liable to be judged in a non-theological perspective (a political perspective, for instance) at variance with its genuine scope. I find the need and the basis for the clarification of perspective in Scripture itself—both in the Pauline and even in the Matthean understanding of fully revealed law as radically "no prohibition." I feel that one can appreciatively probe this paradox of gospel law and bring it to bear on *Humanae Vitae* by contrasting revealed Christian law with political law, the latter as understood by John Courtney Murray, S.J. (1960).

In politics one hardly views law precisely as an ideal, much less as a personal ideal, and never as becoming perfect as our heavenly Father is perfect. The standpoint of politics or policy usually dictates that we consider law *primarily as a minimum norm of action binding under some sanction.* Grace does not enter this perspective, nor does the Christian ideal of perfect justice. Norm of action pure and simple—and minimal—not ideal action rendered possible by grace, defines the horizon. Christian politics, like Christian philosophy or Christian thinking in any area of human reason, lies open to grace; but it does not focus on grace, nor does it focus, therefore, on the ideal which only grace makes possible.

THE MEANING OF THE GOSPEL LAW

The law of Christ differs radically. Indeed, a minimum norm is enunciated: those who (characteristically) perform this, that, and the other sinful act will not enter the kingdom of God (cf. 1 Cor 6:9ff.). But Christ's law does not focus on the sanctioned norm of action, much less on the minimum norm. It focuses on and even "prescribes" the ideal made possible by grace and understanding in Christ. Thus it is that chastity and heroic renunciation of earth-bound goods exemplify the acme of Christ's law—precisely as counsel in eschatological (historically final and definitive) perspective, not as expected minimum norm of conduct binding under pain of sin and sanction. Christ's law *includes* "the counsels" and, indeed, finds its fullest expression in them.

Thus it is, too, that Christ can proclaim in the beatitudes God's grace and forthwith state His law in terms stricter than those of any Pharisaic school. For He focuses the whole law in a fundamentally different way, and His prescriptions differ accordingly. It is the *perspective of grace* which explains everything, precisely as the dominant perspective. Each action God will judge in line with His all-penetrating favor, which reaches beyond the human power-structure and human expectations. Human precept is not the ultimate criterion, nor is human understanding. He who becomes angry with his brother is liable to judgment (Mt 5:22); one is not to swear even by his own head (Mt 5:36). Pluck out your eye if it scandalizes you! Even one betrayed by his wife is expected to live as a eunuch for the kingdom of heaven (Mt 19:12; cf. Quesnell [1968]). More than Semitic hyperbole is involved in passages like these. All this is fundamentally a way of voicing and "prescribing" an *ideal*: perfect justice (the theme of the Sermon on the Mount, Mt 5–7); "for those to whom it is given . . . let him who can take it, take it" [Mt 19:11–12]). In this jolting perspective, and only thus, the whole mind of God and consequently the whole law, Christ's law of perfect justice and holiness, can be fulfilled to the letter. What is expected on the part of the reader is a way of *understanding* the letter; for the letter in Matthew is mystery.

Humanae Vitae MUST BE INTERPRETED AS AN EXPRESSION OF THE GOSPEL LAW

Within this context of the strictly formulated ideal, notably as we find it in Matthew, we can construe the pope's encyclical as basically evangelical. He levies no disciplinary sanction (remarkable, really!). He focuses for the most part on a realizable ideal, even as he "prescribes" it. One will follow God most faithfully if he follows Pope Paul's practical norms to the letter; for they quite closely resemble Matthean *ideals,* even though they are expressed in terms of a negative cast. As evangelical ideals, however, they are not "nice things to do if they were humanly possible" or "if I feel like it," but ideals true to the gospel vision of what is actually possible by grace (even if not binding under sin or serious sin). This law is supremely demanding, but it is not radically prohibitive. Some points are undoubtedly closer to the minimum than others. Some (e.g., abortion, the first on the pope's list [Paul VI, 1968, n. 14, p. 40]) may perhaps even stand as the very minimum norm. But the total, i.e., "catholic" perspective, which ultimately governs everything, is not precisely that of a norm binding under sin, much less one binding univocally under grave sin.

To discern this perspective and the focus of the supremely demanding law which is radically "no prohibition," nothing substitutes, of course, for discerning interpretation of the formulated law according to the inner law of the Spirit. The ideal is there, and it is operative; it must also be *understood* by a connatural principle, wisdom (cf. Mt 5:13; 1 Cor 2:12–13). This observation entails a twofold caution. On the one hand, let us not debase the evangelical ideal which the pope tries to provide by judging it primarily in the myopic Pharisaic perspective of political norms and sanctions (the perspective of our enlightened press), in which the ideal yields place to "things which must be done, or else. . . ." If Pope Paul is hard to understand and accept, so is Christ Himself in the New Testament. On the other hand, let us remind ourselves that we are to interpret Pope Paul ultimately in the light of the *gospel* and of the mind of Christ, not on the basis of a philosophical moral theology as such.

One may object that the encyclical is largely and perhaps basically an ethical document in the manner of Jacques Maritain; that it is really written from the standpoint of a Christian philosophy and not from the standpoint of the law of the gospel. The not infrequent distinction between "natural and evangelical" (Paul VI, 1968, n. 18, p. 42; cf. also nn. 23–24, p. 44) under the general heading "divine law" gives substance to this objection, especially in the light of n. 4 (Paul VI, 1968, p. 36). I admit that I am seriously disconcerted by this phraseology, but I do not think that it follows from such expressions that the pope is really exceeding his authority or that he effectively excludes the line of interpretation which I have proposed. Paul VI certainly does not want to be accepted as an ecclesiastical moral philosopher. We owe it to him, then, and to the Lord for whom he speaks, loyally to discern what we may feel sure he really means in accordance with the office he exercises. His letter is not mainly "personal" but "institutional," like all official Church documents. Our effort to grasp this official document may have to take the form of what has been called "benign interpretation"— as is so often the case with Church documents of admittedly more weighty character. Even if this is the case with *Humanae Vitae*, there is a quite legitimate basis for this mode of interpretation in the total context of what the pope stands for and of the shared faith of all Catholics.

No papal document is meant to be taken simply on the basis of its reasoned arguments or of the strictly personal suppositions of the author; every papal document must be taken in the total institutional context of Catholic teachings and, therefore, ultimately in the total context of the gospel itself. "Benign interpretation," therefore, as an attempt to understand a given document of the *magisterium,* is valid according to what proves necessary to make the document say what the speaker *officially* represents. It is both easier to propose such an interpretation and more necessary in justice and charity to do so, when the speaker (whatever be his inevitable personal shortcomings in the field of modern communication) is sincerely attempting to exercise his office responsibly and without pretense. I believe that the interpretation which I have offered has solid critical justification precisely as a theological interpretation of an ecclesiastical, papal document, even if one chooses to call it a "benign" interpretation.

CONCLUSION

A closing, practical word from St. Paul: "Whatever is not from faith [i.e., from the Christian's charismatic understanding of his newly restructured relationship to God in Christ] is sin" (Rom 14:23). This statement stands as the Apostle's practical advice for all in the Roman community, and it means forming one's conscience with help from pondering the apostolic guidelines. For St. Paul, "conscience" is the understanding of the way one stands before God—an understanding which reaches its maturity in a reflex awareness of the faith-relationship, and thus can entail a fulfillment of the understanding of faith itself. St. Paul recognized that, living in the same community at Rome, there were those "strong" in faith and "weak" in faith. The difference centered upon certain concrete practices or observances which were considered quite serious at the time. No schism resulted in the Roman community; no schism need have resulted. St. Paul obviously disagreed with a number (the "weak," who insisted upon certain clear-cut norms and practices); he squelched no one. Resolutely, however, he insisted that each one live in charity with others and form his conscience faithfully before God. But, somewhat boldly (Rom 15:15), Paul, perhaps the most prophetic Apostle, had offered to his unseen and mostly unknown audience at Rome his own charismatic vision of faith and law, and had given them a solid, corresponding principle of responsibly charismatic interpretation.

REFERENCES

Murray, J. C. (s.j.) *We hold these truths: Catholic reflections on the American proposition*. New York: Sheed & Ward, 1960.

Paul vi. *Humanae vitae*. Encyclical letter of July 25, 1968. *Acta Apostolicae Sedis*, 1968, *60*, 481–503. English translation: Human life. *Catholic Mind*, 1968, *66* (September, no. 1225), 35–48.

Quesnell, Q. (s.j.) Made themselves eunuchs for the kingdom of heaven (Mt 19, 12). *Catholic Biblical Quarterly*, 1968, *30*, 335–358.

The Conscience of the Theologian with Reference to the Encyclical

FREDERICK E. CROWE, s.j.

Father Frederick E. Crowe, S.J. came to the field of theology with a background in science. His first degree in 1934 was a B.Sc. from the University of New Brunswick. In 1943 he earned an A.B. degree from the University of Montreal, and then in 1953 an S.T.D. from the Gregorian University, Rome. He is editor of Spirit as inquiry: Studies in honor of Bernard Lonergan *(1964) and author of* A time of change *(1968). A member of the Catholic Theological Society of America and the American Catholic Philosophical Association, Father Crowe is a contributor to such periodicals as* Sciences Ecclésiastiques *and* Theological Studies. *Formerly professor of philosophy at St. Mary's University, Halifax, and visiting professor of theology at the Gregorian University, Rome, Father Crowe is currently professor of theology at Regis College, Willowdale, Ontario, Canada.*

The title of this paper refers to conscience and, specifically, to conscience in regard to the encyclical *Humanae Vitae* (Paul vi, 1968). Nevertheless, the course of my reflections as I prepared the paper led me somewhat away from that pair of terms, and I am therefore going to take certain liberties with my topic. I will speak regularly of responsibility rather than of conscience, and I will talk rather of responsibility to the ongoing Church, the Church that has survived the *Humanae Vitae* episode, than about responsibility in regard to the encyclical itself. I do intend to speak of the theologian's responsibility.

I prefer "responsibility," then, as pointing a little more directly to the personal involvement and intervention of the theologian. Conscience is surely the activity of the subject, it is surely personal, but it can refer to a general question on which we form a common moral judgment, though we may be called upon, as responsible persons, to take varying action. Thus, several men may be conscientious objectors to military service, but the responsibilities of a Congressman and those of a drafted student are hardly the same; they differ according to the possibilities of action afforded. To take an illustration from the topic in hand: the conscience of the 87 theologians who issued a statement on *Humanae Vitae* on July 30, 1968, may have been quite the same as mine in regard to the common object, the binding force of the encyclical; but their responsibility was to take the lead in issuing a statement, while mine was the more commonplace one of subscribing to the statement.

In other words, "conscience" seems to refer more directly to the object, while "responsibility" seems to refer more directly to *me* and to what *I* should do. The difference between the two is slight; it is a matter of where the emphasis more *directly* falls; but I think it makes the change worthwhile. There is a principle of maximum concreteness involved, of what I can and ought to do within the limits of my situation. Jesus died for all men, but He could not preach to and teach all men; His responsibility for preaching and teaching was limited to the house of Israel.

The same principle of maximum concreteness is involved in my second change in the topic. The situation in the Church is such today that to *talk about* responsibility is also an *exercise in* responsibility. We are not dealing with matters of merely archaeological interest, but with matters of vital concern to the Church. I mean the whole Church, married or single, lay or clerical, the non-theologian as well as the theologian. For it is not really a matter any longer of what Christian married life should be; it is a matter of what the Church is to be, of how we are to exercise judgment in the Church and determine our practice. If I am to exercise my responsibility with the utmost concreteness in that situation, I must speak to the ongoing Church of today, not to the Church of last year. I will indeed say a word on the conscience and responsibility of the theologian in regard to *Humanae Vitae* itself, but only to set that topic aside with all possible brevity.

THE THEOLOGIAN AND *Humanae Vitae*

The conscience of the theologian in regard to *Humanae Vitae* can be simply described somewhat as follows: the encyclical is the pronouncement of the Holy Father, so the theologian will regard it with respect and study it with due care. It is not an infallible pronouncement; non-infallible pronouncements are fallible, so the theologian will not give the pope unconditional assent on the basis of authority alone, but is obliged to weigh the arguments provided. If his unconditional assent is not required, neither is his absolute obedience. Given sufficient reason, he may dissent; in fact, the reasons are at hand. All these headings could be expanded and, under given conditions, ought to be expanded. But I really do not think that it is appropriate for me to delay any longer on what must be obvious to all of us.

The responsibility of the theologian in the summer and fall of 1968 is a more interesting topic and I will stay a moment on that. I should say, then, that in 1968 the pressing responsibility of the theologian was to the people of God, especially to the "poor" among them—that is, to the uninstructed, the bewildered, the heavy-burdened. A theologian, of course, has various responsibilities to different persons in regard to different values; he has a responsibility to the Holy Father, to his bishop or religious superior, to his fellow-theologians, to his students; he has a responsibility in regard to truth, in regard to understanding, in regard to communication, and so forth. But needs have an order of priority, and so have responsibilities. The need a year ago was the need of husbands and wives to know the options open to them in married life. This came out with great clarity in a meeting of the Société Canadienne de Théologie held in Montreal on September 21, 1968. In an unofficial report of the meeting,* requested by the theological commission of the Canadian Conference of Bishops, it is stated that the right of the poor—i.e., of those not well instructed—to know the whole truth of the matter, was one of the central concerns of the meeting. The theologians present found it unjust and monstrous that better educated persons could profit from the state of doubt in the Church, if the poor were to have a burden imposed without explanation of the whole question of morality and contraceptives.

If the articulation of the need is clear in that statement, the intervention demanded by responsibility was swiftest, most dramatic, and most widely effective in the statement of the 87 theologians issued in Washington, D.C. the day after the encyclical was published. The three final paragraphs of

---

* Unpublished document: L'Encyclique "Humanae Vitae" et la théologie. Rapport . . . non officiel sur la rencontre organisée par la Société Canadienne de Théologie . . . le 21 septembre, 1968.

their statement give the Church teaching, a statement of conscience, the conclusion of the theologians about their own responsibility.

> It is common teaching in the Church that Catholics may dissent from authoritative, non-infallible teachings of the magisterium when sufficient reasons for so doing exist.
>
> Therefore, as Roman Catholic theologians, conscious of our duty and our limitations, we conclude that spouses may responsibly decide according to their conscience that artificial contraception in some circumstances is permissible and indeed necessary to preserve and foster the values and sacredness of marriage.
>
> It is our conviction also that true commitment to the mystery of Christ and the Church requires a candid statement of mind at this time by all Catholic theologians [Washington Theologians, 1968, pp. 3–4].

It is just because of such candid statements as this, that the theologian's responsibility in regard to *Humanae Vitae* can be discussed as an historical question. That is, the responsibility the time called for was discharged. In a similar way the question of conscience has been settled; it was settled within a few weeks of the encyclical's appearance, maybe even a few days. By and large the Catholic world became aware of the options open to it. Its conscience can be regarded as formed. At least, there is the possibility of forming one's conscience in peace. Too many serious believers have assumed as permissible, even obligatory, a practice contrary to that enjoined by the encyclical; too many moderate, obedient theologians have defended the right to dissent; too many episcopal conferences have spoken, respectfully but clearly, on the rights of conscience. The question is no longer a question, and ten thousand headlines in *L'Osservatore Romano* cannot change facts that are now common property.

I do not mean to overlook the continuing need of the people for instruction and support; our responsibility toward them remains. Again, I am not insensitive to the deep feelings that have been aroused in the Church; we have still to remember the saying, "Blessed are the peacemakers." But the indicated responsibilities are not especially those of a pastoral psychology institute. Yet again, we do not know what suffering is in store for dissenters; it may be that things will get worse before they get better; so be it then.* But I refuse to be gloomy. My own opinion is that a principle has been established, my hope is that we will not return again to a curial style of government exercised with the same independence of the people, that we will never revert to such a sharp distinction between the "teaching" and the

---

* This paper was already written when I realized my one-sided concern for fellow theologians, my failure in responsibility toward confessors disciplined by authority for their stand on the encyclical. They were the vulnerable ones; what have we theologians done in their cause? At this point I can only confess my personal negligence.

"learning" Church. I think a chapter has been written; we must look forward to the next.

If this paper, then, is to be not merely *about* responsibility, but also an *exercise in* responsibility, it must regard the present situation and attempt a contribution to the ongoing Church. To my mind we are in a new situation; we are not the Church we were a year ago; there is a new spirit at work; we have a new awareness of our coresponsibility; God has taught us new ways of living as His people; He has sanctioned a new respect for pluralism, and brought more clearly to our attention the legitimacy of dissent within His Church. All this I assume as fact, and I consider it the responsibility of a theologian to try to explain that fact. Our responsibility is to go to the heart of the matter, to what was really involved in the chapter of history just concluded, to teach the deeper truths that will guide the long-range development of the Church's life. It is a matter of analyzing the new situation and of trying to indicate a style of life, a *modus vivendi*, principles of conduct, that suit our new assumption of responsibility. We have to develop a way that combines loyalty with criticism, obedience with dissent, unity with differences of opinion frankly expressed in dialogue. It is a matter really of a new self-knowledge, a knowledge of what man is and how his mind works. The theologian's responsibility is to articulate this. It is more directly theological, then, than pastoral, but perhaps it is the best way he can proceed at the moment toward pastoral goals.

A significant step in the direction of a theology of dissent has already been taken in the brief submitted by twenty professors of The Catholic University of America who were subject by the mandate of the University Trustees to a faculty Inquiry into their stand on the encyclical. Part One of their submission is entitled: On the Responsible Exercise of the Role of the Theologian in the Church in General, and on a Responsible Exercise of This Role in Regard to the Encyclical *Humanae Vitae* in Particular. It is a theological document of high order, calm and dispassionate, historical and systematic at the same time. It justifies dissent from non-infallible teaching in the Church with strict reliance both on historical precedent and on principles of Catholic doctrine. There is a noteworthy contribution to the analysis of the historical situation and to the lines theological understanding must take to be at the service of the Church of the future.

The document is perhaps known to many of you already.* I do not pro-

---

* This brief has been published under the title *Dissent in and for the Church: Theologians and Humanae Vitae,* by Charles E. Curran, Robert E. Hunt and the "Subject Professors," with John F. Hunt and Terrence R. Connelly. New York: Sheed & Ward, 1969.

pose simply to repeat what has already been well done by the theologians involved. What I wish to do is proceed from one theme they introduced to further and more detailed analysis. The document again and again refers to the need of dialogue in the Church today. Why this need of dialogue? It is true that a spirit of courtesy and fellowship will suggest a degree of dialogue corresponding to the social situation and the modern facility in communications, but in my view more fundamental issues are involved than those of the ethics of democracy. We can appeal to the fact of the pluralist world in which we live and to the need we have for remaining open to one another, but that only brings up the further question why it should be a pluralist world, and I would answer that in the same way as the question: Why dialogue?

My contention will be that the very nature of human truth and of the process by which the human mind reaches truth requires dialogue; in all but the simplest truths we simply cannot judge without dialogue. This is surely not an earth-shaking stand to take, but I think it is important to relate my contention to fairly basic ideas of cognitional theory and epistemology, and to apply those ideas to the process by which the learning Church too arrives at truth. We have passed very swiftly from practical questions of great and immediate moment to abstract questions that directly interest only philosopher-theologians. The catch, of course, is in the word "directly." I consider that these "abstract" questions underlie the immediate question and must be solved if we are to have serenity in the Church of God.

My responsibility, as I see it, is to help you learn what learning is, and through helping you to help the learning Church learn what learning is. That is, in speaking to you I am speaking to as much of the learning Church as I can reach at the moment, and I will try to show that, just because of what our minds are and because of the one route they have to truth and being, our learning is not a matter of looking or deducing, though each has its place, but a matter of dialectical process, necessarily involving dialogue. First, I will expose the philosophical ideas we need, trusting that I have not completely misread the philosophers I will be quoting, and then I will proceed to the learning process in the Church.

A PHILOSOPHY OF LEARNING

"Dialectic" is a word with many meanings, some of them distinctly pejorative (Hall, 1967, p. 385). The sense that is common in philosophy today goes back to Heraclitus and his "War is the father of all," but received elaborate formulation and impetus from Hegel; it refers to "the passing over of thoughts or concepts into their opposites and the achievement of a higher unity" (Hall, 1967, p. 388). Hegel's special contribution was the view that the dialectical process is a necessary law, and this both for mind and for reality. "The contradictions in thought, nature, and society, even though they are not contradictions in formal logic but conceptual inadequacies, were regarded by Hegel as leading by a kind of necessity, to a further phase of development" (Hall, 1967, p. 388). In illustration: The notion of being leads to the notion of nothing, and the contradiction in turn to the notion of becoming; in nature, space completes itself in time, and space and time lead to motion and matter; in society, self-consciousness depends on acknowledgment of the other, and is first established through the master–slave relationship—but this only brings into the open the reduced self-consciouness of the slave, and both are finally superseded by the higher attitude of Stoical consciouness that disdains the master–slave distinction (Findlay, 1958, pp. 97–99; 153–159; 274–277).

Now, there is no use denying the fact that the pejorative senses of dialectic are well deserved. Dialectic has been abused, notably by the Sophists who developed specious reasoning for unworthy purposes. Even philosophers have exaggerated the uses of the method; we instinctively react when we see it set forth in a way that denies the principle of non-contradiction. (Incidentally, some students of Hegel absolve him from such a use of the doctrine.) We are too well aware that two contradictory statements cannot both be true; as a matter of fact even the radicals of dialectical thought are witnesses to that impossibility, maybe not in their professed principles, but certainly in their practice. You may have noticed that opponents of the principle of non-contradiction can become as annoyed as anyone else when they are contradicted; try it and see.

But the uses of dialectic need not be exaggerated; we can give the term Lonergan's definition—"a concrete unfolding of linked but opposed principles of change" (Lonergan, 1957, p. 217)—and find it quite acceptable. Then the word means progress by means of opposition. In the sphere of living, there is Lonergan's example of the law of the cross: Christ, by accepting in love and obedience the evil of passion and death, transformed it into good (Lonergan, 1964b, p. 556). In the sphere of thought, the word means the progress of thought by means of opposition; it means thought that is dynamic, always on the go—not, however, in a logical and deductive manner, but in a way that involves alternations and antithetical statements, reconciliations, and eliminations. Dialectic, then, is opposed to deduction. In deduction we proceed from known premises, but in dialectic we do not yet know—we are only on the way to knowing.

My first proposition is that the dialectical process corresponds to the way the human mind must work to reach truth and being: in simpler terms, to know the facts. In primitive man, knowing is largely a matter of seeing and hearing, and in this stage the thinking process is limited to myth-making. A more developed stage occurs with the pre-Socratics, "those Greek thinkers from approximately 600 to 400 B.C. who attempted to find universal principles which would explain the whole of nature" (Guthrie, 1967, p. 441); now myths are overcome and so is the merely practical orientation of knowledge, but the thinking process is limited to deduction. Dialectic is a third stage; we discover, with Socrates, that truth is not in our possession; it is something to be achieved. You will have noticed that the emphases of the three stages correspond roughly to Lonergan's three levels of cognitional activity: experience, understanding, and judgment (Lonergan, 1957). Primitive man is almost confined to experience, the pre-Socratics were largely confined to the level of understanding (more accurately, to its conceptual products); modern man is concerned to verify the truth, to form a correct judgment. But he reaches truth only through a process, and the process is dialectical.

Contribution of John Henry Newman. For the above-mentioned reason the work of Newman is now fundamental. Let us then skip over the Cartesian search for a certitude based on the indubitable fact of my thinking, the radical empiricism that then reduced ideas to sensations, and Kant's tremendous effort to certify scientific knowledge by studying the conditions of its possibility, down to John Henry Newman and *An Essay in Aid of a Grammar of Assent.* Newman has no objection to deductive processes in their place. But his concern, as he repeatedly tells us, is with judgment in "concrete matter" (Newman, 1870, pp. 7, 8, 269, 277, 284, 288, 360, 410–411, and *passim*). "Inference comes short of proof in concrete matters, because it has not a full command over the objects to which it relates, but merely assumes its premises" (Newman, 1870, p. 269). Hence it is ". . . the main position of this Section, the Inference . . . determines neither our principles, nor our ultimate judgments,—that it is neither the test of truth, nor the adequate basis of assent" (Newman, 1870, p. 287).*

What, then, is Newman's basis for judgment?

> It is plain that formal logical sequence is not in fact the method by which we are enabled to become certain of what is concrete; and it is equally plain, from what has been already suggested, what the real and necessary method is. It is the cumulation of probabilities, independent of each other, arising out of the nature and circumstances of the particular case which is under review; probabilities too fine to avail separately, too subtle and circuitous to be convertible into syllogisms, too numerous and various for such conversion, even were they convertible [Newman, 1870, p. 288].

Later Newman illustrates the process by the mathematical procedure of tending to a limit:

* I wonder if we might classify the work of computers as instrumental to Newman's inference? Their "self-teaching" seems to be one of the programmed possibilities, part of a quasi-premise.

We know that a regular polygon, inscribed in a circle, its sides being continually diminished, tends to become that circle, as its limit; but it vanishes before it has coincided with the circle. . . . In like manner the conclusion in a real or concrete question is foreseen and predicted rather than actually attained; foreseen in the number and direction of accumulated premisses, which all converge to it . . . yet do not touch it logically. . . . It is by the strength, variety, or multiplicity of premisses, which are only probable, not by invincible syllogisms,—by objections overcome, by adverse theories neutralized, by difficulties gradually clearing up, by exceptions proving the rule, by unlooked-for correlations found with received truths, by suspense and delay in the process issuing in triumphant reactions,—by all these ways, and many others, it is that the practised and experienced mind is able to make a sure divination that a conclusion is inevitable, of which his lines of reasoning do not actually put him in possession [Newman, 1870, pp. 320–321].

I am not saying that Newman gave us the last word on the question. His very expressions are troublesome, his use of the term "probability" obscuring his stress on the unconditional character of assent. More fundamentally: his distinction between real and notional apprehension is defective; what he lacks on this level is the Augustinian-Thomist procession of concept from understanding. When he transfers his distinction to the level of judgment a still more radical defect shows up: he has no view of being which would enable him to distinguish clearly the object of thought from the object of judgment, and to eliminate the confusion of his notional assent. Thus, only once in the whole *Grammar* have I noticed any emphasis on the word *is* (Newman, 1870, p. 93). What he excelled in doing, and what by his own insistence was all he intended to do (Newman, 1870, pp. 64, 160), was to describe the process that he actually found operative in the act of assent.

Still, he was the great pioneer in a view of how the human mind works when it is reaching out for truth—when it is learning, trying to form a correct judgment. Others have completed his work; the fuller view of cognitional structure, the epistemology and ontology that Newman lacked—all this has been supplied by Lonergan (1957) in his equally pioneering work, *Insight*. The dynamism of mind oriented to truth and being gives the basis of an epistemology; the distinction between understanding and concept shows why Newman was so concerned with images; the distinction of animal and human realism illuminates an obscurity in the relation of Newman's image to reality, and so forth. Some day a study should be made of Lonergan's relation to Newman, but this is not the place for it.

Dialectic a necessary approach to truth. We are at the very heart of epistemology here, and I have no intention of providing a treatise on the subject. But I have to try to clarify that characteristic of judgment which imposes the dialectical approach to truth on the human mind—namely, that judgment is not a matter of looking or deducing, just as being is not something sitting there to be looked at or making itself felt by its influence; it is a matter of approaching the unconditional through conditions fulfilled, just as being occurs contingently through a concatenation of causes.

I think the simplest device is to call your attention to your use of the word "is," or of its equivalent in the word "yes," or, if you like, in the nod of the head that is a sign of assent. I think it will be generally agreed that a dog, however "intelligent" he may be, is hardly capable of uttering "is" or "yes" or of nodding his head in affirmative response to a question for reflection—from which we may conclude that "is" is not the object of an ocular look. But we might then ask whether it is the object of any kind of look. Is there any way of pointing to its objective referent? If a child asks me what "red" is, I can point to the colors of the spectrum, naming each as I point, and he will get the idea: how I use the word "red." Later he will want to understand not only the world of human language but the physical world as well, and again I will point to charts and diagrams so that he may get the idea. But I am pointing to data that are the matrix of an idea; where do I point to demonstrate "is"? To point to a tree, a bird, a man, naming them in turn, may give the idea of tree-ness, bird-ness, man-ness, but hardly the notion of is-ness.

Have we an intellectual intuition of "is"? Some famous men have thought so, but have had difficulty convincing the philosophical world of their position. I myself would say that their position is refuted by the painstaking description Newman undertook of what actually happens when we say "yes" —or, in his words, give assent. And I would say that a view of being arises on the experience of that question for reflection "Is it so?" and the dynamism that not only will not allow "yes" and "no" together, but keeps us on the move till we are able to pronounce one or the other.

But I am not really trying at the moment to prove a position that may be settled only after a few centuries of philosophical reflection. I am maintaining that this view explains why dialectic is a necessary approach to truth, and dialogue is necessary in any community. If you are willing to accept my epistemology provisionally, I think you will see the relevance of Newman to the present question. It is true that he put at the head of his *Grammar* a quotation from St. Ambrose: "Non in dialecticâ complacuit Deo salvum facere populum suum" *—but that refers to a pejorative sense of dialectic. His own process of reaching assent is remarkably like the acceptable sense of the word: "by objections overcome, by adverse theories neutralized, by difficulties gradually clearing up, by exceptions proving the rule, by un-looked-for correlations found with received truths, by suspense and delay in the process issuing in triumphant reactions . . ." (Newman, 1870, p. 321) —what is all this but the dialectic that modern philosophers talk about? His

* "Not by way of dialectic did it please God to bring salvation to His people."

own favorite example (it returns seven times: Newman, 1870, pp. 189, 190, 195, 198, 212–213, 294–296, 318) of the truth, Great Britain is an island, supplies further evidence. How do you justify your assent to that proposition? You consider various ideas: island, peninsula, continental tract. You make various contrary deductions: If an island, then . . . ; But, if part of the continent, then. . . . You reject certain ideas by a *reductio ad absurdum*. And so forth.

What I am saying is this: being is not there like a visible object to be looked at with the eyes, not even with the "eyes" of the mind, and truth is not a matter of letting things appear, even to intellectual intuition. Truth has to be won; it is an achievement. Further, it is not in the general case won by deduction, but by a dialectical process. Newman lists the sequential conjunctions as signs of inference: for, therefore, similarly, and so on (Newman, 1870, p. 263). We might list the adversatives as signs of dialectic: but, however, on the one hand . . . on the other. Finally, when the set of ideas is sufficiently clarified, we can put the question "Yes or No?" Between "Yes" and "No" with regard to a determinate question on determinate being, *non datur tertium*; that is true, but on the way, there is not only a *tertium*, but a *quartum*, and an indefinite number of possibilities. Further, when we reach "Yes," it is not because it loomed out of the darkness, letting itself appear; it is not because it clicked into place with the last movement of a logic-machine; it is because we have reached the unconditional toward which the fulfilled conditions converge much as the polygon converges with the circle.

Necessity of dialogue. My next proposition is that the necessity of dialogue* results from the dialectical process by which truth is won. Truth, in all but the most elementary instances, is not won except by the encounter of many opposing viewpoints, and many opposing viewpoints are not provided except by many persons. I do not deny the role of prophets, of what we would call "men of judgment," but even they utter their words of wisdom on the basis of many contributions. This results, I say, from the dialectical approach that Newman describes. Thus, the datum one man overlooks or forgets, another adverts to. The ideas and possible explanations that do not occur to one will occur to others. The questions that never stir a lazy mind will puzzle the alert, yet perhaps the indolent will foresee practical difficulties to which the more energetic are blind. Implications that escape the dreamer will be drawn out by the logical. Areas of application that are irrelevant to a whole group will deeply concern the stranger. Where one man's temperament inclines him to a too hasty termination of reflection, a more scrupulous type will prolong objections and doubts. And so forth.

There is an extremely simple index of this need of dialogue: the number

* The common root suggests an intrinsic link between dialectic and dialogue, but they have become differentiated as two functions in the cognitional process.

of opinions we require in order to trust a verdict. As adversatives are the sign of dialectic, so the requirement of numbers is a sign of the dialogic factor involved in reliable opinion. But do not reduce my statement to the easily ridiculed position that right and wrong are a matter of counting noses. Advert rather to the fact that in processes of criminal law the judgment of guilt may be committed to as many as twelve persons. What is the implication of this fact? In the supreme court we may have as many as seven men sitting in judgment. Committees are formed of several members. Various speakers are invited to an institute. Peter Berger remarks: "One of the fundamental propositions of the sociology of knowledge is that the plausibility, in the sense of what people actually find credible, of views of reality depends upon the social support these receive" (Berger, 1969, pp. 42–43). Is this a mere gregarious dependence on the crowd? I think not; I believe it rests upon a profound though inarticulate understanding of the working of the human mind. As Bernard Lonergan says: ". . . in its judgments . . . common sense tends to be profoundly sane" (Lonergan, 1957, p. 242). As a movie title had it many years ago: Fifty Million Frenchmen Can't Be Wrong. And, to make the story a little shorter, we believe in universal suffrage, trusting that in the long run the judgment of the people will be better than that of a dictator. If it is not enough for certainty, at least it will provide a fairly safe working hypothesis.

Of course, that last remark brings us face to face with the fact that for a while, maybe a long while, we can all be wrong. A whole country can commit great stupidities at the polls. Fifty million Frenchmen *can* be wrong. There is also the fact that the judgment of one expert may be worth the judgment of a thousand novices. The question of numbers is not simple; there is a sliding scale. But the main point is beyond question: we judge safely in the long run when we judge together, and that accords perfectly with the nature of judgment as I have outlined it. If judgment were a matter of looking, one good looker would suffice, and certainly two or three witnesses would be quite adequate. If judgment were a matter of making deductions from premises, then one keen logician would suffice: better still, a logic-machine, especially if the moving parts are kept well-oiled. But, if judgment is the kind of process that Newman and Lonergan describe, then a wide spectrum of questions, ideas, objections, counter-objections, opinions, is necessary. It is not a matter of dividing work; often, as in a jury, the number merely multiplies the work; it is a matter of dialectic.

We should not ignore the problem of defining what we mean by men of judgment, and of determining in the concrete case who or of what type the men of judgment are. You recognize the delicacy of the task, given the famous proverb that everyone complains of his memory and no one of his judgment. We expect "experts" to be men of judgment in their field, yet we repeatedly find the "experts" disagreeing with one another—in our courts of law, in our civil service, and the like. We have plenty of examples too of men who exercise judgment very well in their business, and are complete fools in love or sport or politics or war. Again, the seniors of the community used to be regarded, with reason, as the men of judgment; Aristotle explained this as the result of experience, Newman (1870, p. 341) agreed, and common sense in general approved. But today there is a new proverb: Don't trust anyone over thirty.

The confusion, however, is not total. The point is that judgment requires a mastery of the whole of the data; one's insight has to be invulnerable. In a developing science, the experts are ahead of the rest of us but are far from having reached mastery; their judgment consequently is insecure. In an age of transition, the old standards which the experience of years once taught have no longer the same validity; the elders must learn along with the youngsters, and so judgment is not so patently on their side. But all this only illustrates more graphically the dialectical process by which we reach judgment. It does not mean that judgment is gone from the earth. There are still the basic human factors, the *existentialia,* in which common sense—that is, the judgment of men everywhere—is "profoundly sane"; a long life still gives one a wiser judgment, provided one has not arrested the learning process at thirty.

THE LEARNING PROCESS IN THE CHURCH

What I have been saying about the nature of judgment and the dialectic by which we come to know is to be applied now, *mutatis mutandis,* to the judgments we make in the Church as we gradually achieve truths we had not previously formulated. There is a basic supposition here which I notice briefly: we are an *inquiring* Church. God may have said all He is going to say on earth, but we have certainly not got all He said into our possession in the form of explicit articles of faith, and so we are in the position of Socrates who did not have truth at his disposal but had to learn. The Church is a learning Church; the *whole* Church is a learning Church. This was as clear as crystal to Origen seventeen centuries ago, when he drew up at the beginning of his *First Principles* a list of the truths given in plain terms by the Apostles, and the questions they did not settle but left for us to investigate (Origen, 1936, pp. 1–6). It ought to be clear to all of us now, over a century after Newman's work on development. It is of very special moment just in this present period of confused stirring.

Given this learning situation, the present concern is to notice that in the Church too investigation proceeds dialectically. Certainly, truths of faith are not to be had by any act of looking, ocular or intellectual. But in the general case they are not to be had by deductions either. Deduction works when there are given terms which can function as premises. But the characteristic of *development,* of significant development as we understand it now, is just that the terms are not given; they are new; we ask questions our fathers could not understand at all. Hence deduction does not work. What does work is the antithesis of ideas, the slow clarification of the question, the gradual elimination of impossible answers—in short, the dialectical process.

The best way to see this is in a concrete example. One classic example is the development of Trinitarian theology, and the finest exposition of this that I know is in Lonergan (1964a, pp. 5–112, 137–154). It runs through more than a hundred pages of packed Latin, some of it to be found in more readable form in the second chapter of John Courtney Murray (1964), but much of it still in the original Latin. What emerges from this study is the dialectical aspect of the two-hundred-year struggle (roughly, from A.D. 180 to 380) to formulate the basic Trinitarian dogma. A deductivist mentality sees only the opposition between orthodoxy, true to its apostolic premises, and heterodoxy, in the mystery of iniquity abandoning those premises. But the dialectical mentality sees Praxeas trying to do justice to the one God of faith but unable to do justice to the data on the distinct reality of Son and Spirit; Tertullian correcting Praxeas but failing to escape a materialist view of the Three; Origen overcoming Tertullian's materialism but faltering at the idea of equality; Arius carrying Origen's trend to a logical conclusion and being rejected by the Council of Nicaea; the Nicene definition itself giving rise to objections that can be met only after the patient and creative work of clarification done by Athanasius. It is a slow march toward the truth, in its gradual stages resembling the approach of the polygon to coincidence with the circle, but in its zigzag course resembling more the tacking of a ship into the wind; better still is to transpose Lonergan's image of a staircase spiraling upwards (Lonergan, 1957, p. 186).

This puts a new light on the conduct of the bishops after Nicaea. It was remarked a century ago by Newman and has been repeated many times since, that it was the bishops who wavered after Nicaea and it was the laity who stood firm in the faith. This is not quite fair to the bishops. They were the theologians of the time, the ones who had to work out the implications of the new dogma; they could not do so except in a dialectical process where idea would be set against idea. Not till the whole new set of ideas had been fairly well worked-out by Athanasius and the Cappadocians could the episcopal minds reach harmony. The laity, I suggest, had the appearance of standing firm simply because they were not moving with the times. That situation is not without parallel today, which is one reason why I make special mention of it. Vatican I and Vatican II represent arcs in the spiraling staircase of ecclesiology that has not yet come to a landing. The comparison of a dialectical process that came to a sort of term long ago with one that is going forward in our own day can be exceedingly illuminating for present questions.

Dialogue needed for the dialectical development of doctrine. My second general proposition was that dialectical progress requires dialogue, and surely it would be laboring the obvious to insist that this applies also to dialectical development of doctrine. But I think it worthwhile to delay a moment on the significance of numbers in this special area of application. Augustine, in a memorable line of one of his works, left us the slogan *"Securus judicat orbis terrarum"* (*Contra epist. Parmen.*, III, 4)—"When the whole world agrees, you can be sure of its judgment." This stray line, almost alone and out of context, reached Newman in a roundabout way, and he tells us in his *Apologia* what a deep impression it made upon him (Newman, 1864, pp. 116–117). As Newman was at once aware, the slogan was valid far beyond the original application to the Donatists. It has become, in fact, a fundamental criterion in the Church. The present point is that it accords perfectly with the dialectical approach to truth. Again, it is not simply a matter of counting noses; it is a matter of insuring that all the relevant questions, ideas, implications, applications, objections, and ramifications will be noticed and confronted with all the relevant data in the given word of God; it is our human guarantee against oversight and error in judgment.

Thus, there is a significance more fundamental than that of a traditionally "sacred" number in the fact that there were twelve Apostles. St. Paul made a point of the fact that the risen Lord was seen by more than 500 Christians at once. The post-Nicene Fathers appealed constantly to the great council (as they thought it to be) of 318 bishops. It is in continuity with such instances that theologians are talking today of the community aspect of faith, that our bishops speak of the coresponsibility of the laity, that collegiality is in the air, that we think in terms of teamwork. Collegiality is in fact the teamwork of the bishops. To come for a moment to my official topic, it is not a trivial worship of numbers when we underline the fact that 87 theologians issued the statement in Washington in July, 1968, or that several hundred theologians subscribed to it, or that a good number of influential conferences of bishops sanctioned in effect the stand these theologians took. (Of course, you can count numbers on the other side too. We have not yet one voice from the *orbis terrarum*. All that I am saying is that numbers have their importance—in this case to establish a probability while we await unanimity in the Church.)

Now, I am concerned not to leave too simple a picture of judgmental activity in the church. *"Securus judicat orbis terrarum"* leaves many questions unanswered. Who speaks for the whole world? If we discover a consensus, have we gone far enough, or do we need an "authoritative" statement? Is the situation like Newman's accumulation of probabilities converging on assent—like it to the extent that the many may voice their opinions but the truth is uttered by one? If there are specially qualified men of judgment in the Church, who are they? Are there different bodies which in different cases exercise judgment?

A generation ago, when a sharper distinction between the teaching and the learning Church was maintained, with theologians occupying a kind of no-man's land, there was indeed something like a division of labor between areas such as France and the Vatican in Rome. We would say in those days that France got the ideas, and Rome judged their orthodoxy. We were not just being facetious; there was a real validity in the arrangement. However, that was an era when the truth was more in our possession; we had not yet begun the great migration in the world of ideas; the premises were well enunciated and a fairly adequate set of terms was understood in a fairly common way. Then a board of judges, given leisure for the purpose, could examine any given idea to see whether it accorded with the premises. Then too the idea of a policeman of the faith in the Holy Office was not altogether ridiculous.

But the situation today is not one in which we study new ideas as possible conclusions from fixed starting-points in traditional premises. It is not a situation in which the main opposition is between truth and error; that will always be a question, but it is the terminal question, and we are not yet ready for it—at least, not on every front; we are engaged in the preliminary steps of the dialectical process. The situation is one in which we must form a new set of concepts, establish new premises, throw back the horizons of thought. It is not directly a matter of confronting the new ideas with the faith of our fathers, simply because the confrontation cannot be made in any easily determined way; when we do attempt the confrontation, we need to penetrate to the fundamental intention of our fathers instead of making a shibboleth of their words. Surely our new ideas must not contradict the ancient faith—in extreme radical eyes this will put me squarely among the conservatives—but today's ideas are so new that confrontation with the ancient faith is not the primary question—and that perhaps in conservative eyes will put me among the radicals.

In an age of such far-reaching transition as this is, we must allow the dialectical interplay of ideas and counter-ideas. We must talk with one another. We must openly admit that our condition is that of inquirers after truth, not possessors of the truth; we must recognize that prior to the question of truth there is an enormous problem of developing understanding. So there must be congresses and institutes, theological commissions, synods, and ecumenical councils, the whole strategy and tactics by which the people of God move toward judgment. And while definitive judgment is delayed, we can trust the people of God to judge what concerns them immediately in practical matters, just as we can trust them to change their judgment later if the weight of evidence shows them to be in the wrong.

However, I asked the question "Who judges in the Church of God?" I would say that this question must be inserted in the larger one of the degree of human participation in divine providence that God wills for His people. Now, it seems clear that God intends an ever-increasing degree of participation in His work. Dietrich Bonhoeffer made the famous remark from his Berlin prison that God is teaching us that we can get along very well without Him. I would say that the Catholic counterpart, and perhaps corrective, is the statement that God wants us to take over more and more of the government of the world, according to our degree of maturity. As St. Thomas would say, the progressive actuation of our potencies calls for a corresponding exercise.

This increasing participation by man in the work of providence can be traced in the very matter of divine teaching. The early prophets were ecstatics; not only were they singled out as individuals, but they hardly knew what they were doing—they were "seized" by the Spirit (Dodd, 1960, Chs. 2, 3). The later prophets were inspired—surely, the word of the Lord came to them—and they still act very much as individuals; nevertheless, they are much more rational: there is a greater degree of human participation. An evangelist like Luke was also inspired in his own way, but his way was to consult the traditions, the written accounts, perhaps even the eyewitnesses. The Church in her councils is not inspired but, as we say in scholastic theology, she has the negative assistance of the Spirit. The pattern is clear; it is toward assignment to men of a larger degree of participation in the divine management of the world; and fuller participation by men means a greater involvement of the multitudes. When one man speaks for God, divine intervention must in the nature of the case occur continually; when the people speak, God can trust them a little more.

I am not forgetting that we are judging in the field of mystery. The originally given word of God is not a philosophical discovery to be developed by mere human ingenuity. We cannot get along without the Holy Spirit. But the question is "Where is the voice of the Spirit to be heard?" The old question was "Who has authority to teach in the Church?" I think a much better perspective is given if we ask "Who are the authorized spokesmen of the Church?" Materially we may come to the same answer, but the perspective is different. To talk of authority puts the emphasis on the individual who has authority, but to call him a spokesman for the Church puts a needed emphasis on the fact that the Spirit is given primarily to the Church, and that it is the judgment of the Church that God intends to guide and protect. Meanwhile the adjective "authorized" retains whatever elements of authority belong by nature in a divinely founded institution.

When we view the matter from this perspective, the question becomes one of analyzing the various factors that determine who, by God's will, should act as spokesman for His Church. It is clear that there has been a certain historical variety in the matter of spokesmen. I wonder if the answer will not vary more or less as human society develops. In the early Church, individual congregations under an apostle were spokesmen to a greater degree. In the patristic age, periodic gatherings of bishops were spokesmen for the Church. Then throughout a long period the head of the college of bishops exercised to a much greater degree the role of spokesman. But perhaps in our more highly organized society, with a possibility of communication that our fathers could not even dream of, the people are much closer to being their own spokesmen. We do talk today of the infallibility of the Church in believing, of the *sensus fidelium,* of coresponsibility of the laity. I am not able to form a judgment on how far this trend will go, but I have been concerned to get to the heart of the matter, and to remain open to development in whatever way God is leading us.

RESPONSIBILITY OF THE THEOLOGIAN TO THE CHURCH

At the end of this long analysis of the learning Church and its situation today, an analysis aimed at helping you form your conscience on some of the urgent questions that agitate us, I should say a word on the general responsibility of the theologian to his Church, the Church that nourished him and made him what he is, the Church without which all his lucubrations would have no more substance than the fantasies of alchemist or astrologer. The question of responsibility always becomes finally quite concrete, and I can merely indicate the general factors that come into play to determine a theologian's responsibility.

Obviously, he has a responsibility for the truth, for maintaining the truth that has been given, for seeking the truth that is not yet given. The corollary that I would draw attention to is his responsibility for exposing our failure to be true to the light—our bad faith and inauthenticity. I say this, fully conscious of the ill-mannered and neurotic tirades to which it leaves us open, of the injustices done daily to our leaders, of ultraconservative reactions thereby provoked; it still remains our task. I think especially of our failure after four-and-a-half centuries to do justice to the challenge of the reformers. Our attitude toward them is still too much a matter of polarization, not one of dialectic. There is, or was, a school among them of dialectical theology which would resign itself to an insoluble contradiction in the object of theology—between God and man, eternity and time, and so on. But I am not referring to that theology as an ideal. The dialectical movement I have tried to expose would not rest in such a static tension, and neither should it rest in the polarization that has characterized Western Christians all these years. The theologian has a special responsibility here in that he owes so much to his Protestant colleagues.

A theologian has a responsibility for ideas, for understanding the truth that God has given and is still communicating to His people. This too is obvious, and so are the immediate corollaries—that ideas must have freedom to occur, that the theologian must be able, without being hailed into the court of orthodoxy, to expose his ideas for the criticism of the public. Naturally this means allowing expression to some rather wild ideas of some rather wild men, but the alternative is the suppression of all ideas, given that the truth, the correct idea, is achieved only dialectically. In any case, today it simply wins unmerited sympathy for wild ideas if we are too eager to forbid them, whereas they would wilt under ridicule if allowed into the open. But these matters do not directly concern the theologian's responsibility. His responsibility is to have the courage and humility to express his own ideas, to speak when he thinks he is right even though he may turn out to be wrong.

A theologian has a responsibility for communicating truth and understanding to others. He is at the service of the Church—of the Holy Father, of the bishops, of the universities, of the people. Corollaries are legion; I limit myself to one. The theologian must remember that there is a style of doing theology—sober, scientific, even pedestrian. He may not responsibly seek the notoriety of headlines or aim at creating a sensation when his job is to help people to understand. I do not wish to belittle the invaluable service being done the Church by journalists today; the cause I have advocated would be lost without them. I am not against theologians' turning to journalism; Church reporting cannot get along without them. I am merely saying that theology is one thing, and journalism is another, and a theologian should decide which is to be his vocation.

When a theologian communicates, he communicates with people, and so we have to take up the delicate question of what people are involved in the area of his responsibility. We could consider classes of people like conservatives and angry young men. Conservatives are people; angry young men are people; the Church is full of people, and people have feelings and rights which a theologian may not ignore. But the real question is more delicate still: what should the responsible theologian's attitude be toward those people who are the Holy Father and the Roman Curia? In general, he may not abdicate his responsibility to stand up and speak out when that is his indicated task. If the Holy Father speaks without adequate knowledge of the question in hand, as I think Pope Honorius did centuries ago, it devolves upon the theologians, naturally after due deliberation and with all humility, to speak their minds, however painful the duty.

Let me insist again that the present question is not one of marital ethics. Fundamentally, the question is one of the *modus vivendi* of the Church today. And the chief difficulty lies in the governing style of the Vatican. I say this with full awareness of the enormous superiority of Vatican political sagacity over ours: We are simply novices in comparison. The trouble is, in my view, that Vatican competence belongs to a world that is gone, like the art of sending smoke signals in modern communications. The very success of Vatican politics in the past makes it all the harder to change styles today. Add the immobility of an entrenched bureaucracy and the opposition to change that is apt to characterize older men; recall, if you are middle-aged, the difficulty you yourself experience in making the transition to the new world in which we live; then perhaps you will appreciate better the difficulties of transforming the Vatican, and value more highly the many steps that have already been taken. If I consider that a theologian has still a responsibility to speak up, it is not because I impugn the real desires of the Holy Father to achieve *aggiornamento,* or am insensitive to the suffering he has undergone, or have forgotten that criticism is cheap and difficulties enormous. It is simply that I consider the measures taken too much a matter of mending fences; the desired change must be more radical; the fences, most of them, must go.

So I come at last to talk of violence, not just because it is in the air and everyone else is talking about it, but because it is germane to our question. We have to ask to what extent violence is necessary for the updating of the Church. Again today there is already a good deal of the violence we knew four centuries ago (I am not now talking about physical violence, but about revolt in the Church), but so far it has occurred in scattered cases. There is some pleading on the part of ultraconservatives for the counter-violence of excommunication. I profoundly hope that the methods of the 1500s will not come into play again on either side, but I recognize that we cannot simply repudiate violence if we follow the Christ who is presented to us in the gospels as excoriating the Pharisees and driving the money-changers from the temple with a whip.

In fact, there are things that do not get done, or whose doing is disastrously delayed, unless there is some form of violence. If the pope is appealing to our obedience, and it is precisely the concept of obedience that is in question, our response cannot help being a form of violence. If our request is for a greater measure of dialogue, and it is precisely dialogue in the measure suitable to the times that is denied us, then the situation is bound to contain an element of violence. But there is violence and "violence." The violence I may employ to protect a child against a pervert is not the violence I employ in my role as theologian helping the Church to learn. Here I think we may take as a working model the action of the 87. Our violence is that mild form shown in their dissent, and defended in the dispassionate brief presented by the professors subject to inquiry at the Catholic University of America, a violence without enmity, a dissent with loyalty, a disobedience with love.

I began this paper with a reference to the need for dialogue, I moved at once to the role of dialectic, and I seem to be ending now with a state of dissent and violence. May I say, as I conclude, that this state is not terminal.

It is merely the violence that is implicit in all dialectic, the conflict of opinions that is an essential element in reaching the truth, a built-in necessity of the human way of learning—that is, it is only a stage in the process toward the terminal position.

REFERENCES

Berger, P. L. *A rumor of angels: Modern society and the rediscovery of the supernatural.* Garden City, N.Y.: Doubleday, 1969.

Curran, C. E., *et al. Dissent in and for the Church: Theologians and Humanae vitae.* New York: Sheed & Ward, 1969.

Dodd, S. H. *The authority of the Bible.* (Rev. ed.) London: Collins (Fontana), 1960.

Findlay, J. N. *Hegel: A re-examination.* London: Allen & Unwin, 1958.

Guthrie, W. K. C. Pre-Socratic philosophy. In P. Edwards (Ed.) *The encyclopedia of philosophy.* New York: Macmillan & Free Press, 1967. Vol. *6*, 441–446.

Hall, R. Dialectic. In P. Edwards (Ed.) *The encyclopedia of philosophy.* New York: Macmillan & Free Press, 1967. Vol. *2*, 385–389.

Lonergan, B. (s.J.) *Insight: A study of human understanding.* London: Longmans, Green, 1957.

Lonergan, B. (s.J.) *De deo trino.* (2nd ed.) Vol. 1. Rome: Gregorian University Press, 1964. (a)

Lonergan, B. (s.J.) *De verbo incarnato.* (3rd ed.) Rome: Gregorian University Press, 1964. (b)

Murray, J. C. (s.J.) *The problem of God, yesterday and today.* New Haven: Yale University Press, 1964.

Newman, J. H. *An essay in aid of a grammar of assent* (1870). London: Longmans, Green, 1930.

Newman, J. H. *Apologia pro vita sua, being a history of his religious opinions* (1864). London: Longmans, Green, 1921.

Origen. *On first principles* (trans. by G. W. Butterworth). London: Society for Promoting Christian Knowledge, 1936.

Paul VI. *Humanae vitae.* Encyclical letter of July 25, 1968. *Acta Apostolicae Sedis,* 1968, *60,* 481–503. English translation: Human life. *Catholic Mind,* 1968, *66* (September, no. 1225), 35–48.

Washington, D.C., Theologians. Statement on the encyclical *Humanae vitae. Catholic Mind,* 1968, *66* (September, no. 1225), 2–4.

The Conscience of the Confessor and the Encyclical

JOHN R. CONNERY, S.J.

Father John R. Connery, S.J. received an M.A. degree from Loyola University (Chicago) in 1942, and an S.T.D. from the Gregorian University, Rome, in 1948. Between 1951 and 1960 Father Connery was the author of more than twenty-five articles appearing in such journals as Theological Studies, The American Ecclesiastical Review, The Homiletic and Pastoral Review, and America. From 1954 through 1959 he provided an annual review of developments in the field of moral theology, called Notes on Moral Theology, appearing each year in the December issue of Theological Studies. Then he served for a period of six years as Provincial Superior of the Chicago Province of the Society of Jesus. Father Connery has now returned to his career of teaching and writing as professor of moral theology at Bellarmine School of Theology, North Aurora, Illinois.

There is perhaps no subject in recent times that has aroused so much interest and discussion both inside and outside the Catholic Church as that of contraception. A. Valsecchi, an Italian theologian who recently published a book on the debate that took place on this matter between 1958 and 1968, advises us that he had to read more than twenty thousand pages of material in preparation for publication. Nor can it be said, at least up to the present, that the encyclical *Humanae Vitae* (Paul VI, 1968) put an end to this controversy. However much he might regret it, one would have to admit rather that the encyclical added a few more issues to the discussion. It is to one of those issues that the present paper is addressed—the relation between conscience and a teaching authority (a variation on an already much discussed subject in this era of situation ethics: the relation between conscience and law). The discussion here is limited to the question as it relates to the confessor.

THE MEANING OF CONSCIENCE

Before pursuing the subject further, it might be well to clarify the meaning of the word "conscience" as it will be understood in this paper. Such clarification is necessary because of the confusion that surrounds the current use of the term. One often hears today of a conflict between "conscience" and the teaching authority of the Church, or one appeals to his own "conscience" against this authority, or one is told that he may follow his "conscience" rather than this authority. This manner of speaking represents some truth, but I think it is also misleading. The basic conflict with a teaching authority, when it occurs, is not on the level of conscience. It is rather between the teaching authority and a dissenting opinion of the subject. The conflict arises between conscience and this authority when the individual forms his conscience on the basis of this opposing opinion rather than of the relevant teaching. Conscience does not pronounce on the rightness or wrongness of acts in general, but on the rightness and wrongness of *this particular act*. In order to do this, it must already be in possession of the knowledge of the rightness or wrongness of an act in general. A dissenting opinion, therefore, is on a different level from conscience, and is indeed prior to it. Ultimately, of course, one must always follow his conscience, since this is the only guide he has to the morality of individual acts. The question is "to what extent is conscience bound to a teaching authority?"

Vatican Council II in the Declaration on Religious Freedom sets down the general norm for the formation of conscience in reference to the teaching of the Church:

> In the formation of their consciences the Christian faithful ought carefully to attend to the sacred and certain doctrine of the Church. The Church is, by the will of Christ, the teacher of the truth. It is her duty to give utterance to, and authoritatively to teach, that Truth which is Christ himself, and also to declare and confirm by her authority those principles of the moral order

which have their origin in human nature itself [Vatican Council II, 1966, n. 14, pp. 694–695].

How does this pertain to the confessor, and, in particular, how does it affect the conscience of the confessor in relation to the papal teaching on contraception as enunciated in the encyclical *Humanae Vitae*? It should be said, first of all, that the confessor, as a member of the faithful, has at least the same obligation toward Church teaching as any other member. It is admitted, of course, that this obligation differs according as one is dealing with infallible or non-infallible teaching. While granting that this should be by way of rare exception, all theologians allow for the possibility of dissent when dealing with merely authentic or non-infallible teaching. Since it seems to be generally admitted that the Church teaching on contraception belongs in this latter category, dissent is a possibility. That it has actually occurred in the Church, and even among priests, is a matter of common knowledge. Although this dissent is serious, it should not blind us, of course, to the fact that the encyclical has also met with widespread acceptance. We are concerned here particularly with the effect both assent and dissent might have on the conscience of the priest when he is playing the role of confessor. Since dissent might seem, at least initially, to constitute a larger problem for the conscience of the confessor, it might be advisable by way of introduction to make a few general comments about the dissenting confessor.

May a priest-confessor follow his own private opinion even though this is opposed to the teaching of the Church when he is functioning in the role of confessor? I am not sure how important an issue this may be, since ultimately it is the conscience of the penitent rather than the conscience of the confessor that is of primary concern in the sacrament of penance. But this much should be said in general. The confessor represents the Church, and in particular he represents his local bishop. Also, the teaching of the Church (even the non-infallible teaching) has the presumption of truth. He should respect these facts and recognize his obligation to represent the teaching of the Church. If a penitent ask him his own opinion, he is certainly free to communicate it, even though it may not agree with the teaching of the Church; but he should make sure that in so doing he does not lessen general respect for the teaching authority of the Church. It seems to me also that in honesty and fairness to his penitent he should advise him that the private opinion of a confessor does not have the status of the teaching authority of the Church—however convinced the confessor may be of his own opinion. This is not to deny that the primary obligation of the confessor is to truth, rather than to any teaching authority. It is merely to say that the teaching authority of the Church, because of the guidance of the Holy Spirit, offers a better guarantee of truth than any private theologian.

PASTORAL FEATURES OF *Humanae Vitae*

It is obviously not enough for a confessor to know, or even to assent to, the teaching of the Church on contraception, in order to function competently in the confessional. The conscience of the confessor is dependent upon the moral law and the teaching of the Church; but just as pertinent to his conscience-decisions in the confessional are the norms of pastoral theology. It is indeed fortunate that in the encyclical itself Paul vi set down some guidelines that can be used for pastoral practice. The confessor will need these to ground his own conscience-decisions.

Anyone making a comparison between the encyclical *Humanae Vitae* (Paul vi, 1968) and its predecessor *Casti Connubii* (Pius xi, 1930), will be conscious of the different pastoral approach of Paul vi. This contrast is a recognition of a vastly different pastoral situation than that which prevailed at the time of *Casti Connubii*. This is entirely too large a subject to go into in any depth in a paper of this kind, but it might be helpful to point out just a few of the differences. First of all, there was not at all the same need for family limitation at that time. An individual couple, just as now, might have had personal reasons for desiring to limit their families, but the population problem was non-existent. In fact, if anything, there was great concern about declining populations, particularly in Western Europe, a concern which did not tend to make one sympathetic toward family limitation. Then, too, the introduction of the artificial contraceptive on a broad basis was relatively recent at that time, and hence easier to reject than today when it is generally accepted by all outside the Church as a legitimate method of family-planning. Thirdly, the recognition by the Church today of the love-giving as well as the life-giving meaning of the marriage act gives her a deeper appreciation of the sacrifice called for on the part of those who must forego or limit this expression of love because of the need of family limitation. The explicit recognition of the love-giving meaning of the marital act came with Pius xii and found expression in his allocution on artificial insemination (Pius xii, 1949), but is not found prior to this. Finally, it is common knowledge that, during the period of uncertainty while the whole question of the contraceptive pill and contraceptives in general was being discussed, many moralists were teaching that the use at least of the pill was probably licit; others were admitting the same for contraceptives in general. For these and many other reasons, the pastoral situation that faced Paul vi was in broad contrast with the world context into which *Casti Connubii* was to fit. It elicited from him a real pastoral concern and sympathy for the faithful who would be faced with a problem of family limitation.

In the pastoral part of the encyclical, Paul VI (1968, nn. 12–19, pp. 39–43) tells us first that the Church must follow the example of Christ in her conduct toward men. She must understand the weakness of men, have compassion on the crowd, and receive sinners. She must do this, however, without renouncing the law. The Church cannot compromise the law in any way. Paul was undoubtedly aware, of course, that God did seem to tolerate such things as divorce, polygamy, and the like in the Old Testament because of the "hardness of heart" of the people; but he evidently felt that, after almost two thousand years of Christian tradition against human interference in the life-giving process, the faithful would be receptive to a reassertion of the traditional teaching. This did not prevent him, however, from being acutely conscious of the support the faithful would need in observing the law.

The pope acknowledges the fact that the teaching of the Church will appear to many difficult to put into practice, and even impossible. He addresses himself to this reaction by admitting that it will demand serious engagement, and much effort—individual, family, and social. He even grants that without the help of God, who strengthens the will of man, it would not be realizable. From recognition of the difficulty he then goes on to encouragement. He recommends both personal effort and appeal for divine assistance through prayer, and particularly through the Eucharist. The faithful should not be discouraged if they are not immediately successful, but should have recourse to God in the sacrament of penance.

In his counsel to priests he urges them to follow the example of the Church and not to compromise on the level of teaching. On the pastoral level, however, the priest should show the patience and goodness Our Lord manifested in dealing with men. Although He was uncompromising with evil, He was always merciful to the sinner; He came to save, not to condemn. The married couple must always find in the attitude and words of the priest a reflection of the love and voice of the Redeemer; he has come to save them from their sins in the name of Christ.

These general guidelines reflect the pastoral attitude of Paul VI toward the faithful who would have a problem with family limitation. I am sure that all will appreciate the truly Christian understanding and sympathy they reveal. The priest who goes into the confessional today must be sure that he understands and assimilates this pastoral approach as completely as he understands and assimilates the law. As we have already indicated, his competence in the confessional depends upon both. He cannot make prudent conscience-decisions without them.

GUIDELINES FOR THE CONSCIENCE OF THE CONFESSOR

We are now in a position to move on to more specific guidelines for the
conscience of the confessor to meet problems of family limitation. These
guidelines, which will be pastoral as well as moral, will draw from the
encyclical as well as traditional treatises on confessional practice.

I think it important to emphasize first that, according to the Constitution
on the Church in the Modern World, the decision regarding responsible
parenthood—i.e., the number of children a couple should have—belongs to
the couple themselves (Vatican Council II, 1966, n. 51, p. 256). The
Church has never taught, in spite of periodic accusations to the contrary,
that married couples have an obligation to have as many children as physically possible. No confessor, therefore, should make any such demand of
a married couple. Nor is it up to the confessor to decide in any particular
case how many children a couple should have. If it is clear to a confessor,
of course, that a couple is acting irresponsibly, either by having more children than they should have or by obvious selfishness, he should remind them
of their responsibilities, but he should do no more than acquaint them with
the various factors that must be taken into consideration in a responsible
decision. The ultimate decision is up to their conscience. But I doubt that
this problem will be the confessor's main concern in reference to the encyclical. It will deal rather with the method of achieving responsible parenthood, at least when it calls for family limitation. In handling this problem
the confessor will have to be prepared to cope with a variety of consciences.
It may be helpful to consider the pastoral handling of some of the more
likely possibilities.

The penitent in good faith. A confessor should be prepared, first of all,
to handle a penitent who in all good faith is not able to grasp the evil of
contraception. When dealing with such cases, he must first assure himself
that he is dealing with genuine good faith, and not with a culpable stance.
This will have to be a prudential decision gathered from the penitent's overall respect for the teaching authority of the Church, his sincere effort to
understand the present teaching, and the general religious tenor of his life.
There are many factors in the present situation which make the possibility
of such good faith quite real, and perhaps not infrequently so, in people
who are otherwise devout and sincere Catholics. Just the fact that there has
been so much public disagreement with the encyclical on the part of priests
and theologians is enough to lead to a certain amount of misunderstanding
on the part of many people. One must consider also the subtlety of the arguments in the encyclical against contraception and the difficulty of grasp-
ing the moral distinction between the practice of rhythm and other methods

of family limitation. Many of the faithful are also aware of the opposition of the Majority Report of the Papal Commission to the position taken in the encyclical (Hoyt, 1968, pp. 15–111). If you add to all this the widespread misunderstanding of the statements of various conferences of bishops on the encyclical, particularly regarding the role of the individual conscience in deciding this problem, you can easily understand how much foundation there is for such good faith.

Karl Rahner even suggests the possibility that we may be dealing here with a situation analogous to that which prevailed in the time of the Old Testament prophets, when polygamy and divorce were accepted by the people. He does not feel that the possibility of such a parallel is eliminated by the fact that no proclamation against these evils existed in Old Testament times. If the moral consciousness of certain people or culture groups is not ready for this kind of teaching, a proclamation will not be effective but will have to await for its effectiveness a later development of moral awareness. As he says:

> Conceived in such a way, it is at least not an absurd question whether the moral norm of the encyclical does not perhaps proclaim an "ultimate norm" which even now means an immediate and contemporary obligation for many different and educated consciences of individuals, but not for the entire community in general at the present level of its moral development [Rahner, 1968, p. 36].

Whatever may be said for this explanation, I do not think that one can question the fact that much good faith will exist in regard to the practice of contraception. Such penitents may range all the way from the theologically educated who feel that they can support their position by solid arguments to the ordinary housewife whose spontaneous and unshakable judgment gives her complete security in the matter. The question that now concerns us is "How will the confessor respond to this good faith, once he has assured himself that it is genuine?"

The options open to the confessor who finds himself in this situation are clearly delineated in the standard treatises on pastoral theology. They are the well-known norms for dealing with a penitent in good faith—i.e., a penitent who thinks he is doing the right thing even when he may not be. Applying these norms to the penitent practicing contraception in good faith, the confessor will have different options according to his analysis of the situation. If in a particular case the confessor thinks that an attempt to get the penitent to accept the teaching of the encyclical will be fruitful, he should certainly make the effort in this direction. But if he feels that it would not be fruitful and would only turn good faith into bad faith, he should ordinarily omit the correction and leave the penitent in good faith. Otherwise, all the confessor accomplishes is to cause sin where there was no sin previously. Also, if drawing the penitent away from contraception would do more harm than good, it would be advisable for the confessor to leave him or her in good faith. Thus, for example, if the confessor judged that the mother of several children, who was practicing contraception in good faith, would give up the practice at his advice, but only at the risk of her life, he should not disturb her good faith. The consequent danger would far outweigh the good to be achieved. There is only one situation in which such a penitent should not be left in good faith: if the good of the community demands it. For example, if one priest knows that another priest is invalidly ordained, he could not leave him in good faith, but would have to inform him. Too much damage would be done to the community if he were left in good faith. But it is difficult to see how the good of the community would be immediately involved in the ordinary contraception case. Moreover, several of the conferences of bishops made specific allowance for cases of good faith in their statements on the encyclical.

Even in those instances in which a confessor legitimately allows a penitent to remain in good faith regarding the malice of contraception, he may be able to bring him to the point where he can appreciate the position of the encyclical as an ideal. If this can be done, I think it would be a real service to the penitent and might eventually develop into complete acceptance. The Austrian bishops (1969) in their statement on the encyclical also advise those who cannot accept the teaching of the encyclical that they have no right to create confusion among their brothers in the faith with their opinions.

The perplexed penitent. The confessor must also be prepared to handle penitents who accept the teaching of the pope but find themselves involved in what seems to be a clear conflict of duties—e.g., reconciling conjugal love and responsible parenthood. Both the Belgian bishops (1968) and the Canadian bishops (1968) consider this case in their statements on the encyclical. It is the case of the *conscientia perplexa* treated in standard moral manuals when the person is faced with two alternatives and sees sin in either option. Catholic moral theology, of course, does not admit any objective conflict of duties, but does not deny the possibility of such a conscience. Basically, then, the confessor is dealing with an erroneous conscience. This situation is somewhat analogous to the case just dealt with and the confessor is faced with another conscience-decision regarding the feasibility of trying to correct the conscience of the penitent. If for one reason or another the dilemma cannot be solved, the penitent, as the Canadian bishops say, "may be safely assured that whoever honestly chooses that course which seems right to him does so in good conscience" (Canadian Bishops, 1968, p. 56).

The doubtful penitent. The priest-confessor will undoubtedly be confronted by penitents who are in a state of doubt about the morality of contraception. Some of these penitents may be just waiting for a confessor to tell them that it is all right to practice contraception. They may even have engaged in some previous shopping-around with this in view. No confessor should allow himself to be maneuvered into a position in which he is being used by a penitent to dodge a personal responsibility. Moreover, I do not know how much valid support even a dissenting confessor can give to a doubting penitent. As the Canadian bishops recently advised, the faithful must recognize that "even the opinion of a number of theologians ranks very much below the level of [authoritative] teaching" (Canadian Bishops, 1969). The dissent, therefore, even of a number of theologians does not remove the obligation of the faithful to listen with respect and openness to such teaching.

But many of those who come to the confessor in doubt will want to do the right thing and will be sincerely looking for help. Although the confessor should not take it upon himself to make a decision for these penitents, he should do everything he can to help them come to a right decision. He should do everything he can to help them understand and assimilate the values the encyclical wishes to inculcate, as well as the teaching derived from these values.

The penitent with difficulties of observance. The confessor will be faced with penitents who have sincerely accepted the teaching of the encyclical, but who may be having practical difficulties observing it. It would clearly be a disservice for a priest who dissented from the encyclical to undermine this acceptance in any way. As Rahner says,

> . . . even today it is quite possible that he will meet consciences who . . . would refuse the "pill." In considering the "authenticity" of the papal doctrine, he certainly has no right to want to "enlighten" such a conscience. Still worse would it be . . . if a priest in confession would undermine the joyous will and Christian courage to have a greater number of children [Rahner, 1968, p. 41].

On the pastoral level, however, there should be no limit to the amount of patience with which the confessor matches their good will. He should try to give these penitents every help he can to make the required abstinence possible for them, but he should not be discouraged at failure. As we have seen, Paul VI himself in the encyclical advises married couples not to be discouraged at failures. There is no more reason why a confessor should be discouraged, even if the failures continue for some time. And clearly as long as the penitent shows repentance and good will for the future, the confessor should never think in terms of refusal of absolution. As is clear from pastoral treatises on the sacrament of penance, such good will is entirely consistent with the knowledge of weakness and the likelihood of future lapses.

Finally, when the confessor is dealing with penitents of good will who make sincere efforts to abstain from contraceptive acts, but who fail in spite of their efforts, there is reason to believe that their guilt may fall short of the objective seriousness of their acts. In other words, there may not be present that depth of personal commitment required for mortal sin. It must be admitted that Paul vi urges those who are still caught in sin to have recourse to the mercy of God in the sacrament of penance, but I do not feel that we have to see in this statement an implication that they are always committing serious sin. Such advice would be salutary, even if there were no question of mortal sin. Besides the support it gives against future sin, a return to the sacrament of penance after a lapse is a splendid sign of the good will of the penitent. A penitent might, of course, be taking a mechanical or even a magical approach to the sacrament, and assume forgiveness without genuine repentance or purpose of amendment, but this should be readily apparent to the confessor.

REFERENCES

Austrian Bishops. Statement of the Austrian Bishops on *Humanae Vitae. Catholic Mind*, 1969, *67* (April, no. 1232), 57–60.

Belgian Bishops. Statement of the Belgian Bishops on *Humanae Vitae. Catholic Mind*, 1968, *66* (October, no. 1226), 53–56.

Canadian Bishops. Statement of the Canadian Bishops on *Humanae Vitae. Catholic Mind*, 1968, *66* (November, no. 1227), 52–57.

Canadian Bishops. Additional statement of the Canadian Bishops on *Humanae Vitae. Documentary Service*. United States Catholic Conference, Press Department. April 24, 1969.

Hoyt, R. G. (Ed.) *The birth control debate*. Kansas City, Mo.: National Catholic Reporter, 1968.

Paul vi. *Humanae Vitae*. Encyclical letter of July 25, 1968. *Acta Apostolicae Sedis*, 1968, *60*, 481–503. English translation: Human life. *Catholic Mind*, 1968, *66* (September, no. 1225), 35–48.

Pius xi. *Casti Connubii*. Encyclical letter of December 31, 1930. *Acta Apostolicae Sedis*, 1930, *22*, 539–592. English translation: On Christian marriage. *Catholic Mind*, 1931, *29*, 21–64.

Pius xii. To Catholic doctors. Address to the fourth international convention of Catholic doctors, September 29, 1949. *Acta Apostolicae Sedis*, 1949, *41*, 557–561. English translation: *Catholic Mind*, 1950, *48*, 250–253.

Rahner, K. (s.j.) On the encyclical "*Humanae Vitae*." *Catholic Mind*, 1968, *66* (November, no. 1227), 28–45.

Vatican Council II. W. M. Abbott (s.j.) (Ed.) *The documents of Vatican II*. New York: Herder & Herder, 1966.

The Conscience of the Penitent
and the Encyclical

GARY MacEOIN

Gary MacEoin was born in Ireland and educated there and in England. His A.B. degree is from the University of London (1941) and his M.A. (1942) and Ph.D (1951) degrees are from the National University of Ireland. He has had a varied career as reporter, feature writer, book and drama critic, and newspaper editor. He has been Caribbean and South American correspondent for Inter-American Press Association, and chairman of the Inter-American Affairs Committee of the Overseas Press Club. Dr. MacEoin received a citation from the University of Florida for outstanding contributions in the field of inter-American relations in 1956, and in 1966 he was the recipient of the annual award of the Catholic Institute of the Press of New York. He is the author of numerous books, among them Latin America: The eleventh hour *(1962);* New challenges to American Catholics *(1965);* What happened at Rome? *(1966); and most recently, in collaboration with Francis X. Murphy, C.Ss.R.,* Synod '67: A new sound in Rome *(1968).*

The title involves an ambiguity: "penitent" implies guilt, an implication which, if accepted, would prejudge the issue. Accordingly, I here understand "penitent" as a Church member who acknowledges authority and who has to make a decision or take an action which brings him into a relationship with the directions given by Pope Paul VI (1968) in *Humanae Vitae*. This spreads the net considerably beyond married couples who must decide whether or not to use contraceptives. It includes the confessor or spiritual adviser they consult. It includes the parents, the grandparents, the entire complex of people whose opinions are respected and whose views serve to form the social and cultural framework within which the parties ultimately make their decision.

Obviously, this is a far-from-homogeneous group. If one thinks of the geographic and cultural extensions of the Catholic Church throughout the world, one can envisage a great variety of situations which influence the concrete decision. The many millions living at or below subsistence level in Asia, Africa, and Latin America are going to decide in a quite different way from those who enjoy the affluent society of Europe and North America. The Australian or New Zealander, faced with the social problem of inadequate population, finds a series of cultural factors quite different from ours.

THE DEMANDS OF A DEVELOPING WORLD

Within our society also, there are various strata of cultural and intellectual development and of personal attitude toward religion. Those, for example, whose ecclesiology has not been influenced by the currents of the second Vatican Council will react to the encyclical in an easily describable way. They will, without question or intellectual examination, accept the decision of the pope as being for them the will of God.

Time prevents me from examining in detail the variety of such responses and their varied motivations. I accordingly limit myself to those—and they are many in our society—who believe that they should study the encyclical, evaluate its arguments, and draw their own conclusions. They are the Catholics who believe it their duty to live in the world of the twentieth century and who recognize that, living in it, they are part of it and are influenced in all they do by the culture of the world to which they belong. They believe that the knowledge developed by man throughout the ages, and at an accelerating pace in our times, has to be the starting-point for all their decision-making. They believe, specifically, that they are in an evolving world, a world in which creation constantly continues, and in which it is the duty of each to contribute to this process of perfecting man together with the entire universe within which he lives.

For them, no necessary conflict occurs between the demands of this evolutionary world and those of Christ's law. On the contrary, the material and natural world (to the extent that a natural–supernatural dichotomy is acceptable) provides the perfect background against which to live a supernatural life and develop the virtues appropriate to the Christian. In order to do this, however, it appears to them necessary to purify Christianity of cultural and other accretions which perhaps once served but now only tend to obscure the reality and prevent the Christian from playing his full part at either the natural or the supernatural level.

THE DEMANDS OF A SCIENTIFIC CIVILIZATION

Here, as I already noted, the man of today has no choice but to begin from the culture into which he is integrated. It is a culture with well-defined characteristics, of which I think the most significant for our present purpose is its domination by the scientific method. As Ciaran Ryan has noted, science is very important in our culture, not only because the culture is largely a direct result of science, but because scientific thinking exercises a profound influence on the general philosophical climate. It serves in many ways as a model of thought, he says, "and in all spheres one hears of the need to adopt a scientific approach. The enormous prestige enjoyed by science derives ultimately from its success, from its ability to tackle and solve problems in a systematic way" (Ryan, 1969, p. 79).

Among the characteristics of the scientific method is a total dedication to the concept of the evolutionary process in which we are engaged. The city we have is not a lasting one. On the contrary, it is constantly in process of being pulled down and rebuilt at a better and more human level. The things we own or control have for us a relative value. I do not mean that we formally deny them an absolute value. But as far as we are concerned, they have simply the value we place on them in the concrete circumstances. A building producing a million dollars in annual revenue will be sacrificed without a thought in favor of another that will produce a million-and-a-half.

I have chosen words which parallel those of conventional Christian asceticism ("We have not here a lasting city"; "all is vanity"; "ashes to ashes") while giving them a very different meaning. In today's thinking, the relativity of material things has a positive content, and that is why I believe that the thinking which this simple example offers is of great importance in relation to the present discussion. Our culture is committed to the belief that everything should be measured by its value for people. Only to the person, the human person, does it give an absolute value. This is a very interesting notion, one to which the conventional Catholic theologian can in principle fully subscribe.

This mood was well described recently by Yves M. Congar, O.P. He was commenting on Pope Paul's charge on Holy Thursday 1969 that "a schismatic ferment" was working within the Church.

I also think that a very general and characteristic viewpoint of the present age has a decisive impact on the current crisis in the Church. People are talking and with reason, of mutation of civilization. The categories, language, and forms of our old Catholic culture, a culture in which a cleric like me still feels at home, no longer carry weight. They seem to have neither an audience nor influence. The world is marked by secularity, while simultaneously telescoping time and space by virtue of its increasing complexity, interdependence, and dramatic conquests. This trend is progressively universalized by the media of communications which keep us violently and immediately in its presence. It has always been true (in principle!) that the Church is at the service of men, and that in this sense the world establishes the agenda for it. Today, that is not only a principle but a fact. The awareness which Christians have of their Christian being tends to identify with their feelings about their situation and their responsibility in the world of men, as far as evangelical values and the charity of Jesus Christ are concerned. . . . These members of the Church are sensitive to what is specifically evangelical and Christian, but they entertain a certain coolness or lack of interest for the specifically confessional and sociologically Catholic [Congar, 1969, p. 31; my translation].

The man Father Congar describes is the same man Leo Joseph Cardinal Suenens of Belgium had in mind when he recently denounced the "essentialist, bureaucratic, static, juridical, and centralizing" spirit of the Roman Curia and called on the local Churches around the world to join in a concerted effort to free the pope from a system that holds him prisoner.

A major reason why change is urgent, the cardinal explained, is the extremely rapid mutation that is taking place in the world. "We are here dealing with a new kind of man who has a new understanding of human nature and a different mentality and scale of values. He is conscious of his personal dignity, of his human rights, and of his inalienable freedom of conscience" (Suenens, 1969, p. vi).

Or, as Hans Küng has put it, "intolerance and duplicity are rightly deeply repulsive to modern man, who has espoused the cause of the freedom of the individual in religious matters and rejects every sort of dishonesty and duplicity" (Küng, 1967, p. 316).

This rejection of dishonesty and duplicity which Father Küng mentions is a principal characteristic of today's man. The youthful rejection of the values of a society it despises for its pharisaism extends to religious institutions insofar as they fall short of their proclaimed ideals. Today's man has a level of straightforwardness, of honesty, and of directness sociologically unknown before our times. There was, of course, a reason that this kind of honesty never flourished before—simply that it was not economically viable. It is today's affluent and mobile society which enables a man to survive while challenging conventional concepts and attitudes.

The man of today would agree with Vatican Council II that the primary task of the Church, as of the world, is to make man more human, and that one of the main places this operation can and does occur is in and through marriage which the Council described in its Pastoral Constitution on the Church in the Modern World as "the primary form of interpersonal communion" (Vatican Council II, 1966, n. 12, p. 211).

The mutation of civilization of which Congar speaks affects not only Roman Catholics and not only Christians. It affects our entire culture. Even though it started in what had been a distinctively Christian culture, it is far from clear to what extent its original motivations and the drives which produced it were Christian. What is clear is that it was vehemently resisted by the Christian—especially the Roman Catholic—institutions, but that it gradually broke this resistance and penetrated their defences.

MAN'S CONTROL OVER THE MATERIAL WORLD

What has all this to do with the reaction to *Humanae Vitae* and specifically what bearing does it have on the "conscience of the penitent"? In my opinion, it is the decisive factor. As I have explained in some detail elsewhere (MacEoin, 1968), I believe that the basic conflict in the Church today is between those who have become part of the new scientific civilization and those who are still emotionally and culturally back in the civilization it has replaced. More concretely, the central apparatus of the Church—including Pope Paul—is dominated by what has become not only a subculture of Western culture, but actually a sub-subculture of the Italian subculture.

The new scientific man is not necessarily aggressive. On the contrary, he is firmly committed to a policy of live and let live, as long as facts do not intervene to force a decision. In consequence, the scientific man who was a believer, although he felt uncomfortable with much of the jargon and greatly rejoiced at Vatican Council II's attempts to lighten the ship, was in general content to ignore what he considered irrelevant. This was all the easier because of the long Catholic conditioning in accepting without question whatever was determined by those in authority—most of all if the authority invoked was that of the pope.

Here *Humanae Vitae* acted as a catalyst. It moved the conflict between the old and the new from the realm of theory, where the principles of the new could live indefinitely in pluralistic indifference with those of the old, to that of practice and action, the specific field of the new. And in doing this, it made a basic tactical error. It claimed its reasoning was self-evidently convincing while shoring it up simultaneously with an appeal to authority against those it did not convince. For the scientific man, authority yields to evidence (as indeed it should for every man, because it is also a well-established principle of traditional Catholic philosophy and theology that there can be no contradiction between truths of different orders).

The ultimate issue, though never expressly formulated in the encyclical, is the extent of man's control over the material world, including his own body and its functions. Are there some things a man is able to do which are forbidden by a law binding in all circumstances so that he may never morally do them? Or are all actions ultimately morally indifferent, our evaluation of their morality depending entirely on our evaluation of circumstances and consequences? Were Napoleon's soldiers retreating from Moscow justified in their daily killing of prisoners no longer able to march, as described in Tolstoi's *War and Peace*, knowing that if left behind alive they would give the pursuing Russians information that would ensure the total destruction of the fleeing French?

One's answer to this question will be mightily influenced, if not absolutely determined, by one's view of the role of man in creation. If one sees this role as essentially static, a period of trial and testing within a framework established in all its particulars by God at the first moment of time of an instantaneous creation, as traditional theology envisaged, then it is easy to agree that purely arbitrary limits to man's moral activity can exist.

If instead, as today's vision (prodded by the charges of alienation which unbelievers reasonably leveled against the old view) proposes, man has been entrusted by God with the task of carrying to perfection an inchoate creation, and given all the tools he needs for that task, then one is forced to question every assertion that the nature of things imposes absolute restriction on certain actions.

Here it is important to avoid semantic confusion regarding the meaning of nature. In the former view, that is natural which was so determined by God in the moment and act of creation. In the latter, it is what man at a given moment judges to be here and now helpful to carry the continuing creation toward its destined perfection. This is the position formulated by P. J. McGrath when he states that "no action can be morally wrong unless it is detrimental to human welfare, nor morally right unless humanly good" (McGrath, 1969, p. 73).

This special function and duty of man has been formulated as follows by Johannes Metz:

> Becoming a human being involves more than conception and birth. It is a mandate and a mission, a command and a decision. A human being has an open-ended relationship to himself. He does not possess his being unchallenged; he cannot take his being for granted as God does his. Nor does he possess it in the same way as the other creatures around him. Other animals, for example, survive in mute innocence and cramped necessity. With no future horizons, they are what they are from the start; the law of their life and being is spelled out for them, and they resign themselves to these limits without question. Man . . . must win his selfhood and decide what he is to be. He must fully *become* what he *is*, a human being, To become man through the exercise of his freedom—that is the law of being [Metz, 1968, pp. 6–7].

Richard McBrien expressed himself in almost identical terms:

> With creation, history emerges as the locus of God's action. God and man are separated from nature, which is shorn of all magical aura. Nothing in nature is worthy of adoration or reverential fear, because God and nature are distinct. Nature, therefore, is not something preordained by God, something to be accepted as a given reality. Nature is the raw material for human initiative and innovation. Neither God nor man [is] defined by their relationship to nature, which means that both God and man are freed for history and that nature is now available for man's use [McBrien, 1969, p. 44].

The conclusion is clear. It belongs to the nature of man to interfere particularly with the nature of things (himself included), taking account of nature but ever seeking to transcend it.

P. J. McGrath has further pointed out that there is not a single natural-law tradition. Rather, he distinguishes four main types: the argument based on natural tendencies; the argument from consequences; the argument based on the natural function or purpose of a faculty; and the argument from rights (McGrath, 1969, p. 60).

THE ARGUMENTS IN *Humanae Vitae*

Humanae Vitae (Paul vi, 1968, n. 17, pp. 41–42) uses the argument from consequences and that based on the natural function or purpose of the sex organs or faculty. In neither case, however, does its reasoning carry conviction within the perspective discussed above.

The statement, for example, that artificial birth control opens a wide and easy road toward conjugal infidelity and a general lowering of morality, and may cause men to consider their wives as a mere instrument of selfish enjoyment, runs counter to the experimental data. In the words of Dr. John Marshall, a member of the papal commission whose recommendation Pope Paul had rejected, "this assertion . . . casts a gratuitous slur . . . on the countless responsible married people who practise contraception and whose family life is an example to all." * In fact, contraception can serve to eliminate one of the causes of mutual infidelity and enable husbands to express an increased respect for their wives as human beings. The further argument that governments will make contraception compulsory if it is ruled lawful hardly seems worthy of serious consideration.

The argument that a particular organ has a specific function and that it is an abuse to use it for other purposes is particularly unconvincing to today's man. He knows that, on the contrary, the faculties have evolved by trial and error to perform an increasing range of functions as required to

---

* Quoted in *Herder Correspondence*, 1968, *5*, 309, from a letter of Dr. Marshall which appeared originally in the London *Times* for July 31, 1968.

establish greater control of the environment. The nose serves to smell, to breathe, to eliminate noxious substances. The tongue has a score of purposes. To use an organ for a new purpose represents an advance toward man's destiny. There is neither morality nor immorality about the physical laws. There is nothing wrong about making water boil at a temperature lower than its "natural" boiling point. Rather, it is highly moral to do so for the right reasons.

The encyclical's exception in favor of the rhythm method of contraception also seems quite arbitrary. What it means is that frustration of "the natural order of the conjugal act" is ruled lawful if done in terms of time but unlawful if achieved by a manipulation in space, this in spite of the fact that we live in a time-space continuum which cannot be separated either in good sense or good physiology.

If one single feature can be isolated which more than any other destroys the credibility of the encyclical for today's man, it is the claim (Paul VI, 1968, n. 6, p. 37) that the pope was committed to follow the teaching which had been clearly formulated by his predecessors. This continuing pretense of Roman theology runs counter to the historical evidence. It appears as nothing more than the frantic clinging to threatened authority by frightened, obscurantist, and self-seeking office holders. Anyone who publicly asserts it, within a few years of the repudiation by Vatican Council II of the Syllabus of Errors in the Declaration on Religious Freedom, exposes himself to suffering a total loss of credibility. Nor is that an isolated example of correction of official errors by Vatican Council II. It reformed the teaching of Pope Pius XII (1943) in *Mystici Corporis* that the mystical body and the Roman Catholic Church were identical (Surlis, 1969, p. 132). And it made "an explicit correction of a canon of the Council of Trent" in its description of the origins of the ecclesiastical ministry of bishops, priests, and deacons (Küng, 1967, p. 418).

The same lack of honesty is apparent in the encyclical's distortion of the teaching of Vatican Council II. Philippe Delhaye has documented this point fully (Delhaye, 1968, p. 1132). The most glaring of the many examples he cites are three passages presented as being the total teaching of the Pastoral Constitution on the Church in the Modern World, when in fact they are merely the views of the minority inserted in the Council document to balance those of the majority.

OTHER CONSIDERATIONS

What is to be thought, in this perspective, of the reactions of theologians and national conferences of bishops? The statement issued by faculty members of the Catholic University of America, Washington, D.C., and signed by more than 650 theologians, taking exception to some of the specific ethical conclusions of the encyclical as "based on an inadequate concept of natural law," is a clear expression of the outlook described here. One may note specifically its major conclusion: ". . . spouses may responsibly decide according to their conscience that artificial contraception in some circumstances is permissible and indeed necessary to preserve and foster the values and sacredness of marriage" (Washington Theologians, 1968, p. 3).

The response of bishops, on the contrary, was primarily political, avoiding confrontation on the theological issues, both those raised directly by the content of the encyclical and the more important consequential issue of the nature of authority in the Church and its mode of exercise (see survey in MacEoin, 1969, p. 8). A typical solution was that of the Belgian bishops. A Catholic who after serious examination of the encyclical came to a different conclusion on certain points "has the right to follow his conviction provided that he remains sincerely disposed to continue his enquiries" (Hoyt, 1968, p. 162).

The problem about this solution and its variants is that it starts from the assumption that the encyclical's teaching on contraceptives is objectively right, and that a concession is being made to the weakness of people unable to live up to the totality of the law. It does not satisfy those who believe that it is positively virtuous to use contraceptives when the fostering of mutual love calls for intercourse although personal or social circumstances would make conception irresponsible. The integrity of consciences should not be sacrificed to considerations of authority. This is a point that was made very specifically by a group of fifteen German moral theologians, professors of faculties and schools of theology. They said that they were convinced that "a decision different from that laid down by the magisterium can rest on a base other than a defective conscience, namely, on an objective foundation" (German Theologians, 1968, p. 13). What is at issue is not the weakness of Christian spouses but their virtuous duty.

The other problem unresolved by the bishops is the extent of the right to public dissent. The Canadian bishops, perhaps the most open in their total evaluation, still felt compelled to affirm that "those who have been commissioned by the Church to teach in her name will recognize their responsibility to refrain from public opposition to the encyclical" (Hoyt, 1968, p. 169). This seems to create an impossible situation for the bishop or pastor who conscientiously believes that the salvation of souls entrusted to him requires him to proclaim the truth as he sees it. Similarly, the widespread efforts to limit discussion to theologians and to professional publications overlook the principle formulated by Vatican Council II that all the people of God can and should contribute to the life of the Church. The point has been made very incisively by Daniel Callaghan:

It is not, I think, adequate to simply say that everyone should follow his own conscience and thus reject the encyclical if his conscience so directs. If one takes seriously all the good reasons in favor of a use of contraceptives—if one, say, follows the thinking of the majority of the papal commission—then it is not merely a neutral matter. On the contrary, there is an obligation on the part of those Catholics who perceive the morality of contraception to positively foster and propagate their convictions. This means doing everything in their power to educate people in the valid use of contraceptives. It means convincing governments that they should listen to the voice of the Catholic people and not to the voice of the Pope on this issue. It means doing everything possible to negate and repudiate the encyclical, putting in its place a very different teaching.

People should of course be free to follow their conscience. But there is much sense in the traditional corollary that they should have an informed conscience; a lot of mischief is done in the name of conscience. In this instance those opposed to the encyclical would seem to have the positive duty of trying to inform the consciences of those who might feel an obligation to follow it: to inform them that they should know all the good theological arguments in favor of contraception; to inform them that they cannot cast off the obligation of making up their own minds on the shoulders of popes and bishops; to inform them that it is possible that good morality might require that they use contraceptives [Callaghan, 1968, p. 558].

This then, I suggest, is the impact of *Humanae Vitae* on the conscience of the enlightened Catholic, an impact quite different from that envisaged by its creators. It has become a challenge to pursue a necessary work of demythologization. Its failure to affect the thinking and behavior of the faithful in the direction sought by its authors indicates the extent to which it is out of touch with the mentality of contemporary man. In that respect, it is itself already a significant contribution to the demythologizing process.

REFERENCES

Callaghan, D. An alternative proposal. *Commonweal,* 1968, *88,* 558–560.
Congar, Y. M. (o.p.) Un "ferment schismatique"? *Informations Catholiques Internationales,* No. 335, Paris, May 2, 1969.
Delhaye, P. The encyclical and the council. *Tablet,* London, November 16, 1968.
Hoyt, R. G. (Ed.) *The birth control debate.* Kansas City, Mo.: National Catholic Reporter, 1968.
German Theologians. *Informations Catholiques Internationales,* No. 322, Paris, October 15, 1968.
Küng, H. *The church.* New York: Sheed & Ward, 1967.
MacEoin, G. Cultural lag in Catholicism's central city. *National Catholic Reporter,* August 14, 1968.
MacEoin, G. Catholics escalate the conflict. *The Lamp.* 1969, *67* (5), 8–10; 28–30.
McBrien, R. P. *Do we need the church?* New York: Harper & Row, 1969.
McGrath, P. J. Natural law and moral argument. In J. P. Mackey (Ed.) *Morals, law and authority.* Dayton: Pflaum, 1969. Pp. 58–78.

Metz, J. B. *Poverty of spirit* (trans. by J. Drury). Glen Rock, N.J.: Newman, 1968.

Paul VI. *Humanae vitae*. Encyclical letter of July 25, 1968. *Acta Apostolicae Sedis*, 1968, *60*, 481–503. English translation: Human life. *Catholic Mind*, 1968, *66*, (September, no. 1225), 35–48.

Pius XII. *Mystici corporis*. Encyclical letter of June 29, 1943. *Acta Apostolicae Sedis*, 1943, *35*, 193–248. English translation: Mystical Body. *Catholic Mind*, 1943, *41*, (November, no. 971), 1–44.

Ryan, C. Science and moral law. In J. P. Mackey (Ed.) *Morals, law and authority*. Dayton: Pflaum, 1969. Pp. 79–90.

Suenens, L. J. L'unité de l'Église. *Informations Catholiques Internationales*, No. 336, Supplement, Paris, May 15, 1969. An English translation appeared in the *National Catholic Reporter*, May 28, 1969.

Surlis, P. The church's message. In J. P. Mackey (Ed.) *Morals, law and authority*. Dayton: Pflaum, 1969. Pp. 127–154.

Vatican Council II. W. M. Abbott (s.j.) (Ed.) *The documents of Vatican II*. New York: Herder & Herder, 1966.

Washington, D.C., Theologians. Statement on the encyclical *Humanae vitae*. *Catholic Mind*, 1968, *66* (September, no. 1225), 2–4.

VIII
THE MATURE CONSCIENCE IN
MULTIDISCIPLINARY PERSPECTIVE

The Mature Conscience in Philosophical Perspective

W. NORRIS CLARKE, S.J.

Father W. Norris Clarke, S.J. has a master's degree in philosophy (1940) from Fordham University, a licentiate in theology (1946) from Woodstock College, and a doctorate in philosophy (1949) from the University of Louvain. He is a past president of both the Metaphysical Society of America and the American Catholic Philosophical Association. He is the author of some thirty-five articles and papers contributed to representative professional journals and to symposia. He has been the American Editor-in-Chief since its inception in 1961 of the International Philosophical Quarterly. *After previous teaching posts at Woodstock College and Bellarmine College, Plattsburgh, N.Y., Father Clarke came to Fordham University in 1955, where he is currently professor of philosophy.*

Before I begin my paper I must confess to a certain embarrassment in attempting to develop this topic. I am not a specialist in ethics at all; in fact I rarely work in that area in my own philosophizing, at least explicitly. It is not possible for me, therefore, to present the professional ethician's approach. I am simply going to set forth briefly and schematically my own reflections, drawn from some modest incidental reading over the years, much talk with my philosophical brethren, and mostly reflections on my own and others' experience, situated in a total philosophy of the person.

Since I am convinced that most if not all of us already instinctively recognize what the mature conscience is, even if we cannot express it adequately, the only merit this paper may have is to help pull together and make explicit what you already know. For, the purpose of all philosophy, as I see it, is the systematic and persistent effort to illuminate and take possession of our own experience in depth, and to situate it in a vision of reality as a whole. And if there is one type of experience that all of us, to the extent that we are human, are experts in, it is moral experience, even though not moral philosophy or theology. Hence I would like to appeal directly to the experience and reflection of each one of you, as to a community of experts, to check the soundness of what I have to say.

SOME PRELIMINARY CONSIDERATIONS

Let us recall briefly what conscience is. It is that inner voice, that judgment of our practical reason, which tells us that a particular action or course of action is morally good (i.e., can be done or ought to be done) or morally evil (ought not to be done). Its direct concern is not with moral principles, although it is nourished by them, but with a concrete moral choice that presents itself here and now for decision.

What is the role of conscience in human life? It is to be the light by which man guides himself in his actions, freely and responsibly, and as wisely as he can toward the fulfillment of his maturity, his self-realization, his destiny, or his last end—however one wishes to put it in philosophical terms. It is thus at the core of the essential dignity of every human person as endowed with reason and free will.

St. Thomas links conscience with the image of God in man. At the beginning of his whole treatise on the moral life in his *Summa Theologiae* (Part I–II), he says that just as God by His reason and freedom exercises providence over the whole universe, guiding all things toward their ends, so too man as His image should exercise providence over his own life and actions, thus guiding himself toward his own end. The moral life thus consists in one's own personal responsible self-guidance toward his final end. And the light of our own reason, by which we guide ourselves, is itself a participation, a living image, of the divine intelligence, a spark of the divine light, as some have put it. Thus it is because each man must be personally responsible for his own moral decisions and make them according to the light of his own reason, that he must always follow his own conscience, even when its judgment is in fact erroneous. As St. Thomas puts it:

Every man is held to examine his own actions in the light of the knowledge which he has from God, whether it be natural, or acquired, or infused. For every man must act according to reason [On Truth, q. 17, a. 5, ad 4].

Let us come now to a consideration of the mature conscience. The mature conscience is a function of the mature person; hence when looked at in philosophical perspective it must be set in the context of a total philosophy of the person (Donceel, 1967, Ch. 13; MacMurray, 1957, 1961; Plattel, 1965; and Walgrave, 1965). In brief, for our purposes here, the mature person is one who has reached a well-developed stage of self-awareness and self-possession, and has situated himself realistically in his thought and action within the real world in which he lives—i.e., within the human community of other human persons in a common world. Hence the primary characteristics of the mature conscience are that its moral judgments be *truly personal* or interiorized, i.e., proceeding from the authentic inner self of the person; truly *social-minded,* seeing his own good as inseparable from the good of others; and *truly prudent* or showing habitual good judgment in deciding, among various conflicting values at stake, what is the best thing to do, here and now. Let me develop each of these characteristics briefly in turn.

CONSCIENCE AS PERSONALIZED

The most basic characteristic of the mature moral conscience and the necessary condition for all else is the habit of making its moral judgments truly personal ones. By this I mean that they proceed truly from within, from one's own moral convictions, according to one's own sincere judgment, in the light of one's own moral ideals and values freely and responsibly accepted as one's own; in a word, when the voice of my conscience is really the voice of my own deepest and most authentic self speaking out to guide my actions. It is a function and natural consequence of developed self-awareness and responsible self-possession of one's actions—in a word, of being an authentic self.

The opposite of this personalization is the habit of making one's moral judgments out of extrinsic motives, or under the domination of extrinsic sources, such as fear, desire of reward, conformity to social pressures or even to authority and law as merely external norms (cf. Monden, 1965). One of the most fundamental elements in the passage from moral immaturity to moral maturity is this passage from extrinsic to intrinsic motivation, from purely external pressure to internalized truly personal morality. Ignace Lepp expresses it as follows:

> As psychological maturity increases, however, the network of moral obligations loses its character of a superego to become a personal moral conscience. In the mature adult this conscience takes the form of a free adherence to the good, recognized as such by the subject. His morality is personal [Lepp, 1965, p. 24].

Nor is the process of internalization for most people ever total and complete, once and for all. There always remain some extrinsic pressures, from society or the unconscious, which we are not able to become fully aware of or fully dominate, and which continue to influence our moral judgments and weaken their full free autonomy. But beyond a certain point of development we and others can know that for the most part our moral judgments proceed primarily from intrinsic and not extrinsic sources. We might add that perhaps never before in history has such a significant proportion of people emerged all around the world, groping and longing consciously and articulately, though with many exaggerations and blind alleys, toward such a truly personal morality.

This inner-sourced character of mature morality is not at all the same as a self-centered subjectivism that does not take into account traditional moral wisdom, community experience and customs, legitimate authority, or the will of God. It opens itself humbly and sincerely to all these, but always in such a way that whatever it accepts from the outside it personally assimilates and turns into its own personal conviction. Even when it judges that it should here follow authority or tradition against its own preference, it does so because it sincerely judges that this is here and now the best thing to do. And the responsibility for this practical judgment, whether it is here and now good for me to obey, can never be abdicated to another in the name of any other virtue, such as humility, obedience, reverence for authority, and so forth.* With respect to God, however, the highest development of the mature conscience is so to internalize and make one's own the will of God that His voice finally becomes identical with that of our own deepest, most authentic self. Here outer and inner voice finally become one in a lived coincidence of opposites.

In order to achieve this personalized moral conscience, however, a strong motive force is needed as an inner dynamo to keep the process going. This is the profound personal commitment to the ideal of the good as such, so that I truly want habitually to respond to the authentic call of the good, wherever it may lead me, rather than merely be concerned with how much I can get away with without running afoul of moral obligation, how far I am bound by duty.

It is really amazing what a difference it makes in one's moral attitudes when one makes this step and seriously takes hold of the pursuit of the good as one's own personal ideal that he truly wants to follow, and commits himself to follow as his own personal goal, not something forced upon him and

* This is the teaching of St. Thomas in the text of which the conclusion was quoted above. In talking about individual conscience and legitimate authority, he makes the point that when we are given a command by such an authority, it is not the subject's business to judge the goodness of the command in itself; but it must be our business to judge whether or not we should here and now obey the command, for every man is held to examine his own actions.

dutifully accepted from without. This gives a clarity and steadiness to moral judgment that has no adequate substitutes.

Note that this profound commitment of the whole person to the good as absolute value is also a commitment to reason, mediated through one's own reason. For, part of the very meaning of "to be reasonable," "to live reasonably," is that we should habitually want to do what our reason judges to be reasonable or fitting to do. To be reasonable and to be moral are really two sides of the same coin. And reason in the concrete must always be one's own reason, responsible to its own vision, no matter how limited, and not merely the reason of another as extrinsic to one's own.

This radical commitment of the person to the call of the good and of reason—or, if you wish, to the call of the good as mediated through reason—cannot, if it wishes to be efficacious, be a commitment of pure passionless intellect or pure spiritual will. It must enlist and draw into itself our emotions, our affectivity, at the deepest level possible. It must, as Ignace Lepp maintains, take on a certain quality of enthusiasm, but "an enthusiasm that comes from the depths of one's being." I agree with him that "the moral élan must spring from the love rather than the knowledge of the good. All efficacious morality must be supported by a mysticism"—that is, some deeply felt dedication to a transcendent or ultimate ideal whose value is somehow intuitively known or experienced, whether this is identified as divine or as immanent in nature (Lepp, 1965, p. 87). The role of emotion or affectivity as a necessary support of a mature moral life seems to me an important factor often overlooked.

The above notion of deeply felt commitment to the good as the inner dynamo of the moral conscience and the whole moral life may help also to illuminate one aspect of conscience that has always filled me with wonder and not a little puzzlement. This is the spontaneous, intuitive, non-analytic character of its judgment in so many cases, even quite complex ones, in which it comes out with clear-cut judgments—"This is right; do it; that's no good, avoid it"—even though we find it very difficult to justify or organize these in any explicit analyzable reasoning. The answer is perhaps the peculiar intuitive connaturality or affinity with the good which results from the radical commitment to the good itself as absolute ideal. This connaturality through love gives a certain intuitive feel or flair for discovering the good wherever it is to be found that is beyond the reach of step-by-step analytic reason. St. Thomas himself gives an important place to such knowledge by connaturality—the term itself is his—in the knowledge of God, of morality, and of spiritual things in general—a place which is often overlooked in our traditional treatises both of epistemology and of ethics.

CONSCIENCE AS UNIVERSAL OR SOCIAL-MINDED

Closely connected with the notion of conscience as personalized or interiorized moral judgment, but worth distinguishing from it explicitly because
of its importance, is the second basic characteristic of the mature conscience: the universal or socially oriented quality of its judgments. The more
a person becomes mature, the more he comes to recognize, and turn to a
truly personal conviction, that his own individual good is joined inseparably
with the good of other persons, in ever-widening circles until his horizon of
judgment finally takes in the entire human race as one and indivisible in
interdependence, destiny, and happiness. In a word, his moral judgments
take on more and more the point of view of the common good, seen in
ever-wider contexts, and recognized as in indissoluble solidarity with his
own authentic personal good and happiness. Existentially this is a wisdom
gained by experience and good living. Philosophically it is rooted in the
very nature of the person, as a self whose very selfhood is instrinsically constituted in relation to other selves. There is no coming to awareness of the
"I" except in relation to a "Thou" and a "We"; there is no unfolding of the
freedom of the person except in relation to the freedom of other persons;
there is no authentic happiness or self-realization of the individual self except
in communion with other selves, including the ultimate Infinite Self of God
Himself. Lepp puts it thus: "Authentic morality must be at once inseparably
subjective and objective" (Lepp, 1965, p. 42). And again: "Society is not a
juxtaposition of individual egoisms but a community whose members are
integral parts. It follows that moral obligation is inseparably individual and
collective, that we ought to pursue the common good and the personal good
in the same moral movement" (Lepp, 1965, p. 60).

An essential part of the growth to maturity is the progressive passage
from a predominantly narrow, self-centered individualist point of view as
a basis for moral judgment to one where the common good—or, perhaps
better, the solidarity of the individual and the common or community good
—takes on predominance. Note that I say the common good, which is not
always the same as the common opinion, community pressure, and the like.
Some psychiatrists have even defined maturity as that state of a personality
in which it is habitually disposed to be at least as much concerned with the
good of others as with its own. Moral education should aim to assist this
development in every possible way. I might add that one of the most interesting and inspiring developments in the evolution of moral consciousness in
our times is the steadily increasing proportion of mature persons, who now
take explicitly as their point of reference in orienting their moral decisions
the good, not just of their own families, or their local community, or even
nation or culture, but of all humanity, of the human race as such. This will

certainly become more and more one of the great moral imperatives of the mature conscience of the future.

An immediate corollary of this universal or social-minded character of the mature conscience is the classic Kantian test for checking the soundness of our moral judgments: so act that your action may become a norm that can be followed by every other person in similar circumstances. In a word, what would happen if every one acted the way I wish to act in such a situation? I am well aware of all the controversies, theoretical and practical, one can get into if he tries to defend this rule rigidly and literally, since no two persons or situations are ever exactly alike. Nonetheless it remains in practice a most helpful and illuminating general guideline or rule of thumb to be taken into account by anyone sincerely wishing to reach a mature decision, if he knows how to use it, not as a straitjacket, but as a magnet to pull him out of the narrow perspective of self-centered interest into the wider horizon of the common good.

It is evident from the above that I am not an advocate of situation ethics, at least in its extreme form, which would claim that every person and every situation is so unique that no general norms can be applied. The truly mature person, it seems to me, is humble enough to admit that he shares a great deal in common with other men, and that similar actions for the most part result in similar consequences—but only for the most part; hence he is sensitive enough to discern the dosage of uniqueness in each case and its relevance for the moral judgment.

CONSCIENCE AS PRUDENT, PRACTICAL INSIGHT

We have considered up to now basic general dispositions and attitudes of the mature conscience. Now we come to the heart of the matter and the most difficult part of our analysis to articulate abstractly. This is the process of actual decision-making, of arriving at the concrete practical judgments of conscience: "This is morally good; that is morally wrong." It is here that the primary virtue of the mature conscience enters in—namely, prudence. I am taking prudence, not in the modern sense of cautiousness, but in the rich, older sense of the insight of practical wisdom, which sizes up what should here and now be done in order to realize the ideal of the good in this concrete situation (Pieper, 1959). This practical judgment goes beyond all merely abstract general principles because it has to judge precisely which principle takes precedence here and now. Its principal task, therefore, is to make a calculation of values—i.e., to weigh the various conflicting values and principles at stake and decide which one takes precedence in this case. For every particular moral judgment involves deciding between at least two conflicting goods or values (since it is impossible for the will to choose what does not present at least the appearance of good). We always choose and pursue some good, whatever we do. But the question is: which good should be given the green light here and now?

What are the basic factors involved in making a mature prudential judgment of conscience? The first requisite is that one be well-informed on his environment and the people in it. I simply must have good information in order to make good mature moral judgments—which are not the same as well-intentioned, sincere ones. This point is sometimes overlooked in discussions of morality, together with its corollary, the obligation to keep reasonably well-informed about the world one lives in. This is one reason that children and adolescents can have good, but not mature, consciences.

The second requisite is to possess a well-developed sense of the consequences of certain types of actions, based on a rich memory-bank of experience, personal and social. If one does such and such, what usually happens? A very large part of moral wisdom, whether in arriving at general moral principles or making practical judgments, consists in developing such a sense of consequences—i.e., good judgment in discerning and evaluating the probable consequences of actions. For, most moral principles—and the more particular they are, the more true this is—receive their justification, not as necessary a priori truths, or by a purely intrinsic consideration of their nature, but rather from an evaluation of the consequences of types of action with respect to endangering or enhancing more fundamental and general values. The empirical side of moral thinking, both philosophical and theological, is considerably larger than has perhaps been traditionally admitted.

Aside from the few great fundamental principles of morality based directly on the basic intrinsic values, such as love and respect for the dignity of all persons, most moral problems are solved by such a consequences-analysis as the following: Such and such a type of action is wrong because it leads to the following consequences, which in turn endanger such and such a more basic value which we are already committed to, or which possesses an ultimate absolute value. Hence it is one of the essential characteristics of mature judgment that it weighs carefully and has an experiential feel for the probable consequences of a projected course of action. As part of this consequences-analysis, we should include here the universalization principle of Kant, mentioned earlier: if every one in similar circumstances were to act in the way I am considering doing, what would the probable consequence be?

The next factor that should enter into the mature moral judgment, one closely connected with the sense of consequences, is a respectful consultation of the traditional moral wisdom, principles, and customs of the social community or communities in which one lives, such as the family, civil society, the Church, and so forth. For these embody the accumulated moral experience and wisdom of society, based on the memory-bank and reflection of that society, spread over a larger duration and scope of experience than the individual can possibly draw on from his own limited experience. It is really impossible to have a purely individual morality and still be human. One must accept at least the basic moral principles of some living community, be member to some social moral consensus, since we cannot be sure even of our own sanity or self-identity except in the context of some kind of mutual ratification and consensus with others.

However, the mature conscience must always keep a certain freedom and critical distance with respect to the traditional or contemporary moral consensus of any social group. The group in question may have become rigidly fixed in certain positions based on too narrow a context or perspective, no longer adequate to their total experience in relation to their environment and each other. Or certain kinds of corruption may have become ingrained in a given society, so that a partial moral blindness has come over them in these areas. This may even become so bad that the mature conscience may feel called upon to speak out against a particular moral principle of his own society, or even leave it for another, in the name of the very fundamental moral ideals he has learned from the same society. The history of the great moral reformers is eloquent with such examples. The mature conscience must always be able to personalize and turn into its own sincere conviction whatever it receives from society around it. But even when one is not personally convinced of the soundness or binding force of traditional moral principles or practice in his society, he must still carefully take into account the consequences of his acting differently with respect to the common good.

So far I have said nothing explicitly about the so-called absolute moral principles, whose claims as absolute transcend the varieties of time, place, culture, historical evolution, and even any consideration of consequences. Should not appeal to them immediately settle many moral decisions, without going through all the above complex calculus of values and consequences? Here I feel myself obligated to amplify my position a little further and perhaps part company with some of you who have stayed with me thus far. If so, my only excuse is that I too must be honest and faithful to my own lights, dim though they be. And at least I will not put forward my position dogmatically, but tentatively and suggestively, as reflecting the drift of my own reflection in process.

It seems to me, reflecting on the nature of human consciousness and morality, with its intrinsically evolutionary character, as well as upon the history of moral thinking, that there are really very, very few particular moral principles which are absolute, transcending all possible diversity of contexts and circumstances. The great, general moral values, such as love and respect for one's fellow man because of his eminent dignity as a person, hence not treating another person as a mere means—these indeed are absolute. But they are very general and formal, and do not tell us directly how to apply these values here and now in real life. I am talking rather about moral principles with a specific content, such as killing, or stealing, justice, the morality of sex, and the like. It seems to me that *almost* all these hold only for the most part, as St. Thomas himself maintains quite explicitly for divorce (prescinding from revelation) and other moral principles, which he holds are not primary precepts of the natural law. I say "almost" since there may well be some principles with specific content that are so closely connected with the preservation or violation of the intrinsic dignity of the human person that they share inseparably in the absoluteness of the latter. But I would be very slow to specify exactly what these are in any detail, nor would I necessarily accept all the ones laid down by St. Thomas. Slavery under certain conditions would come close to it, and so would the taking of an innocent person's human life. But even here I have some difficulty in seeing clearly the absoluteness of the merely physical life of the human person in all possible contexts now and forever.

It seems to me that the whole history of moral thinking down the ages reveals a slow but steady process of mitigating the absoluteness of particular moral principles and partially relativizing them in terms of wider contexts, where they are seen to yield occasionally to more fundamental values. The general principle involved here is that all particular principles are based on limited values involving limited perspectives on reality as a whole. And it is very difficult if not impossible to judge that no wider perspective or horizon of vision will ever occur in which these particular values will come into conflict with a more basic value and have to yield to it. I believe it is quite possible to reach a consensus, even of all mankind, that such and such a principle should be considered inviolate under all present and foreseeable future contingencies. But such a prudent practical judgment and consensus does not yet commit me, it seems to me as a philosopher, to a timeless and exceptionless absolute for all possible human history (cf. Curran, 1968).

Hence it seems to me an inseparable characteristic of the mature conscience that it have the good judgment and courage to know how and when to relativize all or almost all moral principles dealing with specific types of actions, in the name of the few great general moral values which are ultimate and absolute. It takes both mature judgment and courage to be able prudently to do this in order to protect or foster the few authentic absolutes. The effects of such action on others must also be carefully weighed, of course, and the Kantian principle of universalization applied as a check. But I do not see how we can rule out the need and right to do so under certain circumstances; and it seems to me that the mature conscience must be ready to face this challenge and take the risk when one judges it prudently appropriate, even at the risk of condemnation by other good people or even by legitimate authority.

Let me here introduce the final general principle or disposition for making a mature moral judgment. It is that one should make the most deliberate and earnest effort, as far as lies in his power, to situate the problem at hand within the widest possible relevant context of value and reality. It seems to me, in reflecting on the progress of moral thinking down the ages, especially on those moments when the moral wisdom of a society evolves decisively and reverses or notably qualifies previously held moral principles, that what usually happens is that a wider context of reality with new relevant consequences comes into focus, or that it becomes recognized that the previous judgments were made from too narrow a value-perspective, subordinating a higher but less apparent value to a more immediately evident shorter-range one. To know what angle of vision to take on a problem, what set of relevant value perimeters to situate it within, what horizon of consequences to include in one's vision—all this can be done well only by a mature judgment. The general rule is that particular goods of a person should be subordinated to the more general good of the whole person, the goods of an individual person to comparable goods of the community as a whole, the goods of lesser communities to comparable goods of broader ones, and so forth. It is the special characteristic of the mature moral conscience that it not only makes every effort to situate any moral decision in the widest relevant context of reality and value, but also has the good judgment to recognize how far to go in determining the limits of the relevant context in a given case.

After taking into account all the above factors, the mature conscience must finally make its own judgment from within, sizing up the total picture in an act of practical moral insight. This cannot be spelled out in any foolproof abstract formula or legislated in advance by anyone else. It is the ultimate responsibility of the person's own conscience, a burden that cannot be laid on anyone else's shoulders. All that can be said is that it should be done in the light of a profound openness to the call of the good (and to the Spirit of God speaking within one, if he is a religious man), and also a profound loving attentiveness to the whole present context of reality lying before him.

Lastly, once he has made his judgment, the mature moral person will follow out his conscience with what Dr. John Cavanagh, in his paper in this volume, calls very aptly "functional certitude" *—that is, without undue anxiety or endless rehashing of the wisdom of the judgment. For it is also proper to the mature person that, once his decisions are made to the best of his ability, he has a certain detachment or distance from the results of his own actions, leaving them humbly and trustingly to the wider providence of God, who alone has ultimate providence over the whole universe and all of human history.

In summary, the distinctive characteristics of the mature moral conscience are that it has formed the habit of making moral judgments which

* Page 384.

are truly personal, truly social-minded, truly realistic, and truly prudent, all animated from within by a profound and deeply felt commitment to the good as absolute value.

REFERENCES

Curran, C. (Ed.) *Absolutes in moral theology?* Washington: Corpus Books, 1968.
Donceel, J. (s.J.) *Philosophical anthropology* (3rd ed.) New York: Sheed & Ward, 1967.
Lepp, I. *The authentic morality.* New York: Macmillan, 1965.
MacMurray, J. *The self as agent.* London: Faber & Faber, 1957.
MacMurray, J. *Persons in relation.* London: Faber & Faber, 1961.
Monden, L. (s.J.) *Sin, liberty, and law* (trans. by J. Donceel [s.J.]). New York: Sheed & Ward, 1965.
Pieper, J. *Prudence* (trans. by R. & C. Winston). New York: Pantheon, 1959.
Plattel, M. G. *Social Philosophy.* Pittsburgh: Duquesne University Press, 1965.
Walgrave, J. H. *Person and society.* Pittsburgh: Duquesne University Press, 1965.

The Mature Conscience in Theological Perspective

EWERT H. COUSINS

Ewert H. Cousins received his A.B. degree from Spring Hill College in 1950, an S.T.L. from St. Louis University in 1959, and a Ph.D. from Fordham University in 1966. He is a member of the Society for the Scientific Study of Religion, the Association for Applied Psychoanalysis, and an associate member of the Catholic Biblical Association. He has published in Continuum *and* Franciscan Studies *and has contributed a chapter on* Psychoanalysis and Spiritual Transformation *for a forthcoming publication under the editorship of Benjamin Wolman which is to have as its title* Psychoanalysis and Catholicism. *Currently, Dr. Cousins is an associate professor in the theology department at Fordham University.*

A mature person is one who faces reality and faces it in its deepest dimension. The child grows to maturity by opening himself to reality—to its limits, its crises, its possibilities, and its fullness. If one achieves maturity by opening himself to the depths and complexity of reality, then the Christian has a special task. For the Christian reaches maturity not only by opening himself to personal, social, and political reality, but by becoming increasingly aware of that level of reality from which revelation has removed the veil of darkness. Illumined by faith, the Christian must penetrate the mysteries of revelation and allow them to transform every facet of his life and bring him to spiritual maturity. For the Christian, then, conscience is not merely a matter of a personal ideal or of social norms. The Christian's conscience and his moral decisions are bound up with the mystery of Christ and the life of the Spirit. His conscience has its ontological roots and its ultimate meaning in the Trinitarian life; and his concrete moral decisions are caught up in the mystery of the fall, the incarnation, and redemption, and the eschatological fulfillment of the kingdom. The Christian, then, grows to maturity not merely by reaching adulthood in the family and state, but by reaching spiritual adulthood in the Church and the life of the Spirit. For the Christian, the mature conscience is one that is illumined by the Spirit and conformed to Christ, and through Christ is united to the Father. In this context we will explore the Christian's conscience in its theological perspective and attempt to draw into relief those qualities that are a mark of its maturity.

THEOLOGICAL METHOD

The theologian's task is complicated, for he must examine human experience in the light of revelation and in the life of the Church. Although he knows that revelation illumines human experience and that grace transforms human possibilities, he can never grasp the extent of that transformation nor comprehend the ultimate dimension of the mysteries. Yet he is assured by the statement of Vatican Council I that "if human reason, with faith as its guiding light, inquiries earnestly, devoutly, and circumspectly, it does reach, by God's generosity, some understanding of mysteries, and that a most profitable one" (Denzinger & Schönmetzer, 1965, #3016 [#1796]). The Council goes on to say that human reason can do this by exploring "the similarity with truths which it knows naturally and also from the interrelationship of mysteries with one another and with the final end of man" (Denzinger & Schönmetzer, 1965, #3016 [#1796]). Following the method outlined by the Council, we shall examine the mature conscience by bringing it in contact with the mysteries of Christian revelation. In this way we enter into a dialogue between revelation and human experience. We will examine human experience in the light of revelation and revelation in the light of human experience. By correlating these two poles, we hope to clarify each in the light of the other. Thus by viewing the mature conscience in the light of the Christian mysteries, we can bring to the fore new dimensions of its richness and complexity.

We shall begin by examining the mature conscience in its personal and social dimensions and then view it in the light of the mystery of Christ, seen primarily through the Pauline and Johannine writings. Secondly, we shall view the mature conscience in the light of the mystery of the Spirit working in the processes of history. For maturity involves not only growth toward the ideal of Christ, but also the anguish of growing in history as an individual, a nation, and a world community. Only by situating the mature conscience in the mystery of Christ and the Spirit can we view its ideal possibilities and its tragic and problematic historicity—as the Spirit works to bring man to the full stature of his identity in Christ.

INTERIOR MORALITY

If we examine human experience, we observe that the mature person does not look upon the moral law as something merely outside himself: as a command of his parents, a decree of his Church or government, a taboo of his culture, an impersonal law of nature, or an edict of God. If he looked upon law as something merely extrinsic to himself, he might respond to situations like a child who submits slavishly to the voice of his parents. Or like a rebellious child, he might reject the law as an infringement on his freedom. Or he might submit to the law out of a sense of abstract duty or helplessness, yet with rancor within, crying out in the depths of his soul like Prometheus against the injustice of a tyrannical Zeus. Unlike the submissive or rebellious child, the mature person realizes that the moral order, while extrinsic to himself, is also most intimate to his subjectivity. Like Socrates he believes that doing evil destroys what is noblest within us; therefore it is better to suffer injustice than to commit it (Plato, *Gorgias*). Finally, like Socrates he would be willing to face death rather than go counter to his deepest moral convictions (Plato, *Crito, Phaedo*). In his authentic moral decisions, he knows that his own deepest self is at stake.

When the mature person discovers the moral law at the heart of his subjectivity, he does not fall into subjectivism or relativism—that is, into a type of moral solipsism in which his own autonomous will determines the law. This would be to reduce maturity to the state of a childish tantrum in which willfulness prevails. The mature discovery of the moral self is much more profound and paradoxical than that. At the very moment when autonomous subjectivity is touched, the moral self is most universalized. At the moment one realizes that an absolute moral demand touches his deepest subjectivity, he becomes aware that this demand is capable of being universalized to all subjectivities. Thus in discovering his moral self, the mature person grasps finite subjectivity as such. Hence he realizes that any man in these circumstances should feel the absolute demand of the moral ought. At the same time his moral awareness becomes most personal, it becomes most social and universal. It is this convergence of the deepest subjectivity with the greatest universality that Kant expressed in his dictum: So act that your maxim can be made a universal law (Kant, 1923, pp. 38–39). However, this universalizing property of the moral law should not be read primarily with the logic of classification, but with the logic of the coincidence of opposites. The important point here is not that we can easily specify or classify the circumstances in which an action would be right or wrong, for the circumstances are not easily universalized. The important point is that at man's moral center an absolute moral demand converges with the relativity of circumstances, so that in the depths of the moral decision each man becomes universal man. In the moral decision, particular man rises above the endless qualities of classification—above the relativity of circumstances—and becomes his true self, and at that moment reaches the point where his autonomous subjectivity coincides with that of all men.

The reason why one's deepest individuality coincides with the greatest universality is that in their moral centers all men coincide before the absolute call of God. According to Christian theology, each man is an image of God (Ladner, 1959), with God's light shining in the depths of his soul. This divine light touches man profoundly in his moral decision, confronting him with an absolute call at the center of his freedom where he is most unique and at one with all men. Here in the moral decision, where man touches God, the opposites coincide: what is most individual with what is most universal; what is most immanent with what is most transcendent. At this point of convergence moral maturity is reached. The morally mature man is at one with himself, with God, and with the universe. He stands at the farthest remove from the submissiveness or the autonomous willfulness of the child. At this point of convergence he is beyond conflict, for in pursuing his true self he is pursuing God and in pursuing God he is pursuing all things.

MATURITY THROUGH CHRIST

To achieve this maturity is a difficult task. Man is caught in the mystery of evil: he is a soaring spirit entrapped in finitude; he is split off from his true self—the slave of his own desires, imprisoned in a maze of self-deception, and overpowered by the forces of evil (Dubarle, 1964). In a classic passage in the Epistle to the Romans, Paul describes man's moral helplessness in the face of evil. Overcome by the burden of extrinsicism, Paul cries out against the letter of the Mosaic Law. But it is not merely the extrinsicism of the Mosaic Law or its ritualistic prescriptions that Paul inveighs against, but moral consciousness itself. "If it had not been for the law," Paul says, "I should not have known sin. I should not have known what it is to covet if the law had not said, 'You shall not covet' " (Rom 7:7). Moral consciousness is indeed ambiguous. At the same time that it awakens man to his highest ideals, it stirs the law of sin within his members. "The very commandment," Paul says, "which promised life proved to be death to me"

(Rom 7:10). Paul describes the warfare within: "For I delight in the law of God, in my inmost self, but I see in my members another law at war with the law of my mind and making me captive to the law of sin which dwells in my members" (Rom 7:22–23). Paul cries out against the intolerable demand of the moral ought and the burden of guilt it imparts: "Wretched man that I am! Who will deliver me from this body of death?" (Rom 7:24). Paul answers that it is Jesus Christ:

> For God has done what the law, weakened by the flesh, could not do: sending his own Son in the likeness of sinful flesh and for sin, he condemned sin in the flesh, in order that the just requirement of the law might be fulfilled in us, who walk not according to the flesh but according to the Spirit [Rom 8:3–4].

It is Christ who overcomes the forces of evil and liberates man to become his true self. Christ removes the extrinsicism of morality and touches man's deepest subjectivity. As Image of the invisible God, He awakens the image of God in man. As Son of the Father, He draws man into adoptive sonship:

> For you do not receive the spirit of slavery to fall back into fear, but you have received the spirit of sonship. When we cry, "Abba! Father!" it is the Spirit himself bearing witness with our spirit that we are children of God, and if children, then heirs, heirs of God and fellow heirs with Christ, provided we suffer with him in order that we may also be glorified with him [Rom 8:15–17].

In the Spirit we are united to Christ. The mature Christian is one who in the depths of his moral self has "put on Christ" (Gal 3:27), who with Paul can say: "It is no longer I who live, but Christ who lives in me" (Gal 2:20).

Throughout the centuries, Christians have reached moral maturity by meditating on the life of Christ, by imitating His virtues, and by adopting His fundamental moral attitudes (Häring, 1963, pp. 51–53). This does not result in a moralism or a mere surface copying of his virtues, but involves a total transformation of the personality, resulting in a new spiritual identity and attitude toward the world. In the Johannine writings this attitude is described in terms of love and the Trinitarian life. In the discourse at the Last Supper, Christ tells His disciples:

> As the Father has loved me, so have I loved you; abide in my love. If you keep my commandments, you will abide in my love, just as I have kept my Father's commandments and abide in his love. These things I have spoken to you, that my joy may be in you, and that your joy may be full. This is my commandment, that you love one another as I have loved you [Jn 15:9–12].

This is the mature Christian attitude: law has been subsumed into love (Gilleman, 1959, pp. 253–279). The commandments have been completely interiorized and lifted up to the divine level, for Christ has drawn the Christian into the intimate love of the Trinitarian life. Christ prays that "they may all be one; even as thou, Father, art in me, and I in thee" (Jn 17:21). Christ promises to send the Spirit, who will draw men into the Trinitarian life because, as theologians will explain later, the Spirit Himself is the love of the Father and the Son.

Having been drawn into the Trinitarian life of love, the mature Christian is assimilated in his moral self to the Trinity. He realizes himself as image of the Trinity and shares in a special way in the mystery of creation and the incarnation. In the technical terms of moral theology, conscience "is a judgment of the practical reason on the moral goodness or sinfulness of an action" (Jone, 1953, p. 38). As incarnate spirit, man must express himself in his actions in space and time. His conscience is his guide, the faculty that directs this expression so that his actions will be the adequate expression of his moral self as image of God. Having united himself to Christ, the Christian is swept up into the mystery of the generation of the Son from the Father. As perfect image of the Father, the Son adequately expresses the reality of the Father; and as the Word of the Father, He is the vehicle for all expression in creation and ultimately in the incarnation. The Trinity is the mystery of perfect expressionism—both internally in the processions and externally in creation and the incarnation. Through union with Christ, the Christian strives to approximate the perfect expressionism of the Trinity. Through the guidance of his conscience in the incarnate moral decisions of his life, the Christian grows toward the maturity of the ideal expressionism revealed in the Trinity.

THE SPIRIT IN HISTORY

Although Christ has given us the ideal of maturity and has inaugurated the era of the resurrection, we have not yet reached the goal. We are a pilgrim Church, involved in the processes of history. The Spirit has been promised and has been sent, but He works slowly through human institutions and human culture. Although Christ has revealed the ideal, we do not know how the fullness of the ideal will be incarnated in history. Yet because of the power of the Christian ideal, we may fall into a moral triumphalism and take on the attitude of the idealistic adolescent who feels that he has the fullness of truth and must convert the world overnight. The mature adult, on the other hand, faces up to the ambiguity and complexity of living in history. And the Christian realizes that history in its ultimate dimension is the work of the Spirit.

What are the marks of maturity for the Christian who is open to history and the Spirit? The first quality of the mature conscience is a sense of ambiguity and limitation. Although the absolute ideal of the moral ought presses heavily upon him, the Christian realizes that there is much he cannot achieve. He is not at the ἔσχατον, but *in via*. He realizes that his own finitude, the powers of evil, and his historicity set limits to his moral achievement (Schoonenberg, 1965, pp. 63–123), and that success is ultimately not his, but the work of the Spirit. Although he bears within himself the remembrance of paradise, he will acknowledge that he now lives east of Eden and after Cain. He will strive earnestly to reinstate paradise; but he realizes that after the fall this is an arduous and complex task, for life is ambiguous, and before the final judgment we cannot neatly divide the sheep from the goats. Hence he will not be disillusioned, like the adolescent, when he discovers that his idols have clay feet. Nor will he rail in outraged indignation against the evil forces in the universe. For, even in his most inspired prophetic moments, when he calls divine judgment on society, he will realize that he himself is not innocent and at that very moment may be the victim of illusion and the pawn of evil. But he will not be discouraged, for he has confidence in the redemptive work of Christ and the power of the Spirit.

The second quality of the mature conscience is a certain tragic sense—an awareness that maturity involves suffering and that true spiritual growth takes place through the mystery of death and resurrection. Although the mature Christian knows that the good will triumph in the end, he realizes that this does not follow the neat formula of a Western movie. Like the dreamy adolescent, one might believe that spiritual maturity or moral reform happens automatically or is easily bought. But as the Christian begins to mature and becomes aware of ambiguity, one thing becomes increasingly clear to him: that profound moral growth, both personal and collective, follows the way of the cross. Christ's victory over evil did not liberate Christians from suffering and death. To live in history and to be led by the Spirit toward the Christian ideal is to become increasingly involved in the mystery of Christ's death and resurrection. If, for example, a Christian feels constrained to protest against unjust institutions or warfare, he will not expect to be rewarded like the good little boy by his parents or like the adolescent who has won honors in school. He will rather expect to be persecuted—especially by those who represent justice. He will anticipate being rejected, reviled, and punished. He realizes that his efforts may fail or that they will bear fruit only in the next generation when his contribution is forgotten. He will accept all this gladly, for he knows that this is the way the Spirit works in history.

The third mark of the mature conscience is a sense of responsibility. As one matures, his sense of responsibility enlarges. As a child, he is expected to respond to the rules of the family, but when he passes through adolescence, he takes responsibility for himself, his life, his destiny; as an adult he shares the responsibility for other lives—his own family and to a varying extent the community. At the present time, man's responsibility is enlarging in a remarkable way. Through communications, he is breaking out of his tribal consciousness into a global community. Through science and technology he is moving into space and shaping his environment, even the forms of life of the future. As horizons enlarge, new moral issues emerge and a new dimension of moral consciousness is called for. Man must begin to think of morality in a new perspective, for he is gradually becoming responsible for his future and for history itself (Lepp, 1965, p. 85; Monden, 1965, pp. 168–69).

At one time man could enjoy the moral security of the child in the family. He could learn the moral demands of his social relations in a closed society, as expressed in the ten commandments, and live up to these. But the world is much more complex than the desert tribal culture in which the ten commandments were formulated. The man of the future must enlarge his sense of moral responsibility from the tribal circle to the world community and the community that is in an historical process. His most urgent moral question should not be merely "What should I do here and now?" but "What contribution can I make to the expansion of human freedom and moral consciousness in history?" To move into the larger world of moral responsibility is both challenging and frightening. If we have no place to ground our hope, we may hesitate to step into this larger world and turn from the responsibility of the future. It is here that the theology of the Spirit can come to the Christian's aid. If the Christian can enlarge his concept of the Spirit from the one who gives individuals strength to perform good moral actions to the one who guides history itself, then he will have the hope and the courage to accept the responsibility of his new moral position in the world (Cousins, 1969, pp. 171–176)

THE CATHOLIC AND HISTORY

At the present time the Catholic community is in a state of transition, since Vatican II has ushered in the age of the Spirit and plunged the Church into the world. Many Catholics are learning for the first time what it means to live without childhood security or adolescent triumphalism. They are discovering a deeper security and a more realistic vision in the mystery of the Spirit as that mystery unfolds in the processes of history. Coming out of their closed world, they have learned to accept the consciences of other men and to acknowledge the ambiguity of the moral sphere. They have enlarged their moral sensitivities from the personal to the social sphere and have abandoned their conservatism to raise a prophetic voice against institutions. While many are disturbed by the changes, and fear that they have been thrown into a moral relativism, others are beginning to sense that under this loss of bearings is the mystery of the Spirit working in the world.

As the Catholic is entering more deeply into the present and the future, he is beginning to read his past history with more sophistication. Instead of seeing the Church as providing moral security in each age by giving definitive solutions to all problems of conscience, he can read history more dialectically. He can see the Spirit working through the Church and the structures of society—often in struggle and ambiguity—to bring moral consciousness into concrete reality. He can accept the fact that it is not always easy to form one's conscience in a given age. For each period of history seems to have a problem area where the moral values are so bound up with change in the structures of society that a simple solution seems impossible. When Europe was changing from a feudal to a capitalistic society, the moral status of usury was clouded. At the time of the Reformation, when Europe was being torn into new religious and political divisions, issues of personal loyalty became excruciatingly complex. In our age the issue of birth control has become such a storm center that one is impelled to see behind it some radical change taking place—not merely in economic, political, or religious structures, but in man's basic relation to nature. Man's power over nature and life has reached a critical point in the twentieth century; for man is on the verge of changing his basic attitude from passive observer to active creator. How far and in what ways should this power extend so that he can maintain human dignity and the moral value of life? The ultimate solution to questions of this kind, and the moral dilemmas they create, usually lies in the future. The new economic form of capitalism emerged so that the moral issue of money-lending could be seen clearly; the religious and political divisions of Europe have settled to the point where a mood of ecumenism prevails at the present. Perhaps the solution to the birth-control issue will be seen only when man develops more fully the very scientific and economic resources that brought the issue into the fore. But in the meantime our age may have to endure the moral anguish of bearing the cross of history so that the next age will be able to reach a satisfying moral solution. It is a sign of maturity for a given age to bear courageously uncertainty and confusion so that the next age may have, through the help of the Spirit, an enlarged moral consciousness.

The chief need of our times, then, is for the virtues of the Spirit, especially for the gift of the discernment of spirits so that the Christian can penetrate beyond his personal moral dilemmas to see the larger historical issues at stake. At this time, the Christian must not be entrapped in the childish security or the adolescent triumphalism of a closed moral world. He must not only accept change, but through confidence in the Spirit he must be in the advance of the development of moral consciousness. But this requires that he accept the marks of a mature conscience—its responsibility, its tragic sense, its awareness of ambiguity and limitation—so that he can have the courage to bear his cross of historicity and the confident joy to make a positive contribution to the development of the kingdom as the Spirit transforms the universe in the image of Christ.

REFERENCES

Cousins, E. Teilhard and the theology of the Spirit. *Cross Currents,* 1969, *19,* 159–177.

Denzinger, H., & Schönmetzer, A. (s.j.) (Eds.) *Enchiridion symbolorum.* (33rd ed.) Barcelona: Herder, 1965. English translation from: Clarkson, J. (s.j.), *et al. The Church teaches.* St. Louis: Herder, 1955.

Dubarle, A. M. (o.p.), *The biblical doctrine of original sin* (trans. by E. M. Stewart). New York: Herder & Herder, 1964.

Gilleman, G. (s.j.) *The primacy of charity in moral theology* (trans. by W. Ryan [s.j.] & A. Vachon [s.j.]). Westminster, Md.: Newman, 1959.

Häring, B. (c.ss.r.) *The Law of Christ* Vol. I (trans. by E. Kaiser [c.pp.s.]), Westminster, Md.: Newman, 1963.

Jone, H. (o.f.m., Cap.) *Moral theology* (trans. by U. Adelman [o.f.m., Cap.]). Westminster, Md.: Newman, 1953.

Kant, I. Fundamental principles of the metaphysic of morals. In *Kant's critique of practical reason and other works on the theory of ethics* (trans. by T. K. Abbott). (6th ed.) London: Longmans, Green, 1923.

Ladner, G. *The idea of reform: Its impact on Christian thought in the age of the Fathers.* Cambridge: Harvard University Press, 1959.

Lepp, I. *The authentic morality* (trans. by B. Murchland [c.s.c.]). New York: Macmillan, 1965.

Monden, L. (s.j.) *Sin, liberty and law* (trans. by J. Donceel [s.j.]). New York: Sheed & Ward, 1965.

Plato. *The dialogues of Plato* (trans. by B. Jowett). 2 vols. New York: Random House, 1937.

Schoonenberg, P. (s.j.) *Man and sin* (trans. by J. Donceel [s.j.]). Notre Dame: University of Notre Dame Press, 1965.

The Mature Conscience as Seen by a Psychiatrist

JOHN R. CAVANAGH

John Richard Cavanagh received both his B.S. and his M.D. degrees from Georgetown University. He is a fellow of the American Psychiatric Association, and a diplomate in psychiatry of the American Board of Psychiatry and Neurology. Since 1939, Dr. Cavanagh has been a special lecturer in pastoral medicine and psychiatry at the Catholic University of America. A past president of the Guild of Catholic Psychiatrists, he was for many years editor of the Bulletin *of the Guild. Since 1964 he has been a member of the Papal Commission on Population and Birth Control. Dr. Cavanagh is the author of an impressive number of books, among them the following:* Fundamental marriage counseling *(1956, 1963)*, Fundamental pastoral counseling *(1962)*, The popes, the pill, and the people; a documentary study *(1965), and* Counseling the invert *(1966)*. At the present time, Dr. Cavanagh is principally engaged in the private practice of psychiatry in Washington, D.C.*

The goals of morality and the ideals of maturity are synonymous. Their apparent difference is caused by the fact that the orientation of the psychiatrist differs from that of the theologian. Objectively, however, the facts of morality and maturity remain identical. For example, a psychiatric description of a mature attitude toward the Ten Commandments might read something like this:

> What man with a proper sense of reality, with true humility and capable of love, would be inclined to disrespect his God? Who would deliberately dishonor his father or mother, especially if the parents loved each other and gave security to their children, while preparing them for emancipation? The sexually mature person is not interested in masturbation or other sexually immature activities. If he is maturely capable of love and married to an equally adult person, he is hardly concerned seriously with adultery and divorce. He is prepared for responsible parenthood. One with good self-understanding and insight, who had resolved his own personal anxieties, will not be tempted to gossip or bear false witness against his neighbor, any more than one who can and does enjoy work, play, and love, will be seriously tempted to steal.

But the fact that this identity exists between objective morality and subjective maturity proposes a question, "What is a mature conscience and how is it formed?"

"Conscience" is not a term frequently used in the vocabulary of a psychiatrist. Instead he is likely to speak of superego.

THE SUPEREGO

The *superego* is the closest psychiatric equivalent of the *conscience*. Freud in his description of superego said: ". . . the superego, you may call it, the conscience" (Freud, 1933, p. 106).

Freud arrived at his concept of the superego in an interesting fashion. He observed how psychotic patients frequently had delusions. Such individuals often had the delusion of being watched. This was, the patient believed, an effort on the part of others to catch him doing something that was forbidden and for which he might be punished. Freud stated that the strong impression he received from this clinical picture never left him. He asked himself how it would be if this picture were in harmony with reality:

> Under the strong impression of this clinical picture, I formed the idea that the separating off of an observing function from the rest of the ego might be a normal feature of the ego's structure; this idea has never left me, and I was driven to investigate the further characteristics and relations of the function which had been separated off in this way [Freud, 1933, p. 85].

The ego, it is evident, "can take itself an object . . . can treat itself like any other object, observe itself, criticize itself . . . or put one part of the ego over against another part" (Freud, 1933, p. 86). Freud concluded from this that the ego can be split. One's conscience, he reasoned, can most easily be separated from one's ego and set over against it. Thus, "conscience" can punish one with painful reproaches after the individual has done wrong, and can make him feel remorse for it.

In early life, the superego is formed by incorporating the attitudes of the parents or parental surrogates. Later on, as the years pass, the youth accepts the standards or the superego of his parents. The superego, having incorporated the parental authority, assumes the parental functions. The superego may be considered a successful example of identification with parental vetoes and an introjection of parental principles.

The functions of the superego are (1) self-observation, (2) formation of moral judgments, and (3) formation of ideals. "The superego is the representative of all moral restrictions, the advocate of the impulse towards perfection . . . —in short what people call the higher things of life" (Freud, 1933, p. 95).

The superego is also "the vehicle of the ego-ideal, by which the ego measures itself, towards which it strives, and whose demands for ever increasing perfection it is always striving to fulfill" (Freud, 1933, p. 93).

Hinsie and Shatzky in their dictionary also state that "it is the superego that is conscience." They continue, "Conscience, therefore, may be defined as those psychical organizations that stand in opposition to the expression of instinctual actions" (Hinsie & Shatzky, 1953, p. 115).

I am reluctant to disagree with such distinguished authorities but I must do so. Conscience and superego are not the same. The superego contains unconscious elements. I would agree that the conscious portion of the superego and conscience were similar, but the conscience has no unconscious portion. The factors which enter into a judgment of conscience are all in consciousness at the time the judgment is made. When the judgment of conscience is made, after much deliberation and research, some of the previously unconscious factors of the superego may become conscious. Unconscious factors may influence conscious decisions but are never coercive. This is based on the concept that our motivation must, in the same way, be known to us. We may, therefore, say that the conscience and the conscious portion of the superego are similar.

THEOLOGICAL DEFINITION

Turning for a moment from psychology to theology, the definition of conscience provided in the standard textbooks of moral theology is that conscience is the judgment of the practical reason about the moral goodness of a particular act.

Bernard Häring says that "conscience, man's moral faculty, with its knowledge of values and freedom is the subjective source of good" (Häring,

1961, p. 135). Deep within himself, man is conscious of a law that calls him to love good and avoid evil, and it is in his free and deliberate obedience to this law that man achieves his greatest dignity.

In speaking of conscience the English edition of the Dutch Catechism notes that "All men, believers and unbelievers, know the voice of conscience" (*A new catechism*, 1967, p. 15). Conscience, then, is a universal concept, even though it is not always known by the same title. Thus it remains the constant teaching of the Church that each man must be guided by the profound law of his conscience. The Second Vatican Council in its Pastoral Constitution on the Church in the Modern World declares: "In fidelity to conscience, Christians are joined with the rest of men in the search for truth . . ." (Vatican Council II, 1966, n. 16, p. 214).

The role of conscience is essential in the Christian life, for it is conscience that directs man to pursue the good. In the final analysis, each man must follow his own conscience, even if that conscience is erroneous or founded on invincible ignorance. Cardinal Newman affirmed this principle in stating: "I have always held that obedience to one's conscience, even if the conscience is erroneous, is the best way to the light," and in the Washington controversy of 1968 even Cardinal O'Boyle (1968) agreed with this particular point.

I have stressed the Catholic teaching on conscience and erroneous conscience from the standpoints of the psychiatrist and the theologian so that they may be placed in perspective, and to distinguish these concepts from "freedom of conscience," a concept that I believe is poorly understood. As Häring emphasizes, "there can be no absolute freedom of conscience for the simple reason that conscience does not free one from the law" (Häring, 1961, p. 150). When ignorance or error is present, the person must follow his conscience, but his options are limited. When a particular issue is impossibly complex, or when adequate information for an accurate decision is lacking, the individual may choose that course of action which his conscience indicates as most consistent with his principles and values.

A further discussion of these basic concepts is beyond the scope of this paper, but I would refer the reader to Häring's (1961) *Law of Christ*, Delhaye's (1968) *The Christian conscience*, or the essay of Warren Reich (1968) on "The individual conscience and marriage today" in *Marriage in the light of Vatican II*, or *Christian morality today* by Curran (1966, Ch. 2).

However, since the free conscience is not within our scope at this time, I shall limit myself to the mature conscience.

MATURITY

A few words now on maturity. An early postulate for the study of maturity is the recognition that personality and maturity are concepts referring to developmental realities which, while they may achieve workable proportions relatively early in life, continue to expand during the lifetime of the individual. They renew themselves from within during adolescence, when the individual is facing society for the first time on his own, and, in the early years of marriage when he is adapting to an intimate contact with another person, it should reach its optimum level. His future adjustment will, in large measure, depend upon his acceptance or rejection of mature attitudes during this period. There can be little doubt that the individual's milieu during early life will have a tremendous influence over his adolescent and later emotional and sexual development. His future mental health and mental adjustment will depend upon his acceptance of a realistic adjustment.

To orient this discussion, one should first define maturity—as, e.g., *the capacity of an individual to react in terms of the requirements that a situation imposes* (Schneiders, 1955, p. 435).

One can say that maturity in the person occurs on several levels and roughly can be expected to develop in the following order:

1. Emotional maturity;
2. Sexual maturity;
3. Intellectual maturity;
4. Social maturity.

Together and in their fullness these would be the qualities of the *completely mature person*. Such a person develops not only from within. Self-actualization which leads to maturity is not only an internal change. It is a change which results from a need for social actualization which includes the acceptance by others as well as self-acceptance.

Maturity is a developing process. Essentially it is a learned process. This learning starts early in life. It is involved with conscious and unconscious factors. Many of these are the result of a continuing process whereby the immature attitudes are passed from mother to daughter, less frequently from father to son. Such individuals may then approach adulthood with immature attitudes toward life in many of its aspects. In many instances the problems confronting them are the result of uncontrolled fertility. Such problems may cause even those previously mature to regress to the emotional state of an earlier period of development.

In those already mature, regression to more immature levels may occur in those couples confronted by ambivalent matters such as uncontrolled fertility and problems of responsible parenthood. Ideas which cannot converge in morally acceptable conduct may cause disabling conflicts. The prospect of prolonged periods of sexual abstinence because of serious physical illness in the wife, which would require abstinence for the duration of the child-bearing period, would require a high degree of maturity.

THE MATURE CONSCIENCE

If we combine the concepts described above from conscience and maturity we will arrive at a definition of mature conscience. The person with a mature conscience is one who, when confronted by difficult decisions in the ethical order, carefully evaluates, insofar as he can, all aspects of the matter. On this basis he comes to a practical judgment about what is right and what is wrong. Then he acts on the matter with a functional certitude—that is, without unreasonable fears and doubts.

Following this discussion, it is appropriate to give a definition of conscience. The descriptive terms given above lead to this definition:

> It is in this inner sanctuary that man becomes aware of the law that calls him to pursue good and avoid evil. It is here also that he refines his hierarchy of values and that he reflects upon his responsibility to himself and to others. In light of the law, the values, and the responsibilities, a man determines how he will act. We call this decision the judgment of conscience.*

It is obvious that there must be many varieties of conscience. In the scope of this paper only the mature conscience will be discussed.

Maturity of conscience gives great freedom of thought and activity because the mature person is not restricted by taboos, fears, obsessions, or ambivalence, or other restrictive forces. Such maturity gives an incentive to seek greater freedom which gives even greater maturity and hence greater peace of mind.

A mature conscience is well-informed concerning the facts and is molded in conformity to the individual's capacity to discern realistically and react emotionally to the requirements imposed on him by a situation. It thus forms a confident, subjective, moral judgment.

CONFLICT WITH AUTHORITY

What happens when there is a conflict between an individual and the claims of authority? Conventionally, it was taken for granted that the judgment of authority prevailed against conscience. If the individual rebelled, he was regarded as having a deliberately misguided conscience. There was, it is true, a theology of good faith for the ill-informed and the ignorant. However, there "really was no developed theology of good faith as applied to the fully aware and well-informed conscience [the mature conscience], where the individual decided that something judged wrong by authority was

---

* Personal communication to the author from Rev. James T. McHugh, Director, Family Life Bureau, United States Catholic Conference.

not wrong—or at least was not wrong in his case" (O'Callaghan, 1969, p. 14). Theology is now confronted by this situation.

The national hierarchies of a number of countries have upheld the right of the properly informed conscience in the matter of birth control. They have stated that the responsible decision of conscience, taken after serious consideration of all the factors involved, must be respected.

Although this is a sensitive area and the principles are not completely agreed upon, there are certain theological guidelines. A directive of the magisterium must be treated with respect and evaluated as objectively as possible. Such a directive will always demand a positive response—i.e., what Vatican II's Constitution on the Church calls "a religious submission of will and of mind" (Vatican Council II, 1966, n. 25, p. 48). The encyclical *Humanae Vitae* refers to this as a loyal internal and external obedience (Paul VI, 1968, n. 28, p. 46). What do these terms mean to a psychiatrist?

Internal assent. Does this expression mean a real intellectual conviction? But how can one convince oneself—or does one have an obligation to be convinced? It is impossible completely to submit one's intellect and will to such a demand. In the concrete case, where doubt exists it can only mean respect for authority with a humble readiness to seek the truth and put aside prejudice.

External obedience. Does this expression mean that one refrains from and suppresses all discussion, and refuses to entertain any question? It certainly cannot mean this. Or does it mean that one must act in one way even though one thinks in another way? This would be to abdicate reason or to be guilty of gross dishonesty—laying oneself open to a kind of "moral schizophrenia." All external obedience can mean is that one fairly states the position of authority and gives it full objective weight and force. One does not deny that there is a serious debate and major difficulties in the general moral situation.

Those who have taken all reasonable steps to form their conscience and are unable to accept the conclusions, e.g., of the encyclical *Humanae Vitae,* are in a more complex situation. In principle, they are entitled to follow their conscience—they cannot be accused of the specific guilt of contraception (O'Callaghan, 1969, p. 14).

The individual with a mature conscience does not lightly arrive at a conclusion that an official teaching of the Church, e.g., on contraception, should not be followed. Instead, before having arrived at a firm conviction, the individual with a mature conscience will seek answers to his questions in various places:

1. He will ask what the sciences—e.g., biology, medicine, psychology, and

others—have to say on the subject. What are their conclusions? If these agree with the teaching authority of the Church he can arrive at fairly solid conclusions.

2. If there is disagreement between the teaching authority and science then further investigation is indicated.
3. If the teaching is not infallible, then the possibility of change is granted, and the methodological doubt, first adopted to insure objectivity and with the conviction that faith builds on reason, has become a real doubt. It demands further study since the norm of morality must be a certain one to avoid evil as much as possible [Swift, p. 49].
4. If the doubt persists then he must seek the advice of others, granted that they are experts in the field. Sometimes the complexity of the problem surpasses the capability of the ordinary individual to grasp the complicated arguments. To rely, then, on the judgment of an expert is by all means to act prudently.

After such study, the individual is prepared to form his judgment conscientiously. This is the approach of the mature person. It is reasonable to presume that the mature person has a mature conscience. Admittedly, there are varying degrees of maturity—total maturity may be achieved by relatively few. One does not need to be exceedingly mature to act in a mature way.

It is one of our duties as psychiatrists, psychologists, and clergymen to educate our fellow men in the various aspects of maturity. We must encourage them to think for themselves, to be free to form judgments as long as it is not harmful to others. We should be prepared to encourage them in free thinking and so enable them to see life in a broader perspective; liberate them from their taboos, obsessions, fears, and phobias; impress upon them that they are part of the magisterium of the Church (Maguire, 1968, p. 105)—that they are part of the Church, and not peons or slaves.

The person with a mature conscience is a free person who, after adequate study and introspection, decides on what he considers his responsible participation in his religion.

REFERENCES

Curran, C. E. *Christian morality today*. Notre Dame, Ind.: Fides, 1966.

Delhaye, P. *Christian conscience*. New York: Desclée, 1968.

Freud, S. *New introductory lectures on psychoanalysis* (1933). New York: Norton, 1961.

Häring, B. (c.ss.r.) *The law of Christ: Moral theology for priests and laity* (trans. by E. G. Kaiser). Westminster, Md.: Newman, 1961.

Hinsie, L., & Shatzky, J. *Psychiatric dictionary*. New York: Oxford University Press, 1953.

Maguire, D. C. Moral absolutes and the magisterium. In C. E. Curran (Ed.) *Absolutes in moral theology?* Washington: Corpus Books, 1968. Pp. 57–107.

A new catechism: Catholic faith for adults (trans. by K. Smyth). New York: Herder & Herder, 1967.

O'Boyle, P. *An instruction: The Catholic conscience.* Washington: Archdiocese of Washington, 1968.

O'Callaghan, D. Theology and the encyclical. *Catholic Marriage Advisory Council Bulletin,* 1969, *8*(3), 10–16.

Paul VI. *Humanae vitae.* Encyclical letter of July 25, 1968. *Acta Apostolicae Sedis,* 1968, *60,* 481–503. English translation: Human life. *Catholic Mind,* 1968, *66* (September, no. 1225), 35–48.

Reich, W. The individual conscience and marriage today. In J. T. McHugh (Ed.) *Marriage in the light of Vatican II.* Washington: Family Life Bureau, U.S. Catholic Conference, 1968.

Schneiders, A. A. *Personal adjustment and mental health.* New York: Rinehart, 1955.

Swift, F. American reaction to Janssens. *Louvain Studies,* 1966, *1,* 19–53.

Vatican Council II. W. M. Abbott (s.j.) (Ed.) *The documents of Vatican II.* New York: Herder & Herder, 1966.

The Mature Conscience in Political-Science Perspective

JOHN A. ROHR, s.j.

Father John A. Rohr, S.J. received A.B. and Ph.L. degrees from Loyola University (Chicago) in 1957 and 1959 respectively, an M.A. degree from Georgetown University in 1964, an S.T.L. from Woodstock College in 1966, and finally a Ph.D. from the University of Chicago in 1970. Although still at the beginning of his academic career, Father Rohr has already published articles in such journals as America, Continuum, National Catholic Educational Review, Journal of Church and State, *and the* American Ecclesiastical Review. *A member of the American Political Science Association, Father Rohr is currently assistant professor of political science at Loyola University, Chicago.*

The topic I have chosen as an indication of the political scientist's approach to the formation of a mature conscience is that of the selective conscientious objector. The religious convictions of conscientious objectors to military service have been recognized in the laws and public policy of the United States from the earliest days of the Republic. The objectors' privileged position, however, was based for many years on the supposition that they would meet the following conditions: (1) their objection must stem from their religious training and belief, not from views that are essentially political, economic, or sociological; (2) they must oppose all wars, or, in the wording of the Selective Service statute, war in any form.

The strictness of the first requirement—that of religious training and belief—gradually eroded over the years. As recently as World War I the exemption was restricted to members of the historic peace Churches. By the time of the Second World War the privilege covered any form of religious training and belief, although the federal courts differed among themselves in their interpretation of what constituted a "religious" belief. In the Seeger case of 1965 the United States Supreme Court broadened the understanding of religious belief to include all but the hard-core atheist. In the spring of 1969 a Federal District Court in Boston declared unconstitutional this discrimination against those with no religious beliefs whatsoever. The Supreme Court has not reviewed this case as yet.

While the liberalization of the religious clause has reflected the growing secularization of our society, the second requirement for conscientious objection—objection to war in any form—has maintained its pristine vigor. If the Supreme Court follows the reasoning of Judge Wyzanski in the Boston case to which I just referred this could be changed, but for the present it is quite clear that the law of the land does not permit a man to select the wars in which he will fight. For the conscientious objector, war is a package deal. If he would fight in any war, he must fight in every war. There is no provision for *selective* conscientious objection whereby the man who would have fought against Hitler could refuse on grounds of conscience to fight against Ho Chi Minh.

The absence of such a provision has provoked a vigorous public debate in which such unlikely allies as the American Catholic Bishops (1968, pp. 26–27) and the American Civil Liberties Union have joined forces in urging reform. In this paper we shall examine the implications for the mature conscience in the case for selective conscientious objection (or sco as it is usually called).

THE ROLE OF CONSCIENCE IN CIVIC LIFE

Ordinarily, a discussion of conscience and politics moves along on two different levels. First, one must consider the substantive merits of a particular policy—what good does it accomplish, what risks does it involve, how much will it cost? It is on the basis of these considerations that the citizen decides whether or not his government has acted unjustly—*e.g.* segregated schools are immoral, the war is unjust. Once the citizen has decided that a law or policy decision is unjust, the next question is what he should do. Can he avoid getting involved in the injustice? Should he resist and, if so, to what extent—a severe fine? imprisonment? death? Or should the injustice be tolerated as a lesser evil? Our investigation of the case for sco need not move on these two levels because the role of conscience in political life is intrinsic to the sco debate. Here the problem of conscience does not follow upon and judge a particular policy decision. It is itself the basis on which a policy decision for or against sco must be made. The substantive merits of selective objection are of particular relevance to a consideration of the *mature* conscience. Ralph Potter (1969) of the Harvard Divinity School offers as one of his reasons for supporting sco the hope that such a policy would elevate and refine the public argument on war and peace. Paul Ramsey (1968, pp. 91–137) and John Courtney Murray (1968) applaud Potter's attempt to connect selective objection with enlightened public debate, but they feel that he has reversed the temporal sequence. They would first look for an assurance that there is throughout the land a high degree of moral maturity before they would approve sco. Without this civic maturity, the risks involved in selective objection would outweigh the possible advantages.

Unfortunately, the concern that men like Murray, Potter, and Ramsey show to connect the case for sco with the level of public argument is not typical of the arguments one encounters in the literature supporting selective objection. All too often these arguments are structured in terms of the individual alone, in splendid isolation from his fellow-citizens. Underlying this tendency, there is, I believe, a fundamental misunderstanding of the role of conscience in civic life. In the remainder of this paper I shall review and criticize the arguments for selective objection that suggest this tendency. I cannot, of course, present all the arguments for and against selective objection. That would take us far beyond the purpose of this Institute. Our focus will be limited to those defects in the case for sco which result from an inadequate understanding of the role of conscience in civic life.

THE "LEAP OF FAITH" TENDENCY

The most serious defect in the argument for selective objection is the tendency to deduce public policy from private conscientious imperatives. I call this tendency "the leap of faith" because it seems to be an occupational hazard of clergymen. With the dignity of the human person as a cover, the argument leaps from the conscientious convictions of the individual to public policy, without the slightest concern for public order. *America* made this leap when it opened an editorial on selective objection in the following manner:

> Every man is obliged to follow his conscience. Yet, under current legislation, there is no legal protection for the young man who, though not an absolute pacifist, is forbidden by his conscience to fight in the Vietnam war [*America*, 1967, p. 73].

The editorial went on to exhort the reader "to push new legislation that will respect the selective objector's freedom of conscience."

The leap of faith is an ecumenical venture. It is not restricted to Roman Catholics. The Fourth Assembly of the World Council of Churches called for "pressure to have the law changed" to recognize selective objection simply because good men oppose particular wars on grounds of conscience (World Council of Churches, 1968, p. 1). Before we apply "pressure" or "push" for any legislation, it would seem to be advisable that we look into the possible effects of such legislation upon the nation's defense posture. The *America* editorial and the World Council statement are innocent of any such concerns.

THE CONSCIENCE OF THE LEGISLATOR IN SCO

This tendency to ignore the public interest in leaping from personal belief to public policy is caused by an overemphasis upon what no opponent of sco need ever deny—namely, the duty of every man to follow his conscience. From this principle one might well conclude that a citizen morally opposed to the war in Vietnam should refuse to fight. This is a question of civil disobedience and, as such, is quite distinct from the discussion of sco. Selective objection concerns the *government's response* to the dissenter, not the dissenter himself. It is the conscience of the legislator, not that of the citizen, that must be the focus of the debate on sco. No legislator can responsibly support a bill which, in effect, exempts certain citizens from civic burdens because of their conscientious scruples. Such a principle would justify conscientious objection to sending one's children to integrated schools. The conscience of the legislator is committed to promoting the public interest. He must be assured that when the government accommodates the consciences of some of its citizens it does not harm society at large. Proponents of sco must show that their cause would not seriously impair the nation's ability to prosecute a war effectively now or in the future. This is a difficult burden, but there is no reason to think it cannot be borne. Indeed, one might argue that if sco had been the law of the land, there would have been much less domestic resistance to the war in Vietnam, since no one opposed to the war on grounds of conscience would have been drafted; this, in turn, might have facilitated the government's war effort. This, of course, is sheer speculation, but it is the sort of consideration that proponents of sco ignore at their peril. When they prattle on about the citizen's duty to follow his conscience, they only belabor what no one denies. In so doing they fail to take seriously the conscience of the legislator. To meet *his* conscientious needs, the argument must not be structured *exclusively* in terms of man *versus* the state. Rather, the case for sco must show the harmony between the interest of the dissenter and the public interest.

THE SELECTIVE OBJECTOR AND THE CONSCIENTIOUS OBJECTOR

A second argument for sco which suffers from a misunderstanding of the role of conscience in civic affairs is the effort to assimilate the position of the selective objector to that of the conscientious objector. This argument is used frequently by Catholic selective objectors. Its structure is quite simple. The religious training and belief of Quakers and Mennonites obliges them to object to all wars, while that of Roman Catholics obliges them to object only to unjust wars. The law has granted sco status only to those who object to all wars. This constitutes a form of discrimination against the adherents of the just-war doctrine because their objections are no less conscientious simply because they are restricted to unjust wars. It is both unfair and unconstitutional to favor the religious beliefs of one group over those of another. While this argument raises some interesting constitutional issues—e.g., has the Selective Service Act made the Quaker religion the established Church in America?—it is quite deficient on the more fundamental level of basic fairness. The tendency to interpret the present requirements for conscientious objection as discrimination against just warriors in favor of pacifists stems from considering public morality in terms of the individual's *response* to public policy, rather than in terms of the policy itself. With such an attitude, the difference between selective objection and total objection grows dim. Both involve moral decisions against war, but one is respected and the other rejected. Can this be right?

If we approach the question from the point of view of the legislator, the striking difference between total and selective objection becomes quite clear. The selective objector goes through the same conscientious process as the legislator. They both weigh the pros and cons of going to war before reaching their decision. The only difference between the selective objector and the legislator is that they arrive at different conclusions. The legislator decides that a recourse to war is just, while the selective objector reaches the opposite conclusion.

The pacifist makes an entirely different type of conscientious judgment. He does not soil his hands with the messy empirical data involved in balancing the good and evil that might come from war. No matter what good might be accomplished, he will have none of it. The pacifist is, in the area of war and peace, simply a political dropout. The crux of his case rests on principles that transcend space and time. Government is incompetent in such areas and wisely avoids harassing such men as long as their number is not large enough to pose a threat to a major military effort.

The selective objector, however, challenges the government in an area in which it enjoys some competence—namely, questions of justice. Unlike the pacifist, he takes political arguments seriously. He is no dropout; he is one of us. He presents a threat to his own government because he accuses it of failing seriously in a question of the utmost importance. The pacifist presents no such threat. He condemns all participation whatsoever in the sinful folly of war. In this way he does not single out his own government as the object of his moral indignation. Thus he presents the government with a problem entirely different from that of the selective objector. In considering the merits of approving selective objection as public policy, the legislator must weigh the wisdom of granting some citizens a personal veto over the most important foreign-policy decision a government can make. Unlike the pacifist, the selective objector cannot be dismissed as a tame irrelevancy whose eccentricities a liberal government can easily indulge.

THE JUST-WAR DOCTRINE IN SUPPORT OF SCO

The case for sco does not stand or fall on the alleged similarity between selective and total objection. However, the fact that such an argument is even attempted betrays a disturbing bias against taking seriously the moral dimensions of a government's decisions.

The same bias appears in appeals to the just-war doctrine to support sco. Here the proponents of sco state with considerable accuracy the traditional norms for a just war—declared by legitimate authority, right intention, civilian immunity, and so on. Frequently, however, one important aspect of the just-war doctrine is overlooked. The forgotten norm is the one that forbids participation only in those wars that are known to be unjust with *moral certitude*. In the just-war tradition, doubts are resolved in favor of the government. Proponents of sco eagerly enlist the just-war doctrine in their cause. They do so for good reason because this enables them to show that the case for selective objection is not simply the creature of the Vietnam resistance movement. It has a long and honorable history and cannot be dismissed as a cover for *ad hoc* foreign-policy objectives. However, those who appeal to the just-war doctrine must take it as it really is. They may be selective in the wars they will support, but they cannot be selective in applying the norms of the just-war doctrine and still base their argument on that doctrine.

This, however, is precisely what is being done. In Chicago, for example, a prominent anti-war activist offered the following advice in a letter circulated among his friends:

> Thus, if we are convinced that the war in Vietnam is unjust (or even if, after a reasonable effort to gather some data we have serious reservations about it,) then let us die to ourselves and to the false cult of respectability and conformism and let us resist the war in some concrete way.

A young man in San Francisco outlined his reasons for opposing the war in a letter to his draft board. His closing sentence read: "If I am wrong, then it is the obligation of our government to refute all points in order to prove me wrong."

Two years ago there was a seminarians' conference on the draft held in Cambridge. One of their resolutions stated that, "The spirit of these principles [of the just-war doctrine] demands that every war be opposed until or unless it can be morally justified in relation to these principles."

In commenting on this resolution, the late John Courtney Murray, a cautious supporter of sco, remarked "The dear seminarians have got it backward." He went on to explain:

> The root of the error here may be simply described as a failure to under-stand that provision of the just-war doctrine which requires that a war should be "declared." This is not simply a nice piece of legalism, the prescription of a sheer technicality. Behind the provision lies a whole philosophy of the state as a moral and political agent. The provision implies the recognition of the authority of the political community by established political processes to make decisions about the course of its action in history, to muster behind these decisions the united efforts of the community, and to publicize these decisions before the world.
>
> If there is to be a political community, capable of being a moral agent in the international community, there must be some way of publicly identifying the nation's decisions. These decisions must be declared to be the decision of the community. Therefore, if the decision is for war, the war must be declared. This declaration is a moral and political act. It states a decision conscientiously arrived at in the interest of the international common good. It submits the decision to the judgment of mankind. Moreover, when the decision-making processes of the community have been employed and a decision has been reached, at least a preliminary measure of internal authority must be conceded by the citizens to this decision, even by those who dissent from it. This, at least in part, is what Socrates meant by respect for the "conscience of the laws." This is why in the just-war theory it has always been maintained that the presumption stands for the decision of the community as officially declared. He who dissents from the decision must accept the burden of proof [Murray, 1968, pp. 26–27].

Murray's remarks make it clear that the imposition of the burden of proof upon the dissenters is not some sort of statism. It is simply a corollary of the principle which holds that political society is a complex network of moral relationships.

THE SUGGESTED DICHOTOMY OF POLITICS AND MORALITY

The seminarians are not alone in ignoring what Murray has called "a whole philosophy of the state as a moral and political agent." Some senior members of their profession have gone beyond denying the government a presumption of justice, and have suggested a dichotomy of politics and morality. To be sure, this is never done explicitly. If it were, it would be the end of sco, for the thrust of the case for selective objection is aimed at a government sensitive to moral values. Nevertheless, the tendency to separate morality and politics is unmistakably present in sco literature. The reason for this self-defeating tendency is, I believe, caused, once again, by a faulty understanding of conscience.

The problem arises when critics of sco ask how such a policy would be administered. Who would qualify as a selective objector? It is an important question and one that could prove embarrassing to sco apologists, because they must, as we have seen, offer the government some reasonable assurance that the privilege will not be used so widely that the nation could not fight a war effectively. A common response is to distinguish objection on political grounds from objection on grounds of conscience. In an article that belies the political sophistication he has shown elsewhere, Roger L. Shinn gives this response in its purest form:

> If a man says, "I think this war is not the most effective way to serve the national interest," he would not be a conscientious objector. If he says, "I profoundly believe that this war is morally evil," he probably is a conscientious objector [Shinn, 1967, p. 63].

Shinn's statement suggests a distinction without a difference. How can a war possibly be moral if it is not in the national interest?

The national interest is not the highest norm of morality. The fact that a war is in the national interest does not make it just. But if a war is not in the national interest, it is certainly unjust. To wage a war for a cause that does not affect a nation's interest is military adventuring at its worst.

Shinn concedes that the difference between political and moral judgment is not always clear-cut. Nevertheless he defends his morals–politics test by pointing out that "We can tell a hot day from a cold day, even if we are not certain about every day" (Shinn, 1967, p. 63.) The image is interesting because, at first, it seems to blur his sharp distinction between the political and the moral. A closer look at Shinn's thermometer, however, reveals how serious he is in distinguishing politics and morals. The two come together only when the mercury is near the middle. *Real* politics and *real* morality are as different as hot and cold!

As we have seen, this kind of thinking is disastrous for sco. The case for sco must resist the temptation to confer upon the individual a monopoly on moral insight. It must take seriously the moral dimensions of public policy precisely because it is public policy. sco must not become mired in a view of civic morality that limits the discussion to the individual's response to policy decisions.

Perhaps it is a moral revulsion toward war that prompts selective objectors to withhold from the government a presumption of justice and even to dichotomize politics and morality. This moral revulsion is a valuable asset in our society as long as it is centered on war and not on the political process. Before a nation goes to war, it would do well to impose a heavy burden of proof on those who favor such a policy. But once the decision for war has been made, the burden of proof must shift to those who dissent. If this burden does not shift, it would mean that the decisions of government hold no moral value precisely in their capacity as decisions of government. This can be the case only in a corrupt regime. Then, however, the salient political problem is not sco but flight or revolution. As long as the basic character of a regime is just, its decisions must be considered just until proven otherwise. This must be the basic stance of the mature conscience toward life in the πόλις.

ADDITIONAL CONSIDERATIONS

Our discussion has by no means exhausted the arguments for and against sco. Needless to say, there are many approaches that are not vulnerable to the points I have made in this paper. One of these is the argument for selective objection to the American involvement in Vietnam on the grounds that there has been no declaration of war. Since the argument parlays requirements peculiar to the American Constitution with the factual situation in Vietnam, it is necessarily limited in its application to the United States' presence in Vietnam. Thus, it would not represent total victory for selective objectors. But this is no reason to despise the argument. We might keep more of our finest young men out of prison if we lower our sights and settle for an argument that addresses only an *ad hoc* situation.

Another approach some political scientists would applaud is the effort to isolate war from every other policy decision. Is there something peculiar to war that would permit us to suspend the ordinary norms of civic responsibility in this area alone? If a persuasive argument could be developed along these lines, we would then be assured that in accepting sco we were not stepping on a slippery slope that would commit us to support sco in other areas as well. Unfortunately, some proponents of sco move in the opposite direction. Instead of narrowing the implications of sco, they wonder aloud and in print whether these very principles could not be expanded to include selective objection to paying certain taxes. In so doing they play into the hands of their adversaries by legitimating the fears that sco could destroy the fabric of society by making every man his own legislator.

CONCLUSION

In conclusion, then, the political scientist's perspective on the mature conscience is one of concern that we do not disregard the public interest in the name of conscience. In the specific area of selective objection to military service, this concern would manifest itself by asking proponents of sco to give some reasonable assurance that their proposal would not seriously hinder a future military effort, which, at least in the eyes of the government, is justified. On the broader issue of conscience *versus* political authority in general, the same concern would prompt the political scientist to insist that evidence of severe conscientious hardship cannot be decisive in a public-policy debate. It is only the first half of the argument. One must still show how accommodating the conscientious scruple will promote—or at least not substantially impair—the interests of society. Finally, this political scientist would be extremely uneasy with any argument in defense of conscience that could, by implication, undermine the moral foundation of positive law.

REFERENCES

America. Editorial: The selective conscientious objector. *America*, 1967, *117*, 73.
American Catholic Bishops. Collective pastoral: Human life in our day. *Catholic Mind*, 1968, *66* (December, no. 1228), 1–28.
Murray, J. C. (s.j.) War and conscience. in J. Finn (Ed.) *Conflict of loyalties: the case for selective conscientious objection.* New York: Pegasus, 1968. Pp. 19–30.
Potter, R. B. *War and moral discourse.* Richmond, Va.: John Knox Press, 1969.
Ramsey, P. *The just war.* New York: Scribner, 1968.
Shinn, R. L. The selective conscientious objector again. *Christianity and crisis,* 1967, *27*, 61–63.
World Council of Churches, Fourth Assembly. Statement on human rights. *New York Times,* July 16, 1968.